BEFORE THE WELLS RUN DRY

Before the Wells Run Dry

Ireland's Transition to Renewable Energy

Edited by

Richard Douthwaite

The Foundation for the Economics of Sustainability

in association with

**GREEN
BOOKS**

**THE LILLIPUT
PRESS**

First published in Dublin (September 2003) by Feasta,
The Foundation for the Economics of Sustainability
159, Lower Rathmines Road,
Dublin 6
Tel: (01) 4912773
Email: feasta@anu.ie
www.feasta.org

Distributed in Ireland by the Lilliput Press, 62-63, Sitric Road, Arbour Hill, Dublin 7.
Tel: (01) 6711647
Email: info@lilliputpress.ie   Website:www.lilliputpress.ie

Distributed in the UK by Green Books Ltd., Foxhole, Dartington, Totnes, Devon, TQ9 6EB
Tel: (01803) 863 260
Email: sales@greenbooks.co.uk Website:www.greenbooks.co.uk

Feasta is registered as an educational charity No. 13052

A CIP record for this title is available from the British Library.

ISBN 1 84351 037 5
Printed in Dublin by Betaprint
Designed and typeset by Roisin Meacle, Email: info@roisinmeacle.com

CONTENTS

Part One: World conventional energy supply prospects   29

The world's oil and conventional gas reserves are being rapidly depleted and at some point, production will begin to decline. How soon will the decline begin and can other conventional sources of energy - coal, tar sands and nuclear - be developed to prevent shortages occurring?

Part Two: Do renewable energy sources have the potential to fill the gap?   71

It will take considerable time and energy to develop renewable energy sources and to adapt the economy to their use. Despite this, renewables may not be able to supply enough power for economic growth to continue at anything like its present rate.

Part Seven: The potential for renewable energy in Ireland   287

Two elements are crucial to the development of renewable energy sources in Ireland – the quality of the resource and the quality of the people involved in developing it. This section reviews both – and the obstacles people face.

Part Eight: The way ahead   309

It is crucially important that the world begins making the massive investments required to start the switch to renewables now, before oil and gas production peaks, so that enough fossil energy is available. Waiting a few years could condemn millions to misery.

Acknowledgments

The publication of this book would have been impossible without two things. One was the work that each of the authors put into writing the very careful, detailed papers it contains. In many cases these go far beyond what those who wrote them were able to say in their 20- or 30-minute slots at the conference on which the book is based. Feasta is very grateful indeed for the trouble they took. Their names are listed in the contributors' section along with those of Gerard O'Neill, Euan Baird, Harry J. Longwell and David Morris who generously allowed us to fill gaps in the book's coverage by reprinting material they had written for use elsewhere. David Morris was, in fact, hoping to speak at the conference but we were unable to get sponsorship for him to travel from the US. We are also grateful to Sunny Lewis, Editor in Chief, Environment News Service, for allowing us to reprint two news items his service carried earlier this year. On a personal level, the editor would like to express his thanks to John Jopling for his sound advice and also for his meticulous help with the proof-reading, to Kevin Healion for his work in assembling the articles in Part Seven, and to B9 Energy for wind and biomass illustrations.

Besides authors, the book's other essential ingredient was money. The initial grant for its publication was secured from the Green Group in the European Parliament by Nuala Ahern MEP long before most of its contents had been written and, when it became apparent that it was going to be roughly twice as long as originally envisaged, Sustainable Energy Ireland provided a matching sum to enable printing to go ahead. We are very grateful to both, particularly as neither donor attempted to influence the content or coverage of the book in any way. Indeed, the opinions the writers express – including those of the editor – may or may not be shared by any of the organisations whose logos decorate this page. The two grants will enable some copies of the book to be distributed free and others to be sold at a price most people should be able to afford.

Since this book would never have appeared had the conference not taken place, Feasta would also like to thank those who made that possible. In particular, we acknowledge the financial help we received from ESB Independent Energy, Airtricity, GE Wind and Comhar, the National Sustainable Development Partnership.

The Greens
European Free Alliance
in the European Parliament

TIPPERARY
INSTITUTE

COMHAR
AN PHÁIRTÍOCHT
FORBARTHA
INMHARTHANA
NÁISIÚNTA

Independent
Energy

SUSTAINABLE
ENERGY
IRELAND
Renewable Energy Information Office

Meitheal
Na Gaoithe

. . . and thanks

Equally vital were the contributions made by our partners in organising the event – the Tipperary Institute and the Renewable Energy Information Office of Sustainable Energy Ireland. Pádraig Culbert, Chief Executive of the Tipperary Institute, welcomed the conference to its campus. Kevin Healion, Clifford Guest, Seamus Hoyne and Ciarán Lynch invited the renewable energy organisations to participate in the event and made most of the on-site arrangements for it with the help of their colleagues Derek Blackweir, Michael Bulfin, Sandie Byrne, Michael Cox, Caitríona Daly, Kate Dwyer, Paul Fennessy, Sean Lydon, Paddy Maguire, Liam Noonan, Catherine-Ann O'Connell, Agnes Quinn, George Ryan, Michael Ryan, Patricia Ryan and Tara Ryan. Jim Casey, Mayor of North Tipperary County Council helped by chairing a session. We should also thank Emma Greene and Sally-Ann Morrissey of the Tipperary Energy Agency, John Fogarty of Templederry Community Development Group, and the other organisations that promoted the event: the Association of Irish Energy Agencies; the Geothermal Association of Ireland; the Irish Bioenergy Association; the Irish Hydro Power Association; the Irish Solar Energy Association; the Irish Wind Energy Association and Meitheal Na Gaoithe. *The Irish Farmers' Journal, The Sunday Business Post, The Irish Times* and the local papers in the Tipperary area were particularly helpful in publicising the event. Dunne St. John Catering provided excellent food during the conference and Hairy O'Gorman provided a reliable minibus service between the Institute and the Anner Hotel where many participants stayed. The hotel was comfortable and its staff pleasant – our thanks to them for that.

At the Renewable Energy Information Office, we must thank Rosemarie Ahern for preparing the conference leaflet and sending out e-mail publicity shots, Paul Dykes who provided mailing lists and looked after the leaflet's printing and delivery, Xavier Dubuisson who chaired a conference session, and Paul Kellett for his support and encouragement.

Feasta members who helped with the conference included David O'Kelly, Davie Philip, Enid O'Dowd, Kaethe Burt-O'Dea, Joe Glynn and Michael Lemass. We would also like to thank the staff at the Courthouse Centre, Tinahely, Co. Wicklow, who handled the bookings with enthusiasm and care.

Contributors

 **Gerard O'Neill** is a graduate of the University of Ulster at Jordanstown (BA 1st Class hons in Social Policy and Public Economics) and of the London School of Economics (MSc Econ in Economics). He worked as a management consultant at Henley Centre for Forecasting in London during the 1980s, moving to Dublin to take up the position of Business Planning Manager in An Post in January 1988. He had primary responsibility for the company's business strategy plan, and was secretary to the Executive Committee of An Post.

He left An Post to set up the Irish franchise of the Henley Centre in October 1989. This quickly established itself as an innovative consulting company, specializing in the business implications of social, economic and technological trends.

In 1998, Henley Centre Ireland was renamed Amárach Consulting, to position the company more clearly as the leading provider of business forecasting and predictive market research services in Ireland. Clients include AIB, Guinness, Microsoft, ESB, An Post, eircom and Tesco.

He has been a director of the Irish Direct Marketing Association and Chairman of the Marketing Society. He is a member of the Information Society Commission's Futures Group. He is a professional member of the World Futures Society and ESOMAR. He is also the Irish member of the International Association of Energy Economics.

 **Richard Douthwaite** was born in Sheffield, Yorkshire, in 1942. He worked as a journalist in Leeds, Oxford and London before studying economics at the University of Essex and the University of the West Indies, Kingston, Jamaica. He set up and managed a boatyard in Jamaica on behalf of the island's fishing co-ops before spending two years as Government Economist in the British colony of Montserrat. He has lived in Westport, Ireland, since 1974 and he and his wife Mary ran their own manufacturing and mail-order business there with twelve employees for ten years. He then went back to journalism, specialising in business, financial and environmental matters to do with the West of Ireland.

His book, *The Growth Illusion: How Economic Growth Enriched the Few, Impoverished the Many and Endangered the Planet,* was first published in 1992 and was re-issued in an extended and updated second edition in 1999. A major section of his other major book, *Short Circuit* (1996) deals with the ways that communities can adopt to make themselves less dependent on supplies of fossil energy.

He has made a special study of rural sustainability. He is a founder of Feasta and is co-editor of its publication, the *Feasta Review*. He has acted as economic adviser to the Global Commons Institute (London) for the past ten years, during which time GCI has developed the Contraction and

Convergence approach to dealing with greenhouse gas emissions which has now been backed by a majority of countries in the world, most recently the UK. He is currently working on a voluntary basis with groups in Mayo and Donegal on a project that should lead to widespread community investment in wind turbines.

PART ONE:

WORLD CONVENTIONAL ENERGY SUPPLY PROSPECTS

Colin Campbell obtained his doctorate in geology from Oxford University in 1958 and has worked since as a petroleum geologist with companies including BP, Texaco, Fina and Amoco. He was Exploration Manager for Aran Energy, Dublin, in 1978-9. More recently he has been a consultant to the Norwegian and Bulgarian Governments, and to Shell and Esso. In 1998, he and a colleague, Jean H. Laherrère, were largely responsible for convincing the International Energy Agency that the world's output of conventional oil would peak within the following decade. He is the author of two books and numerous papers on oil depletion and has lectured and broadcast widely. He lives in Ballydehob, Co. Cork.

David Frowd headed the energy group in Shell's Scenarios Team until March, 2003. The department is known as Global Business Environment (PXG) within Shell International Ltd. He had been a member of the Scenarios team since 1998, and was directly engaged in the building of the 1998 and 2001 Global Scenarios. He was also involved with the building and use of scenarios at the country and business level. His spheres of interest include worldwide hydrocarbon resource assessment, longterm oil prices and OPEC behaviour. He joined Shell as a petroleum engineer after graduating from Leeds University in Mining Engineering. He worked in several countries including the UK, Gabon, and Peru, usually in economics or commercial posts such as project evaluation, commercial agreements and acquisitions and divestments. He was head of Joint Ventures for Norske Shell, and from 1993 to 1997 was head of Strategy and Planning in The Hague.

Harry J. Longwell is Executive Vice President of Exxon Mobil Corporation. Before the merger of Exxon and Mobil, he was Senior Vice President, member of the Management Committee and Director of Exxon Corporation. His primary responsibilities included the corporation's oil, gas, coal and minerals exploration and production activities.

After graduating from Louisiana State University in 1963 with a petroleum engineering degree, he began his career with Exxon as a drilling engineer in Exxon Company. He served as Operations Manager in the Production Department of Exxon USA in Houston from 1980 to 1983, when he was named Vice President for the department with responsibility for the company's U.S. production activities.

In 1986 he moved to London as Vice President of Exploration and Production in Europe. He returned to the U.S. later that year as Executive Assistant to the Chairman and the President of Exxon Corporation in New York. He became Vice President of Exploration and Production for

Exxon Company, International in Florham Park, New Jersey, in 1987, Senior Vice President in 1988 and Executive Vice President in 1990. He was named President of Exxon Company, U.S.A. in 1992. He was elected a Senior Vice President of the Corporation effective January 1, 1995, and was elected a Director in October 1995. He was named Executive Vice President of the Corporation in 2001.

John T. McMullan, B.Sc., M.A., Ph.D., D.Sc., C.Eng., C.Phys., F.Inst.P., F.Inst. Energy, is Professor of Physics and Director of NICERT (Northern Ireland Centre for Energy Research and Technology) in the University of Ulster, Coleraine, Northern Ireland. He has been closely involved with energy R&D, technology and policy for 30 years, and his primary research interests lie in the technical and economic assessment and optimisation of advanced power generation and fuel conversion systems, particularly those based on coal, biomass, waste and other renewable energy sources, and including the analysis of their environmental impacts.

His input into energy R&D, development and policy have included membership of the UK Technology Foresight Energy and Natural Environment Panel and the chairmanship the UK Technology Foresight Energy Futures Task Force. He has also been a member of the UK Technology Foresight Zero Emissions Power Generation Task Force, chairman of EC Steering Committee for Clean Electricity and Heat Production R&D and a member of the UK Technology Foresight Task Force on Clean Coal Utilisation. He has published over 270 books and papers.

Euan Baird has been chairman of Rolls-Royce plc, the world's No. 2 civil jet engine maker, since February 2003. He was previously the chairman, president and chief executive officer of the oilfield services company Schlumberger Ltd. He was born in Aberdeen in 1937. He attended Aberdeen University and Trinity College, Cambridge. He received an M.A. degree in Geophysics from Cambridge University in 1960. In 1995 He received the LL.D. from Aberdeen University in 1995 and from Dundee University in 1998. In 1999 he received a D.Sc. from Heriot-Watt University in Edinburgh.

He joined Schlumberger in 1960 as a field engineer. He became a member of the British Prime Minister's Council of Science and Technology in 2000, and a member of the board of Scottish Power that same year.

Ian Hore-Lacy became Head of Communications with the World Nuclear Association in London in 2001. This effectively expanded his previous and continuing role as General Manager of the Uranium Information Centre in Australia, which he has held from 1995. His function is primarily focused on public information provision via the Web. He now splits his time between London and Melbourne. The Uranium Information Centre was set up in 1978 to provide a clearinghouse for information on uranium and the nuclear fuel cycle for electricity generation. He is a former biology teacher who joined the mining industry as an environmental scientist in 1974. He is author of *Nuclear Electricity,* the sixth edition of which appeared in 2000. It has been probably the most widely used school resource in Australia dealing with nuclear power.

PART TWO:
DO RENEWABLE ENERGY SOURCES HAVE THE POTENTIAL TO FILL THE GAP?

David Elliott is Professor of Technology Policy in the Faculty of Technology at the Open University and Director of the OU Energy and Environment Research Unit. He trained initially as a nuclear physicist and worked for the UK Atomic Energy Authority at Harwell and the Central Electricity Generating Board in Bristol. At the Open University he has been looking at energy policy issues and in particular at renewable energy policy. He is co-ordinator of the Network for Alternative Technology and Technology Assessment (NATTA) and editor of its journal, *Renew*. See http://eeru.open.ac.uk/NATTA/rol.html

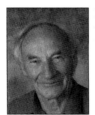

Malcolm Slesser graduated in chemical engineering and worked in the oil, synthetic fibres and nuclear industries before taking up a post at Strathclyde University, where he eventually became Professor of Energy Studies. He has taught in the USA and Brazil, and was for three years head of systems analysis with the European Commission in Italy. He retired to an honorary position at Edinburgh University in 1981 and for seventeen years led a research team in Natural Capital Accounting, fulfilling many contracts, and teaching many foreign and native postgraduate students. He is currently chairman of the Resource Use Institute. He has published ten books, over thirty refereed papers and many articles. He is a well-known mountaineer and Arctic explorer.

Olav Hohmeyer is an economist by training. He studied in the USA (Tougaloo College, Miss.) and in Germany, where he graduated from the University of Bremen in 1980 and received his PhD in economics from the same university in 1989. After two years of research work at the University of Oldenburg, Germany, he joined the Fraunhofer-Institute for Systems and Innovation research in Karlsruhe, Germany, where he did research in the field of energy and environmental economics and policy for 11 years. He is well known for his work on the social costs of energy. Since 1983 he has co-ordinated and lead national and international research projects first as a senior researcher and later as deputy head of two different departments of the institute. From 1994 to 1998 he was head of the Department of Environmental Economics and Management of the European Centre for Economic Research in Mannheim, Germany, where he was responsible for more than fifty research projects. More recently he has worked on new policy instruments to combat global climate change. He was appointed professor at the University of Flensburg in July 1998.

David Fleming read History at Oxford from 1959 to 1963, and then worked in manufacturing (textiles), marketing (detergents), advertising and financial public relations, before taking an MBA at Cranfield in 1968. From 1977 to 1995 he practised as an independent consultant in environmental policy and business strategy for the financial services industry. He edited a manual on the formation and management of investment funds in the Former Soviet Union, which was published in 1995. He was the Ecology (Green) Party's economics spokesman and press secretary between 1977 and 1980. It was at this time that he started to develop the concept of his forthcoming book *The Lean Economy.* In order to research the economics underlying the concept he took an MSc in economics at Birkbeck College, University of London in 1983 and a PhD in 1988. He was Honorary Treasurer and then Chairman of the Soil Association, the UK's leading advocate of organic farming, between 1984 and 1991. He has been a regular contributor to *County Life,* and has published in *Prospect* and other journals, and in the academic literature. He was editor of *The Countryside in 2097,* published in 1997, and gave the 2001 Feasta lecture.

Werner Zittel was born in Munich in 1955 and took a diploma in Physics at the Ludwig-Maximilian University in 1982. His thesis was on nuclear reaction theory. He was awarded a doctorate in Physics by the Technical University, Darmstadt, in 1986. His thesis was on laser fusion. From 1982 to 1987 he worked at the Max-Planck-Institute for Quantum Optics doing design studies for solar pumped laser devices.

Since 1989 he has worked at L-B-Systemtechnik GmbH, Ottobrunn, Munich, a small strategy consulting company focussed on sustainable energy and transport strategies. LBST is a founding member of the European Business Council for a Sustainable Energy Future, which acts as a business NGO at climate negotiations to promote the enforcement of the Kyoto protocol and to support "climate friendly" policies and technologies. He has been concerned with greenhouse gas emissions - particularly methane - by industry, scenarios for introducing renewable energy, introduction scenarios and the infrastructural requirements of a hydrogen based energy economy, and the analysis of fossil-fuel depletion.

PART THREE:
HOW ENERGY AVAILABILITY WILL LIMIT IRELAND'S DEVELOPMENT OPTIONS

David Crane holds degrees in Environmental Chemistry, Parallel Computing and Ecological Economics from the University of Edinburgh. He has worked with environmental simulation modelling for over ten years, and has consulted to the European Union, the Australian CSIRO and to private utility companies. He worked closely for many years with the Centre for Human Ecology in Edinburgh, and remains a Fellow of that organisation. He is currently based in Bristol where he divides his time between simulation modelling for sustainability and Information Technology consulting.

Lawrence Staudt received a B.Sc. and M.Eng degree from Rensselaer Polytechnic Institute in the USA. He worked as engineer and engineering manager of Enertech, a wind energy company involved in the California wind farms in the 1980s. He came to Ireland in 1985, doing research toward a Ph.D. for Enertech at University College, Dublin. During this time Hurley Staudt Associates carried out the first wind energy survey of Ireland. He worked for the Electricity Supply Board for nine years working in the area of power station control systems, and during this time was a founder director of the Irish Wind Energy Association (IWEA) and a vice president of the

European Wind Energy Association. He left ESB in 1998 to become the first chief executive of the IWEA, a post he held for three years. He subsequently spent one year with Airtricity in the area of wind farm development, before taking up his present position as a lecturer in engineering at Dundalk Institute of Technology where he is involved in the development of its Centre for Renewable Energy. He is a co-director of Celtic Wind Turbines, and holds a patent for an aspect of small generator technology.

PART FOUR:
EU POLICIES AND ENERGY SECURITY

Nuala Ahern is the Green Party M.E.P. for Leinster. She was first elected to the European Parliament in 1994 and re-elected in 1999. She entered politics in 1991 when she was elected to Wicklow County Council. During her term of office she has been Vice-Chair of both the committee on Industry, External trade, Research and Energy and of the Petitions committee. She is also a member of the Culture committee.

She became involved in politics through community action in Wicklow to prevent sewage pollution in the sea. She is a founder member of the Irish Women's Environment Network, which has made important contributions to the removal of toxic products from the home. She is a longterm anti-nuclear campaigner, beginning with the campaign against a nuclear power plant in Carnsore Point, Co. Wexford in the late 1970s. She grew up in the Cooley peninsula of North Louth which is very close to the plutonium reprocessing plant in Sellafield on the west coast of England. She is an active anti-Sellafield campaigner. She joined the Green Party in 1989 and was a founder member of the Wicklow Greens.

Andy Gouldson holds BA, MSc and PhD degrees and has lectured in environmental policy within the Department of Geography and Environment at the London School of Economics since 1995. He is also a member of the LSE Centre for the Analysis of Risk and Regulation.

His research focuses on the nature of the relationship between industrial development and the environment and on the influence of different forms of policy and regulation. At the broadest level, his work on the theory of ecological modernisation considers the nature of industrial progress and the ability of modern societies to recognise and respond to the side effects of continued economic development. He has also worked extensively on environmental policy and regulation where his research has examined the impact that different forms of policy can have on the environmental and economic performance of large and small firms and on the development and diffusion of new technologies. This work has emphasised the origins and influence of different regulatory styles, the existence of various barriers to innovation in regulated firms and the need for policy to establish imperatives, incentives and capacities for change if new technologies and techniques are to be more widely adopted.

Most recently, he has examined the influence that access to information, gained particularly through community 'right to know' legislation, can have on the relations between regulators, industry and stakeholders in the field of environmental risk regulation. He has also been working with the Scottish Environmental Protection Agency to develop methodologies for Regulatory Impact Assessment.

He is Editor of the journal *European Environment* and is co-author of the book *Environmental Management and Business Strategy* (with R. Welford - Pitman Publishing, 1993). His latest books are *Regulatory Realities* (with J. Murphy - Earthscan, 1998) which examines the implementation and impact of environmental regulation in the UK and the Netherlands and *Integrating Environment and Economy* (with P. Roberts - Routledge, 2000) which assesses the relations between economic and environmental policies and plans at the local and regional levels.

Dan Plesch is a Senior Research Fellow at the Royal United Services Institute in London. He was educated at Nottingham and Bristol Universities and has a BA in History and a qualification in Social Work. In 1987 he founded the British American Security Information Council (BASIC), in Washington, DC, and directed the Council until this year. His research and policy advocacy experience includes: arms control and conflict prevention measures; the European code of conduct on arms exports; the adoption of measures on the control of small arms by a range of multilateral institutions; and successive review conferences of the nuclear non-proliferation treaty and the NATO Strategic Concept. His own research has also included Western nuclear weapons doctrine, nuclear weapons safety, US-NATO dynamics, and the politics of intervention. He has written for a wide range of publications including *The Guardian, The New York Times* and *The Washington Post*. He is one of the few Britons to be asked to testify to the Foreign Relations Committee of the US Senate.

PART FIVE:
THE ATTITUDE OF THE ELECTRICITY COMPANIES TO RENEWABLE ENERGY

Anne Trotter is Manager, Transmission Access Planning at ESB National Grid, where she is responsible for completing the planning studies and analysis associated with transmission connections. She graduated from Trinity College Dublin with an honours degree in Electrical & Microelectronic Engineering in 1990. She joined ESB in 1990 and worked in Distribution Department, Dublin Region and Southern Region before joining National Grid in May 2001.

Owen Wilson is Manager, Group Health, Safety and Environment with the Electricity Supply Board (ESB) and has been involved in the environment and energy area at national and European level for over ten years. He is a member of the Emissions Trading Advisory Group and Inventory Data Users Group which were set up under the National Climate Change Strategy. He is a member of the Energy and Climate Change Group of the World Energy Council and of the Environment and Sustainable Development Committee of Eurelectric, the representative group of the electricity industry in Europe. He is also a member of the Industrial Board Queen's University Environmental Science and Technology Research (QUESTOR) Centre, which supports applied scientific research and is a Director of Conservation Volunteers Ireland. He has written and co-written papers and reports on environment and energy.

Declan Flanagan was responsible for trading and regulation within the Airtricity Group at the time he wrote his paper. He was responsible for pricing and forecasting, contract management and relations with regulatory bodies in the various markets in which Airtricity is active. He now heads Airtricity's expansion into the United States. Before joining Airtricity in 2000 he worked in Energy and Environmental Policy with the Irish Business and Employers Confederation and before that as a consultant in the utilities sector. Airtricity is currently developing renewable energy projects in the Republic of Ireland, Northern Ireland and Scotland and is a leading player in the area of green credits, both through the Renewable Energy Certificate (RECs) scheme and the UK Renewable Obligation.

PART SIX:
HOW A RENEWABLE ENERGY ECONOMY WILL AFFECT RURAL LIFE

Bernard Rice works at the Teagasc Crops Research Centre at Oak Park in Carlow where he is Acting Head of the Crop Production and Engineering Department. He is a mechanical engineer, and has worked on farm machinery, crop storage and production and utilisation of energy on farms.

Folke Günther, M.Sc., has a background as a field biologist and as a farmer as well as his university career. He has worked eight years as a lecturer in Human Ecology at Lund University and is a Ph.D. student at Dept. of Systems Ecology, Stockholm University. The title of his thesis is 'Ecological Adaptation of Human Settlements'. One of the conclusions from this work is that ecological adaptation is a good way to attain sustainability. He is also involved with ecological engineers and permaculturalists working on biological water purification.

David Morris is one of the United States' leading authorities on policies that strengthen local and regional economies. For 25 years, he and his organisation, the Institute for Local Self-Reliance, have promoted economic ideas that enable communities to extract the maximum amount of value from local resources.

He has written five books, and dozens of technical reports. His most recent book, *Seeing the Light: Regaining Control of Our Electricity System,* discusses the potential of a decentralised, renewable-fuelled electricity system. He coined the term the "carbohydrate economy" almost 20 years ago to signify an industrial economy based on plant matter, where farmers own the manufacturing facilities. His 1992 book, *The Carbohydrate Economy: Making Chemicals and Industrial Materials* from *Plant Matter,* helped to popularise the term. He is currently editor-in-chief of the quarterly newsletter, *Carbohydrate Economy.* He has worked with the Minnesota farm community to help design and implement the so-called Minnesota model in which 15 largely farmer-owned ethanol plants provide 10 percent of the state's transportation fuel. He currently serves on a congressionally created advisory committee to the Departments of Energy and Agriculture on expanding the use of plant matter for industrial and energy purposes.

Michael Doran joined Rural Generation Limited in 2001 as its business development manager. In 1983 he was the founder partner in a multi disciplinary firm of surveyors, architects and project managers with offices in Northern Ireland and in the Republic. He left the practice in 1998 to work as an Interim Manager specialising in business start-ups, business development and turnarounds. He is a Chartered Surveyor and a member of the Association of Project Managers.

Charlie Pinney was born in Dorset in 1950 and educated at Eton and Nottingham University where he studied both Zoology and Philosophy. Between 1969 and 1979 he farmed 250 acres in Dorset using draught horses. In 1974 he founded the Western Counties Heavy Horse Association. In 1975 he introduced the Ardennes breed to Britain and opened the studbook. He devised the "Heavy Horse Handling Course" for the Agricultural Training Board which became adopted nationally. He still runs training courses in heavy horse use both privately and for agricultural colleges. In 1979 he founded Carthorse Machinery to design and manufacture horse-drawn farm machinery. The business won the Prince Philip Cup for the PINTOW chassis system at the Royal Show in 1996.

Between 1982 and 1986 he was a member of the "History with a Future" project committee evaluating current and potential uses of draught horses. He is a member of the Joint National Horse Education and Training Council Heavy Horse Committee and National Verifier for the NVQ Heavy Horse module and National Standard Setter for the Road Driving Assessment. He has written extensively in the technical press on horse farming. In 2000 he moved to a 600-acre organic mixed farm in Scotland to continue developing new horse machinery.

Tom Woolley is Professor of Architecture at Queens University, Belfast and Director of the Centre for Green Building Research. He has been involved both as a practising architect and as a teacher and researcher in environmental building design for much of his career. For the past eight years he has concentrated on looking at the impact of the building industry on the environment and this has led to the publication of the *Green Building Handbook*. This work emphasises the importance of the toxic and damaging impacts of conventional materials on the eco system and human health as well as issues such as energy.

A founder member of the UK Ecological Design Association and a member of the committee of the Association of Environment Conscious Builders, he is also a member of the International Board of the Ecological Building Network and the advisory board of the European Green Building Network. He has chaired the Northern Ireland Building Regulations Advisory Committee for the past four years and is a consultant on the Design Advice Towards Greener Buildings Scheme. He is involved in architectural practice with Rachel Bevan Architects carrying out new ecological projects, work with rural community groups and historic building renovation.

PART SEVEN:
THE POTENTIAL FOR RENEWABLE ENERGY IN IRELAND

 **Kevin Healion** is from Rosenallis in Co. Laois. He studied biotechnology at Dublin City University and environmental engineering at Trinity College, Dublin. His first job was as an environmental consultant specialising in sewage sludge management and renewable energy production from wood. He now lives in Co. Tipperary and teaches on the Degree in Rural Development and Certificate in Renewable Energy courses at the Tipperary Institute. He is secretary of the Irish Bioenergy Asssociation.

 **Douglas Gordon** lives in Dublin. He has worked in environmental management and monitoring for many years. He took part in the EU-funded study of Ireland's geothermal resources in 1980-81. The huge potential of the solar-related geothermal energy that this study revealed led to his involvement in the Irish Solar Energy Association. He is professionally involved in non-chemical water treatment systems.

 **Seamus Hoyne** has a Bachelor of Engineering and a Masters of Engineering from the University of Limerick. He is Leader of the Tipperary Institute's Certificate in Renewable Energy course. His current project and research work includes wood pellet heating systems and community involvement in renewable energy. He was Secretary of the Irish Bioenergy Association (IrBEA) from 1999 to 2002. He was the full-time manager of the Tipperary Energy Agency (http://www.tea.ie) and continues in that role on a part-time basis. He is chairperson of the Association of Irish Energy Agencies (http://www.tea.ie/aiea.htm).

 **David Miller** was the chairman of the Irish Hydropower Association for fifteen years and is now the president of the European Small Hydro Association. He lives in Co. Offaly where he is part owner of a commercial small hydro station which has been selling into the national grid since 1982.

Inge Buckley has a BSc in Economics and Business. She moved to Ireland from Denmark in 1971 and for 17 years was Vice-Consul in charge of the commercial section of the Danish Embassy in Dublin. She is a member of the Marketing Institute of Ireland and was chairman of the Irish-Danish Business Association from 1998 to 2000. She set up Scan Energy & Environmental Services in 1990 and has held the agency for Vestas wind turbines in Ireland since 1991. She was a founder member of the Irish Wind Energy Association and has been a member of the IWEA Council since its foundation. She was IWEA chairman from 2000 to 2002. She is a member of two bodies advising the Irish government on its energy policies, the Wind Strategy Group and the Grid Investment Committee. She is also a member of IBEC's Energy Strategy Group.

Brian P. Connor graduated in 1962 and took a post as a research assistant in the Geology Department at University College, Dublin. In 1968 he joined Tara Exploration and Development Company Ltd as an exploration geologist. Two years later he moved to P.D. Buckley & Sons Ltd. of Mallow, Co. Cork, as company geologist and in 1972 he joined Amoco Minerals Ireland as a consultant geologist on base metal exploration. From 1976 to 1991 he was managing director of Geoex Ltd., a hydrogeological and environmental consulting firm. He left to establish Brian P. Connor & Associates Ltd., a consultancy on the sustainable development of natural resources including renewable energy resources, which was contracted by the EU to research low temperature geothermal energy technologies. His firm also promotes the utilisation of European technologies in Ireland. He is a Fellow of Geological Society of London and a member of International Association of Hydrogeologists.

PART EIGHT:

THE WAY AHEAD

 **Jackie Carpenter** BSc CEng MIMechE FRSA is Director of Energy 21 and the current President of the Women's Engineering Society. She went to an all-girls school and studied pure maths, applied maths, physics and chemistry at A level. She took a degree in Mechanical Engineering at University College London and worked in a variety of engineering companies for several years. At age 25 she began a career break and raised two daughters, with motherhood as her main occupation for eight years. She returned to work as assistant to the Chief Engineer at a small Johnson and Johnson factory and then joined Vickers (which later became Brown and Root) where she worked for nine years. She started at Vickers as a junior project planner and became a chartered engineer and a senior project manager managing multimillion-pound projects within a few years. Eventually she became the most senior woman engineer in the company and was transferred to London as a member of the UK and Europe strategy team.

She has had a great love and respect for the natural world since her schooldays and has spent many hours working as a volunteer in nature conservation. The Rio conference in 1992, which set the scene for sustainable development, was a great inspiration and in 1993 she decided to set up her own business and became a consultant in renewable energy. Increasing opportunities to develop more appropriate technologies, in harmony with nature, led her to become part of a team which set up a charity, Energy 21, whose mission is "to generate a greater awareness and understanding of renewable energy". She is now Director of Energy 21 in Stroud, Gloucestershire.

Glossary and Abbreviations

Bar: a unit of pressure roughly equal to an atmosphere. (A bar is 100,000 newtons per square metre and an atmosphere is 101,325 newtons per square metre.)

BAU: business as usual.

Bbls: barrels.

B/d: barrels per day.

BWR: Boiling Water Reactor.

C: carbon.

Ca: calcium.

CCGT: Combined Cycle Gas Turbine.

CHP: Combined Heat and Power.

Cwt: hundredweight.

Ebcus: emissions-backed currency units.

Entropy: a measure of the extent to which the energy in a system is available for doing work. Entropy increases as energy is dispersed when it is used.

ERE: Energy Requirement of Energy – the energy required to produce energy.

GER: Gross Energy Requirement.

GHG: Greenhouse gas.

Gt: giga-tonnes. Giga stands for 1000 million.

GW: gigawatt, equal to 1,000 megawatts.

H: hydrogen.

HMC: human-made capital.

IFIAS: International Federation of Institutes of Advanced Study.

IPCC: Intergovernmental Panel on Climate Change.

Joule: a unit of work or energy. It is the work done when a force of one newton moves an object one metre. It is equal to 4,187 calories.

K: potassium.

KJ: kilojoules or 1000 joules.

LNG: liquid natural gas.

Mecu: million ecu. An ecu is now considered equal to a euro.

Mt: million tonnes.

Mha: Million Hectares

MW: megawatt. A megawatt is a 1,000 kilowatts.

MWe: a megawatt of electrical energy.

MWth: a megawatt of thermal (heat) energy.

N: nitrogen.

Na: sodium.

NEA: Nuclear Energy Agency, part of the OECD.

NGL: natural gas liquids.

O: oxygen.

P: phosphorus.

PJ: petajoules. The prefix peta- stands for 10^{15}.

psi: pounds per square inch, a measure of pressure.

PV: Photovoltaic.

PWR: Pressurised Water Reactor.

$GDP: Gross Domestic Product expressed in dollars.

S: sulphur.

SEK: Swedish crowns.

SERs: Special Emission Rights.

SRC: Short Rotation Coppice.

SWU - separative work unit, a measure of the effort needed to separate the U-235 and U-238 atoms in natural uranium in order to create a final product that is richer in U-235 atoms.

Tcf: trillion cubic feet.

TCO$_2$: tonnes of carbon dioxide.

TNO: the Netherlands Organisation for Applied Scientific Research..

Toe: tonnes oil equivalent.

TWh: terawatt-hour, equal to a million megawatts or a billion kilowatts.

UNFCCC: United Nations' Framework Convention on Climate Change.

W/cap: watts per capita

Introduction:
The energy required to produce energy

This book is based on the papers given at a conference, *Ireland's Transition to Renewable Energy*, held at the Tipperary Institute in Thurles over three days in Autumn 2002. The event was organised by Feasta, the Dublin-based Foundation for the Economics of Sustainability, the Renewable Energy Information Office of Sustainable Energy Ireland and the Tipperary Institute itself. It drew its inspiration from the work of Dr. Colin Campbell, who has been arguing authoritatively for some years that the world's oil supply will begin to contract during the current decade as a result of resource depletion.

Feasta has been interested in Dr. Campbell's ideas since it was established in 1998 and he spoke at the *Money, Energy and Growth* conference it organised at Trinity College, Dublin, in March 2000. The three themes indicated by the title of the Trinity conference ran through the Thurles one and will be apparent in this book. This is because although the Thurles conference was designed to be an impartial enquiry into Ireland's energy future rather than the presentation of a particular point of view, the questions the enquiry was designed to answer were naturally those that the organisers – and in particular, Feasta, since it took the main responsibility for assembling the programme – thought were significant.

Feasta sees its task as to identify the characteristics that the world will have to possess to become economically, environmentally and socially sustainable. Once it has done this, it should be able to establish which features of the present system need to be changed and how this should be done. Feasta's work so far has led it to believe that continual economic growth is incompatible with sustainability and that a sustainable world can only be powered by energy from renewable sources. It has also identified the present money-creation system as a barrier to the achievement of sustainability. This is because, since almost all the money now in use was originally issued as a debt, unless people borrow just a little more each year than than they or others repaid during the previous one, (the increase is required because the retained earnings of the lenders have to be borrowed back), the money supply will contract and this will limit the amount of trading that is possible.

If this happened, the poor trading would discourage further borrowing and could thus lead to a depression setting in. The only way to avoid this is by ensuring that economic growth takes place every year, so that is what every government on the planet seeks to do. The snag is that generating the necessary growth almost always involves higher levels of energy use. Consequently, if fossil fuels are no longer available in increasing quantities, unless nuclear energy or renewable power sources can be developed rapidly enough not just to make up the increasing shortfall but also to provide extra energy each year, the world economy could go into a serious decline.

Accordingly, the Thurles conference opened with Colin Campbell putting his case, a representative of a major oil company responded by saying that oil will be abundant for at least 25 years, and after some discussion, the meeting went on to explore what other sources of energy might become available and how well they might be able to compensate for the missing oil when it became necessary for them to do so. In particular, the meeting asked, would other power sources enable current rates of economic growth to continue?

It became very clear during the event that the depletion of oil and gas reserves would leave few areas of human life unchanged and that, to bring about a favourable outcome, it was crucial to take the right decisions now. Perhaps the most important decisions involve deciding how the remaining fossil energy supplies should be used. At any time, the size of the world's energy supply is determined by the amount of energy that has been invested as capital into developing energy sources and by the amount of energy these sources require as a regular input to produce their energy output. So energy as capital is the energy required to sink coalmines and oil wells, to build nuclear power stations and to erect wind turbines, while input energy is the power required to use that capital equipment. In the case of the coalmine, it is the energy required to pump out water, to pump in air, and to run the conveyor belts, the cutting equipment, the cages that lift the coal to the surface, the washery and the rest. And, of course, energy is needed to transport the energy to the consumer, whether this is via an electricity grid or a road/rail/sea delivery system.

The point being made here is that energy both as capital and as an input is needed to produce an energy supply. Renewables and nuclear stations usually require much more capital energy during their set-up stages than do their fossil equivalents but the latter generally consume more income energy to produce a continuing power supply. Moreover, as the most easily exploited sources of oil, gas and coal are gradually used up, the amount of input energy required to continue to supply these fuels to the market tends to rise. Eventually, the point will be reached at which the amount of input energy used for their production comes close to the output energy that the fuels deliver usefully when burned. At that point, it will be useless to

continue production because, although there might be a lot of fuel left in the earth, it will no longer be a net energy source. Unless improved extraction technologies cut energy inputs, it might as well not be there.

The portion of the fossil fuels still in the earth that can be extracted and burned in a way that delivers a net energy gain is an endowment that can either be spent on meeting humanity's daily running costs or invested for the future. However, the current generation does not have a completely free hand in deciding the split between these two uses because over the centuries since coal began to be mined, people have developed ways of supporting themselves that require a lot of energy to run. Until renewables and/or nuclear sources have been developed enough to supply that energy, a lot of fossil fuel will have to be consumed to do so instead. In other words, for some considerable time, the world will only be able to turn a fraction of each year's gas, coal and oil output into capital energy to use to develop energy alternatives.

TRAPPED IN MISERY

This means that, even leaving climate-change considerations apart, the world's transition to non-fossil sources of energy must not start too late or proceed too slowly. If it does either, there could be insufficient energy left to be spent as capital on the construction of energy sources to replace fossil fuels and the world could be trapped for generations in a miserable low-energy-use economy that would lead to the premature deaths of hundreds of millions of people.

The question of when a determined switch away from fossil fuels should begin and how quickly should it be carried out cannot be left to the energy markets to decide because once oil and gas prices start to rise as a result of increasing scarcity, it will already be too late. Too late, that is, to make the transition without denying energy supplies to the weakest, most marginal consumers in the world – in other words, to the really poor - unless some sort of rationing is put in place. This denial would not merely mean that the poor had to use less kerosine for their lights at night and for their cooking stoves. The price of tractors, transport and fertilizers would rise, pushing up the cost of food, which would mean that, although undernourished already, they would have to manage on even less.

On a world level, then, the availability of energy is determined by the amount of fossil energy left in the earth, the amount of energy it takes to extract it, and by the amount of energy that has been invested in developing fossil, nuclear and renewable energy supplies. Until now, there has been enough readily-extractable fossil energy left for the supply of fuel to increase year after year. As a result, the availability of money rather than energy has been the constraint governing the level of economic activity. However, when the global production of fossil energy begins to fall because sources which once supplied fuel for little effort are becoming depleted and considerably more energy has to be put in to fossil sources to get any energy out, the money supply will cease to determine how much economic activity goes on around the world. The energy supply will do so instead. From that day on, increasing the amount of money in circulation will have no effect at all on overall energy supply. It will simply cause an energy-price inflation. Indeed, energy will replace money as the true measure of value and conventional money will be valued according to how much energy it can buy. This will be, of course, a complete reversal of the present situation in which energy is valued in money terms rather than vice versa.

Because this fundamental change in the nature of money is almost certain to happen within the next 25 years, a lot of the discussion in this

book is in terms of how much energy it takes to produce energy rather than the monetary cost of producing it. A related reason for discussing energy sources in this way is that money costs and benefits have already shown themselves to be false guides to energy policy and prospects. For example, as David Morris describes in his paper in this book, tax reliefs have enabled alcohol produced from grain to provide 10 percent of Minnesota's transportation fuel. A praiseworthy step towards a sustainable energy supply? Not at all. According to David Pimentel of Cornell University, producing a U.S. gallon of alcohol consumes 131,000 BTUs from fossil sources in planting, growing and harvesting the corn, then crushing, fermenting and distilling it. That same gallon releases only 77,000 BTUs when burned. "Put another way, about 70% more energy is required to produce alcohol than the alcohol actually contains" Pimentel says. If energy was being counted rather than money, this wasteful activity would stop overnight.

FAULTY FORECAST

The American Petroleum Council also has also fallen into the trap of counting money rather than energy. It forecast in 1972 that when the price of a barrel of oil exceeded $6, shale oil extraction would be economic. Although the $6 price has been exceeded by a factor of two, three or four for most of the period since, the shale oil has stayed in the ground. The faulty forecast arose because the APC thought that the costs of extracting shale oil were unaffected by current energy costs whereas the extraction costs are essentially determined by the price of oil to the industries that make the inputs and the capital equipment that the shale oil processors require. An energy-in/energy-out analysis would have shown just how sensitive the extraction process was to changes in energy prices.

To avoid the discussion at the conference or in this book falling into this trap we asked those writing papers about particular energy sources to say, if they possibly could, how many units of energy the sources they were describing supplied for each unit of energy put in. This approach was so foreign to a major oil company that it changed its mind about sending a speaker. "Your suggestion to measure the energy intensity of all activities necessary in the provision of future sources of energy has certainly fallen on fertile ground here" a senior figure in the company wrote, asking to be sent copies of the conference papers. "We will be learning more from the results of the conference then we are currently able to contribute."

A spokesperson for another major oil company also found the approach novel and commented: "I am somewhat confused by the theme of the conference as you state it, that availability of energy is not a function of price, but rather the energy required to release or extract the energy. That all costs of labour and capital can ultimately be resolved to a cost of energy is true, but the purpose of price is precisely to encapsulate those costs." Up to a point, Lord Copper, but, as in the Minnesotan case, those prices can go wrong. Consequently, as energy is about to replace money as the real measure of value anyway, we decided that we had better start costing it in its own terms.

The book opens with the text of Dr. Campbell's conference talk. We are, however, unable to present the full counterview advanced by David Frowd, who was at the time the head of the energy group in Shell International's scenarios team. He has since retired. In his talk, Frowd flashed several slides packed with figures on the screen much more quickly than anyone in the audience could note anything down. He then left the conference before anyone could ask him privately for the full details. He subsequently refused to make the slides or the data on which he based his conclusions available and the transcript we had made of his talk was

meaningless without these figures. "We don't want a debate," he said. It is hard to see his presence at the conference as anything more than a spoiling exercise designed to prevent firm conclusions about when oil and gas output might begin to decline from emerging. After all, once Shell's customers recognise that scarcity is going to make their oil deliveries much more costly in a few years' time, they will start switching to other energy sources, damaging the company's market now. Is that why a debate isn't wanted?

LAST DAYS OF OIL

While we have done our best to present Frowd's arguments fully and fairly, we have also printed the opinions of the second in command of the world's largest oil company, Exxon-Mobil, Harry Longwell, who though he agrees with Dr. Campbell's views on the decline in the rate at which oil is being found (he uses one of Campbell's graphs in his article) nevertheless expresses confidence that the oil industry 'has the resources to meet future global energy demand for some considerable time.' Other oilmen have been even more forthcoming. In February, 1999, for example, Mike Bowlin, the chairman and CEO of a major California-based oil company, ARCO, better known by its old name, Atlantic Richfield, said that the world was entering 'the last days of the Age of Oil'. His company was therefore looking to a future in which motor fuels from renewable sources played a bigger part. ARCO has since been taken over by BP.

This introduction has been written to be as neutral as possible. The conclusions that I, personally, draw from the material in this book come at the end. It should be said that Feasta, the Tipperary Institute and Sustainable Energy Ireland do not necessarily stand over all the opinions expressed in these pages. Nor do I. The conference was designed to be a wideranging enquiry and that is exactly what it was.

This book is more wide-ranging still as we have taken the opportunity to print five or six items which cast an interesting light on, or supplement, the conference papers themselves. The advantages of a methanol economy over a hydrogen one, the prospects for oil from tar sands, and the sequestration of carbon dioxide are examples of the topics covered by these additional papers. So is the panel on Ireland's growing dependency on oil on the opposite page.

The major disappointment of the conference was that, although the speakers were all leaders in their fields and the attendance was good, very few of those responsible for making decisions involving energy issues bothered to come. Feasta and its partners hope that this book will enable them to pick up on the ideas they missed. Ireland's future will be largely determined by whether or not they do.

Ireland's Alarming Reliance on Oil

Gerard O'Neill

Which country is more dependent on oil for its energy - Ireland or Saudi Arabia? The answer, surprisingly, is Ireland - in fact ours is the 7th most oil-dependent economy in the world, and the third most dependent in the EU (after Portugal and Greece, 5th and 6th in the world respectively). Oil makes up 60% of primary energy consumption in Ireland, compared to an EU average of just 43%. Indeed, Ireland is even more dependent on oil for its energy than the United States: the latter is ranked 30th in the world in terms of oil-dependency, with oil providing 40% of it total energy requirements.

It wasn't always this way. Up until the mid-1990s, Irish oil consumption per capita was below the EU average. However as the chart below shows, we've had a Celtic Tiger in the tank during our economic boom, with the result that Irish oil consumption per capita doubled between 1989 and 2001, whilst that of the EU and the world as a whole remained unchanged:

It is worth noting that EU oil consumption in the chart is now lower than it was during the 1973 oil crisis, whilst ours is considerably higher.

In some respects, Ireland's growth in oil-dependency is not surprising. After all, we have limited indigenous sources of fossil energy, and so we are dependent on imported oil to 'fuel' our economic growth. Indeed, econometric modelling by Amárach shows that during the period 1986 to 2001:

- A 1% increase in Irish GDP lead to a 1.8% increase in oil consumption, but that
- A 1% increase in EU15 GDP lead to only a 0.6% increase in oil consumption.

It would appear that Ireland has an 'oil hungry' economy relative to the European Union as a whole. This has important implications for the future: the bottom line is that our continued economic success is crucially dependent on an expanding global supply of oil at current or lower prices.

Our current standard of living requires that we import some 9 million tonnes of oil every year. If our economy is to grow in the medium term by, say, a modest 3% per annum over the next 5 years, then we will have to import over 12 million tonnes by 2008 - right in the middle of the period in which, if Colin Campbell and other experts are right, the world supply of oil will be beginning to contract.

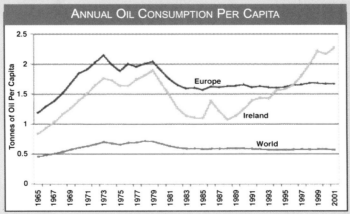

Source: Amárach calculations based on BP Statistical Review 2002 & Eurostat 2003

Part One
World Conventional Energy Supply Prospects

The world's oil and gas reserves are being rapidly depleted and at some point, production will begin to decline. How soon will the decline begin and can other conventional sources of energy - coal, tar sands and nuclear - be developed to prevent shortages occurring?

A   When will the world's oil and gas production peak? by **Colin Campbell** plus panels on tar sands and Shell's approach to oil depletion

B   Exxon-Mobil's view of the future of oil and gas by **Harry J. Longwell**

C   The role of coal in achieving energy sustainability **John T. McMullan** plus panel on sequestration by **Euan Baird**

D   Renewable energy and nuclear power by **Ian Hore-Lacy**

When will the world's oil and gas production peak?

by Colin Campbell

The world's oil and gas production will start to decline within most people's lifetimes. Although this will have a dramatic effect on lifestyles and the course of civilization, vested interests have deliberately kept both policymakers and the public in the dark.

Resource depletion is easy to grasp. As every beer drinker knows, a glass starts full and ends empty. Oil and gas are fossil fuels formed in the geological past. This means that they started running out on the day we started using them. But I think this business of running out has confused many people. It is not really the issue. What matters much more than when the last drop of oil will be used is when production will reach its peak and begin to decline. So the primary interest of my work is to try to determine when the peak will happen.

Why do we need to know?

Well, because the world runs on oil, that's obvious: 40% of all traded energy is oil; 90% of transport fuel is oil. And as gas depletes, too, a diminishing supply will have a big impact on electricity generation. Furthermore, oil and gas are critical inputs in agriculture and for the production of petro-chemicals. So I think there is no more crucial factor to take into account in today's world. I suggest that the onset of decline speaks of recession, if not depression. It speaks of starvation because the population of the world has risen six-fold exactly in parallel with the increase in oil production, so logic tells you the decline of oil will have a serious impact on population. It speaks of conflict, or at least great political and geo-political changes.

So if the dates on which oil and gas production peak are so crucial, why aren't we told when they are?

That is, I think, perhaps an even more interesting subject than the fact of depletion itself. Why is depletion not at the top of every agenda? After all, measuring the size of an oil field is not that difficult. It is well within the capabilities of experienced engineers and geologists. And the world has been thoroughly explored. Surely then, we can have a good idea about how far along the depletion curve we are.

Is the glass half empty? If the turning point is that important, and so easily determined, why aren't we told when it is?

I think the short answer is that those who know don't wish to tell us, and those in government prefer not to know, because politically it is always easier to react to a crisis than to anticipate one. If I'm right, we have two vested interests: one group of people who don't want to reveal what the situation is, and the other group of people who don't want to hear it in any case. The importance of books like this is to try to raise the issue in the public domain.

Confusion is the means by which the truth about depletion is concealed and obscured. Even the definitions are confusing. There is no standard definition of what we are talking about. The distinction between conventional and non-conventional oil, or unconventional as it is sometimes called, is often made but the terms are used in very different ways by different authors. The problem arises because there are many different types of oil, each with its own characteristics and depletion profile.

Which types are conventional and which not? It is obvious that producing oil from a Middle East well, or a North Sea well, is a very different business from digging up a tar sand in Canada with a shovel. These are the two extremes of a wide range of different oil categories; each needs to be analysed, measured, and have its depletion profile developed.

The more we go into detail, the greater the confusion. How are gas liquids - the liquids that condense from gas - to be treated? Then there is the issue of refinery gains: the refining process adds volume so that more comes out than goes in.

And what about war loss? When they burnt up all that oil in Kuwait, was this production? In the sense that it reduced reserves it was production, but it certainly wasn't supply. The statistics for gas variously refer to "dry" gas, from which the dissolved liquids have been removed; or "wet" gas; or "marketed" gas. Flaring gas, re-injecting to support pressure, and operating usage are further causes of confusion. There is such a maze of conflicting, uncertain, weak definitions that everybody is talking at cross purposes.

On top of this we have confused reporting. As I said, estimating reserves is a scientific business. There is a range of uncertainty, certainly, but it is not an impossible challenge to get a good idea of what a field contains. Reporting the result, however, is a political act, whether a company is reporting to a government, or an employee is reporting to his or her superiors. I worked in the oil industry for many years and I don't think I ever told the truth about the size of a prospect. This was not the game we were in. As we were competing for funds with other subsidiaries around the world, we had to exaggerate. So the reporting issue is extremely confused and is another main reason why depletion is not well understood. Furthermore Stock

Exchange rules were introduced to encourage understatement, because to overstate was close to fraud. So the Stock Exchange rules were designed primarily to understate the size of the reserves. There was no problem about saying they were less, but there were great risks if you exaggerated. For most purposes this doesn't matter in the least: it was just the way the industry runs. But if we want to model depletion, we need valid reserve estimates, and above all, valid dates.

So I come to the issue of confused dates. An oil field is found when the first borehole is drilled into it. An oilfield contains what it contains, for the simple reason that it was filled in the geological past. Consequently, all the oil ever to be recovered from it, whatever the technology used and whatever the economic conditions, is logically attributable to the first discovery. After all, if we had not been born, we would not have a career of any kind. So I think that the date of a field's discovery is quite as important as the amount of oil or gas it contains.

REALITY AND ILLUSION

Figure 1A1 shows the importance of the date issue. The lower curve shows public domain data on reserves. They've been growing consistently since 1950. There was a great surge in the late '80s. It is eminently reasonable for somebody looking at this data set to extrapolate it onwards, and many economists do just that giving governments the false impression that the reserves keep on growing for ever. That's what this plot would suggest. But then if we backdate the reserve revisions to the date on which the fields concerned were discovered we get an entirely different picture. We find that peak rate of discovery came in the mid '60s and that it has been falling ever since. If we extrapolate this firm trend of falling discovery on out, we get a firm picture what of left to find and produce. The contrast between

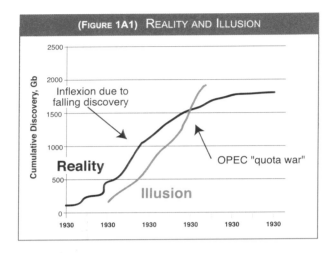

the upper line produced by backdating and using real numbers and the lower line, which is what is in the public domain, has confused many analysts.

Then there is the data itself, another source of confusion. Companies don't really like to talk too much to each other directly about their reserves but they do like to know what each other is doing. Accordingly, they collaborate with commercial firms to put the information together in an industry data base. The problem is that it costs you over $1 million to get into it. This puts it out of range for most analysts who turn instead to two trade journals, the *Oil and Gas Journal* and the *World Oil* who have done a heroic job over many many years compiling the information from governments and from industry where they can, but as trade journals they are not competent to judge the validity of the information they compile. There's also the *BP Statistical Review of World Energy,* the bible for most analysts, many of whom mistakenly think that the statistics in it have the tacit blessing of a major international oil company. They don't. They are simply reproduced from the *Oil and Gas Journal*. And lastly, we at the Association for the Study of Peak Oil, ASPO, are trying in a humble way not to mislead by putting out the best data that we can assemble.

	Abu Dhabi	Dubai	Iran	Iraq	Kuwait	Neutral Zone	Saudi Arabia	Venezuela
1980	28	1.4	58	31	65	6.1	163	18
1981	29	1.4	58	30	66	6.0	165	18
1982	31	1.4	57	30	65	5.9	165	20
1983	31	1.4	55	41	64	5.7	162	22
1984	30	1.4	51	43	64	5.6	166	25
1985	31	1.4	49	45	90	5.4	169	26
1986	30	1.4	48	44	90	5.4	169	26
1987	31	1.4	49	47	92	5.3	167	25
1988	92	4.0	93	100	92	5.2	167	56
1989	92	4.0	93	100	92	5.0	170	58
1990	92	4.0	93	100	92	5.0	258	59
1991	92	4.0	93	100	95	5.0	258	59
1992	92	4.0	93	100	94	5.0	258	63
1993	92	4.0	93	100	94	5.0	259	63
1994	92	4.0	89	100	94	5.0	259	65
1995	92	4.0	88	100	94	5.0	259	65
1996	92	4.0	93	112	94	5.0	259	65
1997	92	4.0	93	113	94	5.0	259	72
1998	92	4.0	90	113	94	5.0	259	73
1999	92	4.0	90	113	94	5.0	261	73
2000	92	4.0	90	113	94	5.0	258	77

(FIGURE 1A2) SPURIOUS REVISIONS

The sudden jump in oil reserves in 1988. The figures are in billions of barrels

Table 1A2 illustrates this flawed database It shows that in 1985, Kuwait added 50% to its reported reserves, although nothing particular changed in the reservoir. It did so because OPEC quota was based in part on reserves: the higher the reserves, the higher the quota. That action, incidentally, greatly upset its neighbour Iraq and was one of the causes of the Gulf War. Then moving to Venezuela, in 1988 it doubled the size of its reserves, doing so by including the huge amounts of heavy oil that had been known for years, but which it now decided to include in the resource base for no particular reason. Its action then caused Abu Dhabi, Dubai, Iran and Iraq to retaliate with enormous, overnight increases in reported reserves to protect their OPEC quota. It is interesting to note that the Neutral Zone, which is owned equally by Kuwait and Saudi Arabia, had two owners with no motive to change the numbers.

The table also shows another anomalous feature. Is it at all plausible that Abu Dhabi has had exactly 92 billion barrels of reserves for twelve years despite their depletion as a result of production? For reserves to stay the same despite production means production has to have been exactly matched by new discoveries or by reserve revision. I accept that the early numbers were too low, having been inherited from the private companies that ran the fields before they were being expropriated. Some increase was called for, justified and reasonable. The point is

that nothing happened in 1988, and the revisions, whatever the true number might be, have to be back dated to the discovery of the fields concerned, many of which had been found up to fifty years before. This emphasises the critical importance of back dating the numbers properly.

As you have to find oil before you can produce it, the past discovery trend shows us by extrapolation how much there is yet to find in the future, and, if we deduct how much has been produced so far, how much is left to produce in the future.

Figure 1A3 shows Shell's record of discovery since 1885. It's absolutely remarkable that the actual discovery matches so closely the theoretical curve. Shell can be extremely proud of this record, because it shows that they were using the very best of technology and were very efficient, searching the world for the biggest and best prospects. Their performance was outstanding, but the graph also tells us that they have found about 80% of all they can ever hope to find no matter how hard they try. Other companies were very much less successful. *Figure 1A4* shows that poor old Amoco really found nothing with the last 500 wildcats it drilled, a performance vastly inferior to Shell's and of course it has now disappeared, merging with BP, for very obvious and good reasons.

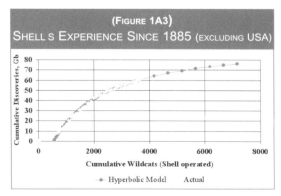

(FIGURE 1A3)
SHELL S EXPERIENCE SINCE 1885 (EXCLUDING USA)

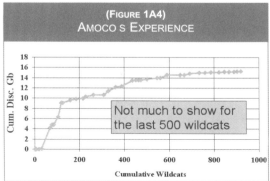

(FIGURE 1A4)
AMOCO S EXPERIENCE

USA

Let us now look at the United States in *Figure 1A5*. Discovery peaked in 1930, roughly, with the East Texas field (just off to the left of the curve). It has been falling ever since. Despite having all the technology, all the money, all the incentive, they just weren't able to counter this downward trend. And here we see the peak of production that followed the peak of discovery after a time lag of forty-one years. And there is really nothing at this late stage that can reverse the downward trend of the 48 contiguous US states. Certainly we can add something for the deepwater, but that is a different category. And it explains, incidentally, why the United States government officially states that access to foreign oil is of vital national interest, justifying military intervention.

NORTH SEA

Now let us look at the North Sea in Fig 1A6. It shows a very similar pattern. Discovery very clearly peaked in 1973 and it's a long time since a giant field was found there. The corresponding production peak was predictably passed in the United Kingdom in 1999, and output is falling fast. Norway is not far behind, as now admitted by the Norwegian authorities. So there is a simple and very obvious relationship between the peak in discovery and the peak in output

WORLD - CONVENTIONAL OIL

Figure 1A7 shows the world picture. The vertical bar shows discoveries, with the spikes being the very large Middle East fields. Peak discovery was in 1964. The grey line shows the theoretical bell-shaped curve that would have been achieved had it been an entirely open environment of production and consumption. There

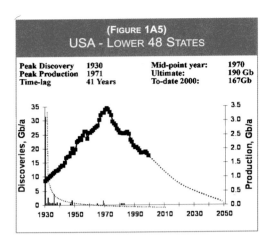

(FIGURE 1A5)
USA - LOWER 48 STATES

Peak Discovery	1930	Mid-point year:	1970
Peak Production	1971	Ultimate:	190 Gb
Time-lag	41 Years	To-date 2000:	167Gb

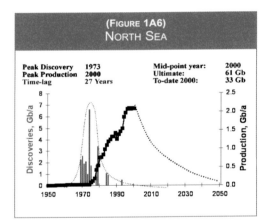

(FIGURE 1A6)
NORTH SEA

Peak Discovery	1973	Mid-point year:	2000
Peak Production	2000	Ultimate:	61 Gb
Time-lag	27 Years	To-date 2000:	33 Gb

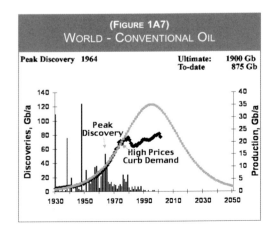

(FIGURE 1A7)
WORLD - CONVENTIONAL OIL

| Peak Discovery 1964 | Ultimate: | 1900 Gb |
| | To-date | 875 Gb |

was a close match until the oil shocks in the '70s, when high prices restricted demand. This means that the actual production peak will be lower and later than would otherwise have been the case, but the good part about that is that the rate at which output eventually falls will be less rapid. The graph covers conventional oil only.

CONVENTIONAL OIL SCENARIOS

No one can predict the near-term future with any confidence on the brink of war but one has to do one's best. The middle line in *Figure 1A8* supposes that conventional oil production will stay more or less at its present level until 2010 because recession will reduce demand. After that, however, my guess is that the five main Middle East producing countries will no longer be able to increase their output by enough to offset declines in the output elsewhere and a long-term decline in output will begin. Of course there are other scenarios. You can picture a decline from now on, represented by the lower line, or you can have an economic recovery for a few years, giving the higher curve shown by the upper line, but a more rapid decline in output when that eventually begins. In all of these scenarios, however, the midpoint of depletion, which more or less corresponds with peak production, comes around 2005.

PRODUCTION FORECAST

Figure 1A9 sums up the story as well as I can put it together. The grey area is conventional oil as I define it, with a plateau up to 2010 and the onset of long-term decline then. The darker area above it is the heavy oils from Canada and Venezuela that I think will continue to increase in production. Then we have deep-water oil, a rather special and very difficult environment, where I picture a peak coming also around 2010. This might be a bit optimistic, but that is how it sits at the minute. And then there is polar

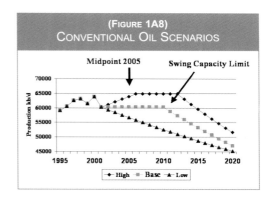

(FIGURE 1A8)
CONVENTIONAL OIL SCENARIOS

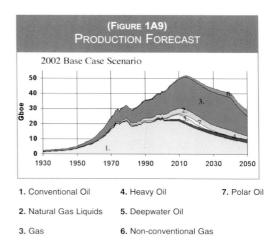

(FIGURE 1A9)
PRODUCTION FORECAST

1. Conventional Oil   4. Heavy Oil   7. Polar Oil

2. Natural Gas Liquids   5. Deepwater Oil

3. Gas   6. Non-conventional Gas

oil. The Russians tell me that they have hopes for large new discoveries in their Arctic regions. I am not sure how valid that is, or whether it will happen, but I give them some credit for that. Then we have gas liquids, they are an increasingly important fuel for the future, and of course they derive from gas. Gas itself is number 3. I expect output to reach some sort of plateau around 2015 if new pipelines to Central Asia and the Middle East are constructed. And then at the top we have a few non-conventional gases, such as coalbed methane.

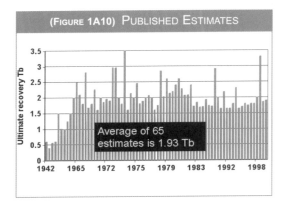

(FIGURE 1A10) PUBLISHED ESTIMATES

I have published this graph in various places and was immensely gratified and impressed to find on my recent visit to Norway, that this very plot was reproduced in a BP article in an official Norwegian publication. I wouldn't give much for the author's future in the company, because the company does not encourage such revelations. But truth does somehow filter out in the strangest ways.

PUBLISHED ESTIMATES

There are other estimates. How does what I have shown you compare? Well, *Figure 1A10* shows 65 estimates of the world's oil reserves published over almost as many years. Of course we don't exactly know what definitions the various authors were using but by and large it gives a rounded number of 2 trillion. Many of these estimates were by major companies, Shell, BP, Mobil and so on. So, when I say that the amount of conventional oil ultimately recoverable is 1900 trillion barrels, I'm not far off the average of 65 published estimates by the industry itself and by everybody else qualified to pronounce on it. My figure cannot therefore be regarded as an extraordinarily unreasonable one.

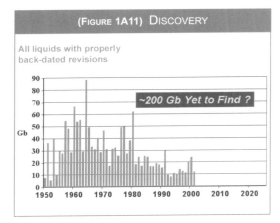

(FIGURE 1A11) DISCOVERY

DISCOVERY

Figure 1A11 plots discoveries with proper back dating to the time each was found. It shows that the rate of discovery has been falling since 1964 and it is pretty easy to see that if the downward trend continues, only around 200Gb more will be found.

ABSURD SCENARIOS

Shell is famous for its energy supply scenarios up to 2050, which the company publishes under heroic names. The grey line in *Figure 1A12* shows Spirit of the Coming Age which

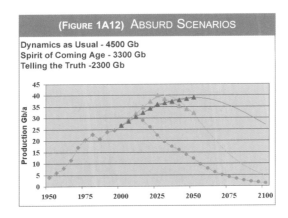

(FIGURE 1A12) ABSURD SCENARIOS

- public acceptance and planning permissions. Failure to obtain planning permission has seriously impeded the uptake of projects under the UK Renewables Obligation legislation;
- market operation. For example, the operation of the New Electricity Trading Arrangements (NETA) in the UK is having the effect of driving down wholesale electricity prices to the extent that power stations are being closed – including new, highly efficient gas-powered combined cycle units. NETA currently operates against CHP and renewables, and even against central plant that is taken out of service for maintenance;
- failures or flaws in national energy policy, or failures in the implementation of policy, for example, through unrealistic or uncertain timescales;
- the stability of companies over a sufficiently long period, especially in the current climate of multiple acquisitions. The ARBRE project in the UK has now closed after a series of changes in ownership of the company building the power station. This project was intended to act as a technology demonstrator for the use of energy crops. Its failure has potentialy

disastrous implications for the UK biomass programme as it has destroyed the confidence of those farmers who were willing to take a long view and plant the energy crops to be used in the ARBRE power station.

The last point illustrates a serious rate-limiting step in the implementation of a biomass programme. The success of any such programme depends critically on the power plant operator having confidence that he will have access to an adequate supply of fuel for a long enough time (typically 15 years) to ensure a return on the capital investment. Simultaneously, the fuel provider must have confidence that there will be a market for his crop to allow his investment to be recouped. The ARBRE experience has seriously damaged this mutual confidence. One solution to this chicken and egg problem could be to use existing or new coal plant to provide the necessary buffer to ensure a flexible biomass market that would allow biomass supply to build up – in turn giving the power plant developers confidence that fuel will be available for the lifetime of their plant.

Acknowledgments

The quoted data has been taken from publications and the web-sites of World Coal Institute, International Energy Agency, USDOE Energy Information Agency, and the Geological Survey Offices of USA, Australia and Canada.

The prospects for sequestering carbon dioxide

Euan Baird

If carbon dioxide buildup in the atmosphere needs to be dealt with, it is by no means an intractable problem. Carbon dioxide is not the sort of radioactive or chemical pollutant that concerns regulators when present at the part-per-billion levels. It is a natural part of our environment. Without carbon dioxide, plants would not grow and our planet would be a more extreme and inhospitable place. Thus, we only need to guard against having too much of a good thing in our atmosphere.

Carbon dioxide released by the combustion of fossil fuel is most conveniently vented to the atmosphere. Unfortunately, the atmosphere is a relatively small reservoir of carbon and appears to be particularly sensitive to the addition of more. The biosphere is also a small carbon reservoir that releases carbon dioxide back to the atmosphere as readily as it absorbs it. In contrast, the ocean reservoir of dissolved carbon dioxide is 50 times larger than either the atmosphere or biosphere and can easily absorb much more. In addition, carbon dioxide dissolved in the oceans will precipitate to create carbonate formations and sub-sea sediments that sequester huge quantities of carbon for hundreds of million of years. However, the natural transfer of gas to the ocean is slow with respect to atmospheric ventilation due to the long deep-ocean circulation times of about 550 years. It would make a lot of sense, therefore, to bypass the atmosphere and store the carbon where it is destined to wind up anyway – in the oceans and inside the earth. The U.S. Department of Energy estimates that 200 years of carbon emissions from burning fossil fuels at current rates can be absorbed, or sequestered, by two sources alone – the oceans and depleted oil and gas fields.

Bypassing the atmosphere to accelerate the normal carbon dioxide sequestration cycle has been the subject of much debate. Research programs have been designed to make sure that all the consequences of this solution are properly understood. We need to make sure that we do not solve one environmental problem by creating others. Not only do we need to ensure that industrially sequestered carbon dioxide does not harm people, we also have to check that it has no important negative impacts on any part of our natural world.

Our operational solutions must be deliberately incremental so that no single action carries too great a risk. Sequestering carbon in the deep ocean and in deep geologic formations is just that kind of incremental solution. The target reservoirs are huge and already contain vast quantities of oxidised carbon. The injection of carbon dioxide can be continuously monitored to detect any deviations from our predictions, and operations can be stopped for evaluation at any time.

Probably the most straightforward proposal is to sequester carbon dioxide in depleted oil and gas reservoirs. In fact, the industry already does this when it uses carbon dioxide floods to enhance the tertiary oil recovery process. These reservoirs have a good track record for stability, having trapped hydrocarbons in the subsurface for millions of years. However, this is not a guarantee of future stability. Does the cap rock of the reservoir rock itself degrade as a result of pressure cycling or from being in contact with the slightly acidic solutions produced when carbon dioxide dissolves in water? These are questions that need answers.

Another attractive option is to bury carbon at sea. Shallow injection is futile, as the gas will quickly rise to the sea surface and reenter the atmosphere. However, carbon dioxide is considerably more compressible than water even in its liquid state. At pressures above 3,000 meters, liquid carbon dioxide is denser than seawater. Injected at this depth, the carbon dioxide will fall to the seafloor, dissolve rapidly to form bicarbonate ions and eventually precipitate as carbonate. Ocean sequestration involves the considerable cost of compressing gas to 4,500 psi and piping it miles offshore. But there are other possible ways to achieve the same effect that need to be investigated, such as taking advantage of the fact that carbon dioxide forms a dense, solid hydrate at modest depths within the ocean. While work proceeds on the feasibility of oceanic sequestration, it is important to address the environmental issues associated with the process.

First, can the oceans absorb the necessary amount of carbon dioxide, and how would oceanic acidity be affected? Even though it already contains 140 trillion tons of dissolved carbon, the ocean is grossly undersaturated in carbon dioxide. The oceans can easily absorb the 35 trillion tons that would result from burning all the world's remaining proven reserves of coal, oil and natural gas. The addition of 35 trillion tons of carbon would decrease the pH of the oceans by 0.3, which is well within the natural range of variability of seawater at various depths and in different parts of the world.

Second, as carbon dioxide slowly dissolves, it creates local plumes of acidity. Are these plumes detrimental to fish or other life at the sea floor? Scientists at Monterey Bay Aquarium Research Institute in California have undertaken small-scale tests by discharging liquid carbon dioxide onto the seafloor and then watching the behavior of the marine fish.

Fish swim up to the liquid blob, investigate it, and then calmly swim away, apparently with no ill effects. Current research is now focused on immobile and microscopic invertebrates found at, and under, the sea floor.

If one theme runs through the thinking about carbon dioxide sequestration, whether in the ocean or in geological formations, it is that more research is needed. However, bypassing the atmosphere by sequestering carbon dioxide directly in the oceans has the makings of a very elegant solution to controlling "man-made" carbon dioxide emissions to the atmosphere.

ADDRESSING THE CARBON ISSUE

I have covered this particular approach to carbon dioxide sequestration in some detail not because it is necessarily the best or the only possible solution, but because it is typical of the highly responsible and rigorous research work that is being undertaken by universities, institutes and oil companies to find cost-effective ways to mitigate the environmental cost of using fossil fuels. There is a growing understanding in our industry that a carbon-sensitive world offers us opportunities as well as threats. If the accumulation of "man-made" carbon dioxide in the atmosphere is a global problem, the separation, compression, transport and storage of it elsewhere will become huge businesses. Who else has the technical expertise, financial strength and global management skills to help stabilise the composition of the earth's atmosphere? The petroleum industry has the unique capabilities and the motivation to solve the carbon problem. Let me mention some of the initiatives that have been started recently to address the carbon issue.

BP, ChevronTexaco, Shell, ENI and several other oil companies are collaborating on a project to reduce the cost of carbon dioxide separation from stack gas.

Offshore Norway, Statoil responded to the concerns about hydrocarbon emissions by developing a system capable of separating one million tons of carbon dioxide per year from natural gas coming from the Sleipner reservoir and reinjecting it into the shallower Utsira formation. The process is being monitored using time-lapse 3D seismic surveys – an interesting adaptation of technology that was designed to monitor producing reservoirs.

Princeton University, BP and the Ford Motor Company have joined to find "credible methods of capturing and sequestering a large fraction of carbon emissions from fossil fuels." Together, the two companies will spend $2 million a year for the next 10 years to support this project.

Stanford University has formed a consortium of leading technology companies including Schlumberger, ExxonMobil and General Electric to address world energy and environmental concerns through the development of a portfolio of practical energy technologies that address the potential long-term risks of climate change. The 10-year Stanford University Global Climate & Energy Project (G-CEP) is designed specifically to accelerate the development and use of low greenhouse gas emission technologies. The involvement of Schlumberger will focus on the hydrocarbon reservoir addressing carbon dioxide sequestration issues.

During the 1970s, the future of our industry was threatened by concern over the supply of oil. Our response was to harness the creativity of our people and invest heavily in new exploration and development technologies. The results are impressive. Today, the remaining proven oil reserves are estimated to be 2,450 billion barrels, almost five times higher that the estimate of 550 billion barrels made by the Club of Rome in 1972. The price of oil has been stabilised at a low level, and consumer confidence in supply restored so that oil demand has grown robustly for the last 17 years.

Consumer concerns about the environmental costs of burning fossil fuels present a similar threat to the future of the oil and gas industry. Our challenge is to develop environmentally acceptable energy solutions that will allow the world to continue to benefit for as long as possible from the convenience and cost effectiveness of oil and gas and prevent any premature move to more expensive energy sources. These solutions will come through ongoing partnerships between the best academic institutions and industry to accelerate the development of commercially viable technology.

Given this growing industry commitment to confront the environmental costs associated with the use of our products, I am convinced that once again we will surprise our customers, critics and perhaps even ourselves by our ability to adapt to ever-changing customer needs. I am equally certain that oil and gas will continue to be the best source of energy solutions for most of this century.

An extract from the Dewhurst Lecture at the 17th World Petroleum Conference, Rio de Janeiro, September 3, 2002

Renewable Energy and Nuclear Power

Ian Hore-Lacy

The two best ways of investing energy to produce energy are wind turbines and nuclear power. However, nuclear is a much better way to provide base-load electricity. Wind power would have to be converted into hydrogen and back again to achieve the same result.

Why consider nuclear power in a book about the transition to renewable energy? In my view, because nuclear is complementary to renewables in moving to a sustainable and largely carbon-free energy future. The reason I say this is that in most countries, the demand for electricity has a very large continuous component - see *Figure 1D1*. This requires a reliable supply of electricity which cannot be readily met from intermittent wind or solar sources since their electricity cannot be stored on a large scale.

Nuclear is simply the most appropriate technology for the job of providing clean base-load power. (Hydrogen may one day be made on a large scale from electricity, or directly from nuclear energy by thermochemical means and then stored on a large scale for turning back to electricity, but such developments are many years away. Even then the hydrogen will be in higher demand for transport.)

ENERGY BALANCE

The economics of electricity generation are important. If the costs of building and operating a power plant cannot profitably be recouped by selling the electricity, it is not financially viable. But as energy itself can be a more fundamental unit of accounting than money, it is also essential to know which generating systems produce the best return on the energy rather than the money invested in them. Determing this involves Life Cycle Analysis (LCA).

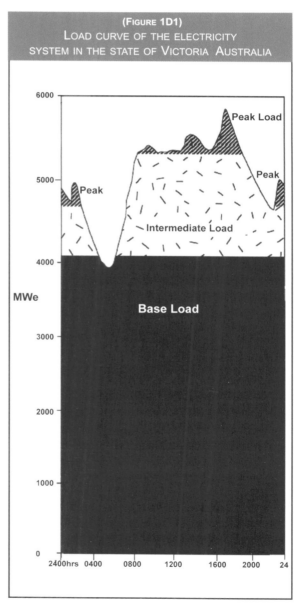

(FIGURE 1D1)
LOAD CURVE OF THE ELECTRICITY
SYSTEM IN THE STATE OF VICTORIA AUSTRALIA

Analysing the energy balance between inputs and outputs, however, is complex because the inputs are diverse, and it is not always clear how far back they should be taken. For instance, oil expended to move coal to a power station, or electricity used to enrich uranium for nuclear fuel, are generally included in the calculations. But what about the energy required to build the train or the enrichment plant? And can the electricity consumed during enrichment be compared with the fossil fuel needed for the train? Many analysts convert kilowatt-hours (kWh) to kilojoules (kJ), or vice versa, but this requires them to make assumptions about the thermal efficiency of the electricity production.

Some inputs are easily quantified, such as the energy required to produce a tonne of uranium oxide concentrate at a particular mine, or to produce a tonne of particular grade of uranium hexfluoride at a uranium enrichment plant. Similarly, the energy required to move a tonne of coal by ship or rail can be identified, although this will vary considerably depending on the location of the mine and the power plant. Moving gas long distances by pipeline is surprisingly energy-intensive.

Other inputs are less straightforward such as the energy required to build a 1000 MWe power plant of a particular kind, or even that to construct and erect a wind turbine. But all such energy inputs need to be amortised over the life of the plant and added to the operational inputs such as fuel. Also the post-operational energy requirements for waste management and decommissioning plants must be included. There is no such thing as a free kilowatt-hour!

As well as energy costs, the environmental and health consequences of energy production that do not appear in the financial accounts need to be considered as well. Recent studies have plausibly quantified them in financial terms, and I will comment on those at the end.

Many energy analysis studies done in the 1970s seem to have assumed that if nuclear generating capacity was expanded very rapidly, it would require so much energy for fuel production and construction that, for a few years, inputs would exceed overall outputs. To determine whether or not this would happen requires the dynamic analysis of the whole energy system and is not attempted here. The 1970s studies were also driven by a perception that primary energy sources including uranium would become increasingly difficult and expensive to recover, and would thus require undue amounts of energy to access them. This notion has since re-surfaced.

The figures in *Figure 1D2* are based as far as possible on current assumptions and current data for enrichment, mining and milling, etc. Where current data are unavailable, that from earlier studies is used. For nuclear power, enrichment is clearly the key energy input where the older diffusion technology is used - it comprises more than half of all the energy used in the lifetime of the plant. However, with centrifuge technology, enrichment takes far less energy than the construction of the plant itself. Indeed, the difference between the two processes is so great that, overall, an input of only a third of the energy is required to build and operate a nuclear plant using centrifuge technology than one fuelled by the older diffusion method.

As yet, no energy-input figures seem to have been published for the fuel cycle that the UK has been using - the closed cycle involving reprocessing at Sellafield, a point that some Irish observers find upsetting. However, this probably uses less energy overall because, although reprocessing requires extra energy, 25% less enrichment will be required. It is also important to recognise that precise energy figures for plant construction are not readily available, although several studies use a factor converting monetary inputs to energy.

(FIGURE 1D2) LIFE CYCLE ENERGY REQUIREMENTS FOR A NUCLEAR POWER PLANT			
	GWh (e)	TJ (th) Annual	PJ (th) 30 year
Inputs			
Mining & Milling (180 t/yr U₃O₈ at Ranger)		37	1.26
Conversion (ConverDyn data)			5.63
Initial enrichment diffusion @ 2400 kWh/SWU	576		6.23
Urenco centrifuge @ 63 kWh/SWU	15		0.16
Reload enrichment diffusion @ 2400 kWh/SWU	201	2175	65.25
Urenco centrifuge @ 63 kWh/SWU	5.3	57	1.71
Fuel Fabrication (ERDA 76/1)			4.32
Construction & Operation (ERDA 76/1)			24.69
Fuel storage, Waste storage, Transport (ERDA 76/1, Perry 1977), Decommissioning allow			1.0
Total (diffusion enrichment)			**108**
Total (centrifuge enrichment)			**39**
Output: 7 TWh/yr	7000	75.670	**2 270** PJ
Input percentage of lifetime output, thermal		(diffusion)	4.8%
		(centrifuge)	1.7%
Energy ratio (output/input), thermal		(diffusion)	21
		(centrifuge)	59

Assumptions:

Fuel Cycle: 1000 MWe, 30-year life, 80% capacity factor, enrichment with 0.30% tails (3.0 SWU/kg for initial 80 t fuel load @ 2.3% U-235, 4.3 SWU/kg for 3.5% fresh fuel @ 19.5 t/yr), 45,000 MWd/t burn-up, 33% thermal efficiency.

Calculations: Electrical inputs converted to thermal @ 33% efficiency (x 10 800, kWh to kJ)

Other figures for front end: Cameco mines in Saskatchewan input 32 TJ per 180 t U3O8 over 1992-2001 including some capital works. Urenco enrichment at Capenhurst input 62.3 kWh/SWU for whole plant in 2001-02, including infrastructure and capital works.

Other figures for construction (but not operation) of 1000 MWe PWR power plant are: 13.6 PJ (Chapman 1975, recalculated), 14.76

PJ (Held 1977, if converted direct), 24.1 PJ (Perry et al 1977).

Energy payback period. If 30 PJ or 25 PJ is taken for diffusion and centrifuge enrichment respectively as the energy capital cost of setting up, then at 75 PJ/yr output the initial energy investment is repaid in 5 months or 4 months respectively at full power. Construction time for nuclear plants is 4-5 years.

The only data available for storage and disposal of radioactive wastes, notably spent fuel, suggests that this is a minor contribution to the energy picture. This is borne out by personal observation in several countries - spent fuel sitting quietly in pool storage or underground is about as passive as you can imagine. Decommissioning energy requirements may be considered with wastes, or (as Vattenfall) with plant construction.

Recent studies have compared different means of generating electricity in energy and greenhouse terms. Here are some of their results, together with earlier data. The energy ratio is simply output divided by input for the full life cycle. Unlike some others in use, the R3 energy ratio employs a convention which converts between electrical and thermal energy, including a thermal efficiency factor, so is used here. Nevertheless the reciprocal percentage, the input as a percentage of a plant's lifetime output, may be more meaningful.

(FIGURE 1D3) LIFE CYCLE ENERGY RATIOS FOR VARIOUS TECHNOLOGIES		R3 Energy Ratio. (output/input)	Input % of lifetime output
Hydro	Uchiyama 1996	50	2.0
	Held et al 1977	43	2.3
Quebec	Gagnon et al 2002	205	0.5
Nuclear (centrifuge enrichment)	see Table 1D2.	59	1.7
PWR/BWR	Kivisto 2000	59	1.7
PWR	Inst. Policy Science 1977*	46	2.2
BWR	Inst. Policy Science 1977*	43	2.3
BWR	Uchiyama et al 1991*	47	2.1
Nuclear (diffusion enrichment)	see Table 1d.	21	4.8
PWR/ BWR	Held et al 1977	20	5.0
PWR/BWR	Kivisto 2000	17	5.8
	Uchiyama 1996	24	4.2
PWR	Oak Ridge Assoc.Univ. 1976*	15.4	6.5
BWR	Oak Ridge Assoc.Univ. 1976*	16.4	6.1
BWR	Uchiyama et al 1991*	10.5	9.5
Coal	Kivisto 2000	29	3.5
	Uchiyama 1996	17	5.9
	Uchiyama et al 1991*	16.8	6.0
	Inst. Policy Science 1977*	14.2	7.0
unscrubbed	Gagnon et al 2002	7	14
Natural gas- piped	Kivisto 2000	26	3.8
piped 2000 km	Gagnon et al 2002	5	20
LNG	Uchiyama et al 1991*	5.6	17.9
LNG (57% capacity factor)	Uchiyama 1996	6	16.7
Solar	Held et al 1997	10.6	9.4
Solar PV rooftop	Uchiyama 1996	9	11.1
utility	Uchiyama 1996	5	20.0
amorphous silicon	Kivisto 2000	3.7	27
Wind	Resource Research Inst. 1983*	12	8.3
	Uchiyama 1996	6	16.7
	Kivisto 2000	34	2.9
	Gagnon et al 2002	80	1.3
Biomass forestry waste	Gagnon et al 2002	27	3.7
plantation	Gagnon et al 2002	5	20

* In IAEA 1994, TecDoc 753.

These figures show that energy ratios are clearly sensitive not only to the amount of energy used to build the power source and supply it with whatever it needs to run, but also to the proportion of the time at which it is delivering power – in other words, its capacity factor.

This is particularly true where a significant amount of energy is required to build the power plant. The higher the energy input to build the plant, the more output is needed to amortise it. With technologies such as wind, where a turbine will only be producing whenever the wind blows, and then at a rate dependent on the wind speed, a longer period is required to cover the inputs due to lower capacity factors. Energy payback period for the construction of a nuclear power plant is 3-4 months, which compares favourably with all except gas combined cycle.

The Liquid Natural Gas (LNG) figures quoted are for natural gas compressed cryogenically and shipped to Japan and used largely for peak loads. The solar and wind figures relate to intermittent inputs of primary energy, with inevitably low capacity utilisation and relatively high energy costs in the plant (for silicon manufacture in the case of solar cells, or steel and concrete for wind turbines).

The Swedish utility Vattenfall has undertaken a thorough life cycle assessment of its Forsmark nuclear power station, which has three boiling water reactors totalling 3100 MWe net. These started up in 1980-84 and run at 86.4% capacity. The energy analysis figures (input as % of output, transport included, 40 yr plant life, with PJ figures calculated from % on basis of 3272 PJ output) are shown in figure 1D4 below.

The Vattenfall Life Cycle Analysis study tracks energy inputs further back than others, and so is only comparable with data based on similar methodology. Even so, some major variances are unexplained - notably refining and conversion.

Uchiyama (1996) points out that hydro, nuclear and fossil fuel plants have high energy ratios of output over inputs because of their higher energy density as well as capacity factors. Wind and solar, however, are under 10 because of their lower energy density, or output in relation to plant volume and hence materials used.

(FIGURE 1D4) ENERGY ANALYSIS OF A SWEDISH NUCLEAR POWER STATION		
	input as % of output	PJ (calculated)
Mine	0.44	14
Refining & conversion	3.18	104
Enrichment (80:20 centrifuge:diffusion)	3.00	98
Fuel fabrication	1.34	44
Plant operation	0.28	9.2
Plant build & decommission	0.27	8.8
Waste management	0.11	3.6
Waste build & decommission	0.01	
Total life cycle:	**8.70%**	**285 PJ**

LIFE CYCLE ANALYSIS: GREENHOUSE GASES

A principal concern of life cycle analysis for energy systems today is their likely contribution to global warming. This is a major external cost.

If all energy inputs are assumed to be from coal-fired plants that release about one tonne of carbon dioxide per MWh, it is possible to derive a greenhouse contribution from the energy ratio. With major inputs, this is worth investigating further.

Uranium enrichment in USA is by diffusion and some of this capacity is supplied by coal-fired plants. If a national average, allowing for different sources of power, is applied, this input has a value of around 650 kg CO_2/MWh. This gives a greenhouse contribution for nuclear power of about 40kg/MWh overall. In France, however, which has the world's largest diffusion enrichment plant, electricity is supplied by on-site nuclear reactors (which also supply the grid). Because of this, the greenhouse contribution from any nuclear reactor using French-enriched uranium is similar to a reactor using centrifuge-enriched uranium -- less than 1kg /MWh for the enrichment input, and less than 20 kg/MWh overall.

Rashad and Hammad conclude that the life cycle CO_2 emission coefficient for nuclear power, on the basis of centrifuge enrichment, is 2.7% of that for coal-fired generation. This is consistent with other figures based on fossil fuel inputs.

Adding further confirmation to figures already published from Scandinavia, Japan's Central Research Institute of the Electric Power Industry has published life cycle carbon dioxide emission figures for various generation technologies. Vattenfall (1999) has published a popular account of life cycle studies based on the previous few years experience and its certified Environmental Product Declarations (EPDs) for Forsmark and Ringhals nuclear power stations in Sweden, and Kivisto in 2000 reports a similar exercise for Finland. They show the CO_2 emissions in the table below.

The Japanese gas figures include shipping LNG from overseas, and the nuclear figure is for boiling water reactors, with enrichment 70% in USA, 30% France & Japan, and one third of the fuel to be MOX. The Finnish nuclear figures are for centrifuge and diffusion enrichment respectively, the Swedish one is for 80% centrifuge

(FIGURE 1D5) RELATIVE CARBON DIOXIDE EMISSIONS FROM DIFFERENT ENERGY SOURCES			
g/kWh CO_2	Japan	Sweden	Finland
coal	975	980	894
gas thermal	608	1170 (peak-load, reserve)	-
gas combined cycle	519	450	472
solar photovoltaic	53	50	95
wind	29	5.5	14
nuclear	22	6	10 - 26
hydro	11	3	-

OTHER EXTERNAL COSTS

The report of ExternE, a major European study of the external costs of various fuel cycles, focusing on coal and nuclear, was released in 2001. The European Commission launched the project in 1991 in collaboration with the US Dept of Energy (which subsequently dropped out), and it was the first research project of its kind "to put plausible financial figures against damage resulting from different forms of electricity production for the entire EU".

The external costs are defined as those actually incurred in relation to health and the environment and quantifiable but not built into the cost of the electricity to the consumer and therefore which are borne by society at large. They include particularly the effects of air pollution on human health, crop yields and buildings, as well as occupational disease and accidents. In ExternE they exclude effects on ecosystems and the impact of global warming, which could not adequately be quantified and evaluated economically.

The methodology measures emissions, their dispersion and ultimate impact. With nuclear energy the (low) risk of accidents is factored in along with high estimates of radiological impacts from mine tailings and carbon-14 emissions from reprocessing (waste management and decommissioning being already within the cost to the consumer).

The report shows that in clear cash terms nuclear energy incurs about one tenth of the costs of coal. In particular, the external costs for coal-fired power were a very high proportion (50-70%) of the internal costs, while the external costs for nuclear energy were a very small proportion of internal costs, even after factoring in hypothetical nuclear catastrophes. This is because all waste costs in the nuclear fuel cycle are internalised, which reduces the competitiveness of nuclear power when only internal costs are considered. The external costs of nuclear energy averages 0.4 euro cents/kWh, much the same as hydro, coal is over 4.0 cents (4.1 - 7.3 cent averages in different countries), gas ranges 1.3-2.3 cents and only wind shows up better than nuclear, at 0.1-0.2 cents/kWh average.

The EU cost of electricity generation without these external costs averages about 4 cents/kWh. If these external costs were in fact included, the EU price of electricity from coal would double and that from gas would increase 30%. These particular estimates are without attempting to include possible impacts of fossil fuels on global warming. See also web: http://externe.jrc.es/

Another European treatment of production and external costs, specifically of power generation in Switzerland, has recently been done by the Paul Scherrer Institut and shows that the damage costs from fossil fuels range from 10% (gas) to 350% (coal) of the production costs, while those for nuclear are very small. A summary is accessible on the web: http://gabe.web.psi.ch/eia-external%20costs.html

An earlier European study (Krewitt et al, 1999) quantified environmental damage costs from fossil fuel electricity generation in the EU for 1990 as US$ 70 billion, about 1% of GDP. This included impacts on human health, building materials and crop production, but not global warming.

The ExternE report proposes two ways of incorporating external costs: taxing the costs or subsidising alternatives. Due to the difficulty of taxing in an EU context, the subsidy route is favoured. EC guidelines published in February 2001 encourage member states to subsidise "new plants producing renewable energy ... on the basis of external costs avoided", up to 5 c/kWh. However, this provision does not extend to nuclear power, despite the comparable external costs avoided. EU member countries have pledged to have renewables (including hydro) provide 12% of total energy and 22% of electricity by 2010, a target that appears unlikely to be met. The case for extending the subsidy to nuclear energy is obvious, particularly if climate change is to be taken seriously.

Consideration of external costs leads to the conclusion that the public health benefits associated with reducing greenhouse gas emissions from fossil fuel burning could be the strongest reason for pursuing them. Considering four cities - New York, Mexico, Santiago and Sao Paulo - with total 45 million people, a 2001 paper in *Science* presents calculations showing that some 64,000 deaths would be avoided in the two decades to 2020 by reducing fossil fuel combustion in line with greenhouse abatement targets. This is consistent with a 1995 WHO estimate of 460,000 avoidable deaths annually from suspended particulates, largely due to outdoor urban exposure.

The World Health Organisation in 1997 presented two estimates, of 2.7 or 3 million deaths occurring each year as a result of air pollution. In the latter estimate: 2.8 million deaths were due to indoor exposures and 200,000 to outdoor exposure. The lower estimate comprised 1.85 million deaths from rural indoor pollution, 363,000 from urban indoor pollution and 511,000 from urban ambient pollution. The WHO report points out that these totals are about 6% of all deaths, and the uncertainty of the estimates means that the range should be taken as 1.4 to 6 million deaths annually attributable to air pollution.

OTHER CONCERNS ABOUT NUCLEAR POWER

In discussions of the relative merits of different means of producing electricity, several concerns are commonly raised regarding nuclear power. This is not the place to treat them comprehensively, but I will attempt a paragraph on each of four:

RESOURCES

Uranium is abundant. The world's present measured resources of uranium in the IAEA-NEA lower cost category (3.1 million tonnes) and used only in conventional reactors, are enough to last for almost 50 years. This represents a higher level of assured resources than is normal for most minerals. Further exploration and higher prices will certainly, on the basis of present geological knowledge, yield further resources as present ones are used up. This is indicated in the figures if those covering estimates of all conventional resources are considered – 15.4 million tonnes, which is 240 years' supply at today's rate of consumption. This figure still ignores unconventional resources such as phosphate deposits (22 Mt) and seawater (up to 4000 Mt). But before recourse to them, widespread use of the fast breeder reactor could increase the utilisation of uranium sixty-fold or more. It is well-proven but currently uneconomic due to low uranium prices. Using uranium for electricity is responsible in relation to allowing for the needs of future generations.

WASTES

Virtually all wastes from the civil nuclear fuel cycle are contained and managed. Certainly none cause any harm to people or the environment, nor pose any significant credible threat, with the possible exception of reprocessing where high-level wastes are in liquid form for a time. High-level wastes mainly comprise, or are derived from, spent fuel. They must be shielded and cooled, neither of which is difficult or complex. As spent fuel, they are in stable ceramic form, and if reprocessed they end up thus. Storage under water or in shielded concrete structures is simple and safe. For final disposal some 50 years ex reactor, they will be encapsulated and placed in deep repositories, well down towards where radiogenic decay of uranium already heats the earth. The distinguishing feature of radioactive wastes is that their toxicity decays, unlike most other industrial wastes - after 40 years from reactor, the radioactivity of spent fuel has decayed to one thousandth of its original level, and it is producing less than one kilowatt of heat per tonne. Apart from renewables, nuclear power is the only energy-producing industry which takes full responsibility for all its wastes, and fully costs this into the product.

SAFETY

From the outset, the safety of nuclear reactors (where one has a very high energy density) has been a high priority in their design and engineering. About one third of the cost of a typical reactor is due to safety systems and structures. The Chernobyl accident in 1986 was a reminder of the need for this (normal safety provisions being largely absent there), whereas the comparable Three Mile Island accident in 1979 showed that such safety measures work - no-one was harmed. In fact, and despite Chernobyl, the safety record of nuclear power is better than for any other major industrial technology. And it is improving with newer reactors.

WEAPONS PROLIFERATION

An early concern as nuclear technology emerged from its military chrysalis was that civil nuclear power should not enable more countries to acquire nuclear weapons. Under the Nuclear Non-Proliferation Treaty a safeguards system was set up to detect and deter any diversion of fissile material from civil to military use. It is arguably the UN's most successful program, and early prospects of 20-30 countries with nuclear weapons have been averted. Today, the flow of material is from weapons stockpiles to civil use, filling about one fifth of world uranium demand. One in ten light globes in the USA are now lit by ex-Russian military uranium.

The WNA web site www.world-nuclear.org has information papers on all these issues and many more.

Part Two
Do renewable energy sources have the potential to fill the gap?

It will take considerable time and energy to develop renewable energy sources and to adapt the economy to their use. Despite this, renewables may not be able to supply enough power for economic growth to continue at anything like its present rate.

A A sustainable future - the limits to renewables
by **David Elliott**

B Using the net energy concept to model the future
by **Malcolm Slesser**

C Switching the European economy to renewable energy over the next 50 years
by **Olav Hohmeyer**

D Building a Lean Economy for a fuel-poor future
by **David Fleming**

E The prospects for a hydrogen economy based on renewable energy
by **Werner Zittel**

A sustainable future? The limits to renewables

by David Elliott

Although vast quantities of energy arrive daily from the sun, capturing it is always going to be limited by technical, ecological and land-use constraints. The most serious barrier to capturing it at present, however, is that other energy sources are artificially cheap.

Can renewable energy save the world from climate change by replacing fossil fuels? It is relatively easy to outline a series of 'technical fixes' for the climate change problem which would allow most of us to continue to live much as at present, at least for a while. Shell's 1995 scenario[1] suggested that, in theory, renewables could be supplying possibly 50% of world energy by 2050 and, in 1993, the Stockholm Institute's scenario for Greenpeace suggested that, if we wanted to, we could have a world system based almost entirely on renewables by 2100, even assuming continued growth at 2% a year in energy use.[2]

Since these studies emerged, renewables have developed rapidly - for example, there is now 24,000MW of wind power in use around the world - and it has been argued by Amory Lovins that demand for energy can be dramatically reduced by clever 'Factor 4' and even 'Factor 10' energy efficiency measures[3]. So the prospects for a shift to a sustainable future are looking promising.

Indeed, there is something of an emerging consensus that, as the UN/World Energy Council 'World Energy Assessment' report, published in 2000, put it "there are no fundamental technological, economic or resource limits constraining the world from enjoying the benefits of both high levels of energy services and a better environment". A little more cautiously, the report adds "A prosperous, equitable and environmentally sustainable world is within our reach, but only if governments adopt new policies to encourage the delivery of energy services in cleaner and more efficient ways"[4]

However, the consensus is not complete. Although renewables are seen as playing a rapidly increasing role in this optimistic future, the strategy that is seen as being required also relies on continued use of fossil fuels, albeit more efficiently, and possibly also on the expanded use of nuclear power. Most environmentalists cannot countenance the latter option: they argue that, quite apart from the uncertain economics, why try to solve one problem (climate change) by creating another (radioactive pollution)? In addition, there is the possibility, argued forcefully by Colin Campbell and others, that the economically extractable reserves of oil and gas, may not be sufficient for their continued use on a large scale for very long. If that is so, we will have to move even faster to renewables.

Certainly, the WEA's fairly leisurely approach to replacing fossil fuels with renewables may not be adequate in the face of the climate change threat. We may not simply be able to wait for fossil fuels to run out (or rather to become prohibitively expensive). Sheikh Yamani is alleged to be the original source of the now familiar view that 'just as the Stone Age didn't end because people ran out of stones, the Oil Age won't end because we run out of oil.'

So there are plenty of reasons why we should

consider moving rapidly to a more sustainable approach, based on the use of renewable resources and the adoption of more efficient ways of using energy. That will not be easy. The development of the new green energy systems involves many technical challenges, and many believe that it will in practice be difficult to actually achieve major energy efficiency gains.

In addition, there are many strategic and political battles to be won - for example, that to obtain the necessary funding. However, in this paper I will try to explore the basic resource problems that face this approach. For not everyone believes that there will be sufficient renewables energy resources to meet growing demand, especially as the developing countries industrialise.

RESOURCE LIMITS

My first question is - how much renewable energy will be available? Looking a long way ahead is obviously difficult. But some broad patterns are clear. The chart below produced by energy analyst Gustav Grob shows the relatively short period during which industrialisation occured, based on fossil fuel[5]. It is followed, after the projected demise of fossil fuels, by continued and accelerated expansion of energy use, based on renewables, up to about twice the current level of energy use. If true, that is good news. That period of expansion could allow the developing world an opportunity to catch up with the industrial countries, although of course, alternatively, it could allow the industrial world to continue to expand ahead of the rest.

But, either way, subsequently, according to this chart, growth can continue but not at such as rapid rate. Technical, ecological and land-use limits impose what Grob calls a 'natural limit' on the amount of additional energy we can obtain from renewable sources, although we can raise this limit as we develop better renewable energy technologies and learn how to use natural energy flows more efficiently. Estimates vary as to what the ultimate limit actually is. Some, like the Australian ecologist Ted Trainer, put it much lower than Grob[6]; others, mainly the technophiles enthused by the potential of renewables, put it much higher - maybe ten times or even more.

For example, since some solar PV cells can convert sunlight to electricity at 15% efficiency, compared to the 1% efficiency of photosynthesis, then, given the huge solar input to earth, there are potentially very large amounts of extra energy available. In reality, for good or ill, the

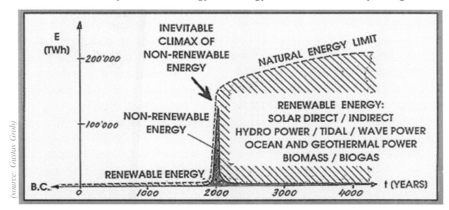

From an historical perspective, the use of non-renewable energy sources appears as a brief spike (the dark area above). Will renewable energy sources be developed to take over as fully as the chart shows?

BEFORE THE WELLS RUN DRY

PART TWO: DO RENEWABLE ENERGY SOURCES HAVE THE POTENTIAL TO FILL THE GAP?

amount of energy that can in practice be obtained from natural renewable sources like solar may not be as large as these figures imply. While the amount of solar energy falling on the earth is very large (around 90,000TW equivalent), given the limitations of geographical access, only about 1000 TW is in any way actually available to us to use[7]. That is around 70 - 80 times current global energy generation (13TW). However, in practice there are technical limits on how much of this can actually be converted into useful energy. This is due to constraints on the efficiency of conversion and the diffuse and intermittent nature of much of this resource, as well as land access limits.

LAND USE LIMITS

Well before the use of renewables begins to expand to the energy limit, there will be land-use conflicts and, in particular, conflicts between the natural ecosystem and the emergent human-managed ecosystem. It has always been that way, ever since we started farming. As we have spread our influence across the planet this issue has become crucial to the survival of the planet - indeed many 'deep greens' say it may already be too late.

At the same time, if Grob's estimate is anywhere near right, there is not an indefinite amount of room for economic expansion available ahead, so surely, within this more limited arena, it must be possible to have some sort of co-evolutionary balance between the human system and the natural system. Clearly they must not conflict: they must be part of the same overall system.

We are already fighting out some of these issues in terms of the debate over the location of wind farms and similar issues could emerge over other renewable energy options such as the growing of energy crops. The key point is that renewable energy sources are mostly diffuse

and the energy collection system must therefore cover large areas.

Some are however worse than others. For example wind turbines cover relatively small areas and wind farms can produce up to twenty times more energy per hectare than energy crop plantations of short rotation coppice. Growing oil seed rape and the like for liquid biofuels is even worse in terms of energy per hectare - by a factor of perhaps ten. However energy crops have the advantage that they can be stored, although so far they look like generating electricity at much higher prices than wind[8].

The opposition to wind projects in the UK is quite serious. It has meant that around 70% of project proposals have been blocked in recent years, so that the UK is falling behind in its attempt to obtain 10% of its electricity from renewables by 2010[9]. Opposition is also mounting to large hydro around the world not just on the grounds of the social dislocation resulting when large areas are flooded for reservoirs, but also since it now seems that some hydro projects in warm climates can generate methane gas which makes a major contribution to climate change[10].

Most of the other renewables are seen as more benign and as having less land-use implications. For example most PV solar modules would be located of rooftops and on walls and so have no land take implications. Offshore wind, wave and tidal stream system obviously have no land use implications.

ENERGY LIMITS

It is sometimes argued that the main limitation to renewables will be that more energy will be needed to construct the equipment than it will produce over its lifetime. Fortunately this is a fallacy - a misreading of arguments about the 'embedded energy' debt. As it happens, the embedded energy costs associated with renewables are mostly low and usually less than for other energy technologies.

Thus, a review of energy payback times by Hydro Quebec has indicated that, over their full lifetime, typically, wind turbines generate around 39 times more power than is used in their construction and operation. For comparison, nuclear power plants are estimated to only generate around 16 times the energy needed for construction and operation, including the provision of fuel (which of course wind turbines get free). Combined Cycle Gas Turbines are even worse, only generating fourteen times the energy needed for their construction and operation.[11] See page 315 for Hydro Quebec data.

It is true that some renewable options are less attractive in this sense but even PV solar, the most energy intensive renewable energy technology, still manages to generate 9 times more energy than is needed for cell fabrication, and that is using current types of cells. The newer PV technology now emerging is far less energy intensive.

Large hydro, whatever other problems it may have, is about the best deal, generating, according to the same study, around 200 times more energy than is consumed in construction - presumably because of the large capacity of the plants and their very long lifetimes (perhaps 100 years or more before major equipment replacement is needed).

Interestingly, however, energy crops do not come out very well on this analysis, presumably due to the high requirement for mechanised energy for planting, harvesting and in particular transportation of the bulky fuel to power plants. Biomass plantations are estimated to only return five times the energy needed to grow and collect them. As noted above, liquid biofuels have even lower energy output to input ratios than solid biofuels.

However, the use of forestry residues seen as much better, yielding 27 times the energy needed to collect them (growing is presumably seen as free).

Of course these energy calculations need to be set in the context of the value of the energy produced. Electricity from energy crops would replace electricity produced from fossil sources that produce carbon dioxide gas. As long as the rate of energy crop planting balances the rate of harvesting, the overall process can be roughly neutral in carbon dioxide terms since plants absorb carbon dioxide while growing. If land is not scarce then electricity generation from energy crops could therefore be seen as valuable in environmental terms. Of course, in a market system, there are also other types of value. For good or ill, fuel for vehicles commands a high price at present, so it may be that liquid biofuels will be the preferred energy crop despite the high energy input to output ratios. That certainly seem to have been the case in continental Europe.

CAPITAL LIMITS

Rather than embedded energy being a constraint, the main limit to the rapid expansion of the renewables could be financial. Most energy technologies are capital intensive to some degree. Quite apart from the reticence of individual investors and companies to back new technologies like renewables, there may not be sufficient financial resources available overall to permit the expansion, much less the renewal, of even the present conventional types of energy system.

In part, of course, this is due to the high embedded energy content of energy technologies, but there are also other key elements - especially in the more advanced conventional energy systems which use expensive high technology, large amounts of rare materials, and highly-skilled and expensive construction personnel.

BEFORE THE WELLS RUN DRY

PART TWO: DO RENEWABLE ENERGY SOURCES HAVE THE POTENTIAL TO FILL THE GAP?

In addition to being complex, most conventional projects are also physically large and take many years to plan and build. This adds to the cost of borrowing money. The result is that, to put it simply, energy technology is expensive. Worse still, it seems to have become more expensive over the years.

In his celebrated 1976 book *The Poverty of Power*, Barry Commoner argued that in its drive to increase the rate of profit, capitalism relied on ever more capital-intensive forms of production and energy production was no exception[12]. Indeed it was one of the most capital intensive. However the gains made in each successive wave of investment were falling - or, rather, the cost of each productivity gain was growing faster than fresh capital (that is, resources) could be created. Basically, he argued, the capitalist system, which has to keep improving productivity and expanding to survive, was running out of the resources it needed to do so. Commoner's quasi-marxist model of endemic economic crisis may be less fashionable these days, in part because the capitalism has learnt how to increase productivity with technologies that permit lower levels of resource (that is, capital) use.

In the energy sector, the end point of the old resource-intensive model was nuclear power, with reactors costing up to $3000/kW - three times as much as coal plants. By contrast, modern combined cycle gas turbines (CCGTs) can be installed at around $500/kW. It interesting in this context that, in its current attempt to get back in the game, the nuclear industry is trying to develop new plants with the target of getting capital costs down to $1000/kw. That seems some way off, with, for example, the much hyped South African pebble bed modular reactor being perhaps ten years away. Its costs are still very speculative, too. By contrast, wind projects are now being installed at $750/kW and $500/kW is seen as likely soon[13].

Even so, given that most of the world's power plants will have to be replaced over the next few decades because they are reaching the end of their lives, there could be shortages of the resources needed to do so. This problem is clearly worsened by the huge expansion in energy demand both in the industrial countries and in the developing ones. There may simply not be enough financial resources to permit this expansion, whatever type of technology is used.

Some renewable energy technologies are less resources-intensive and thus cheaper than conventional technology. Wind power for example is now marginally competitive with CCGT's in some contexts. But most renewables are more expensive, at least for the moment. So their widespread adoption may be difficult - unless companies are willing to choose green options for their longer-term environmental (and commercial) benefits and consumers are willing to pay more for green power (for their, or their 'descendents', longer-term welfare).

Clearly it is unfair that clean green energy technologies have to compete with dirty fossil fuel based systems, but for the moment, in the absence of a system reflecting the environmental costs in the price we pay, the playing field is far from level. This limitation is however not like the ones I have discussed before - it's a construct of our society and its economic basis, and as such, it can be changed.

REVALUING ENERGY

One of the reasons why renewables sometimes look expensive is because of the way we value energy. The conventional system is based on large centralised power plants that are usually some distance away from the power user. They are seen as providing instant power reliably at a flick of a switch. Their environmental costs are assumed to fall somewhere else.

Most renewables by contrast have very low environmental costs but are intermittent, offering only variable sources of energy. Some renewables, like hydro and biomass, are reliable, although weather dependent to some extent, but energy is only available erratically from the sun, winds and waves, and that from the tides depends on the lunar cycle.

Let us take these issues one at a time. First, the environmental costs issue. There are of course various ways of reflecting the environmental costs and benefits of energy technologies in prices - by adding a surcharge, by some sort of energy and carbon tax, or more generally by subsidising options seen as desirable. This is not the place to explore all the ramifications of green pricing. But, as a striking example, on the basis of the figures produced by the EU EXTERNE study on environmental impacts, renewables could be condoned on environmental grounds even if they cost twice the price of conventional power.

Extra cost resulting from environmental damage (to be added to conventional electricity cost - assumed as 0.04 euro/kWh average across the EU) **in Euro cents/kWh**

Coal	5.7
Gas	1.6
Biomass	1.6
PV solar	0.6
Hydro	0.4
Nuclear	0.4
Wind	0.1

Source: The ExternE 'Externalities of Energy' report, 2001, European Commission ExternE Programme, DG12, L-2920 Luxembourg.

As can be seen, the extra environmental cost associated with the use of wind is miniscule compared with coal or even gas, and four times less than nuclear. Given that there are actually wind projects going ahead at below 2.5p/kWh (less than 4 euro cents/kWh), then clearly there is something wrong with our current way of valuing these options.

Part of the problem is the second issue mentioned above, the belief that renewables are unreliable, due to the intermittency of the energy sources. In fact this intermittency is not too much of a technical problem. If renewables only supply up to around 20% of the total electricity generated in a country and their power is fed into the national grid, then the local variations in renewable availability are balanced out. However, for larger proportions of renewables we would need some way to store the energy. But by the time we have reached that point it should be possible to use hydrogen as a storage medium- generated from renewable sources by the electrolysis of water and then transmitted along gas pipelines, perhaps initially mixed in with natural gas, to the point of use. Hydrogen can be burnt as a heating fuel or in a power station to generate electricity, with no emissions except water, and can also be used to power fuel cells to generate electricity.

These, and other generation systems like small gas-fired combined heat and power (CHP) units, are small enough to be used to supply power to individual homes. The same is true for photovoltiac solar cells although they are still very expensive.

However, we can look forward to an energy system which has a range of sizes of generation plant, some quite large (e.g wave, offshore wind) some small enough to be in individual homes (PV solar, fuel cells, micro-CHP units). These micro power systems would all be linked via the electricity grid which would help to balance out local variations in energy production.

They would be backed up by power from non-variable renewable sources like energy crops

BEFORE THE WELLS RUN DRY

PART TWO: DO RENEWABLE ENERGY SOURCES HAVE THE POTENTIAL TO FILL THE GAP?

and by gas supplies generated increasingly from renewables too[14].

The end result would be a robust decentralised energy system with the advantage that, on average, much of the power would be generated locally, from local sources, with only excess being exported via the grid and imports only being required to meet occasional shortfalls. Surprisingly, such a system could also supply cities as well as rural areas since most cities have sufficient roof space to provide for most of their power needs, averaged out, via PV solar, with this energy being backed up by waste digestors and pyrolysis units, converting the cities' wastes into energy. (waste is one thing in which cities are self-sufficient!).

Such a system would avoid the large energy losses incurred by shunting large amounts of power over very long distances via the grid, as happens with the present system. Currently, the advantage offered by generators embedded in local power systems is not recognised in the way we value power. Indeed, small local generators are often penalised as offering only small amounts of unreliable power. If renewables are to expand rapidly and replace fossil fuels, we need a new approach to the economic evaluation of distributed and dispersed renewable

energy sources.

The precise mix and size of technologies will depend on the context. In some areas of the world off-grid generation from renewables makes sense. Indeed, for most of the 2 billion or so people who currently do not have access to electricity, it is likely to be their only option. PV solar is the obvious option, along with direct solar heating and cooling, and modern biomass technologies. Micro hydro also has a lot of potential. But there are also locations where larger grid-linked options make sense. For example India and China both have ambitious wind programmes. However, plans for large, environmentally invasive hydro projects could be replaced by large tidal current projects, like the 2.2 GW tidal fence being considered as part of a causeway between a series of islands in the Philippines.

In most of the industrialised countries, wind, on and offshore, looks like being the largest single option, with offshore wave and tidal power being the next largest for those with access to this resource (for example they could each supply 20% of UK electricity). Wave and tidal are still relatively expensive but as the technology develops, prices should drop as is already happening for solar PV. Energy crops remain uncertain economically as I have described,

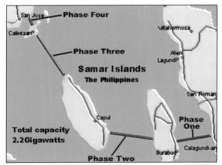  

Tidal Power in the Philippines: Rapid tidal currents between islands could be used to generate large amounts of electricity with tidal turbines installed along causeways. The UK has developed some pioneering designs for free-standing tidal current turbines like the ones shown.

and, although the resource is vast in many parts of the world, it requires land and a good water supply.

Direct solar heating has many attractions even in the cloudy north and heat supplying options could begin to make headway as fossil fuel prices increase. The main problem so far has been the difficulty in competing in the heating market with cheap gas.

Basically, it is the same story in every field. The main current limits are economic - as reflected by the current market valuation of conventional fuel sources. Only when that problem is resolved will we have to face up to the other limits I have identified.

CONCLUSION

As we have seen, while for the moment the constraints are mainly economic, in the longer term, there could be relatively tight environmental and technical limits to renewable energy-based human economic activity, at least of the current sort, ultimately imposed by the constraints of natural energy availability but reinforced by social and economic factors. We may be able to deal with some of the social and economic factors - for example, we may be able to convince people that it makes sense to pay more for green energy and to accept some visual intrusion from wind farms for the greater good of the planet. Then come the wider environmental limits - the need to maintain biodiversity and not impinge unduly on the natural processes that maintain the Earth's ecosystem. That could get increasingly hard if populations and affluence grow.

The overall renewable energy resource limit is even harder to deal with. Of course you might say it provides a welcome ultimate limit on our ability to damage the ecosystem by continued economic expansion. Technical fixes, like

devices that use energy more efficiently, can obviously help stretch these energy resources. However, most of the easy and cheap energy saving opportunities will be rapidly exhausted early on and it is hard to see how efficiency gains, through clever new Factor 4 type innovations, can continually keep pace with the seemingly inexorable rise in energy demand of around 2% yearly. If we want to expand human energy use beyond these limits then we would have to find other sources of energy. Some people look to nuclear fusion, hot or cold, others to as yet even more unproven options like the so-called 'free energy' techniques. There is even talk of their being large amounts of hydrogen gas produced by bacteria deep underground.

Options like this are very speculative and might have their own environmental, economic and social limits. For the moment then, we are stuck with trying to operate within the technical, environmental and social limits of the climate and weather system related renewable energy sources. The simple point is that, on a finite planet with a finite energy flux coming in from the sun, there are inevitably resource limits, and renewables cannot help us escape these.

Some people fear that, sooner or later, we will have to face up to radical social, economic and cultural changes. Not everyone sees change in lifestyles as a problem - some say that we would all benefit from a shift in emphasis from the quantity of consumption to the quality of consumption. Some say we should do this sooner rather than later since the environmental and social problems associated with our current way of life are becoming urgent. Indeed, some say we have already gone beyond the ecological carrying capacity of the planet, and are living on borrowed time - borrowed from future generations.

But rising material expectations are locked into, reinforced by, and reinforcing, the global system of economic expansion. We all seem to want more! Even some of the altruistically-minded argue that global economic growth is the only hope for the developed world - if only in terms of allowing for some 'trickle down' to the less well off!

With billions of new consumers potentially joining the race as the developing countries industrialise, it is easier to think in terms of just changing the technology and then just hoping for a more enlightened approach to consumption to emerge. That surely is not good enough. We cannot just keep trying to rush blindly forward believing that we can fix any problems that crop up. Most technical fixes have a downside - they create unexpected problems themselves. And they clearly cannot allow us to continue with materialistic growth for ever. To put it simply, it certainly looks as if environmentally sustainable technology can be developed and provide a technical fix for a while but what we also need is to create a sustainable society - and that's a larger project.

REFERENCES

1. Shell, *The Evolution of the World's Energy System 1860-2060*, Shell International, London, 1995
2. Greenpeace, 'Towards a Fossil Free Energy Future', Stockholm Institute report for Greenpeace International, London, April 1993.
3. von Weizsacker, E. Lovins A, Lovins, H., *Factor Four*, Earthscan, London, 1994
4 UN /WEC, *World Energy Assessment: Energy and the Challenge of Sustainability*, Development Programme, UN Department of Economic and Social Affairs and the World Energy Council, 2000.
5. Grob, G. 'Transition to the Sustainable Energy Age', *European Directory of Renewable Energy Suppliers and Services*, James and James, London, 1994.
6. Trainer, T., *The Conserver Society*, Zed Books, London, 1995.
7. Jackson, T. 'Renewable Energy: Summary Paper for the Renewable Series', *Energy Policy*, Vol.20 No.9, pp 861-883, 1992.
8. Elliott, D. 'Land use and Environmental Productivity' Renew 133, Sept-Oct 2001, pp 22/24
9. Elliott, D. *Windpower in the UK*, NATTA Compilation report Vol.IV, Network for Alternative Technology and Technology Assessment, Milton Keynes, 2002
10. World Commission on Dams, *Dams and Development: A new framework for decision making*, Earthscan, London 2001.
11. Hydro Quebec energy payback comparison paper at: http://www.hydroquebec.com/environment/comparaison/pdf/ang4.pdf
12 Commoner, B. *The Poverty of Power*. Jonathan Cape, London, 1976.
13. Milborrow, D. evidence to the Performance and Innovation Unit's Energy Review, see *Renew* 136, March-April 2002, p.29
14. Hewett, C., *Power to the People*, Institute for Public Policy Research, London, 2001.

Using the net energy concept to model the future

Malcolm Slesser

The transition to a renewable-based economy is not going to be easy. We shall need all the oil and gas we can get to fuel it and models show that, even then, it is going to be hard to maintain economic growth while keeping unemployment low.

The objective of a net energy calculation is to determine the overall amount of primary energy dissipated in order to bring one unit of fuel into use. The result will vary with the energy type, the degree of depletion of the source, and the nature of the deposit. It will also vary with time and technology. The approach is a uniquely valuable concept in economic analysis, payback time estimation, life cycle analysis and the efficient allocation of capital resources between competing energy technology systems.

It is also a very simple concept, though certain procedures have to be taken if the results of analysis are to be meaningful. The most important of these is system boundary: this has to be fixed to ensure that everything is taken account of from the moment a primary resource leaves the ground (or wherever) to its delivery to the market as a directly usable fuel.

DOING THE SUMS

The first step in calculating net energy is to determine what are all the inputs, other than labour and management, that are drawn in when a primary energy source is extracted and transformed into a marketable fuel or fuels. If there is capital stock involved, as must almost certainly be the case, then its embodied energy, amortised, must be included. If there are material inputs, their embodied energy must also be counted. *Figure 2A1* offers a scheme for this analysis.

It is clearly advantageous to have an agreed set of conventions for such calculations so that numbers can be compared, and conclusions reliably drawn. In 1974, following the first OPEC oil price hike, there was a flurry of energy analysis calculations ranging from the energy to produce a loaf of bread to the production of a kWh of electricity via a nuclear reactor. The chaos of methods at that time, not dissimilar from the disparity of corporate accounting conventions today, called for action. The International Federation of Institutes of Advanced Study (IFIAS), which was launched in the aftermath of the Stockholm Environment Conference in 1972, asked me to pull together a group to work out an appropriate set of conventions. I was given *carte blanche* to travel round the world to find appropriate activists. The group that met in Guldmedhytten, Sweden, in 1974 comprised economists, engineers, system analysts, chemists, physicists, academics and corporate managers. In one week of resolute discussion they produced a set of conventions summarised in the booklet called 'Energy Analysis, IFIAS Report 6'. Amazingly there was a 100% consensus.

Unfortunately this book was not given an ISBN number and with the demise of IFIAS is now unavailable. I am told it can be obtained from the British Library, Boston Spa. However an adequate summary is given in chapter 12 of my 1978 publication *Energy in the Economy*. A less detailed but wider ranging exposition, also published in 1978, is still available from the

BEFORE THE WELLS RUN DRY

PART TWO: DO RENEWABLE ENERGY SOURCES HAVE THE POTENTIAL TO FILL THE GAP?

International Institute for Applied Systems Analysis.[2]

The IFIAS convention defined two important units of account:

GROSS ENERGY REQUIREMENT (GER)

(I quote) 'The gross enthalpy of combustion released at standard state of all the naturally occurring energy sources which must be consumed in order to make a good or service available'. The standard state is the one frequently adopted in physico-chemical texts, namely 0°C and 1 bar pressure.

ENERGY REQUIREMENT FOR ENERGY

If one now subtracts from this GER the available enthalpy in the fuel delivered, the difference is the net energy. IFIAS called this the Energy Requirement for Energy, ERE.

ERE = GER per unit enthalpy of delivered fuel. Note the use of the word 'requirement'. One often hears the use of the word 'energy cost' used in the sense of the amount of energy embodied or used to in producing something. This could also imply monetary cost, hence the strict use of the world 'requirement' in the IFIAS conventions.

Another convention well worth following is to use distinct numeraires for electricity and heat (enthalpy). Thus watt-hours or a multiple thereof for electricity (which has high thermodynamic potential), and an enthalpic unit for heat, such as Mega-joule (MJ), Giga-joule (GJ), Tonnes oil equivalent (TOE) or even barrels (of oil). Unfortunately several statistical sources, such as in the UK, have chosen to use watt-hours as representing heat units. So if using such sources beware.

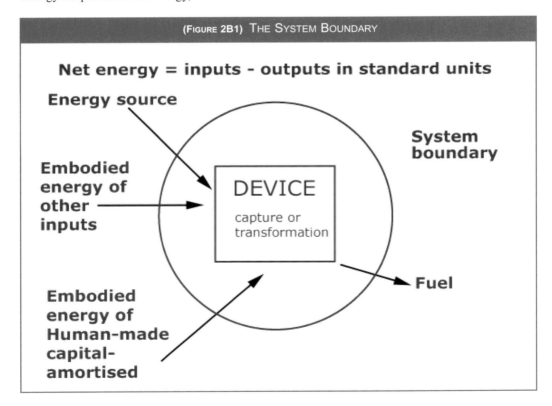

(FIGURE 2B1) THE SYSTEM BOUNDARY

Net energy = inputs - outputs in standard units

Energy source

Embodied energy of other inputs

DEVICE
capture or transformation

System boundary

Fuel

Embodied energy of Human-made capital-amortised

It may be seen that with such a definition ERE is always greater than unity, and the larger the value the poorer the yield and the more energy that is dissipated in converting it into a fuel useable by the market. For example the ERE of North Sea oil is in the region of 1.03, whereas tar sands in Canada are closer to 1.15. An important criterion, often overlooked, is the area requirement, that is the net energy per unit area. This is a particularly important criterion when evaluating biomass-to-energy proposals, such as alcohol from maize, or heat from wood fuel.

Working out the numbers for any particular fuel type and source is complicated by the fact that it almost always invokes a contribution of electricity. Now 1 kWh of electricity has, by definition, a heating value if 3.6 MJ. However creating this from some heat source will require between 2.5 and 3.5 times 3.6 MJ, according

the fuel type and technology transformation. This is because electricity has a very high thermodynamic work potential. The potential efficiency of conversion of heat to work may be determined through the Carnot equation[3].

The fuel used will also have gone through some extraction and purification processes. The upshot, for the case of the UK is that to deliver 1 kWh to a commercial user in the UK in year 2002 dissipates 14.3 MJ primary energy per kWh delivered.

Two conceptual problems arise when the electricity source is from nuclear energy or renewables. Some international statistics attribute to electricity a value of 3.6 MJ/kWh, while others attribute the heat dissipated in the transition. This latter is the more accurate representation, but not perfect since, for example, not all nuclear fuel is burnt. It is a reminder to us all

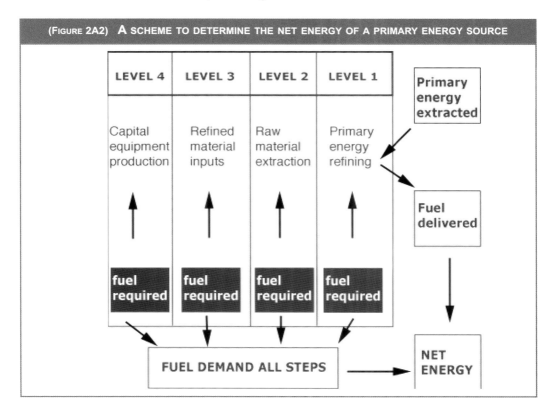

(FIGURE 2A2) **A SCHEME TO DETERMINE THE NET ENERGY OF A PRIMARY ENERGY SOURCE**

BEFORE THE WELLS RUN DRY

Part Two: Do renewable energy sources have the potential to fill the gap?

that energy statistics are far from precise and are affected by a number of questionable conventions.

In the case of renewables, except for the energy embodied in the structure (of, say, a wind or wave turbine), there is no fuel requirement. In my view it is correct to take the primary energy content of the delivered electricity as being the fossil energy embodied in manufacturing and the delivering the turbine to site and its subsequent maintenance. With this convention the primary energy of wind turbine electricity in the UK today may be said to be around 0.2 MJ/kWh.

Heat and Work

It is not heat that drives the economy, but thermodynamic work. In the UK about 55% of all heat is converted to thermodynamic work, often at very low efficiency as in a petrol engine. Strictly speaking all energy analyses ought to be conducted in these terms, but the data requirements are formidable. Indeed there is only one now famous example of this being done, that of Berry and Fels. The alternative, advised by the IFIAS group, is to express GER and ERE in terms of energy sources of a standard quality - the definition of this being the extent to which the heat of combustion could be turned into work. As it happens hard coal, natural gas and hydrocarbons have values within 2% of each other, and since no analysis can be that accurate, this is the adopted standard. Note that wood fuel and alcohol fuels have considerably lower potentials. Electricity has almost 100% availability as work

Models

These calculations are made vastly easier if there is at hand an energy numeraire (i.e. Natural Capital Accounting/ ECCO) model of the economy. Such models are constructed to

determine the elements of each conversion and then to assemble them as an overall system average. This average value will change as the energy mix changes through time.

Thus a fairly accurate value can be determined at any moment in time for the average amount of primary energy dissipated to deliver one unit of marketable heat to the market. In the ECCO model framework this is known as SYSGER - System GER (GJ in per GJ delivered). Such models also deliver another useful average, FEREL: the average fuel energy required to deliver one unit of electricity (GJ per kWh). This can be taken back to primary energy by multiplying FEREL by SYSGER to get GEREL - the average primary energy input to produce one kWh of electricity, which as remarked above is about 14.3 for the UK in 2002.

Such models exists for the UK, Scotland and many other countries. David Crane and Larry Staudt have developed an ECCO model for Ireland that is described in this book.

Renewable Energy Sources

The application of the above principles to renewable energy sources is simple. The inputs are human-made capital, that is to say output of the manufacturing system, its delivery to site and erection and its expected lifetime maintenance and the infrastructure of delivery. This input can then be set against the output expected over its anticipated lifetime. Since most renewable systems deliver electricity how does one measure the net energy? Well, let us suppose that a particular wind farm cost £700,000 per MW capacity (1.05 million Euros). Using UK data, from the UK ECCO model we know that the energy intensity of human-made capital in a given year was (18MJ/£). Hence an approximate value for the energy embodied in the turbines, etc. will be 12,600 GJ. Let us add another 20% for lifetime maintenance, making 15,000 GJ over its lifetime of, say, 30 years.

The potential yield from a one MW turbine is 8760 MWh/year (8760 hours in a year) or 283 thousand kWh over 30 years. However the wind does not always blow. UK averages are about 28% (load factor 0.28) of this potential. Thus the yield over its lifetime is about 75 million kWh. That makes the energy embodied about 0.2 MJ/kWh.

Taking UK figures, as remarked above, the GEREL for the UK is 14.3 MJ/kWh. Hence had these 75 million kWh been generated from fossil or nuclear sources, the equivalent of 1.05 million GJ of primary energy would have been required. The initial energy investment, therefore is returned within 15,000/1,005,000 = 0.43 of a year or 5 months.

From this data set it is easy to calculate how much carbon dioxide will be reduced. If one has an ECCO model this data will be generated automatically

Note, however, that as the fossil or nuclear sector becomes more thermodynamically efficient, or as renewables penetrate, the relative advantages will diminish. That is, the payback time will increase. Eventually with a 100% renewable electricity there is potential for, as it were, energy breeding.

There are other renewable energy systems such as photo-voltaics where the pay-back times are not so favourable. The energy embodied in these devices depends on the type of cells. There are highly efficient cells used in space satellites, whose net energy is certainly negative, but in such a situation this is not the important criterion. However for terrestial uses, there is no point in a negative net energy system. It would be like a farmer having to use all his crop to plant next year's crop and have to buy in more seed as well. The energy embodied in photo-voltaic cells is certainly falling. A recent figure quoted in then literature was 100,000 GJ/MW. Such cells tend to have lower load factor than wind turbine. 13% is often quoted. On this basis the pay-back time would be about 6 years.

ENERGY STORAGE

The Achilles heel of renewable-generated electricity is the variable output and low load factor, which means that if there were ever to be a high degree of replacement of conventional means of generation, some means of storage are needed. Two obvious ones spring to mind: pumped storage and conversion of electricity of hydrogen by electrolysis of water, a well developed technology. It takes 385 kWh to create one GJ of hydrogen, but at low voltage. As a renewable based economy develops one assumes that it will become more and more electrically driven, but storage will remain expensive in net energy terms. The single greatest problem will be in transport fuels, where fuels cells will be the dominant device using methanol or hydrogen. The key thing to look at here is that the supply train will now be reversed. Instead as now, of a flow from primary energy to fuels to electricity, we shall have electricity to hydrogen to fuel cells.

EXAMPLE

The transition to a renewable-based economy is not going to easy or cheap. We shall need all the oil and gas we can get to fuel it. A recent study I helped to carry out for the European Commission[6] showed that for the European Union to switch to a renewable energy economy was not going to easy, especially if we expect to hold on to what seems to me to be three entrenched criteria:
• that unemployment should be kept low
• that self-sufficiency in energy should be main tained or raised.
• that material welfare should grow annually

In fact the study, which used an ECCO model of the European-15 showed that all three criteria could not be met simultaneously.

BEFORE THE WELLS RUN DRY

PART TWO: DO RENEWABLE ENERGY SOURCES HAVE THE POTENTIAL TO FILL THE GAP?

Compromises on material welfare - the growth rate - were inevitable. In fact the three targets set for us by the European Commission were to
  • Achieve an acceptable level of unemploy ment.
• Meet the 1997 Kyoto international protocol commitments on carbon dioxide emissions.
• Increase the European Union's self-sufficiency in energy supply.

Each of these targets requires a set of policies to achieve it. According to conventional thinking the policies might be as follows:
• To reduce unemployment: further expansion of the economy by borrowing externally.
• To reduce carbon dioxide: massive investment in energy conservation.
• To increase self-sufficiency in energy: major investment in renewable energy systems for electricity generation.

To avoid burdening the reader with a torrent of results, the effectiveness of each set of policies in attaining its aims was judged by comparing it with a benchmark called business-as-usual (BAU). Here we assumed that all current policies and trends in the European Union continued unchanged over the next fifteen years to 2015.

Of course, such an unchanging evolution of the economy will not happen. As events unfold, new initiatives, new technologies and new options will be grasped. However it is useful to be informed of what might happen if nothing is done because then politicians can take time by the forelock and obviate some of pitfalls lying ahead!

Here is the business-as-usual (BAU) outcome for the European Union's current fifteen countries (EU-15) for the year 2015 compared to 1999:
• Economic growth is about 2% annually.
• Manufacturing output is up 50%.

• The material standard of living is up 20%.
• Primary energy demand is up 50%.
• Carbon dioxide output is up 45%.
• Self-sufficiency in energy falls to 25%.
• Unemployment is very high, maybe even 30%.

If we adopt Keynesian policies and borrow to make the economy expand faster to reduce unemployment, we calculated the results in 2015 would be:
• Growth rate: 40% higher than BAU.
• Manufacturing output: 90% greater than BAU.
• Material standard of living: 70% higher than BAU.
• Primary energy demand: 45% higher than BAU.
• Carbon dioxide output: 60% higher than BAU.
• Unemployment falls to 4%.

However the cost of all this was a huge rise in EU-15 external debt. Moreover the employment objective was met at the expense of reduced environmental and physical sustainability. We concluded that non-indigenous growth was not a sustainable path, nor the right way to reduce unemployment.

What happens if we concentrate on cutting carbon dioxide emissions by massive investment in energy efficiency measures? Here is the outcome by 2015.
• Growth rate: much the same as BAU.
• Manufacturing output: about the same as BAU.
• Material standard of living: 15% less than BAU, i.e. practically no rise at all from the year 2000.
• Primary energy demand: 30% lower than BAU.
• Carbon dioxide: meets the Kyoto commit ment.
• Unemployment: much the same as BAU - unacceptably high.

In short, this strategy shows a huge improvement in output per unit energy use and a significant reduction in carbon dioxide, meeting EU commitments. However it does nothing for the curse of unemployment and the material standard of living falls.

So what happens then if we make greater energy self-sufficiency the priority since, in both tests described so far, the EU-15 became increasingly dependent on fuel imports even with a major effort towards conservation? Could a fast track investment programme in renewable energies improve matters? To investigate, we assumed a deliberate government-led programme of investment in renewable energy systems: a mix of wind turbine and photovoltaic. Such a policy would be considered wildly uneconomic, at least in the early stages. We assumed too that the resulting growth in renewables would be accompanied by a learning curve resulting in an eventual halving of the amount of human-made capital required per unit of power over the trial period. This was the outcome by 2015:
- Growth rate: 45% less than BAU.
- Manufacturing output: 25% more than for the year 2000, but 11% less than BAU.
- Material standard of living: 24% down on BAU.
- Primary energy: demand 20% less than BAU.
- Self-sufficiency in energy: better than BAU with 33% of electricity from renewable sources.

- Unemployment: even higher than BAU.

So, although self-sufficiency in energy was improved, the other outcomes made this an unattractive policy. The reduced output and increased unemployment were directly due to the massive diversion of capital to investment in renewables which, because of their low load factors, require about three times as much investment per unit output as conventional or nuclear energy sources.

What was clear from these trials is that though it is possible to solve one problem, all three cannot simultaneously be solved. This is an important insight and leads to a search for a set of policies that better meets one's aims.

CONCLUSION

A renewable-based economy is certainly possible so far as the supply side - nature - is concerned. The investment requirements are going to be formidable - greater than with nuclear power. The transition will take time and require the embodiment of much energy. To make this transition we shall need all the fossil fuels we can get. And the sooner we start the easier it will be. We certainly will have to start before it becomes 'economic' using that word in its traditional sense. This is where examining new energy proposals in the light of net energy are immensely valuable.

REFERENCES

1. Slesser, M, (1978), *Energy in the Economy*, Macmillan, London, ISBN 0-333-21495; chapter 12
2. Slesser, M (1978), *Energy Analysis: its utility and limits*, RM-78-46, IIASA, 2361, Laxenburg, Austria
3. The Carnot equation states that the maximum fraction of a quantity of heat that can be turned into work (in the thermodynamic sense) is given the ratio **(temperature of the heat source - temperature of surroundings (sink)) / temp of heat source**, in units of absolute temperature. Thus 100% efficiency of conversion is unattainable
4. Berry, S & Fels, M (1973), 'the energy cost of automobiles', *Science and Public Affairs*, Dec. issue.
5. That is Gibbs Free Energy. These data were published by the American Physical Society in 1974
6. Modelling a socially and environmentally sustainable Europe, Contract SOE1-CT96-1018, under the Targeted socio-economic research programme (TSER), technical report published by the Wuppertal Institute, Germany, 1998. In this study the European Union 15 countries are treated as a single entity.

Switching the European economy to renewable energy over the next 50 years

Olav Hohmeyer

According to a German study, it is possible for the European economy to phase out the use of both nuclear energy and fossil fuels by 2050 while maintaining living standards. Doing this, however, requires decisions to be taken now, so that future energy demands are minimised.

1. ENERGY USE AND SUSTAINABLE DEVELOPMENT

Emissions of carbon dioxide account for about 55% of the human influence on the greenhouse effect (Loske 1996) and most of these emissions come from energy conversion processes. If the Intergovernmental Panel on Climate Change (IPCC) is right and the anthropogenic greenhouse effect is real (see IPCC 2001, p. 4), greenhouse gas (GHG) emissions need to be reduced enough to restrict long term global surface temperature changes to less than 3°C (see IPCC 2001, p. 22).

This is especially true for CO_2 emissions, the main cause of the problem. The IPCC scenarios show that if CO_2 concentrations are to be stablised at 450 parts per million (ppmv), a level that ought to limit temperature change to less than 3^0C, the present emission level of 8 giga-tonnes of carbon a year (Gt C/a) would have to be reduced by about half by 2050 and to about 1 Gt C/a by the year 2200. As WRE450, the lowest line in *Figure 2C1 (a)*, shows, emissions of CO_2 would need to peak within 10 to 15 years from now to allow a transition to an emission pathway leading to a long term concentration of approximately 450 ppmv.

Because the CO_2 emissions from energy conversion processes are caused by the combustion of fossil fuels, the use of these fuels has to be reduced massively within the next fifty years. Industrialised nations have contributed most of the past increase in GHG concentrations in the atmosphere, so the United Nations Framework Convention on Climate Change (UNFCCC) assumes that these countries will take special steps (UNFCCC Article 4) to prevent dangerous interferences with the global climate. The German Parliament's first commission on global climate change concluded that industrialised countries should reduce their GHG emissions to 20% of their 1990 emission level by 2050 (Deutscher Bundestag 1991, p. 867). See *Figure 2C2*. This 80% cut means that the use of fossil fuels has to be reduced accordingly.

Since the reactor accident at Chernobyl there has been serious doubt whether nuclear power can safely replace fossil fuels for energy generation to the extent required to achieve this level of reduction of GHG emissions. In countries like Germany, Austria, Sweden or Denmark there is massive resistance in the population to even the modest use of nuclear power. Moreover, as the uranium resources available seem to be as limited as our reserves of oil and natural gas, and since the problem of very long term storage of spent nuclear fuel has not yet been solved, it seems to be rather unlikely that a future energy system will primarily be based on nuclear energy.

If we accept these two assumptions, a future

(FIGURE 2C1) EMISSIONS, CONCENTRATIONS, AND TEMPERATURE CHANGES CORRESPONDING TO DIFFERENT STABILIZATION LEVELS OF CO_2

(a) CO^2 emissions (Billions of tonnes of carbon)

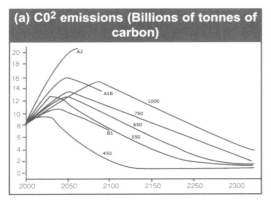

(c) Global mean temperature change (°C)

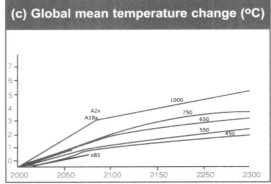

(c) CO^2 concentration (ppm)

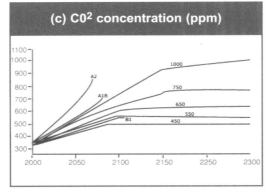

(Source IPCC 2001, p. 20)

(FIGURE 2C2)
SUGGESTED CO_2 EMISSION REDUCTIONS BY 2050

Reduction Targets Proposed by the Enquete Commission
Designed to Reduce Energy-Related CO_2 Emissions
by the Years 2005 and 2050
(Percentage data relative to 1987 emissions
of the respective group of countries)

Group of Countries	Percentage Reduction Targets (relative to the 1987 emissions of the group of countries involved)	
	By the year 2005 at least	By the year 2050 at least
Western and Eastern industrialised nations taken together..........................	-20	-80
Economically strong Western industrialised nations with particularly high per-capita emmissions	-30	-80
European Communities total	-20 or -25	-80
Developing countries total	+50	+70
Worldwide	-5	-50

BEFORE THE WELLS RUN DRY

PART TWO: DO RENEWABLE ENERGY SOURCES HAVE THE POTENTIAL TO FILL THE GAP?

sustainable energy system has to be based on renewable energy sources. Considering that the Earth will provide us with suitable living conditions in the solar system for something like 800 million years, that the internal resources of the planet are definitely limited by its physical size, and that the only resource income from outside the planet is solar radiation, it is quite obvious that this outside energy income will be the only long term energy source for a sustainable energy supply. Knowing the solar energy income is about $3.5*10^6$ EJ/a and the anthropogenic world energy consumption of 1999 was about 406 EJ/a (see BMWi 2002, p. 39) it is quite obvious that the amount of direct and indirect solar energy available will be sufficient to cover the energy needs of mankind for all the time this planet will be habitable. The remaining lifetime of the sun is estimated to be about 5 billion years. Thus, there will certainly be sufficient solar energy available for the entire time that human beings may live on this planet.

Renewable energy sources are used to only a limited extent at present. They provided only 3.2% of the world consumption of commercial fuels in 1998 (Fischer 2002, table on world energy consumption). This limited use is due to the relatively high internal costs of the use of renewable energy sources. As energy markets do not take into account the external cost of the environmental and health damage caused by the use of fossil fuels or nuclear energy, investors choose to develop conventional rather than renewable energy sources (see e.g. Hohmeyer 1988, p. 108f). Thus, a transition to a renewable energy based sustainable energy system will need a policy framework that internalises the long term external costs of all energy sources including long term impacts on global climate change.

As renewable energy sources will be relatively expensive compared with present conventional ones, future energy systems can be expected to use energy far more efficiently. What would such an energy system look like and could the transition to it be possible within the time frame set by the necessity to avert a catastrophic global climate change?

2. SUSTAINABLE ENERGY SCENARIOS FOR THE EU

In 1993, a European research consortium, the LTI-Research Group, reported on what might be involved if the fifteen countries that were then members of the EU, the EU15, attempted to develop a sustainable, renewables-based energy system by 2050. Would it be possible to phase out nuclear energy while at the same time reducing CO_2 emissions by 80%? (LTI-Research Group, 1998, p.1). Most of the rest of this paper is based on the results of the LTI project.

2.1 ASSUMPTIONS OF THE LTI PROJECT

As the LTI project had a broad perspective on sustainable development, some basic assumptions were made beyond the energy system. The most important of these were:

• **General assumptions**
- the population of EU 15 will grow from 140 million in 1998 to 164 million people in 2050 by 2050 the standard of living in EU 15 will all be at the current Northern Europe level
- industrial, commercial and living areas will be developed to minimise transportation demand
- 10% of all land area will be set aside for nature preservation
- consumption patterns will change to reduce meat imports and to allow for food production with only 20% of the present input of fertilisers

• **Assumptions concerning energy demand**
material use by industry will be reduced by a factor of 4 thanks to careful product design.

- recycling rates will be doubled.
- energy consumption in industry will be reduced accordingly.
- floor space will increase to 42 m2 per capita
- household size will decrease to 2.24 persons per household.
- heating demand for buildings in Northern and Central Europe will be reduced from 150 kWh/m2*a to 30-40 kWh/m2*a.
- energy efficiency of household appliances will be increased by 60-85% .
- the tertiary (service) sector will grow by 50% by 2050.
- the transport of goods will decrease by 60% since industry will be using less materials.
- short and medium distance flights will be abandoned in favour of rail transport.
- 50% of all journeys will be by public transport.
- people will travel shorter distances due to changed spatial patterns.
- passenger cars will use only two litres of fuel per 100km and trucks will use only 2/3 of their present diesel consumption.
- the overall energy demand per capita will be reduced from 4500 W/cap in 1990 to 1700 W/cap in 2050.

• **Assumptions concerning energy supply**
- the renewable energy sources considered in the scenario were biomass, solar radiation, wind energy, and hydropower. The share of each was based on expert judgement.
- 500 W/cap will be produced by biomass.
- PV modules will be installed on 30% of the suitable roof area supplying 150 W/cap.
- solar thermal collectors will be installed on 50% of the suitable roof area supplying 330 W/cap.
- wind energy will contribute 50 W/cap from on-shore and 160 W/cap from off-shore installations.
- solar power plants will contribute 180 W/cap.
- no large hydropower plants will be added.
- the use of small hydropower sites will be.

increased from 20-25% today to 90% in 2050 with a total contribution of hydropower of 140 W/cap.
- heat pumps will utilise environmental heat to supply 90 W/cap.
- no more than 80W/head, 5% of the total energy demand, will be supplied by fossil fuels no energy will be imported by the EU15.

Some of these assumptions like the ban on the import of energy or the changes in diet are rather restrictive. Most restrictions on lifestyle could be relaxed, however, if substantial imports of secondary energy produced by renewable energy sources outside the area of EU15 were allowed. Most of this would be electricity and hydrogen produced in Northern Africa, where a vast solar radiation resource is available.

2.2 TIME REQUIRED FOR A TRANSITION TO A SUSTAINABLE ENERGY SYSTEM

The 50-year timeframe adopted by LTI was chosen on the basis that the transition to a sustainable energy system needs to be achieved by 2050 in order to decrease GHG emissions sufficiently to stabilise the concentration of CO_2 at about 450 ppmv. Did the study show that this was long enough to allow for all the necessary changes and adjustments to be made?

The productive capital stock of an economy is turned over at intervals anywhere between four (computing equipment) and 40 years (coal or nuclear power plants). Only the stock of private and public buildings, pipelines and large hydropower dams usually has an average turnover time of considerably more than 50 years. Thus, almost all the capital stock existing today will either be renewed or fundamentally renovated by 2050. This allows almost all energy relevant equipment to be rebuilt or, in the case of buildings, fundamentally renovated at least once before 2050. No capital stock has to

BEFORE THE WELLS RUN DRY

PART TWO: DO RENEWABLE ENERGY SOURCES HAVE THE POTENTIAL TO FILL THE GAP?

be retired prematurely. Consequently, with no stranded investment to be written off, investment costs can be minimised.

Substantial changes in energy investment policy need be made early on, however. Investments in new power plants need to be considered in the light of their contribution to GHG emissions over their entire expected lifetime. This is especially important in the case of large coal power plants that can be expected to operate for 40 or more years after completion. No large coal-fired power plant should be built in the EU again. A single 700 MW power plant would emit about 3 million tonnes of CO_2 per year, a large part of the total amount of the emissions permitted for the whole of Germany in 2050, 200 million tonnes per year. The operation of such a plant would close off many other CO_2 emitting activities.

Another policy area where rapid change is required is that new buildings and factories should be sited to reduce unnecessary transport as otherwise it will take decades to bring about considerable energy savings in transportation. Because energy and transport are currently cheap, environmental damage is not costed and there are big differences in wages between various parts of the world, we are putting in place systems that are extremely transport intensive. The internalisation of all the external costs of transport would be a big step forward as it would bring about a long-term change in the location of production relative to the markets where the products were to be sold.

With short-lived energy-relevant equipment like cars we can improve the situation gradually. Although, by 2050 average consumption of passenger cars should be 2 litres of fuel/100km, we do not need to jump to the 2 litre car by next year as the stock of cars will be turned over a number of times before 2050.

Although most technologies for renewable energy production and the more efficient use of energy are available today, many of them have not enjoyed the cost reductions that will come about when they mature and move into mass production. As we have seen in the case of wind energy during the last twenty years, the costs of energy technologies can be reduced along technical learning curves (see *Figure 2C3* below and e.g. Dieckmann 2002). Broadly speaking, the cost reductions until the late 1980s can be attributed to improvements in wind energy technology while most of the cost reductions since are due to series production and learning about the production process. The rounded curve is a fitted trend line with the estimated function given in the graph.

The Danish and German success with wind energy shows that fair competitive pricing as a result of the internalisation of external costs is necessary for the market diffusion of a renewable energy technology. Indeed, fair pricing seems to be as important as the development of the technology itself as it permits all further technology development and cost reductions to be achieved by private agents in the energy markets.

As a result of the increased price paid for wind energy in Germany since 1991 - the increase was based on a first estimate of the difference in external costs between wind and fossil sources - the installed capacity of wind turbines rose from less than 68 MW in 1990 to more than 10,000 MW in 2002. (10,639 MW by September 30th 2002). This was despite the fact that Germany has a rather unfavourable on-shore wind energy resource. In addition, applications to install turbines with a capacity of about 59,000 Mw in offshore wind parks have been filed with the federal administration as a result of the increased rate paid for offshore wind electricity since April 2000.

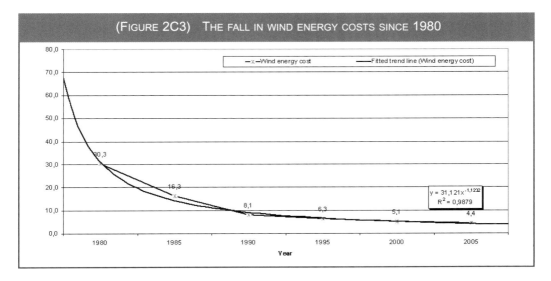

(FIGURE 2C3)   THE FALL IN WIND ENERGY COSTS SINCE 1980

Although this rate of capacity growth is rather impressive, there is a danger that instruments for increased market diffusion like paying higher prices for electricity fed into the public grid can be used too early. Pushing the diffusion of an immature technology can cause substantial losses to society. If a technology is in an early phase of technical development and a number of competing basic designs are available, one of these designs might be cheaper than the others when the massive diffusion policy is introduced.

As a result, manufacturers will invest substantial sums in production facilities for the cheaper technology and rush to market offering that design, which will accordingly develop faster than its rivals. The manufacturers will then become reluctant to try other designs in order not to risk their investment in a specific production technology and in their specialised know how. But the design they chose might turn out to be more expensive in the long run than competing designs with a higher initial cost. The reduced interest loans available to purchasers of PV equipment under the German 100,000 roof programme combined with the high price paid for the electricity they feed into the public grid - approximately 0.5€/kWh - may be locking man-

ufacturers into the production of polycrystalline silicon cells rather than thin film cells.

2.3 THE PATHWAYS CHOSEN IN THE LTI PROJECT

The LTI project assumed that, on average, each person in the EU15 would reduce their total primary energy consumption to 1700 W/cap in 2050. This compares with a consumption of 4500 W/cap in 1990. Renewable energy sources would supply 95% of this reduced amount of power as nuclear energy would be phased out by 2010, coal was not to be used after 2045, and oil and gas would only be used in rather small quantities.

Looking at the different sectors of the economy in *Figure 2C5* we find that industry's demand falls from 1060 W/cap in 1990 to 400 W/cap in 2050, household energy demand (without transportation) is reduced from 844 to 296 W/cap, and the energy demand for transport goes down from 1033 to 144 W/cap. The reductions in transport are due to both increased efficiency and rather drastic reductions in the distances travelled. This last assumption may well be contested. The energy demand from the commercial

BEFORE THE WELLS RUN DRY

PART TWO: DO RENEWABLE ENERGY SOURCES HAVE THE POTENTIAL TO FILL THE GAP?

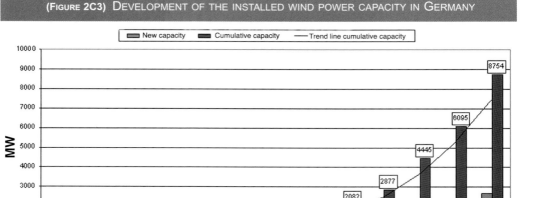

(FIGURE 2C3) DEVELOPMENT OF THE INSTALLED WIND POWER CAPACITY IN GERMANY

(Source BWE 2002)

sector (services) goes up, however, from 329 to 389 W/cap. This is due to a radical restructuring of the economy with more services being necessary because of lower levels of material use.

If this overall reduction in energy consumption can be achieved, less than half the primary energy needed in 1990 will be necessary to run the EU15 in 2050. *Figure 2C6* shows how this fall can be used to phase out fossil fuels and nuclear energy apart from a small amount of mineral oil (80 W/cap), which will be used in transportation. As conventional fuels are phased out over the 50 years, renewable energy sources will start to play an increasingly important role. While these energy sources supplied only about 3% of all primary energy in 2000 their share increases to 95% of all energy used in 2050. *Figure 2C7* shows the phasing in of the different renewable energy sources in EU15 under the sustainable energy scenario. In 2050 the largest share of all renewables will come from biomass (500 W/cap), which has a central role to play in the future energy system, as it can be used to produce liquid fuels for transportation and it can be stored without energy-

consuming conversion processes. Second in volume will be solar thermal heat contributing 330 W/cap. While the use of biomass and hydropower already supply substantial amounts of energy today, it is assumed that solar thermal heat like most of the other renewable sources start to contribute sizeable amounts only after 2000. Third in volume will

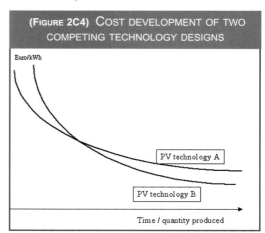

(FIGURE 2C4) COST DEVELOPMENT OF TWO COMPETING TECHNOLOGY DESIGNS

If support for photovoltaics is given too soon, the interior technology, A, might become entrenched in the market.

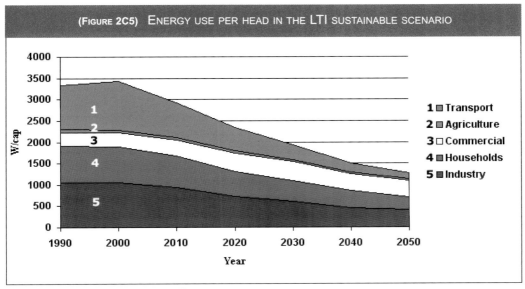

(FIGURE 2C5) ENERGY USE PER HEAD IN THE LTI SUSTAINABLE SCENARIO

(Source: LTI-Research Group 1998, p. 75)

be wind energy contributing about 210 W/cap with most of the resource being located in coastal areas and more than two thirds being generated from offshore wind farms. Solar thermal power plants located in Southern Europe will contribute about 180 W/cap to the electricity generation of EU15. For both wind and solar thermal power plants, the installations will mainly be large central installations feeding into an integrated European electricity grid. By contrast, photovoltaic electricity production (PV) will be done by decentralised installations on roofs contributing about 150 W/cap. Comparing the available resources and the present system costs for wind and PV would lead me to somewhat different assumptions concerning the scenario with substantially larger share of wind energy (which is comparatively inexpensive and only used to 17% offshore) and a rather small share of PV (which is by far the most expensive source of energy used) in the overall system. As *Figure 2C7* shows, all renewable energy technologies expand at a similar pace between 2000 and 2050, most rapidly between 2020 and 2040 and rather more slowly after that.

The project checked not only whether the total amount of energy would be adequate to meet the system's needs but also whether there would be enough at different times of year and different times of day.

By 2050 only 82 W/cap of oil will be used in the system, solely in transportation. Even if one does not agree with all assumptions LTI made, the reduction pathways for specific energy use and the expansion pathways for the use of renewable energy sources calculated for the group's scenario show that a transition to a sustainable energy system is possible for EU15 within the next 50 years, the time span available for such a transition with respect to global climate change.

2.4 ENVIRONMENTAL EFFECTS, COSTS AND EMPLOYMENT IMPACTS OF THE TRANSITION

As shown is *Figure 2C8*, the CO_2 emissions due to the use of energy in EU15 can be reduced by 90% in 2050 as compared to the starting point in

BEFORE THE WELLS RUN DRY

PART TWO: DO RENEWABLE ENERGY SOURCES HAVE THE POTENTIAL TO FILL THE GAP?

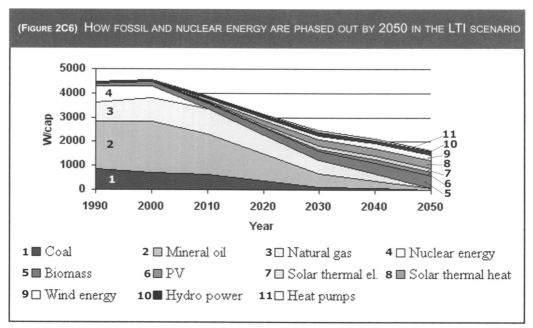

(FIGURE 2C6) HOW FOSSIL AND NUCLEAR ENERGY ARE PHASED OUT BY 2050 IN THE LTI SCENARIO

1 ■ Coal 2 ☐ Mineral oil 3 ☐ Natural gas 4 ☐ Nuclear energy
5 ■ Biomass 6 ■ PV 7 ☐ Solar thermal el. 8 ■ Solar thermal heat
9 ☐ Wind energy 10 ■ Hydro power 11 ☐ Heat pumps

(source: LTI-Research Group 1998, p. 96)

1990. Thus, more than the necessary reductions in greenhouse gases (80%) is possible within the given time frame. What is more, other important pollutants will be reduced simultaneously by 63% at the minimum (NOx) and 99% at the maximum (SO2). Thus, the resulting energy system is not just climate friendly but it will reduce pollution in many important aspects quite drastically. Nevertheless, it will be necessary to find additional ways of reducing emissions of volatile organic compounds (VOC) and of nitrogen oxides, NOx.

We may conclude that it is possible to change the energy system of EU15 into a sustainable energy system by the middle of this century and thus achieve the necessary reductions in greenhouse gases (GHGs) to stabilize their concentrations at comparatively low levels - provided that other countries change their energy systems too.

The costs of the sustainable energy system are not prohibitively high. *Figure 2C9*, shows that the 'total annual cost' of a conventional system would be €182 billion compared with €254 billion for the sustainable system. If the external costs of the conventional system apart from the global warming are taken into account, its cost rises to €218 billion a year. And if the cost of global warming is added too, the total is €754 billion a year. Thus, we can conclude that the sustainable energy scenario achieves its goal, namely the reduction to GHGs below critical levels, at comparatively low cost.

Finally, the direct and indirect employment effects of the sustainable energy scenario have been analysed and compared with those of conventional energy sources. This analysis resulted in gross annual employment effects of the sustainable scenario of 3.8 million person-years in 2050 which compare to 3.2 to 3.4 million person years of employment that would be

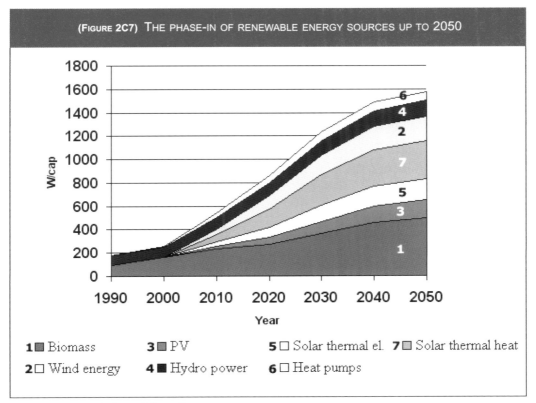

(Figure 2C7) The phase-in of renewable energy sources up to 2050

1 ■ Biomass   3 ■ PV   5 □ Solar thermal el.   7 ■ Solar thermal heat
2 □ Wind energy   4 ■ Hydro power   6 □ Heat pumps

(Source: LTI-Research Group 1998, p. 97)

(Figure 2C8) How emissions would fall

Pollutant	1990 (1000t/a)	2050 (1000t/a)	Reduction (% of 1990)
CO_2	3 060 000	308 000	90%
NO_x	10 800	4 010	63%
SO_2	19 800	175	99%
CO	38 300	11 600	70%
VOC	6 520	1 760	73%
Particulates	2 320	215	91%

(Source: LTI-Research Group 1998, p. 126)

BEFORE THE WELLS RUN DRY

PART TWO: DO RENEWABLE ENERGY SOURCES HAVE THE POTENTIAL TO FILL THE GAP?

created by conventional energy sources. Thus, the net impact of the sustainable scenario on employment would be positive in the range of 340,000 to 580,000 person-years in 2050. Although such employment effects should not be the prime reason for making the transition to renewable energy systems, knowing that the net effect on employment will be positive makes for an easier decision.

3 CONCLUSIONS

Looking at the issue of the time required for a European transition to renewables from the perspective of the necessary transition to avoid substantial human interference with the global climate system, which at the moment seems to be the most urgent reason for such a change, we can conclude on the basis of some first evidence that such a transition is:

• possible within 50 years
• can reduce CO_2 emissions more drastically than required by climate policy
• will reduce other pollution substantially
• will only be modestly more expensive than conventional energy supply strategies (in terms of internal costs)
• will be substantially less expensive for society if the full external costs are taken into account and

• will have positive net employment effects within in the European Union.

Nevertheless, this paper does not address the question of the minimum time required for such a transition from the present system to a sustainable energy system based almost exclusively on renewable energy sources. Looking at the operational lifetime of a large conventional power plant of about 40 years, it is plausible that it will take in the order of at least 30 to 40 years to achieve such transition without creating problems of stranded investment and the resulting substantial costs to society. If necessary for other reasons, however, a transition can probably be achieved in a substantially shorter time span, if stranded investment and high costs to the economy are accepted. At the moment this does not seem to be necessary.

Drawing the conclusion that the transition is possible within the given time frame underscores at the same time the fact that such a low cost transition will only be possible if we take the necessary steps as soon as possible. We need to decide within the next few years not to invest into long-lasting high CO_2 emission technologies any more. Which is to say that no coal fired or nuclear power plants should ever be built in Europe again.

(Figure 2C9) How costs compare

Cost of the reference case and the renewable energy system in the EU in 2050

	Electri-city	Low-tem-perature heat	High-tem-perature heat	Conven-tional energies	Renew-able ener-gies
Final energy demand (W/cap)	3761	576	236	1190	1190
Final energy demand (TWh)	1210	1860	760	3830	3830
Full load hours (h/a)	4500	1600	2500	-	
Installed capacity (Gwp)	269	1160	304	1730	2300
Investment cost (ECU/kWp)	900	135	82	-	
Efficiency of the power plants (%)	55	98	92	-	
Primary energy (TWH)3	2200	1890	827	4920	
Cost (in billion ECU)					
Annual cost 2	8.5	21.5	6.7	36.7	
Annual fuel cost 4	61.2	58.4	26.1	146	
Total annual cost	69.6	80.0	32.8	182	254
Annual fuel cost E15	62.9	70.1	26.8	160	
Total annual cost E15	71.4	91.6	33.4	196	254
Annual fuel cost E26	74.7	75.1	31.2	181	
Total annual cost E26	83.1	96.7	37.8	218	254
Annual fuel cost E37	458	191	68.6	717	
Total annual cost E37	466	213	75.3	754	254

Note: The costs of the conventional energy system of the reference case (Column 'Conventional energies') and of the renewable energy system of the Sustainable Scenario (Column 'Renewable energies') do not include the cost of the use of oil in the transport sector of 19.1 billion ECU in the EU in 2050.

1) Demand for electricity: 314 W/cap; transport sector: 144W/cap; 82 W/cap of oil have not been added because they are also used in Sustainable Scenario, the rest amounting to 62 W/cap is added to electricity (simplifying assumption).
2) Including capital cost and O&M cost, but without fuel cost.
3) This value is calculated with the help of the installed capacities and specific efficiencies.
4) The assumed producer fuel prices in 2050 are: gas (power plants): 28 mECU/kWh, gas (industry): 32 mECU/kWh, oil (HEL): 36mECU/kWh, oil (HS): 24mECU/k Wh (cf. Figure 2.25>).
5Including a low estimate for external cost without global warming (CEC 1995a): gas 0.8 mECU/k Wh, oil 11.5 mECU/kWh.
6) Including a higher estimate for external cost without global warming (Hohmeyer 1994): gas 6.1 mECU/kWh, oil 11.5 mECU/kWh.

(Source: LTI-Research Group 1998, p. 115)

LITERATURE

Bundesministerium fur Wirtschaft und Technologie (no year): Energiedaten 2002 - Nationale und internationale Entwicklungen, Berlin

Deutscher Bundestag (ed.) (1991): *Protecting the Earth - A Status Report with Recommendations for a New Energy Policy*. Third Report of the Enquete Commission of the 11th German Bundestag 'Preventive Measures to Protect the Earth's Atmosphere'. Volume 2. No publisher, Bonn

LTI-Research Group (ed.) (1998): *Long-Term Integration of Renewable Energy Sources into the European Energy System*. Physica-Verlag, Heidelberg

Loske, Reinhard (1996): *Klimapolitik im Spannungsfeld von Kurzzeitinteressen* und *Langzeiterfordernissen*. Metropolis Verlag, Marburg

IPCC [Intergovernmental Panel on Climate Change] (2001): *Climate Change 2001: Synthesis Report*. A Contribution of Working Groups I, II, and III to the Third Assessment Report of the Intergovernmental Panel on Climate Change. [Watson, R. T. and the Core Writing Team (eds.)]. Cambridge University Press, Cambridge, U.K.

Albrecht, Birgit et al. (eds) (2001): *Der digitalte Fischer Weltalmanach 2002*. Fischer Taschenbuch Verlag, Frankfurt a. M.

Hohmeyer, Olav (1988): *Social Costs of Energy Consumption: External Effects of Electricity Generation in the Federal Republic of Germany*. Springer-Verlag, Berlin

Vahrenholt, Fritz (2001): Globale Tendenzen der zukünftigen Energieversorgung. Manuscript published on the internet as PDF document retrieved on October 18th 2002 from www.ipp.mpg.de/de/presse/pi/13_01_vahrenholt.pdf

BWE (2002): Zahlen zur Windenergie. Table retrieved on October 27th 2002 from www.wind-energie.de/informationen/informationen.htm

Diekmann, Jochen (2002): Förderung der Windenergie erfolgreich. DIW-Wochenbericht 9/02. Retrieved as html-file on October 26th 2002 from www.diw.de/deutsch/publikationen/wochenberichte/docs/02-09-2.html

United Nations (1992): United Nations Framework Convention on Climate Change. Retrieved as PDF-file on October 20th 2002 from http://unfccc.int/resource/docs/convpk/conveng.pdf

Building a Lean Economy for a fuel-poor future

by David Fleming

There are solutions to the coming energy deficit, but they will have to be radical. This paper describes the whole-systems thinking that will be required, and outlines "Domestic Tradable Quotas" - an energy rationing system that could help to take us there.

The political economy of the future must learn to live without the cheap and reliable flow of energy which empowers and fuels the market economy of today. The solution, in part, is to develop new ways of providing and using energy but, more fundamentally, it demands new thinking about locality and community. In the "Lean Economy" of the new century, the connection between people and place will be re-established; joined-up local energy will need joined-up local cultures.

Local energy solutions will form systems connected at all four levels of the energy sequence. The four levels are:

1. Capture: land (environment) as an energy source.
2. Production: energy generation and storage.
3. Service: the use of energy to provide energy services.
4. Use: the use of energy services in daily living.

The suggested (2035) target for capture and production combined is to provide energy equivalent to 25 percent of the present (renewables 15%; coal 10%). The needed 75% fall in demand will come from a 50 percent reduction in the energy needed to produce a unit of energy services and a further 50 percent reduction in

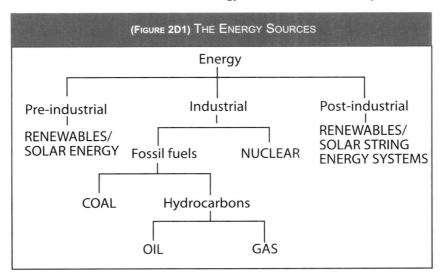

(FIGURE 2D1) THE ENERGY SOURCES

Energy

Pre-industrial — Industrial — Post-industrial

RENEWABLES/ SOLAR ENERGY — Fossil fuels — NUCLEAR — RENEWABLES/ SOLAR STRING ENERGY SYSTEMS

COAL — Hydrocarbons

OIL — GAS

By the 2030s, interruptions in the supply of oil and gas, combined with high prices, will rule them out as a serious mainstream fuel source. Nuclear will contribute little. Coal will be an important source, but it is estimated to contribute no more than 10 percent of the total energy available in 2000, the remaining 15 percent being supplied by renewables – i.e. pre-industrial sources, with the difference that they will be more efficiently conserved and produced.

BEFORE THE WELLS RUN DRY

PART TWO: DO RENEWABLE ENERGY SOURCES HAVE THE POTENTIAL TO FILL THE GAP?

the use of energy services: the potential for supply is roughly one third of the potential of learning to cope with less.

1. CAPTURE: THE LAND AS AN ENERGY RESOURCE

Among the many ways in which the energy sources of the Lean Economy will differ in principle from those on which we have depended so far, there is one in particular that will shape the world of the future. Solar energy in its various direct, indirect and related forms, including sun, wind, plant materials and the tides, is – in contrast with the fierce, concentrated power of oil, gas, coal and nuclear – widely dispersed.[1] It needs land and sea, both on the surface and at depth; it needs winds, the surfaces of buildings and living systems such as woodlands, harvested fields and the water harvests of plants and algae.

This requirement for landscape and waterscape as a source of energy bears comparison with the requirement for land as a source of food. It also places very large towns and the cities of the modern world at a disadvantage: they have relatively little space in which to capture energy; although they have plenty of roof surface on which to install solar panels, this will not be enough to power the energy services on which cities depend: transport, heating, lighting, water supply, sewage disposal, and the industry and services which form the substance of the urban economy. In other words, cities are poorly endowed with energy resources, and hungry for energy services; the realistic model for the future, however, is in total contrast with this: smaller settlements – social cities, smaller towns and villages – that are rich in land and skilled in their ability to sustain their wants and needs in ways which require little energy.

In the Lean Economy, every stretch of land and water, on the surface and at depth, will be a potential source of energy in some form. And to be most useful, that land will need to be local: the high-voltage national grids will become obsolete, and although hydrogen, generated from the electricity produced by, for instance, arrays of marine turbines, can be transported for long distances, the costs of buying and transporting it will place it, in general, beyond the reach of local economies. The implications of this for the physical pattern of land in the Lean Economy will be decisive.

2. PRODUCTION: ENERGY GENERATION AND STORAGE

The defining characteristic of renewable energy is: *connections*. The production and storage of energy, together with inspiration and ingenuity in finding ways in which energy services are provided and used, are like beads on a string, forming integrated "solar string" energy systems.

A solar string is a system which integrates energy-generation, energy-storage, energy-conservation, energy distribution, energy-services and energy-use. No part of the system exists only as a producer or consumer; each part, and each participant, contributes in some way to the functioning and stability of the system as a whole. The relationship between renewables and the solar string is similar to the relationship between organic production and permaculture: organic production is a method of growing, whereas permaculture is a design system; renewables are a method of energy generation, whereas the solar string is an energy design system. As in the case of permaculture, a solar string is conceived and sustained for a specific community and place.

The following tour along the solar string begins with generation and storage, the two key agents of energy production in the Lean Economy.

Generation

Light from the sun (photovoltaics). When sunlight hits a very pure crystal of semiconductor material, such as silicon or germanium, which is doped with the right quantity of the right chemical, electrons are knocked loose from the atoms to which they are attached, producing an electric current. The efficiency with which photovoltaic cells are now able to convert the energy contained in sunlight into usable energy can be as much as 30% or more, and it is constantly improving. There are some disadvantages: photovoltaics are less effective at higher latitudes and on cloudy days and, of course, they do not work at all at night. And yet, this is a technology with promise. As Janet Ramage writes,

Of all the new energy systems, the solar cell in many ways shows the greatest potential for really widespread use. Countries with plentiful sunshine, who have not yet developed full national power systems, can avoid all the paraphernalia of large power-stations, transmission networks, and the rest by installing clusters of solar cells to supply power as and where it is needed, for a town, a village, a factory or even a single household.[2]

The technology is still in its early stages; it is at about the same stage today that the internal combustion engine occupied in the 1890s;[3] as it develops, the cost falls, roughly halving between 1990 and 2000, with further potential for deep cost reductions.[4] It is flexible, capable of being applied on a small scale, providing as little as a single light, and then building up incrementally; it can be attached as cladding on walls and roofs and, per acre of land, photovoltaics produce much more energy than can be obtained from plant material (biomass).[5] There is a sense here of informality, of the birth of a small-scale, domesticated technology – like the hand-mills of the middle ages which challenged the authority of the millers. Local energy confers local empowerment.

Heat from the sun (solarthermal).[6] Energy leaves the sun as electromagnetic radiation, travelling through space until it reaches the atmosphere and surfaces of the earth, whose molecules it pushes around, producing heat. About a third of this energy is absorbed by the atmosphere before it reaches sea level, but some of what remains can be collected by solar thermal panels and used for purposes such as domestic water heating, or brought to the high temperatures needed to drive a turbine to generate electricity.

Solar-powered turbines can be used in combination to deliver large amounts of power, and they have the advantage that they adapt well to hybrid systems – for instance, switching to a methane-powered system at night. There is still a long way to go in developing the technology; for instance, control systems to keep the sun's energy concentrated on the collector throughout the day are not yet standard. It is, however, already well placed to become one of the prime sources of electric power in the solar economy.[7]

Wind

Wind energy can deliver a lot of power. A typical wind turbine in 2000 had an output of around 225 kilowatts, producing a theoretical 2 million kilowatt-hours (kWh) per annum, which reduces to about 700,000 kWh after allowing for the inconstancy of wind-speeds. This is enough for all the energy needs of about 30 households (excluding transport) using energy in the inefficient way that was standard in 2000, or about 60 households that had achieved reasonable progress in the efficient use of energy.[8]

There are good reasons for constructing turbines on a large scale and in places (such as at sea) where there is a lot of wind: the amount of power produced by a turbine is dramatically greater in the case of very large turbines sited in

BEFORE THE WELLS RUN DRY

PART TWO: DO RENEWABLE ENERGY SOURCES HAVE THE POTENTIAL TO FILL THE GAP?

the windiest places, rising with the square of the diameter of the turbine and with the cube of the wind speed.[9] And yet that "efficiency" argument is not decisive. If a locality can make good use of wind as part of its range of energy sources, even if only on a small scale and in a not-particularly windy place, the case for one or more wind turbines may still be strong: in the Lean Economy it is appropriateness rather than efficiency that matters.

As installations are developed and costs decline, the limitation of wind will not be the quantity of energy that can be supplied by wind, but its regularity. The wind tends to ease off at sunset every day, and there are days of calm and of storm when wind turbines produce next to nothing. They must therefore be part of a system which can store energy, and which uses a variety of sources, each of them with a particular contribution to make to the local energy network.

Biomass

"Biomass" is a useful catch-all term for wood, kitchen waste, the residue of harvest, sewage from humans and other animals, and the various forms of fuel that are derived from them. It comes in three forms: solid, liquid and gas. The solid form is the most familiar; it is the fuel of log fires; it comes in straw bales, burning smokily in inefficient furnaces at low temperatures, and in compressed straw that burns more cleanly. It is solid biomass that fuels the fires that still boil cooking-pots, with an efficiency of some ten percent or less, in many communities in the less developed world, and the 40% efficient cooking stoves that are being promoted to replace them.[10] Solid biomass is important in that it is widely distributed, it works without clever technology, and it provides a friendly fireside. And yet, the potential of biomass is seriously developed only when it is converted into liquid or gas.

The liquid form consists of ethanol, aka alcohol. A miscellany of biomass – apples, potatoes, corn, wood, sugar-cane waste and suitably sorted domestic rubbish – can be fermented, breaking down into a concentrated fuel. With cellulose fibres such as wheat straw, corn leaves and wood, the presence of a tough natural tar called lignin effectively protects the starches and prevents them from breaking down but this is being overcome with the use of enzymes. The fuel that is derived from fermentation is used "neat" in suitably adapted engines or, in normal car engines, in a mixture with petrol called "gasohol".[11]

Then there is biomass in the form of gas – equivalent to the coal gas that was standard in the cities of the developed world until the 1960s. Steam, together with air or oxygen is passed over burning solid fuel, producing a hybrid gas consisting of hydrogen, carbon monoxide and methane, together with some carbon dioxide and nitrogen. Any biomass mixture that happens to be available locally can be treated in a simple gasifier, providing an impure gas which will at least burn more cleanly than the original solids. An improvement on this is a sophisticated gasifier which can produce a gas nine-tenths of which consists of hydrogen and carbon monoxide, a highly reactive mixture capable of running a turbine.[12] Alternatively, there is the gas derived from the decomposition of wet biomass in a digester in the absence of air – mainly methane (natural gas), together with the bonus of a nitrogen-rich fertiliser. And a further variant is the somewhat impure methane that is produced by the diverse mixture of biomass contained in rubbish dumps.

Biomass, though not a particularly efficient way of harnessing solar energy (it captures only around one percent of the energy that is available to it), has some powerful advantages. First, it is easy to store in any of its three forms, particularly as a liquid or gas. Secondly, anaerobic

digesters do a good job of waste-disposal, producing fertiliser along with the methane.
Thirdly, biomass does not monopolise the land
on which it is grown. Solar thermal systems, in
effect, take over the land, covering the surface
and leaving little or no space for biological life
– which is the reason why most of the large-
scale solar systems so far have been built in
deserts. Biomass fuel, such as fast-growing
poplar and willow, along with, say, fruit trees,
sustains a living landscape, and can at the same
time be a provider of lubricants, plastics, paper
and construction materials; fuel is derived from
the bits that are not wanted, using waste in a
way which, in the end, is very efficient.

Biomass is therefore complementary with the
other renewable energy sources, illustrating the
solar-string principle: it maintains the connections and variety intrinsic to the energy systems
of the Lean Economy. That diversity is taken
further still with the other energy sources discussed below; none of them are major sources
in their own right but, taken all together, the
renewables come together to form a realistic
solar economy.

Other energy sources

Solar architecture can make such effective use
of solar energy that no other power sources are
needed whether for heating buildings in winter
and cooling in summer.[13] There is energy from
wave power, tides and marine currents.[14] There
are micro-hydro systems, driven by small dams
and by run-of-the river turbines, and medium-
sized hydroelectric schemes, now well-established throughout the world;[15] large hydroelectric systems, despite their profoundly destruc-
tive environmental and human consequences,
will be an inheritance which it would be reasonable for the solar economy to continue to
use during the few decades of their remaining
useful life. Ocean thermal energy may be a possibility in the lower latitudes.[16]

And nuclear fusion energy is still not ruled out:
the theory that very large amounts of energy are
released when two deuterium nuclei fuse
together is sound enough; the only problem is to
persuade them to do so. Hot fusion continues its
long and difficult research programme and
could be within sight of building a functioning
prototype;[17] the search for ways to make fusion
occur without initial recourse to high temperatures has some enthusiastic supporters, but
there is no sign yet that any of the fusion alternatives will be providing energy in reliable high
volume in less than the fifty-year time horizon
for renewables as a whole.[18] And geothermal
energy can make virtually inexhaustible supplies of heat available locally as a source of
energy, but the possibility of doing so is in practice distributed unevenly: the Philippines,
Iceland and New Zealand have the advantage.[19]
Finally, there are small but useful quantities of
methane or be extracted from coalmines.[20]

Storage

Almost all the renewable energy sources produce an irregular flow of energy – and some of
them switch off entirely for some of the time –
so storage is essential. Some forms of energy
can be easily stored. Coal and biomass, in all
their forms – solid, liquid and gas – are excellent storage media. Heat itself can be stored –
for instance, in a well-insulated house, or in the
classic ceramic stove which, for an hour or so,
burns wood fiercely and completely, and then
continues to heat the house for the rest of the
day.[21] Although electricity cannot be stored, the
energy it contains can be held on stand-by in
other forms. Some of them have evident limitations: fly-wheels, compressed air and supercapacitors, for example, are better for smoothing
out fluctuations than for storing energy over
long periods;[22] batteries store energy chemically, but they are heavy, expensive, and a waste-
disposal problem; pumped storage lifts water
uphill and then releases it to drive a turbine, but

BEFORE THE WELLS RUN DRY

PART TWO: DO RENEWABLE ENERGY SOURCES HAVE THE POTENTIAL TO FILL THE GAP?

it is limited by the existence of suitable high-level reservoirs. There is, however, one storage systems that is particularly interesting and has the fewest drawbacks – hydrogen.

Hydrogen can be produced by electrolysis or by direct solar action on water;[23] it can then be stored and transported to be used in fuel cells in which it recombines with oxygen, releasing energy. Fuel cells are pollution free (their waste product is water); they are efficient, recovering between 35 and 65 percent of the energy potential provided by the hydrogen; they can work on any scale between a large conventional power plant and a small box fitted into a car; and the technology is improving, while the price is falling.[24] Hydrogen is not a primary fuel; it is a storage medium; it is unlikely to be distributed in the same comprehensive quantity, still less at the same price, as natural gas in its prime, but it will be of critical importance as a storage and transmission medium in the solar economy. And there are signs that very recent technologies, such as the use of liquid nitrogen as an energy source, may be able to expand the range of technologies with neat portability of the fuel cell.[25]

3. SERVICE: THE APPLICATION OF ENERGY

The five main types of energy service are space-heating; process heat (that is, heat above 1000C, used for all purposes from domestic cooking to industrial chemistry); electric drives for equipment including lighting; transport, which will be considered later; and the energy embodied in materials. Strictly speaking, this last "energy service" is covered by the other four, but it is useful to think of it separately. It refers to the energy that was required to mine or cultivate the materials, to transport, refine and process them. The reason why it is useful to think of this separately is that the quantity of material and the quantity of energy are deci-sively linked: a reduction in the material input per unit of service (MIPS) leads to a more-or-less corresponding reduction in the amount of energy required.[26]

All five energy services will take advantage of the technologies and inventions of the industrial era. Here are some illustrations of the ways in which, respectively, households, industry and services, agriculture and transport, will in the future be able to get the services they need from the reduced flow of energy available to the Lean Economy.

Households

The uses of energy that matter most to households are cooking, heating and appliances. Improvements in energy efficiency are relatively hard to achieve in the case of cooking, but opportunities exist. Pressure cookers and microwaves, both long-established technologies, can deliver substantial savings when they are routinely used; there are improvements to be made in the design of cookers and their temperature control; cookers based on induction (magnetic fields) will offer energy savings in the future; and solar cookers make good use of free energy on sunny days. Even these modest-sounding improvements are expected, over fifty years, to multiply up to a doubling of energy-efficiency, and a doubling (factor 2 improvement) is the baseline from which household appliances start: refrigerators are expected to require some 85 percent less energy per unit of output in 2050; freezers and lighting are on course to reduce their energy requirement by 80 percent, and washing machines by 70 percent (factors of roughly 7, 5 and 3).[27]

The really substantial potential for domestic energy efficiency, however, lies in domestic heating. The case is presented persuasively by the environmental scientists, Amory Lovins and Hunter Lovins, in collaboration with the businessman Paul Hawken, in their book, *Natural Capitalism*.[28] The key is to recognise that, even in cold winters, houses can often be expected to receive enough solar energy to maintain a comfortable temperature so that, in theory at least, the central task is to turn the solar energy that falls on the house into useful heat, and then to stop that heat escaping. Before beginning to think about this up-beat solution, it is advisable to be aware of its limitations: the potential for solar energy in buildings is reduced in those cases where a house is shaded by, for instance, tall neighbouring buildings; large houses with upper floors have the disadvantage of a lot of interior space to be heated, relative to the surface area exposed to the sun. There are also practical snags in imposing on an old house, built in the age of coal or wood, the new sleek technologies of the solar age. Energy saving strategies that may seem quite reasonable in principle have to cope (as Vaclav Smil reminds us, in a review of *Natural Capitalism*) with "technical glitches, social inertia, basic human consistency, and personal priorities and preoccupations".[29]

But the means are available. The leading technology is the "superwindow", a simple idea that starts with the "greenhouse" properties of glass, and takes them as far as they can go. The glazing is coated with insulation film, sealed and filled with heavy gas such as krypton or a silica foam. The result is a window that provides intensely effective insulation, trapping heat inside the house. It only remains to apply an equivalent ingenuity to – well, some twenty other efficiency measures ranging from draft-proofing and wall insulation to window-frames insulated to the same standard as the glass, and heat-exchangers (ventilators which use the heat contained in stale air to warm incoming fresh air). Here, then, we have a house which banks its energy, rather than losing it, and when all this is combined with solar panels on the roof – which generate electricity, which is used to pro

duce hydrogen, which drives the fuel cells which supply the energy to do the cooking – so much energy is saved that the house may end up with a surplus to sell to the local grid.

The theory is undoubtedly heart-warming. There has to be a suspicion that it is all too good to be true, and yet houses exist which do indeed match the ideal. The best response is to acknowledge that the energy-efficiency of houses can be taken a long way at a reasonable cost. A 75 percent reduction in the use of energy in the typical households of today is consistent with the needs of a bearable, liveable home.

Industry and services

The industry and services of the Lean Economy have an advantage over those of the market economy, in that they will naturally comply with the standards of "lean thinking".[30] Local, small-scale industry will naturally respond to that central concept of lean thinking – pull: it will produce things when they are wanted: it will be responsive to local needs, rather than burdened with an organisational agenda of its own. On this small scale, the management of a closed system becomes realistic, opening up the prospect of saving energy by saving materials. Energy is saved by recycling materials (e.g. a 90 percent saving in the case of aluminium); but far more is saved by making things to last. Both of these options are possible on a large scale, but are much easier when the task is done at close-range, at a level which manageable, detail-friendly and less transport-dependent, and which explicitly confers on users the responsibility and incentive to make the system work. In the market economy, one of the primary uses of energy is to simplify life: it reduces the need to plan ahead, to find ways to avoid journeys, to make do and mend. The reduced energy available to the Lean Economy, in contrast, will require it to grapple with detail, and to stay within a scale that makes that possible.

BEFORE THE WELLS RUN DRY

PART TWO: DO RENEWABLE ENERGY SOURCES HAVE THE POTENTIAL TO FILL THE GAP?

The energy efficiency of the Lean Economy's industry can be expected to stay on the long-established course of improvements at the rate of about 1.2 percent per year, giving a 30 percent improvement in industry in a generation (25 years).[31] This is Vaclav Smil's estimate for the future advance of energy efficiency, and it may be an underestimate, since the coming shock in the price and availability of oil and gas will provide a powerful incentive for improvement, and the small-scale organisation of the Lean Economy will provide new opportunities for saving. Indeed, the authors of *Natural Capitalism* encourage their readers to expect a tenfold improvement in energy efficiency within a generation. On the other hand, the disruption of the coming transition and the dearth of capital available for investment could slow the rate of advance; there is no reason, therefore, to dissent from Smil's estimate, which is not inconsistent with the LTI-Research Group's careful estimate of a 60 percent improvement in the energy efficiency of industry by 2050,[32] and with the 50 percent improvement required by the Lean Economy by 2035.

Somewhere along that path, probably well into the period of a settled Lean Economy, there are certainly some remarkable technologies to be developed. One is "biomimicry" - which uses biological processes to produce tough materials, with no more energy than, say, the dappled sunlight, cool water and inconsiderable seafood available to a barnacle. This is discussed elsewhere;[33] meanwhile, it is enough to note that there is, in the longer term, more potential for energy efficiency in the Lean Economy's industry than appears at present to be possible. We might hear, in this matter, the voice of Walt Whitman's "little captain", above the noise of the guns, when his ship had been shot to bits by the enemy, and as prelude to turning things around: *"We have not struck"*, he composedly cries, *"we have just begun our part of the fighting."*[34]

Agriculture

Energy savings in agriculture will flow directly from the transition to organic agriculture. The main use of energy in conventional agriculture is the manufacture and transport of fertilisers and pesticides. Fertilisers are made from anhydrous ammonia, derived from natural gas; pesticides are derived from ethylene and propylene, which are obtained by catalytic cracking of oil, or from the methane derived from natural gas. In the future, with the rising cost and declining supply of gas, organic systems will be the only reliable and affordable option.[35]

Food production in the Lean Economy will become less dependent on energy in other ways, too. There are already many farming tasks, such as transport, fruit harvesting, logging and even some cultivation, for which machinery offers no cost benefit, relative to the alternative such as the horse. For instance, it may take the farmer less time to use the horse than to pay for the capital, fuel and maintenance of a tractor for the same tasks. On the small-scale farms in the fuel-scarce Lean Economy, the advantages of horses will be recognised: they are likely to be a routine form of traction, with tractors and heavy machinery used for special purposes when they and their fuel are available, and their costs can be justified.[36]

And then, there are substantial energy-savings opportunities for farming in the technologies of the future. Greenhouses fitted with superwindows will not need to be heated; grain driers can be wind-powered; electrical machinery will benefit from advances in technical efficiency comparable to those of industry. Lean water management[37] will reduce the energy cost of irrigation pumping. If all these advances in energy efficiency are counted, the prospect of a transformation in the energy-efficiency of agriculture become real.[38]

Transport

The idea of cars that run on solar power is not quite the fantasy it seems. This is how they would work. The solar power (that is, all the solar string energy sources, including sun, wind and water) generates electricity, which in turn produces hydrogen from water by electrolysis. The hydrogen is then used in a fuel cell in a car to deliver electricity that drives an electric motor to turn the wheels. There is also a small battery in the car that allows the fuel cell to operate at constant power; when the car needs to accelerate, it draws on its battery power – and the battery is recharged when the car is cruising or at rest. The car is built to a lightweight design, with a carbon fibre body and a small motor, allowing the heavy steel engineering of conventional cars to be drastically reduced or eliminated; this in turn allows the motor and the supporting structures to be made lighter still, and the material savings more than compensate for the high cost of the carbon fibre. This sequence of positive interactions between the many ways of reducing weight and reducing power requirements is known as "mass decomposition", and it is an illustration of the principle of "whole system design" advocated by Amory Lovins and his colleagues at the Rocky Mountain Institute (RMI). They now have prototypes of the car that can run at conventional speeds with a fuel efficiency equivalent to around 200 miles per gallon, and they have called it the "Hypercar™".[39]

Realistic? Well, there is no chance within the foreseeable future, if ever, of deriving enough power from solar energy sources to drive the world's road transport on its present scale, in addition to all the other things for which renewable energy will be required in the future. RMI therefore proposes that, if only as a transitional solution, the Hypercar should run on hydrogen derived from natural gas; the authors are confident that there are "abundant sources – at least two centuries worth" of gas, adding that oil, too, is so abundant that it "will eventually be good mainly for holding up the ground."[40] However, RMI is wrong about this. As Colin Campbell's paper in this book shows, we are already in the midst of the early stages of oil depletion, to be followed swiftly by turbulence and regional depletion in the supply of gas. The gas that RMI has in mind as a replacement for petrol does not exist. There are also some practical limitations to the concept of the Hypercar; the central principle of weight reduction becomes more elusive in the case of goods vehicles and heavily loaded cars, and there may be some safety concerns with respect to the stability of very lightweight vehicles in crosswinds.[41]

For these reasons, the Hypercar can be ruled out as the car which will replace the conventional steel-built, petrol-driven car of the present: there will be no replacement, for there will not be the fuel to drive it. However, the Hypercar will be able to make a contribution to the reduced transport needs of the Lean Economy. Hawken and his co-authors themselves argue for "sensible land use over actual physical mobility – a symptom of being in the wrong place" – precisely the case which is developed extensively in the study of which this paper forms a part. The pattern of land-use developed and sustained by the Lean Economy is designed to be consistent with a reduction in transport on the scale of as much as 90 percent – and the 10 percent that remains will not include the rivers of long-distance traffic for which it is necessary and economic to maintain motorways. That 10 percent remainder, using the undoubtedly excellent technology of Hypercars (modified as necessary for freight) will have a fuel efficiency of the order of four times that of the present day. On these assumptions, the energy needed to fuel transport will be around 97 percent less than that of the present – and fuel for this could indeed be supplied from local solar string sources. [42]

BEFORE THE WELLS RUN DRY

PART TWO: DO RENEWABLE ENERGY SOURCES HAVE THE POTENTIAL TO FILL THE GAP?

> ### WHOLE SYSTEMS THINKING
> ### THE VALUE OF NATURAL CAPITALISM SHOULD BE RECOGNISED, DESPITE THE FLAWS
>
> *Natural Capitalism* is open to criticism on three counts: it has no sense of history — in particular, of the time it would take to bring in the technologies it discusses; nor (secondly), does it consider the economic implications of the technologies it describes; thirdly, its uncritical optimism on oil and gas reduce many of its essential arguments to fantasy. Nevertheless, the same could be said of many other books in the field, and the reason why they show up particularly clearly in *Natural Capitalism* is that, in other respects, it makes a brilliant contribution, not least in its emphasis on "whole systems thinking", which is simply the argument that it is a good idea to think through the way in which they connect up — to work out what the unintended consequences are, to imagine what the desirable but far-from-obvious consequences might be, and to build a connected system. Such a system will almost invariably spill across the boundaries between energy, food, water and minerals, inspired by recognition of what can be done when the seemingly separate parts of a system actually — for worse or for better — connect up.[43]

4. USE: SHOCKS AND CONNECTIONS

The effective use of energy will have two profoundly significant properties. The first is that the reduction in energy supply that is in prospect does not hold out the promise of sustained economic growth in the conventional sense of the word. The conventional sense of "growth" – which measures the money value of consumption, without regard to whether that consumption may actually be desired or even desirable – though very widely criticised, is in fact a very important meaning which we ignore at our peril, for it is growth in this simple sense which ultimately determines such fundamental matters as whether we have jobs and whether we have the money to buy bread. There is no prospect of the reduced energy supply of the future being consistent with growth in that sense, and the economic consequences of this are as serious and as threatening to economic and social order as any other environmental or political issue in the modern world. There are familiar arguments that claim to contradict this; for instance, it is suggested that the renewable energy systems of the future will be a job-creation opportunity, prelude to a new wave of growth. However, the case against this (also argued elsewhere[44]) is strong, particularly if the decline in the availability of oil and gas, and their rise in price, occurs turbulently, with periods of interruptions of supply, rather than down a smooth decline path, with plenty of warning, and untroubled by any other problems occurring at the same time.

That is to say, it is the way in which energy, and energy services, are used – the way in which society accommodates itself to a drastically reduced supply – that is the critically difficult issue, far more testing than the technical fixes of energy efficiency that we have just briefly reviewed. The big energy issue raised, but not answered, in this paper is how society might accommodate itself to this shock – a shock of a different kind, since this one has no evident end-point. This is when the technical fixes are taken as far as they can go – and it is not enough.[45]

The second issue raised by use is marginally simpler and more manageable. The multiple shocks of the future, arising in part from the energy deficit but a consequence also of disruptions in the supply of all the primary goods, including food, water and materials, will require a response in the form of transition to local economies, smaller in scale than those of the present day, but more complex, more robust, richer in diverse talent and resources. And this will be reflected in energy systems in the form of networks without a centre, whose participants both contribute to them and receive from them, and having more in common with the internet than with the present format of large producers of energy providing a one-way service to numerous consumers. In terms so simplified as to illustrate no more than the bare principles, the following discussion shows how the use of energy services connects up positively with all other parts of the local energy economy in the "minigrid".

5. THE SOLAR STRING: THE ENERGY NETWORK

The technology of small-scale local energy generation will require local storage systems and grids based on devolution and detail. The solar string energy sources have two well-defined characteristics. First, most of them are intrinsically small in scale, providing energy close to where it is needed. The main exceptions are large-scale wind-power and hydro-power, both of which are in the main outside local control, requiring long-distance transmission over a grid designed for much higher loads, and for these reasons alone they may have only a minor contribution to make in the future. Secondly, about half the solar-string energy sources are intermittent: wind, photovoltaics and the solar thermal systems depend on weather and the time of day. Those two qualities shape the design of the solar economy. It requires ways of storing energy; and it must be connected in minigrids that share out the task of providing and conserving energy across all producers and consumers within a locality. Energy will not be the reliable service supplied by a benign but remote big

business; it will be a matter of local responsibility, creative intelligence and an engagement with the detail.

There is no aspect of lean production that illustrates more decisively the transition from the obsolescent structures of "capture and concentration" to the devolution and detail of the complex political economy than the coming transformation in the provision of energy. The guiding principle is that of "soft energy" – the use of local systems of renewable energy and conservation, first outlined in 1977 by Amory Lovins.[46] Here is Janet Ramage's more recent description of the principle:

The typical modern power station has an output in the gigawatt range, sufficient for [the electricity consumption of] a million households. It is seen as large, distant, and controlled by a large, distant organisation. The soft energy version would be different. Agricultural and urban wastes, energy crops, wind-farms, small-scale hydroelectricity, and photovoltaics would provide the power, and combined heat and power [which uses power stations' waste hot water to heat homes] would maximise the efficiency with which the fuels were used. Instead of competition between large organisations, each committed to encouraging the use of one form of energy, local control of the full range of available supplies would promote the best use of all resources.[47]

Capture
Use
Provision
Service

BEFORE THE WELLS RUN DRY

PART TWO: DO RENEWABLE ENERGY SOURCES HAVE THE POTENTIAL TO FILL THE GAP?

The Lean Economy would adopt that principle, but it would take it much further, down to the local level of the parish and neighbourhood. The key to the concept of "minigrids" is intelligence, directed to four functions in an integrated system: capture, use, provision (production and storage) and service – and the acronym "CUPS" accordingly stresses the principle of holding local energy in place and in an accessible form. Intelligence is also central in that minigrids will depend on machines that can think – switching between generation, storage and use in response to variations in demand and supply. Seth Dunn and Christopher Flavin put this into context:

... a more decentralised, dispersed control may provide far more resilience than a centralised, hierarchical system. Such a system could evolve along the lines of resilient biological systems – such as ecosystems or the human body – that decentralise control among numerous feedback loops rather than relying on a centralised hierarchy. Just as the brain does not need to track every bodily process for the system to function, power networks need not have a central point through which all information flows.[48]

Intelligence is also engaged in the case of households, in an awareness of domestic solar technologies and of the intrinsic limitations on their use of energy. Minigrids make plain to the community the reality and character of their local control and responsibility. The market economy defers to the consumer as "sovereign": it is a despotic sovereignty – expecting instance obedience, without appeal, to the consumer's slightest whim. The local minigrids of the Lean Economy, in contrast, will introduce some accountability; consumers will be subject to the science of local energy production.

Minigrids have the practical benefits that they can be built relatively quickly, functioning to some extent almost from the moment when they are started, while the network is expanded incrementally.[49] The losses of power that are incurred when power is transmitted over long distances are reduced, not least because of the alternating current (AC) which is used for long-distance transmission; local minigrids are likely to use the less wasteful direct current (DC) system. Overall, there is a degree of reliability in the existence of local networks, with a mix of generation systems and fuels, largely powered by the sun.[50] This is sufficiently recognised for there to be already some progress in the development of diverse small-scale solar energy sources and services, joined together in local grids. The task must now be to follow through the logic fast – finding substitutes for the big centralised power sources in time to sustain a flow of energy when the market economy itself can no longer provide it.

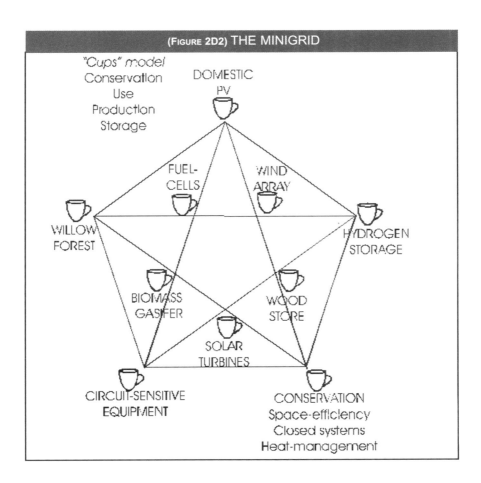

(FIGURE 2D2) THE MINIGRID

The Minigrid. The ten "cups" illustrate some of the range of systems that will operate at intersections of the minigrid. Domestic PV (photovoltaic panels) provides electricity on a very local scale that will need to be stored by, for instance, hydrogen storage, delivering hydrogen on demand to use in fuel cells. Wood from willow forests along streams and rivers and from poplar and fruit trees produces fuel for the wood store; it also combines with straw and biomass of all kinds to produce fuel for biomass gasifiers which, together with solar turbines and energy from the wind array, produce circuit electricity. Circuit-sensitive equipment adjusts its power demand in response to changes in the supply, and is related to the minigrid's critically important conservation systems. These include "space-efficiency", which develops ways of sustaining the local economy with the minimum level of dependence on energy-dependent transport; by establishing and maintaining (substantially) "closed systems" it conserves materials, and the energy embodied in them, in the locality; "heat management" develops high standards of insulation and passive heating with the aid of superwindows and methods of keeping cool with solar-powered air-conditioning and passive cold stores such as north-facing ventilated larders. The essence of minigrids is that they rely on local ingenuity, knowledge, responsibility and the particular opportunities and assets of the place.

BEFORE THE WELLS RUN DRY

PART TWO: DO RENEWABLE ENERGY SOURCES HAVE THE POTENTIAL TO FILL THE GAP?

6. TOWARDS LEAN ENERGY

Domestic Tradable Quotas

This concluding discussion of energy will trace a pathway along which society could travel to reduce its demand for fossil fuels in line with what will actually be available in the future. The critical need is for a wholehearted, collective, cooperative programme to which citizens are fully committed, and which is robust to the shocks that have to be expected in the coming two decades.

There is a convergence of objectives if we have both to reduce carbon emissions to limit climate change and find an equitable way of sharing the declining supply of oil and gas. As discussed above, a suggested target for all fossil fuel use (essentially coal) by 2035 is 10% of turn-of-the-century consumption. The descent of this steep path will not be accomplished without profound turbulence unless society develops a sense of collective purpose – which can be said to exist where the individual is able to fulfil his own designs and purposes most effectively by participating in actions that promote the public good. The conditions that achieve a synthesis of private and collective advantage do not usually happen by accident. The connection needs to be explicitly made – and one way in which it can be made to happen is by an equitable system of rationing such as domestic tradable quotas, DTQs.

There are two main approaches to the task of reducing the demand for fossil fuels. Taxation is the most obvious and widely canvassed one but there are some problems with it. It causes a great deal of resentment, as Britain discovered when protestors against fuel tax brought the country virtually to a halt in September 2000. It is practically impossible to set a rate of tax that changes the behaviour of higher-income groups without causing unacceptable hardship for people on a lower income. And, as the price of

oil and gas rises as a result of scarcity, taxation would only raise it higher still, making a bad situation worse. The other solution is rationing, but in a form which is very different to the coupons-and-scissors memories of the past. In the fair and flexible rationing schemes of the future, a strict upper limit to the quantity of fossil fuels available for the economy as a whole over a specified period will be set and rations based on it distributed electronically among consumers who will then be free to trade their share.

Various tradable rationing schemes have been devised. Those which apply to companies (chiefly relating to sulphur-dioxide emissions) have been developed a long way, and some are being applied in practice. Several "domestic" schemes, which would include consumers as well as firms in the rationing process, have also been suggested. One such scheme, DTQs, has been developed.[52]

DTQs are intended for use within an economy. They are complementary with international permits for trading between nations. It is accepted that the only fair framework for international action has to be one of "contraction and convergence", which would both reduce carbon dioxide emissions, and converge towards a point at which each nation's "right to pollute" is calculated on the basis of their populations.[53] DTQs make it possible for ambitious international targets to be carried out within nations, by giving governments control of the rate at which fossil fuel consumption is reduced, while sharing out the available supply of fossil fuels fairly, and maintaining flexibility in prices so that the market works efficiently.

The proposal is that DTQs should in fact be implemented immediately, taking full advantage of stability and financial resources while they are still available. Some adjustments to the model may be required under post-market conditions.

How Domestic Tradable Quotas work

The scheme works like this. Users are given rations, or quotas, and allowed to buy and sell them, so that if any user cannot cope within his ration, he can top it up, and users who are most successful in keeping their fuel consumption low can sell as much of their ration they can spare.

At the heart of the scheme is the "Carbon Budget" which gives notice of gradual reductions in the upper limit for carbon emissions. The "carbon units" making up this budget are issued to adults and organisations. All adults receive an equal and unconditional Entitlement of units; organisations acquire the units they need from a Tender, a form of auction based on issue of government debt. There is a national market on which low users can sell their surplus, and higher users can buy more.

DTQs are a hands-off scheme, with virtually all transactions being carried out electronically, using the technologies and systems already in place for direct debit systems and credit cards. It has been designed to function efficiently not only for people who participate in it, but also for those who do not – e.g. for overseas visitors, for the infirm and for those who refuse to cooperate.

CARBON UNITS AND SEQUESTRATION

Readers may find it helpful to read the description of Domestic Tradable Quotas before reading this box, which explains how the scheme could take account of sequestration or be used for rationing at a time of fuel scarcity.

It is important to note the units against which the rationing system is measured – namely, "carbon units", the number of kilograms of carbon dioxide produced when a fuel is used. This is the basis for a scientifically objective rating system but, at the same time, there will need to be some flexibility here. This is for two reasons. (1) There is the conceivable possibility that an effective and large-scale sequestration technology will become a reality, breaking the link between the use of the fuel and the release of carbon dioxide. (2) The system could be used as an instrument for rationing oil and gas in conditions of limited supply, rather than reducing carbon emissions from all fossil fuels. The solution to both these problems is straightforward: the fuels for which rationing is required could be declared as having a higher, or much higher, carbon rating than other fuels. Carbon units, renamed as, (for instance) "rating points" could be set at a level which directly reflect the total available ration; it would also be possible to impose electronic limits to the number of rating points purchased by an individual. In practice, it is highly likely that (independently of the issue of carbon emissions) a rationing system will be required for oil and gas in the future, and that electronic technology will be used to administer it.

BEFORE THE WELLS RUN DRY

PART TWO: DO RENEWABLE ENERGY SOURCES HAVE THE POTENTIAL TO FILL THE GAP?

How the quota market works

The numeraire of the model is the "carbon unit", defined as one kilogram of carbon dioxide. Nitrous oxide, methane and other global warming gases would be rated in "CO_2-equivalents" – the number of kilograms of CO_2 that would produce the same amount of global warming as one kilogram of nitrous oxide, methane, etc). Estimates of the carbon units ratings of the main fuels and electricity are set out in the Box.

The domestic market (*Figure 2D3*) works as a sequence. At the start, there is the Register (called QuotaCo); this is a computer database that holds individual carbon accounts

for all participants in the scheme, like the accounts that are held for credit cards and collective investments.

TRANSLATING EMISSIONS INTO FUEL[54]	
Estimates of the global warming potential (GWP) of gases released by the production and combustion of fuels. 1 kg carbon dioxide = 1 carbon unit. The GWP of methane and nitrous oxide is measured as carbon dioxide equivalents.	
Fuel	**Carbon units**
Natural gas	0.2 per kWh
Petrol	2.3 per litre
Diesel	2.4 per litre
Coal	2.9 per kg
Grid electricity (night)	0.6 per kWh
Grid electricity (day)	0.7 per kWh

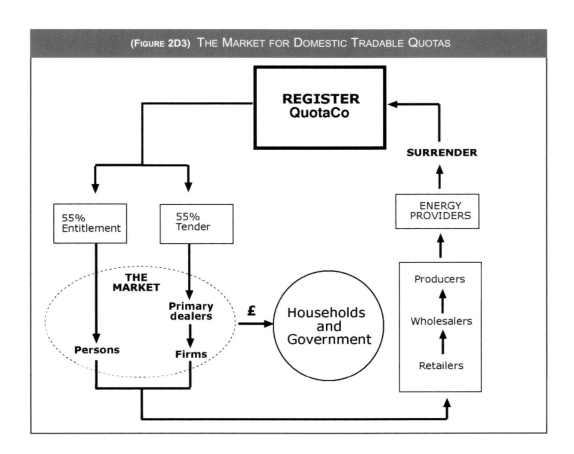

(FIGURE 2D3) THE MARKET FOR DOMESTIC TRADABLE QUOTAS

Carbon units are issued on an annual basis – with an initial issue for one year, topped up each week – and they are placed on the market in two ways. First, there is the Entitlement for all adults: households' consumption of fuel and energy in various forms accounts for about 45% of all emissions in the UK. Carbon units representing this share (45%) of all carbon emissions are therefore issued to adults on an equal per capita basis. (Children's carbon usage is provided for in the existing system of child allowances.) The remaining share (55%) is issued through the Tender to commercial and industrial companies and to the public sector. It is distributed by the banks to organisations using direct credit (for the units) and direct debit systems (for the payments).

When anyone (consumers, firms or the government itself) makes purchases of fuel or energy, they surrender quota to the energy retailer, accessing their quota account by (for instance) using their QuotaCard or direct debit. The retailer then surrenders carbon units when buying energy from the wholesaler. Finally, the primary energy provider surrenders units back to the Register (QuotaCo) when the company pumps, mines or imports fuel. This closes the loop.

Some purchasers will not have any carbon units to offer at point of sale – for example, foreign visitors, people who have forgotten their card[55] or who have used, or cashed-in, all their quota, and small firms and traders that do not bother to make regular purchases of units through their banks. All these must buy quota at the time of purchase, in order to surrender it, but they will pay a cost penalty for this: they have to buy them at the market's offer price and surrender them at the (lower) bid price; the difference between these two prices is the cost of non-participation.

Carbon units can be bought and sold on the secondary market. People who use less than their entitlement can earn a revenue from the sale of their surplus, and people who use more must buy the extra.

The government receives revenue from the tender, and trading revenues are earned by the market-makers who quote bid and offer prices. Purchases and sales of carbon units are made on-line through home computers, through automatic teller machines (ATMs), over the counter of banks and post offices and energy retailers, and by direct debit with energy suppliers.

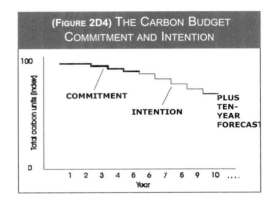

(FIGURE 2D4) THE CARBON BUDGET COMMITMENT AND INTENTION

THE CARBON BUDGET

The 20-year Carbon Budget (*Figure 2D4*), is defined over three periods. Period 1 is a 5-year binding Commitment, which cannot be revised; this is a requirement for an orderly market. Period 2, the 5-year Intention, is inflexible; the presumption is "no change", but it can be revised for stated reasons at an annual review. Period 3 is a 10-year Forecast, which is indicative only.

The Carbon Budget is at the heart of the scheme. First, it guarantees the targets for reduction in carbon emissions. Secondly, it provides a long-term quantity signal. Intentional reductions in carbon emissions take time; people will therefore need to take action now in the light of their knowledge of the quantity of carbon units that will be available in the future. There are automatic rewards (and penalties) in the form of lower (or

BEFORE THE WELLS RUN DRY

PART TWO: DO RENEWABLE ENERGY SOURCES HAVE THE POTENTIAL TO FILL THE GAP?

higher) prices in response to how well (or badly) the economy does in reducing carbon emissions.

The Carbon Budget should be set (it is suggested) by an independent body – like the UK's Monetary Policy Committee. This would relieve the government from having to defend the Budget itself, providing some protection from the political process, and it would allow government to concentrate on helping the economy to achieve the targets that the independent body had set.[56]

Reduction as a collective programme
Withdrawal from dependency on fossil fuels would be an extremely ambitious and difficult programme. It could be carried out only as a joint, cooperative task. It would have to be designed in such a way that it is in the individual's interests not only to reduce his or her own carbon-dependency but also to cooperate with others in encouraging, persuading and collaborating with them to reduce theirs. The claim, now being evaluated in detail, is that DTQs could provide the basis for this cooperation, or "collective purpose". That is to say:

1. It will be in individuals' interests to help others to reduce their carbon dependency
This works in three inter-related ways. First, the fixed quantity makes it obvious to everyone that high consumption by one person means that there is less for everyone else. Your carbon consumption becomes my business: people will want to try to influence each other's behaviour – for their mutual advantage.

Secondly, it is in everyone's interests that the price of carbon units should be low. A high price would increase the cost of industry's purchases of energy, raising prices across the economy as a whole. However, the price of units would be to some degree under the control of the people who used them, since the more they were able to reduce their demand for units, the lower their price. If the public is confident that – by reducing the demand for carbon units –

they can have an effect in keeping prices low, then there is an incentive to cooperate with each other to make it happen.

Thirdly, carbon units lend themselves to local collective initiatives; they can be pooled as a fund, providing the basis for coordinated local action.

2. DTQs provide the framework for establishing carbon reduction at the centre of public policy, aligning social values with individual responsibility.
The DTQ model places everyone in the same boat; households, industry and the government itself have to work together, facing the same Carbon Budget, trading on the same market for carbon units (and all loving to hate the Carbon Policy Committee which sets the budget to which they all have to adapt).

Everyone is given a literal stake, in the form of property rights, in the system. There will be a sense that one's own efforts at conservation will not be wasted by the energy profligacy of others, and that the system is founded on justice. In all these ways, the proposal connects with theoretical studies that have explored the evolution of systems of collective interaction, in which incentives and institutions are mutually reinforcing and self-policing.[57]

ADVANTAGES OF DTQS
1. **Effectiveness**
DTQs are effective. They integrate private preferences with public policy. They give the long-term signal that is indispensable for profound change. They build a framework in which the economy can take effective action.

2. **Equity**
Equity is necessary for political acceptability. DTQs give consumers themselves a central role in the reduction of fossil fuel dependency. There is no sense that there is some government body manipulating the prices and taxes; it is citizens' own scheme.

3. **Efficiency:**

If the claim that DTQs effectively stimulate collective motivation is true, then, at any given quantity of carbon emissions, the fuel price (that is, fuel + quota/tax/other) will be lower under a DTQ regime than under alternatives. This cost-efficiency has economic advantages for incomes and employment.

POTENTIAL OBJECTIONS TO DTQS

1. **Effectiveness**

Suppose that households and industry just gave up and made no effort to reduce their demand for fossil fuels: the prices of carbon units would rise rapidly; hardship stories and the political fall-out could be so awful that the government's nerve could crack and the scheme itself could be abandoned. And yet, all instruments would be vulnerable to a concerted failure of will. DTQs stand the best chance of placing the responsibility where it belongs: in the hearts of citizens.

DTQs would require set-up costs that need to be estimated – but most of the technology and infrastructure already exist and are in place; the principle is much simpler than the paper rationing systems that were used in wartime Europe, and feasibility studies are progressing.

2. **Equity**

No instrument can claim to be entirely equitable. For example, people who live in remote areas would (relative to city-dwellers) have the disadvantage of having further to travel to work, and people with low incomes would have the disadvantage of being less able to buy top-up carbon units on the market than those on high incomes. And yet, there are compensations: people in rural areas would be able to generate much of their electricity; conversely (in a scheme in which collective motivation had been highly developed) heavy users would have the disadvantage that their conspicuous consumption exposes them to public rebuke and ridicule. There may be equity anomalies in the scheme, but not insoluble ones.

3. **Efficiency**

If DTQs caused prices to be volatile, that would be inefficient,[58] but there is no reason why they should be more volatile under DTQs than with any other instrument. For instance, high fuel prices would reduce the demand for quota, tending to reduce its price, so that there is a stabilising effect.

DTQs are a practical instrument designed for reducing carbon emissions within a market economy, and/or for smoothing the transition from the fuel-rich market economy to its fuel-efficient successor. A reduction of fossil fuel consumption, both to forestall climate breakdown and to adjust quickly and fairly to the coming fuel famine, is now intensely urgent.[59] An instrument with DTQs' qualities of effectiveness, equity and efficiency is needed.

CONCLUSION

This paper set about finding solutions to the coming energy famine. It began with a review of the way land will be used as an energy resource in the future, and described the "solar string" technologies that will be available. It showed how energy services can be provided more efficiently with the help of technological advance and "whole systems thinking", but warned that, despite these technical solutions, changes in the political economy at the most fundamental level will be needed to cope with the reduced energy availability in the future. The central idea of the paper is "connections": energy connections in the local solar string energy system or minigrid; material connections between reductions in energy use, material demand and transport; and connections in terms of motivation as citizens are given a clear incentive to reduce their energy dependency and to share out access to energy justly and fairly. Oil and gas depletion was the dark beginning to this story, but it is only by acknowledging that starting-point that there is any possibility of responding to it with the radical decisiveness and clarity that will be needed.

BEFORE THE WELLS RUN DRY

PART TWO: DO RENEWABLE ENERGY SOURCES HAVE THE POTENTIAL TO FILL THE GAP?

NOTES AND REFERENCES

1. Jeremy Rifkin writes, "...highly concentrated nonrenewable energy has shaped today's economy. Solar energy, however, is not concentrated like nonrenewable energy and is therefore unsuited for a largely centralised industrial life-style" (1985), *Entropy*. London: Paladin. For a general introduction to renewable energy see Richard Douthwaite (1996), *Short Circuit: Strengthening Local Economies for Security in an Unstable World*. Dartington, Devon: Green Books.

2. Janet Ramage (1997), *Energy: A Guidebook*, Oxford University Press (second edition), p 274.

3. Christopher Flavin and Seth Dunn (1999), "Coming of Age – the Energy Revolution", *Renewable Energy World* (in http://www.jxj.com/magsandj/rew/1999_04/comingofage.html)

4. Lester Brown et al (2000), *Vital Signs 2000-2001*, London: Earthscan/Worldwatch Institute, pp 58-59. Roger Bentley (Department of Cybernetics, University of Reading) writes, "There is potential for another two- to four-fold cost reduction in the future, plus much larger cost falls in the event of a technological breakthrough". (Personal communication).

5. Producing ethanol from sugar cane in Brazil today is roughly eight times more land-intensive than using photovoltaics to produce an equivalent amount of electricity. Christopher Flavin and Nicholas Lenssen (1995), *Power Surge: A Guide to the Coming Energy Revolution*, London: Earthscan/The Worldwatch Institute, p 187.

6. The distinction between light from the sun (in photovoltaics) and heat from the sun (in solar thermal) is technically a bit spurious. Most solar cells make good use of infra-red energy, while solar thermal collectors use the light energy along with the infra-red. But the distinction is useful for the purposes of this discussion.

7. Ramage (1997), pp 269-273; Flavin and Lenssen (1995), pp 141-151.

8. Calculations based on Ramage's figures for the "leaky house" (25,000 kWh), for the "energy saving house" (12,500 kWh) and for the output of a 225 kW turbine, pp 139, 246. In practice, households would usually try to avoid using wind energy, which is relatively expensive, for home heating.

9. Ramage (1997), p 233.

10. Flavin and Lenssen (1995), p 179.

11. Ramage (1997), p 90. For the technology that extracts lignin from fibre fuels see www.iogen.ca; www.ott.doe.gov/bio-fuels/biofuels.html; and Peter Findlay (2001), "Farming Friendly Fuel", *The Sunday Times*, "Doors", 22 April, pp 16-17.

12. Ramage (1997), p 91.

13. For the literature on solar architecture see, for instance, http://vegastrailer.com/solarbooks/architecture.html Also Ernst von Weizsäcker; Amory B. Lovins and L. Hunter Lovins (1997), *Factor Four: Doubling Wealth – Halving Resource Use*, London: Earthscan, chapter 1.

14. Marine currents: Fred Pearce (1998), "Catching the Tide", *New Scientist*, 20 June, pp 38-41. Tides at different parts of the coastline have the advantage that they are not synchronous either with each other or with the wind.

15. See: Intermediate Technology Development Group's website at www.itdg.org/html/energy/expertise2.htm; Jeremy Thake (2000), *The Micro-Hydro Pelton Turbine Manual*, London: ITDG.

16. Marshall Savage (1994), *The Millennial Project: Colonizing the Galaxy in Eight Easy Steps*. Boston: Little, Brown and Company.

17. See www.jet.uk and www.jet.efda.org; also "hot fusion" on Google.

18. Harold Aspden discusses Nick Hawkins's work with Abrikosov vortices in (1998), "Fusion by Thunder?", Energy Science Essay No. 14, at www.energyscience.co.uk/essays/ese14.htm

19. Ramage (1997), p 297.

20. Association of Coal Mine Methane Operators, www.alkane.co.uk

21. Reinhart von Zschock (1997), "Ceramic Stoves", *Permaculture Magazine*, vol 13, pp 32-34; vol 14, pp 27-29.

22. Information on supercapacitors is being continuously updated and is available on the net. Recommended searches are via Google and Xrefer.

23. Philip Ball (2001), "Water Power: A new Material Helps to Make Clean Fuel from Water", Nature, 6 December. See also references on the technology of water-splitting in endnote 27 of Christopher Flavin and Seth Dunn (1999), "Reinventing the Energy System", p 196, in *State of the World 1999*.

24. Flavin and Lenssen (1995), pp 101-102. See also Seth Dunn (2000), "Micropower: The Next Electrical Era", *Worldwatch Paper 151*, Washington: Worldwatch Institute, pp 24-25.

25. See www.mathtools.net/Applications/Automotive/ Alternative_Fuel_Vehicles/ - 41k - 14 Jan 2003. Also Google search "fuel cell liquid nitrogen".

26. See LTI-Research Group, Ed, (1998), *Long-Term Integration of Renewable Energy Sources into the European Energy System*, Heidelberg, Physica-Verlag. ISBN 3-7908-1104-, pp 54-55. See also the Carnoules Declaration at http://www.fac-torten.co.uk/carnoules_extract.htm

27. LTI (1998), p 66. Also Hill, O'Keefe and Snipe (1995), *The Future of Energy Use*, london: Earthscan, p 79, and Hawken, Lovins and Lovins (1999), *Natural Capitalism*, London, Earthscan. See also a Google search for "solar cookers".

28. Hawken et al (1999), esp chapter 5; Weizsacker *et al* (1997), pp 19-23.

29. Vaclav Smil (2000) "Rocky Mountain Visions : A Review Essay", *Population and Development Review* Vol. 26, No. 1, pp 163-176 (p 171).

30. See James Womack and Daniel Jones (1996), *Lean Thinking*, New York: Simon & Schuster, discussed in The Lean

Economy, chapter 10.

31. Smil (2000), p 168.

32. LTI (1998), p 63.

33. David Fleming (forthcoming) *The Lean Economy*, chapter 14.

34. Walt Whitman, *Song of Myself*, canto xxxv.

35. See, for instance, "Final Report for DEFRA project OF0182", Department of the Environment, Food and Rural Affairs, UK Government.

36. Charlie Pinney (2002), "Bringing Back the Horse", in "Ireland's Transition to Renewable Energy" conference, Thurles, October - 2 November.

37. *The Lean Economy*, chapter 12.

38. Superwindows for greenhouses grain driers: Hawken et al (1999), pp 200, 199. Agricultural equipment, LTI (1998), p 71.

39. See Hawken et al (1999), chapter 2; Weizsäcker et al (1997), .pp 4-9. Also www.hypercarcenter.org

40. Hawken et al (1999), pp 36, 37.

41. For a discussion of the pros and cons of the Hypercar see, for instance, David Barry (2001), "Lovin' Hydrogen", *Discover*, vol 22, 11, at www.discover.com/nov_o1/featlovin.html.

42. LTI (1997) suggest a 50 percent reduction in land-based passenger transport by 2050 that, after taking improvements in the efficiency of vehicles into account, becomes a 90 percent reduction in demand for fuel. LTI (1998), pp 72-73.

43. Whole systems thinking is singled out for criticism by some reviewers, notably Bruin Christensen (2001), "What the Pelican Tells us: Natural Capitalism and Sustainability", http://www.changedesign.org/thinking/.

44. *The Lean Economy*, chapter 7.

45. This is the central question discussed in *The Lean Economy*.

46. Amory Lovins (1977), *Soft Energy Paths*, London: Penguin.

47. Ramage (1997), p 370-371. (Abridged).

48. Seth Dunn and Christopher Flavin (2000), "Sizing Up Micropower", in Worldwatch *State of the World* (2000), p 152.

49. Amory Lovins and André Lehmann, *Small is Profitable: The Hidden Economic Benefits of Making Electrical Resources the Right Size*, Boulder: Rocky Mountain Institute, cited in Seth Dunn and Christopher Flavin (2000), "Sizing Up Micropower", in Worldwatch, *State of the World* (2000), p 152.

50. Dunn and Flavin (2000).

51. The literature on domestic trading in carbon emissions rights at the level of the individual or household does not include a description of the model of domestic tradable quotas set out here; it is sparse, and it discusses – in outline form only – a variety of instruments that have little in common with each other. It includes: Simon Fairlie (1991), "Quotas Against the Great Car Economy", *The Ecologist*, Nov/Dec, pp 234-235; Mayer Hillman (1991), "Towards the Next Environment White Paper", *Policy Studies*, vol 12, 1, pp 36-51; Douthwaite (1992), *The Growth Illusion*, Hartland: Green Books, pp 211-212; Robert U. Ayres (1997) "Environmental Market Failures": *Mitigation and Adaptation Strategies for Global Change*, I, pp 289-309; Paul Koutstaal (1997), Economic Policy and Climate Change: Tradable Permits for Reducing Carbon Emissions, Cheltenham, UK: Edward Elgar; H.R.J. Vollebergh, J.L. de Fries and P.R. Koutstaal (1997), "Hybrid Carbon Incentive Mechanisms and Political Acceptability", *Environmental and Resource Economics*, 9, 43-46; Mark Whitby (1997), "Edge Debate on Transport Hears Call for Major Changes", *Architects' Journal*, 29 May, p 16; and Robert U. Ayres, (1998), *Turning Point*, London: Earthscan.

52. The model of Domestic Tradable Quotas was described in David Fleming (1996), "Stopping the Traffic", *Country Life*, vol 140, 19, 9 May, pp 62-65; David Fleming (1996 and 1997), Tradable Quotas: Setting Limits to Carbon Emissions, discussion papers, London: The Lean Economy Initiative; David Fleming (1997), "Tradable Quotas: Using Information Technology to Cap National Carbon Emissions, *European Environment*, 7, 5, Sept-Oct, pp 139-148; David Fleming (1998), "Your Climate Needs You", *Town & Country Planning*, 67, 9, October, pp 302-304); David Fleming, ed (1998), "Domestic Tradable Quotas as an Instrument to Reduce Carbon Dioxide Emissions", European Commission, *Proceedings*, Workshop 1-2 July, EUR 18451. See also www.dtqs.org.

53. The Royal Commission on Environmental Pollution acknowledges the central role of the concept of Contraction and Convergence. (2000), Energy: The Changing Climate, London: HMSO, Cmnd 4749, p 57-58. See also Aubrey Meyer (2000), *Contraction and Convergence: A Global Solution to Climate Change*, Schumacher Briefing No. 5, Dartington: Green Books, Tom Spencer (1998), "Contraction and Convergence", *Town and Country Planning*. Vol 45, 4.

54. Sources: Petrol and diesel: derived from ETSU (1996), *Alternative Road Transport Fuels - A Preliminary Life-Cycle Study for the UK*, London: HMSO; Table 3.10; and Commission of the European Community (1993), Corinair Working Group on Emission Factors for Calculating 1990 Emissions from Road Traffic. Gas: derived from ETSU (1995), Full Fuel Cycle Atmospheric Emissions and Global Warming Impacts from *UK Electricity Generation*, London: HMSO; Table B2. Coal: derived from ETSU (1995); Table B1. Electricity: ETSU (1995); Table 5.3. Carbon-equivalent indices, on a time-horizon of 100 years, for methane and N2O are, respectively, 21 and 310 times the GWP of CO_2. (IPCC, 1996, Climate Change 1995; Table 4). The assistance of Simon Collings, John Lanchbery and Peter Taylor with this table is acknowledged with thanks.

55. But forgetting a credit card will probably be no barrier to electronic transactions in the future. As other forms of electronic recognition develop, plastic cards are beginning to become obsolete.

56. "Concentration" is one of the key themes of the instrument: it focuses totally on the problem of fuel; other sources of carbon dioxide, such as waste tips and agriculture would come within the remit of different programmes and instruments.

57. Alan Carling (1991) *Social Division* (London: Verso). Alan Carling (1997) 'Rational Vervet: Social Evolution and the Origins of Human Norms and Institutions', Imprints, 2:2, 157-73. Alan Carling (1998) 'Social Selection and Design' Proceedings of the Warwick/LSE Complexity Conference, 112-23. Brian Skyrms (1996) *Evolution of the Social Contract* (Cambridge: CUP).

58. The adverse consequences of price instability are discussed in Martin Weitzman (1974), "Prices vs. Quantities", *Review of Economic Studies*, 41, 4, pp 477-7491; and in William A. Pizer (1998), "Prices vs. Quantities Revisited: The Case of Climate Change", Washington: Resources for the Future, *Discussion Paper* 98-02.

59. Again, the possibility of sequestration calls for some qualification to the case for reducing fossil fuel consumption. If the promise of sequestration comes to pass, then, in the case of coal, reduction in carbon emissions becomes an objective to be distinguished form reduction in demand for the fuel itself.

The support of Elm Farm Research Centre for the preparation of this paper is acknowledged with thanks.

The prospects for a hydrogen economy based on renewable energy

by Werner Zittel

Hydrogen produced from biomass or wind-generated electricity promises to take over the role currently played by oil products in powering the world's transport fleets. Most motor manufacturers are testing hydrogen-powered vehicles and have plans to put them on sale.

A sustainable energy system can only be based on renewable energy. There is no choice in the matter. It is not a question whether we like it or not or whether we feel that our energy needs can be adequately met by renewables. To be sustainable, we have no option but to develop systems that enable us to keep our energy needs low enough so that they can be met by renewable supplies.

This is the context within which this paper discusses building a hydrogen economy. Hydrogen produced from finite energy resources would not solve anything satisfactorily. It has to be part of an integrated sustainable energy strategy.

1. WHY HYDROGEN?

Here are some of the reasons for using hydrogen as part of an integrated energy strategy:
- We will need a carbon-free fuel for mobile applications in the mid-term future. It should have started becoming available before 2010.
- The European automotive industry has committed itself to reducing the average CO_2 emission of the entire European car range on sale in 2008 to 140 g/ km and to 120 g/km in 2012. If this target is not met, the European Commission will enforce it legally. At present, car manufacturers do not know how they can achieve this goal using existing propulsion technologies and conventional fuels while maintaining the present mix of vehicle classes.
- Hydrogen offers the most promising perspective as a fuel for mobile applications, since it can be produced from various sources such as conventional electricity, renewable electricity, conventional steam reforming and the regenerative steam reforming of the products of a biomass gasification process. Hydrogen has the highest energy source flexibility of any alternative fuel and therefore offers the most robust strategy for supplying a clean transportation fuel
- Hydrogen can be used for many purposes ranging from burning for heat as gas, through chemical processes to its conversion to electricity in fuel cells
- Hydrogen, via electrolysis and fuel cells, provides a way of storing large quantities of electricity without running into the raw materials limitations that batteries would present. It can therefore be used as buffer storage to meet peak power demand. Within the next five years it is likely to be used for storing off-shore wind energy and in smaller, stand-alone power systems based on renewable energies. In the longer term - after 2020 - I expect it to be used for large scale applications.

Hydrogen cannot solve the energy problem, but it can help to switch the transport sector smoothly from fossil fuels to renewable ones. In addition, hydrogen can create links between different energy carriers, e.g. between electricity, transport fuel and gas, thus linking heat energy supply with fuel supply and with electricity production.

BEFORE THE WELLS RUN DRY

PART TWO: DO RENEWABLE ENERGY SOURCES HAVE THE POTENTIAL TO FILL THE GAP?

2 COMPONENTS OF A HYDROGEN ECONOMY

2.1 METHODS OF PRODUCTION

Hydrogen emits almost no pollution when it burns so its environmental benefits are determined by the way it is produced. World production is already equivalent to 20-25% of annual natural gas production The following methods are generally used:

1. *As a chemical by product* - Hydrogen is an unavoidable by-product during the production of chlorine, acetylene, styrene or cyanide. It is also produced in petrochemical cracking processes such as the catalytic reforming and cracking of crude oil during upgrading or ethylene production. However, the purity of the hydrogen produced in these ways varies from more than 99.5 percent (chlorine synthesis) to below 60 percent (ethylene production). Even the city gas produced in the last century from coal contained about 50 percent hydrogen.

Most of this hydrogen is mixed with natural gas and burned close to where it was made to produce process heat. However, during the introduction of hydrogen-fuelled transport, it could become available at reasonable cost to supply the first fuelling stations.

2. *From fossil fuels* - Almost half of today's hydrogen demand is supplied by steam reforming natural gas or, in minor quantities, by the partial oxidation of oil products. Most of this production takes place close to the site on which the gas will be used in order to avoid having to transport it. Steam reforming is usually the cheapest way to produce hydrogen and nearly all the gas used for desulphurisation at refineries, for ammonia production for fertilisers, or for methanol synthesis is produced this way. About 30 percent of the energy content of the natural gas input is lost in the conversion.

3. *With electricity* - Another well-established method of hydrogen production is electrolysis - splitting water into oxygen and hydrogen gas. This is the method of choice where cheap electricity is available. Norway has used this method in its fertiliser plants for almost 80 years. Electrolysers are highly modular and can range from very small units producing a few cubic metres of hydrogen per hour - or several kW electric power demand - up to the multi megawatt level. Today's modern electrolysers are optimised to produce hydrogen at a pressure of 30 bar and are designed to cope with a fluctuating electrical power input.

The attraction of electrolytic hydrogen is that its production can be on a small scale, is simple technically, quiet and pollution-free, and gives wide freedom of choice for the primary energy input. It enables hydrogen to be produced close to or apart from the site of the electricity production, from fossil fuels as well as from renewable sources. This feature is ideal for a smooth and steady transition from fossil- to renewables-generated hydrogen.

The various methods of producing hydrogen have very different economic and ecological characteristics. For example, electrolytically-produced hydrogen from coal-fired power plants would result in CO_2 emissions of about 2 kg/kWh or 6 kg/m3. For comparison, gasoline emits about 0.27 kg/kWh during combustion. On the other hand, hydrogen from wind or solar electricity would be almost free of polluting emissions.

Although electrolysis using electricity from intermittent renewable sources involves higher amortisation costs because the plant involved is not able to produce constantly throughout the year, it can still provide cheap hydrogen. For instance hydrogen from large scale hydropower can cost between 2.5 - 5 cents/kWh or 7.5-15 cents/cubic metre. For comparison, consumers in Europe pay about 10 cents per kWh of gasoline, or 1 Euro per litre, including tax. Production using power from large offshore wind farms would cost about 10-15 cents/kWh or 30 - 45 cts/m3. This is roughly in the same range as hydrogen produced from geothermal electricity, assuming that modern low temperature geothermal power generation (hot dry rock, organic rankine cycle) results in electricity cost of below 10 cents/kWhel. The higher electricity production costs are outweighed by the advantage of 8,000 operating hours per year for the electrolyser, instead of about 2,000-3,000 hours per year for wind energy converters.

It takes, on average, about 4 kWh of electricity to produce 1 cublic metre or 3 kWh hydrogen as 20 -25 percent of the energy is lost in the conversion process. Accordingly, the first use of renewable electricity should not be for electrolysis but to replace fossil fuels (predominantly coal) in stationary applications. The electrolytic production of hydrogen could, however, be considered in circumstances like these:

• If electricity is best produced without reference to immediate consumer demand. The surplus electricity can easily be used for hydrogen production.
• If offshore wind energy parks are far from land. Connecting their fluctuating electricity production to the grid directly might be more costly than producing hydrogen at the wind park and piping it to the final destination to satisfy electrical and transport fuel demand.
• If an island is not coupled to the national grid and needs an electricity storage system to become completely independent of outside energy sources. Above a certain size, hydrogen storage is more economic and more ecological than using batteries. Of course, fossil fuel storage would be the cheapest option if one ignored possible supply restrictions CO_2 emissions and external costs.

Logically it might be best use renewable electricity first to replace fossil electricity completely and only when this is done and huge storage problems arise, to convert the surplus into hydrogen. But realistically there are different players with different interests within different demand sectors and the transport sector urgently needs to escape from its oil dependence and the environmental damage that that does. In the early phases of building a hydrogen economy there will therefore inevitably be some straying from the optimum pathway. However, as long as each individual step fits into the overall scheme, it is worth taking it even under sub-optimal conditions.

4. *From biomass* - Using hydrogen from biomass gasification in a fuel cell is a more efficient way of producing electricity than burning the biomass in a thermal generator, even on a small scale. Several options are open. If ten percent of the land in a district is converted to fuel production, biomass harvesting within a radius of 25 km would feed a 5 MW gasification plant. The crude biogas (CO, H2) could then be fed into a high temperature molten carbonate fuel cell which produces both electricity and heat at about 450^0C in sufficient quantities to supply about 3000 houses with heat and electricity. There would also be enough hydrogen to fuel 17 buses with a daily range of about 300 km.

This system has yet to prove itself in practice but all its components are known and technically feasible, though not yet optimised for this use. A prototype would cost close to €10 million to build and then €2 million per year to run. This would cover everything from planting the biomass, the gasification and purification plant, the fuel cell, hydrogen compression and building a transport fuelling station. After a few years' experience, it ought to be possible to reduce the construction and operating costs by about 30 percent. The plant would deliver about 4 million kWh of electricity per year and 16

BEFORE THE WELLS RUN DRY

PART TWO: DO RENEWABLE ENERGY SOURCES HAVE THE POTENTIAL TO FILL THE GAP?

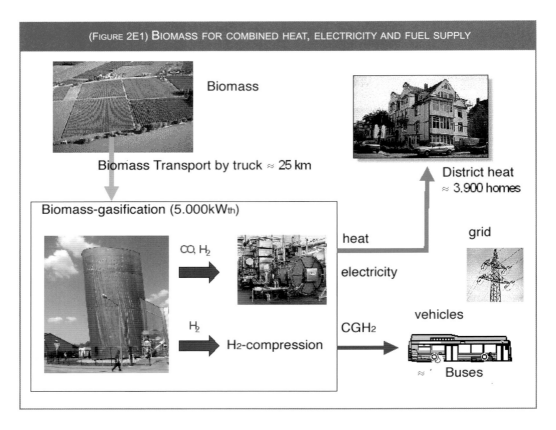

Figure 2E1: Sketch of a biomass gasification plant supplying heat, electricity and transport fuel from agricultural sources such as wood or dedicated crops.

million cubic metres of hydrogen plus 4 million kWh of heat. If the electricity was sold at 10 cts/kWhel and the hydrogen fuel at €1 per litre gasoline equivalent, the annual return would total about €5 million. Biomass gasification offers hydrogen conversion efficiencies somewhat lower than from natural gas reforming, of the order of 60 - 65 percent.

5. *By other methods* - Other production methods like the direct generation of hydrogen by algae or bacteria are already carried out on laboratory scale. We can therefore move towards a hydrogen economy immediately, confident that the future will offer a broader range of hydrogen sources than we know at present.

2.2 STORAGE AND TRANSPORTATION

In principle, hydrogen could be used in mobile applications today but storage improvements are desirable to increase its acceptability for powering vehicles. Two storage methods, liquefaction and compression, have been used in industry for many years. Both have advantages and drawbacks. Liquid hydrogen offers higher energy densities - 2.36 kWh per litre - for long distance transport and for on board storage in automobiles. This is approximately one quarter of the energy density of gasoline fuel. One litre of hydrogen weighs about 70g whereas its energy equivalent, a quarter litre of gasoline, weighs about 200g. However, in order to liquefy hydrogen, the gas must be cooled to - 250 ^{0}C. This process consumes about 14 kWh primary energy per kg of hydrogen in today's liquefaction plants with throughput of 4.4 tons per day. This is about 40 percent of the hydrogen's energy content. Theoretically this figure could be improved by a factor of three in energetically optimised liquefaction plants.

Another serious drawback is that liquid hydrogen boils off when the vehicle is parked. Modern insulation materials limit boil-off losses to approximately 1 percent per parking day. Properly designed tanks are filled with liquid hydrogen leaving a gas cap where the boiled-off hydrogen can accumulate. The hydrogen demand during driving is first met from this cap. During parking, the boil-off is vented to the atmosphere only when a certain pressure in the gas cap is reached (usually above 5-6 bar). In a state-of-the-art design this would happen only when the vehicle had not been used for 4-5 days.

Compressing hydrogen

To avoid the boil-off problem, hydrogen can also be stored at normal temperatures in cylindrical fibre or metal tanks under high pressure. Such tanks are still in the process of optimisation with respect to pressure resistance, durability, conformity and weight. Typical storage pressures are in the 200 - 350 bar range but recently storage systems up to 700 bar have become available. Since the energy consumed by compression scales logarithmically, less is used the higher the input pressure becomes. So compression from 5 bar to 350 bar consumes about 9 percent of the energy in the hydrogen while compression to 700 bar consumes only slightly more (~10 percent). If the initial pressure is 30 bar instead of 5 bar, the energy consumption will almost halve. High pressure hydrogen production technology therefore offers advantages which might outweigh its greater cost.

Other methods

Metal hydrides are another established storage method. Certain metal alloys absorb large amounts of hydrogen when exposed to the gas at certain pressures and low temperatures. Since this process is exothermic, heat is released during absorption. The hydrogen is released from the hydride by heating it. Though metal hydrides can store almost as much hydrogen as the equivalent volume of liquid hydrogen, they are so heavy that the weight of the gas is only 1 - 1.5 percent of the weight of the storage device in working systems.

Recently there has been a lot of research into new storage materials with superior qualities. For instance, highly porous activated carbon can adsorb hydrogen at cryogenic temperatures in quantities far above metal hydrides. In the best cases, it comes close to the densities of compressed hydrogen storage. Although none of the novel materials can yet replace the conventional technologies it is very likely that in the mid-term future some will achieve comparable qualities to today's methods. However, for first (and presumably even second) generation vehicles, either compressed or liquid hydrogen storage will have to be used.

Safety aspects

Special safety precautions must be taken with hydrogen. It mixes three times faster with air than natural gas and can be ignited when the air contains more than 4-5 percent of it. Moreover, ten times less energy is needed to ignite hydrogen than natural gas. However, it is more likely than natural gas to burn rather than explode as its detonation limit - the air-gas mixture which tends to explode rather than to burn - is at about 11 - 18 percent, whereas for natural gas - air mixtures it is 5 - 6 percent, only slightly above the natural gas ignition limit. This means that any ignitable agglomeration of hydrogen is likely to burn whereas natural gas is more likely to explode.

BEFORE THE WELLS RUN DRY

PART TWO: DO RENEWABLE ENERGY SOURCES HAVE THE POTENTIAL TO FILL THE GAP?

The famous accident to the "Hindenburg" zeppelin in 1935 at Lakehurst, New Jersey, was caused by the spark ignition of the aluminium paint covering the outer fabric of the zeppelin's hull - a danger known to the experts at that time. Once ignited, the hydrogen burned but did not explode. Moreover, due to three further characteristics of hydrogen, two thirds of the passengers on board survived that catastrophe. Hydrogen is very light. This caused it to rise rather than spread out and fill the passenger cabin below the hull. Secondly, because hydrogen is the simplest molecule that exists, composed of two identical atoms, it cannot radiate heat. For physical reasons, this is only possible for more complex molecules. Thirdly, hydrogen combustion does not produce smoke in the way that burning oil does. Consequently, although the fire was not far above the heads of the zeppelin's passengers, they were not hurt by the heat or smoke. All the passengers who ran away in the short time between the zeppelin touching the ground and the break-up of the burning hull above the passenger cabin survived.

If cars or aircraft were fuelled with hydrogen today rather than gasoline or kerosene, accidents involving burning fuel would cause fewer severe injuries. Overall, experts agree that hydrogen poses no more risks than natural gas and that it might be safer than liquid fuels. Even so, safety measures including sensors and ceiling ventilation are needed to avoid an ignitable hydrogen-air mixture developing in closed rooms.

2.3 MOBILE APPLICATIONS

Because of its low weight, hydrogen was used for rockets from the beginning of space research. It even has some advantages for fuelling ordinary aircraft, permitting them to carry about 20 - 25 percent more payload. This could - at least partly - outweigh its higher cost. It also is, as we have noted, safer than kerosene,

and, if produced from renewables, would cut the aircraft's carbon dioxide emissions. However, it has to be stressed that its use would increase water vapour emissions which are mainly responsible for contrail formation and infrared reflection. The height of flights is crucial to this phenomenon. As long as an aircraft flies in the troposphere and avoids the tropopause some 8 - 12 km up depending on geographic and climatic conditions, its environmental impact would be much less harmful than with today's kerosene-fuelled aircraft.

Another broad application, if not hydrogen's most important one, will be as fuel for cars and trucks. Although their emissions will be pure water vapour, they will raise local humidity only by several parts per thousand above the normal level. But, provided the hydrogen is produced from renewable energy, no carbon dioxide, hydrocarbon and particulate emissions will be produced. Even nitrogen oxide emissions can be reduced to close to zero if better internal combustion engines are developed while electric drive systems powered by fuel cells will completely cut out all harmful emissions.

For railways, the extra space required for hydrogen fuel is not a critical parameter and electric drive systems based on fuel cells would remove the need for an overhead power supply. Even ships can be fuelled with hydrogen and some small ones have already been converted in ecologically sensitive areas. The space taken for fuel storage is not a problem here either. In short, any oil-fuelled vehicle can be converted to use hydrogen.

Although in principle hydrogen can satisfactorily replace fossil fuels in almost every stationary application, very often other non-fossil alternatives are superior. For instance, heat is better generated from solar energy or biomass burning rather than hydrogen combustion. And

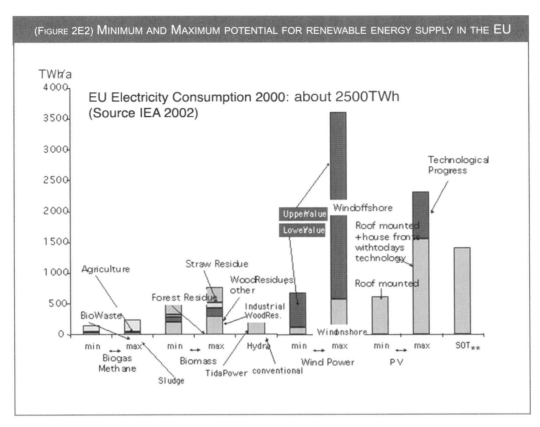

(FIGURE 2E2) MINIMUM AND MAXIMUM POTENTIAL FOR RENEWABLE ENERGY SUPPLY IN THE EU

This chart summarises the broad range of published and estimated possible installations of renewable energy technologies in Europe. The biomass potential is restricted to agricultural, forestry and municipal waste (sludge, wood etc.). The hydropower potential includes tidal power. By far the broadest range of estimates exists for wind energy. The lower figure is based on an estimate by Michael Grubb of the Royal Institute of International Affairs and includes offshore wind produced at sites within 10 km off the coastline and not deeper than 10 m. The upper potential extends these ranges to 30 km distance off the coastline and 30 m water depth. Here it should be noted that already at least one 1GW wind park is being planned at a distance of about 60 km from the German coastline.

The assessment of the photovoltaic (PV) potential varies widely depending on differing assumptions. The lower figure is derived assuming only roof mounted PV installations. The upper figure also includes PV installations on the facade of buildings. This estimate is based on an in-depth analysis for eight cities in the UK and an extrapolation to the whole EU by taking into account different solar irradiation as well as different building characteristics in the other regions. Two estimates are based on these figures. The first assumes that today's conversion efficiencies of about 10 per cent continue, the second that efficiency can be raised to about 13 per cent.

The bar marked SOT represents the potential for building solar-thermal electric power plants in southern Europe. The chart ignores the potential for geothermal electricity production entirely.

BEFORE THE WELLS RUN DRY

PART TWO: DO RENEWABLE ENERGY SOURCES HAVE THE POTENTIAL TO FILL THE GAP?

electricity generation by wind or photovoltaics is much more efficient than producing hydrogen, perhaps by electrolysis, and then burning it in an internal combustion engine with an attached generator, or in a fuel cell, to produce electricity again.

For a long time many people thought that the practical use of hydrogen would only become important when a huge storage system for electricity was needed, perhaps around the year 2050. Apart from this, only niche applications for hydrogen were seen, mainly in stand-alone power systems. For instance, a house or a small village without a grid connection might need to store solar energy from periods with high solar irradiation for use at other times. Storing the power as electricity would need enormous amounts of costly and resource-intensive batteries. In this case, however, the conversion of electricity to hydrogen and its conversion back to electricity during peak power demand has some rationale but a stronger justification comes from the versatility it introduces as the stored hydrogen can not only be used for re-electrification, but also as fuel for cars or for producing heat. It is this link between various uses that, in a fully integrated systems view, makes the hydrogen route superior to alternatives, particularly now that the fuel cell is coming into use.

2.4 THE FUEL CELL - A KEY PART OF THE HYDROGEN ECONOMY

A fuel cell consists of two electrodes (highly porous carbon or another electrically conductive porous material) separated by an electrolyte. Hydrogen gas is fed to one electrode. The hydrogen molecule is decomposed into its constituents on the surface of this electrode, the electrons are stripped off and the two nuclei are separated. The electrolyte is permeable for protons (which are the positive nuclei of hydrogen atoms), but not for electrons. The protons pene

trate through the electrolyte to the other electrode. There they can combine with the electrons and air (or pure oxygen) to form water vapour. Since water vapour has much less energy content than separated hydrogen and oxygen molecules, this process runs by itself. The electrons cannot penetrate through the electrolyte so they have to pass through an electric wire which is connected to the application. The flow of electrons creates the electrical current used by the consumer.

Various electrolytes have been used, some of which allow not only protons but also more complex molecules to penetrate the membrane. The electrolyte determines the specific name of a fuel cell, but the principle always is similar. This main types are the alkaline fuel cell (AFC), the proton exchange membrane fuel cell (PEM), the phosphoric acid fuel cell (PAFC), the molten carbonate fuel cell (MCFC) and the solid oxide fuel cell (SOFC).

Each of these fuel cell types has a different operating regime and application ranges. For instance, SOFC have the highest operating temperatures of about 1000°C. MCFC have an operating temperature of about 600°C. and can consume carbon-rich gases like biogas directly without complicated gas purification processes being carried out first. PEM fuel cells operate at the lowest temperatures but require gas purification first. Moreover, at these low temperatures, the mobility of ions and the pace of the chemical reaction are very slow. The stripping of the electrons at the inner electrode surface needs to be initiated by expensive catalytic materials, predominantly platinum-based metals.

A single fuel cell is composed of the two electrodes at each side of the electrolyte. Many individual cells can be stacked beside each other to form a fuel cell stack. The number of cells within a stack determines the power output.

Once the optimal configuration of a single cell is found, it is very simple to make many more. Fuel cell production is therefore ideally suited to mass production. This should reduce costs greatly. The first fuel cells used large amounts of platinum, making the price too high for commercial use, but successive improvements have helped to reduce the material requirements so much that it seems likely that mass produced optimised fuel cells could become relatively cheap and simple to produce.

Greater Efficiency

Fuel cell drive systems for vehicles should be much more efficient than internal combustion engines. An internal combustion engine is restricted by the laws of thermodynamics to a conversion efficiency determined by the temperatures involved in the combustion process. Consequently, on average, electricity production from heat power stations has only about 33 percent efficiency. Moreover, for cars, the efficiency is also determined by the driving situation, and this is governed by the velocity. At very low speeds - technically speaking, at partial load and low angular momentum - much energy is needed for acceleration. Since during typical driving many stops and acceleration processes are involved, the average efficiency of today's cars is very low, somewhere close to 20 percent.

Fuel cells work completely differently as sketched in *Figure 2E4*. Firstly, they use an electrochemical process, which obeys different thermodynamical limitations so that, theoretically, a conversion efficiency above 90 percent can be reached. Secondly, although their efficiency depends on the load, it is higher rather than lower the less power is required with respect to the maximum available power. In other words, fuel cells are better than the internal combustion engine for accelerating from low speeds. Moreover, the electric drive system has highest efficiencies at low velocities. This

helps to double the overall efficiency of a typical driving cycle. Cycle efficiencies close to 40 percent are already being measured in today's hydrogen cars. With technological progress, fuel cell drive systems ought to become smaller and cheaper. This would allow them to be oversized which, in turn, would increase their energetic efficiency even further.

There is therefore considerable hope that fuel cells will completely replace today's combustion engines in almost all applications in the not too distant future. Bearing in mind the technological revolutions in other fields - such as those from transistors to microelectronics and from mainframes to small personal computers and from wired telephones to wireless small cellular phones - it can be anticipated that a fuel cell revolution could oust the old technology in one or two decades once commercialisation takes off although we are in the very early days at present.

While the fuel cell is the key technological component for using hydrogen in the transport sector and perhaps for some stationary applications as well, there are other conversion technologies which fit well into hydrogen-use strategies such as gas turbines either for fast-response electricity generation and, maybe much more importantly, for powering aircraft.

3. HYDROGEN AND THE TRANSPORT SECTOR

General

To introduce renewable energy into the transport sector various alternatives are possible. These are

- direct use of electricity in electric vehicles,
- direct use of biogas (methane),
- direct use of biofuels (plant oil),
- use of ethanol from lignocellulose,
- conversion of biomass into synthetic fuels (e.g. via the Fischer-Tropsch process),

BEFORE THE WELLS RUN DRY

PART TWO: DO RENEWABLE ENERGY SOURCES HAVE THE POTENTIAL TO FILL THE GAP?

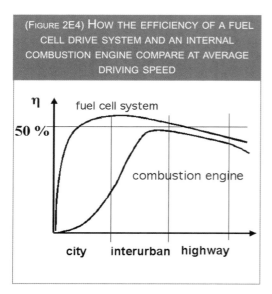

(FIGURE 2E4) HOW THE EFFICIENCY OF A FUEL CELL DRIVE SYSTEM AND AN INTERNAL COMBUSTION ENGINE COMPARE AT AVERAGE DRIVING SPEED

• gasification of biomass and conversion to hydrogen.

Figure 2E5 shows the potential for fuel production from biomass sources in the EU. The total EU transport fuel consumption is about 3,500 TWh of which about 80 percent is for road transport. By far the smallest potential exists for biogas production or for plant oil since only special plants or certain parts of the plants can be used for these fuels. Synfuel, methanol or hydrogen production would make much larger amounts available since nearly all kinds of biomass can be converted to fuels in these processes. But even these quantities would be far from sufficient to fuel the whole transport sector if it is to continue at anything like its present size. As a result, the use of hydrogen from renewable sources is likely to be very important.

As the potential for renewable electricity production is higher than the total EU electricity consumption today, it might be anticipated that a certain share can be used for hydrogen production. *Figure 2E6* shows the hydrogen production potential from renewable electricity generation based on the data in *Figure 2E2*. Obviously, not all this electricity would be used

for hydrogen production but together with the hydrogen which can be produced from biomass and in the long term from other sources, and allowing for the improved energy efficiency of future fuel cell cars, hydrogen is the only renewable energy option which offers the possibility of supplying the whole transport sector. It could be supplemented by the direct use of electricity in vehicles but this option is only a hope at present since all technological developments so far do not indicate that battery technology will become feasible for ordinary cars.

Comparing the most promising fuel paths from well to wheel it becomes obvious that no renewable fuel will be cost competitive with today's diesel or gasoline when compared at a pure cost basis neglecting taxes. Hydrogen will be 4 - 5 times more expensive. On the other hand fuel cell vehicles will be about twice as efficient as today's vehicles thus reducing the fuel consumption by a factor of two. Renewable fuel pathways will also be much less carbon intensive than diesel and gasoline and would reduce the overall carbon emissions considerably.

Environmental aspects

As already pointed out, the environmental and economic aspects of hydrogen strongly depend on the whole fuel chain. *Figure 2E7* and *Figure 2E8* summarise the carbon dioxide emissions and cost per kWh of hydrogen produced from various sources and compare them with today's gasoline and diesel supply. These calculations include all economic costs, but exclude external (ie environmental) costs not included in standard economic calculations.

A road map to hydrogen infrastructure

Car makers are putting a lot of effort into planning the introduction of hydrogen as a fuel for ground transport. Fuelling stations will look very similar to those today and supply either liquid or compressed hydrogen. The hydrogen could be produced centrally, liquefied and delivered to fuelling stations by truck, just like gasoline. Or gaseous hydrogen could be delivered via pipeline just as natural gas is distributed. However, as hydrogen production technologies are highly modular from small to large scale, it would be possible to produce the hydrogen by electrolysis on site using grid electricity or perhaps green electricity from wind power stations or other sources. In the country, hydrogen from biomass might be the technology of choice. This variety of options allows different players to operate fuelling stations. The large industrial integrated company could operate in the way it does today but there should also be scope for small independent fuel producers with limited capital.

Research into hydrogen powered cars started in the late 1970s. BMW started then and now has cars with internal combustion engines and liquid hydrogen storage awaiting commercialisation. Ford is also putting its hopes on internal combustion engines fuelled with hydrogen. By

contrast, Honda, Toyota, General Motors and maybe DaimlerChrysler are putting their money into fuel cell driven hydrogen cars.

In 1996 the world's first hydrogen fuelled bus in regular service with an internal combustion engine started service in Erlangen and later on in Munich, Germany. In 1999 the first public hydrogen fuelling station opened at the Munich airport. At the end of 2002 the following hydrogen fuelling stations were in service or under construction:

• 1996 Erlangen LH2 station. This is a mobile refuelling station for liquid hydrogen. It was built by Linde to fuel the first hydrogen bus in regular public service

• 1999 Hamburg. The W.E.I.T. project financed six small hydrogen fuelled vans and a compressed hydrogen fuelling station. After several years of successful operation the station was dismantled. There are negotiations to reopen it in Milan or another North Italian locality in the near future.

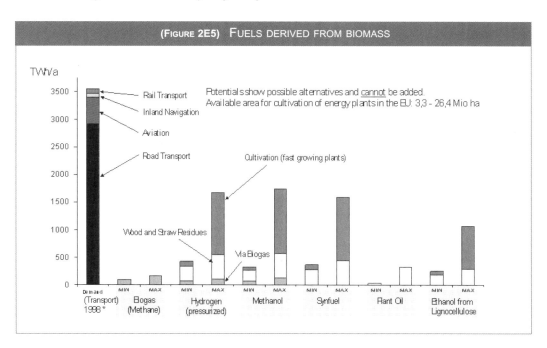

(FIGURE 2E5) FUELS DERIVED FROM BIOMASS

Car makers announce liquid hydrogen refuelling programme

DETROIT, Michigan, April 11, 2003 - General Motors and BMW announced this week that they will jointly develop refuelling devices for liquid hydrogen vehicles. The motor manufacturers said they hope others will join the initiative, which will centre on setting global standards and supply specifications and on finding the best technical and cost-effective solutions.

"We want to accelerate the progress being made on the distribution and onboard storage of liquid hydrogen as the future fuel," said Lawrence Burns, GM's vice president of research and development. "Both compressed and liquid hydrogen hold promise to be used in hydrogen vehicles. The density of hydrogen in a liquid state is especially attractive with respect to fuel distribution and vehicle range."

The goal of the collaboration is to have affordable and compelling hydrogen vehicles for sale by 2010 and the companies need to concentrate on the storage and handling technology to achieve this goal, according to Christoph Huss,

BMW's head of science and traffic policy. We have to start working on a standard so that customers will not be confronted with various systems," Huss explained. "Standardising the refuelling coupler is a must."

Liquid hydrogen provides the most convenient way in transporting hydrogen fuel before a hydrogen pipeline infrastructure is in place, he said, and teaming together will allow GM and BMW to help bring about the liquid hydrogen infrastructure faster.

The car makers say they will follow draft specifications for liquid hydrogen coupling units that have been developed by the European Integrated Hydrogen Project, which are the basis for current negotiations by the United Nations' Economic Commission of Europe (ECE) over a standard for hydrogen-powered vehicles. "BMW and GM want this refuelling system - with the coupler as a core component - to become a global standard" Huss said. - Environmental News Service.

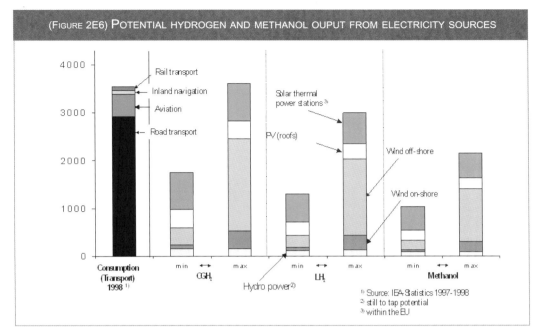

(FIGURE 2E6) POTENTIAL HYDROGEN AND METHANOL OUPUT FROM ELECTRICITY SOURCES

- 1999 Munich. A public liquid hydrogen refuelling station opens at Munich airport. Still in operation.

- 2000 The first North American station opened by the California Fuel Cell Partnership - a government led initiative to accelerate and co-ordinate the introduction of emission free vehicles in California.

- 2001 A liquid hydrogen filling station opened at the BMW site in Oxnard, California

- 2002 Two hydrogen fuelling stations open in Osaka and Takamatsu. Several further hydrogen fuelling stations in the greater Tokyo area are already under construction.

A list of hydrogen refuelling stations for road vehicles can be found at http://www.h2cars.de.

Several companies have put forward introduction strategies for hydrogen vehicles. In Germany, a government-backed industrial consortium (TES - transport energy strategy) composed of car manufacturers and fuel suppliers has sketched a road map for hydrogen introduction. It is anticipated that about 15-20 percent of all filling stations (or app. 2000 filling stations) must offer hydrogen before it will be accepted by the public. The road map assumes that before 2005/2007 only small car fleets operating around individual filling stations will be built to test public acceptance and to prove the every day usage of hydrogen cars. The erection of the network of refuelling stations will require about five years' planning and construction time between 2005 and 2010. At the end of this period, the mass production of hydrogen fuel cell cars might start, delivering about 100,000 vehicles in 2010.

Only Japan and the United States of America seem to have a systematic, government supported introduction strategy for developing a hydrogen infrastructure for vehicles. The Japanese initiative has already had several years of continued strategic and financial support and at the end of January 2003, the U.S. president announced a 1.2 billion dollar introduction

BEFORE THE WELLS RUN DRY

PART TWO: DO RENEWABLE ENERGY SOURCES HAVE THE POTENTIAL TO FILL THE GAP?

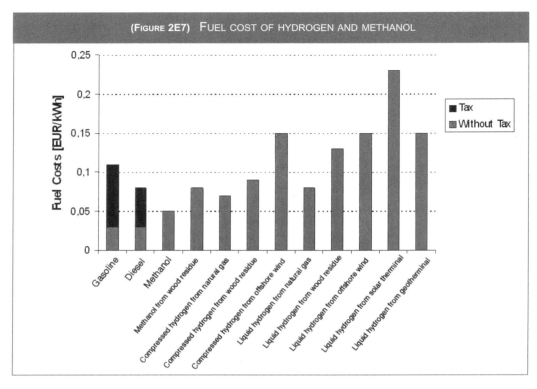

(FIGURE 2E7) FUEL COST OF HYDROGEN AND METHANOL

strategy for hydrogen infrastructure in the US, covering a five-year period.

In Europe, although hydrogen projects have been running for many years now, they are not yet strategically oriented and continuous. The availability of vehicles which consume hydrogen and of an infrastructure with refuelling stations for supplying hydrogen has to be co-ordinated since both are cost-intensive to introduce. Late in 2002, the first initiative at EU-level was launched with the aim of establishing an introduction plan. However, the composition of the steering committee makes some observers think that this initiative is not directed towards hydrogen production from renewable energies but to support hydrogen from nuclear electricity. However, in view of the long lead times and the large financial investment required, I do not think that a hydrogen strategy based on new nuclear power stations could have any mid- to

long term future.

There are plans within the European CUTE (Clean urban transport in Europe) project and the CITYCELL project, both funded by the European Commission, to manufacture fuel cell driven buses to demonstrate and test of technology and public acceptance. Selected European cities will be supplied with three fuel cell buses each and hydrogen filling stations with hydrogen from various sources. There is also the ECTOS-project to convert Iceland's energy economy completely to hydrogen by the year 2030. The first step is to demonstrate buses in Reykjavik. This will be followed by more buses, then private cars and, finally, converting Iceland's fishing fleet completely to hydrogen. Most of the hydrogen will be generated from electricity, while the electricity itself will be produced from Iceland's vast geothermal and hydro resources.

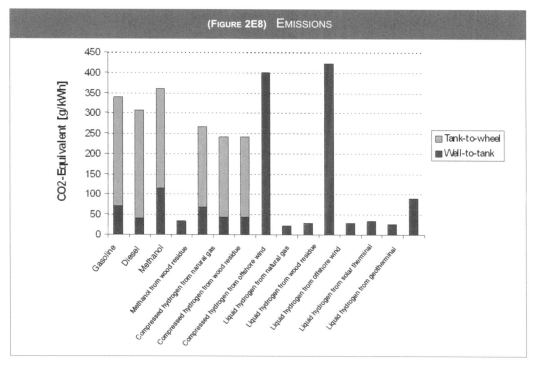

(FIGURE 2E8) EMISSIONS

4. THE CONVERSION OF IRELAND'S TRANSPORT SECTOR TO HYDROGEN

At present, about 1.2 million passenger cars and close to 200,000 trucks use Ireland's roads. The total arable area is 1 million hectare, pasture is 3.3 million hectare and the forested area 0.6 million hectare. The total population is about 3.7 million inhabitants. About 55 percent of all oil consumed in Ireland is used by the transport sector. Road traffic alone consumes about 32 TWh of oil (this corresponds to about 2.76 million tons).

A rough calculation indicates that at least 300 fuelling stations should offer hydrogen to achieve public acceptance of the fuel. This corresponds to 10 percent of all fuelling stations countrywide. If this hydrogen were to be entirely supplied by wind power produced electricity, the total system cost would be of the order of 50 billion Euros or, spread over 30 years, about 2 billion Euro per year. In total about 20 GW offshore wind converters are needed for the power production.

If this hydrogen was completely supplied from biomass via gasification, the total system cost would be in the order of 20 billion Euros, or spread over 20 years, about 1 billion Euro per year. Annually, about 13 million tons of dry biomass would be needed for hydrogen production, or a cultivated area of about 0.7 million hectare. Costs would be similar to those at present but with the difference that a large fraction of the money is now transferred to foreign countries, while domestic fuel production in the countryside would channel the money instead to a domestic labour force.

These very rough figures are intended to give the order of magnitude of the effort to convert the transport totally to hydrogen. In practice, however, a variety of hydrogen sources would be used.

BEFORE THE WELLS RUN DRY

PART TWO: DO RENEWABLE ENERGY SOURCES HAVE THE POTENTIAL TO FILL THE GAP?

REFERENCES:

R. Wurster, W. Zittel: Hydrogen energy, in "Energy Technologies to Reduce CO_2 Emissions in Europe: Prospects, Competition, Synergy". Conference Proceedings, Petten Netherlands, 11-12 April 1994, International Energy Agency, OECD, Paris, 1994, pp 115-158

L-B-Systemtechnik: General Motors Well-to-Wheel Analysis of Energy Use and Greenhouse Gas Emissions of Advanced Fuel/Vehicle Systems - A European Study, download at http://www.lbst.de/gm-wtw, 27 September 2002

A methanol economy rather than a hydrogen one ?

Two technologists living in Switzerland, Baldur Eliasson and Ulf Bossel, believe that a methanol economy might be a better option than a hydrogen one and have placed a paper called 'The Future of the Hydrogen Economy: Bright or Bleak?' on the web drawing attention to some of the problems with hydrogen. The paper seems to have caused many people to doubt whether hydrogen is the solution they had believed it to be, which is why we are discussing it here. Its main conclusions are:

1. PIPELINE LOSSES

Hydrogen should not be pumped for long distances through pipelines because of the amount of energy lost in doing so. Most gas pipelines power the pumps along their length by burning some of the gas they are pumping. With natural gas, which is mostly methane, these pumps take 0.2% of the gas in transit every 100 km. However, because hydrogen is a less-dense gas than methane, a lot more of it must be moved to transport the same amount of energy. Either bigger pipelines must be built, which takes a bigger energy investment, or the gas has to move faster, causing energy losses from the increased turbulence. Eliasson and Bossel (E&B) estimate that about 0.8% of the gas would be lost per 100km and that, if solar energy was used in North Africa to produce hydrogen to send to industrial Europe, only 60-70% would actually arrive.

"Such long distance transport wouldn't be done with compressed gas" Werner Zittel comments. "Why transport electrolytically-produced hydrogen instead of transporting the electricity and converting it to hydrogen at the consumption site? The more decentralised your energy production chain, the shorter the average transport distances for hydrogen." Zittel also says that the E&B loss figures are roughly twice those calculated by his company.

2. DELIVERY PROBLEMS

The low energy density of hydrogen means that a lot more road tankers are going to be needed to get it to filling stations if it goes in compressed rather than liquid form. E&B compare 40-ton trucks, one carry hydrogen at 200 bar, another methane at the same pressure, and others carrying methanol, propane and ordinary petrol. "At 200 bar, the 40-ton truck can deliver about 3.2 tons of methane" they write, "but only 320Kg of hydrogen." As a result, it would take two methane deliveries and 21 hydrogen deliveries to supply the same amount of energy as carried by the petrol tanker. The wish to avoid this problem may be the reason that GM and BMW have chosen to use liquid hydrogen in their cars. (See page 134) Here again, Zittel disputes the E&B estimates. "If liquid hydrogen is transported in a 40 ton truck, about 3,500 kg can be delivered." he says.

3. COMPRESSION COSTS

E&B say that using electricity to make and compress hydrogen at a filling station would involve the loss of over 40% of the energy in the electricity. Zittel responds that it is wrong just to look at this single step and calculate its efficiency. "What has to be done is to look to the whole "well-to-wheel" chain and compare efficiencies of various alternatives over the full chain, not each individual step" he says. "Remember a hydrogen fuel cell is twice as efficient as an internal combustion engine. My firm has carried out analyses of various whole chains for many years for several ministries in Germany, for car companies and for the oil industry (CONCAWE) which did not even favour the hydrogen path. We have analysed about 200 various paths. Our results and assumptions have been crosschecked and discussed by both car companies and oil firms. We are therefore pretty confident that the hydrogen route is best."

In view of these and other problems they claim to have quantified, E&B suggest that a methanol (methyl alcohol, CH_3OH) economy might be a better option than a hydrogen one because methanol is a liquid at normal temperatures and can thus be pumped and stored much more easily. It can also be burned in fuel cells. They write:

The synthesis of methanol requires hydrogen and carbon atoms. In a future sustainable energy world carbon could come from plant biomass, from organic waste and from captured CO_2. Typically, biomass has a hydrogen-to-carbon ratio of two. In the methanol synthesis two additional hydrogen atoms could be attached to every biomass carbon. Carbon from the biosphere may become the key element for in a sustainable energy future. Instead of converting biomass into hydrogen, hydrogen from renewable sources should be added to biomass to form methanol. Carbon atoms should stay bound in the energy chain as long as possible. They are returned to the atmosphere (or recycled) after the final use of energy. But synthetic methanol is one of a number of options to be seriously considered for the planning of a clean and sustainable energy future.

Again, Zittel disagrees. "Over the full well-to-wheel path, methanol is less efficient than hydrogen. Secondly, the direct methanol fuel cell is less efficient and has a shorter life than a hydrogen fuel cell. Thirdly, methanol needs special safety measures to be taken, mainly in repair workshops. According to BMW, it is impossible to ensure these measures are applied in all workshops. This makes it impossible for methanol cars to be repaired around the world without severe safety risks for the repair staff. According to BMW this drawback eliminates methanol from consideration as a motor fuel regardless of any other technical arguments. Finally, my company does not know of any car company that is still considering methanol as vehicle fuel".

The safety aspects that worried BMW arise because methanol is extremely poisonous - less that a cupful can lead to permanent blindness or death - and it doesn't have to be swallowed to be dangerous since the liquid can be absorbed through the skin and the vapour through the lungs. Chronic inhalation or oral exposure may result in headache, dizziness, giddiness, insomnia, nausea, gastric disturbances, conjunctivitis, blurred vision, and blindness. No information is available on the reproductive, developmental, or carcinogenic effects of methanol in humans but birth defects have been observed in the offspring of rats and mice exposed to methanol by inhalation. The United States' Environmental Protection Agency has not classified methanol as carcinogenic.

Another problem is that methanol vapour is heavier than air and, unless there is good ventilation, it will linger close to the ground or in a maintenance pit where the mixture of vapour and air is liable to be set alight by a spark if the concentration of methanol is above 6.7%. and will explode if the temperature is above 12 C. Once ablaze, the flames give out very little light making it very hard to see them or even estimate the size of the fire, especially in broad daylight. Fortunately, methanol vapour has a repulsive, pungent odour so it gives some warning of its presence. However, it is difficult to smell methanol in the air at less than 2,000 parts per million.

Zittel's company plans to publish a detailed response to E&B in mid-2003. "[E&B] sketch spurious scenarios and the results are horrible," he says, "but if you use quite different scenarios they will give you completely different results. [They] take part of today's hydrogen technology and extrapolate it into the future. This is at the same level as people who argue that photovoltaics will never come because today's solar electricity costs about 0.5 Euro per kWh. They ignore the possibility of lower costs from greater economies of scale and longer learning curves. For instance, they calculate the electricity consumption for liquefaction of about 35 %. However, state-of-the-art concepts indicate that this consumption can be reduced close to 20 % when the next generation of liquefiers is built."

Despite the problems, the methanol economy is an option that Ireland should certainly consider, not as an alternative to the hydrogen economy but as a supplement to it. Methanol would allow hydrogen from surplus wind-generated electricity to be combined with biomass grown on farms and the resulting fuel sold throughout Europe. Moreover, the investment required to develop a network of methanol filling stations would be very much less than for its hydrogen equivalent.

The E&B paper is at: http://www.woodgas.com/hydrogen_economy.pdf a second line reading:
The response to it from L-B-Systemtechnik is at :
http://www.hyweb.de/News/LBST_Comments-on-Eliasson-Bossel-Papers_July2003_protected.pdf

SOURCES

The E&B paper is at: http://www.woodgas.com/hydrogen_economy.pdf a second line reading:
The response to it from L-B-Systemtechnik is at :
http://www.hyweb.de/News/LBST_Comments-on-Eliasson-Bossel-Papers_July2003_protected.pdf
For a detailed well-to-wheel analysis of the energy efficiencies of the various fuels that could power motor vehicles, look at
http://www.lbst.de/gm-wtw

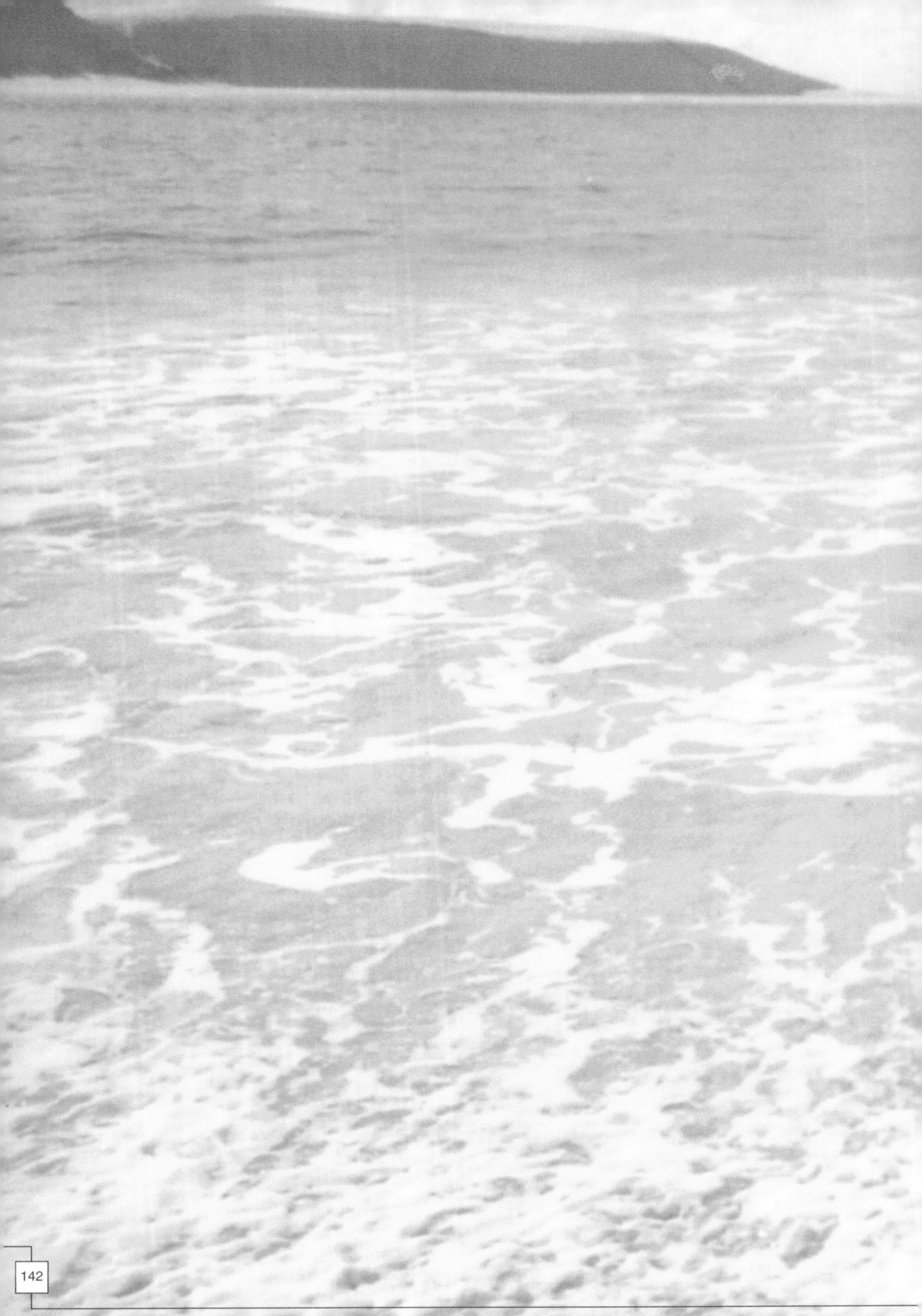

Part Three

How energy availability will limit Ireland's development options

Simulating a Sustainable Ireland
by **David Crane** and **Larry Staudt**

If fossil fuel use is restricted by shortages or by action to slow climate change, the physical composition of an economy rather than the availability of money determines the level at which it can operate. Accordingly, the ECCO computer model focuses on energy and material flows between the various sectors of the Irish economy rather than flows of money.

Simulating a Sustainable Ireland

by David Crane and Larry Staudt

How well can renewable energy meet Ireland's future needs? Feasta commissioned the construction of a computer model of energy flows in the Irish economy to find out. On one of the sets of assumptions set out here, income growth will cease but CO_2 emissions can be halved.

This paper describes a simulation study undertaken with the aim of exploring the potential for renewable energy to make a key difference to the future sustainability of the Republic of Ireland. We begin by looking at the electricity-generating sector itself, and move out from there to consider some complementary technologies that will interact well with renewables-generated electricity in moving Ireland towards a more sustainable state.

The modelling approach we used was ECCO, originally developed by Jane King & Malcolm Slesser (Slesser & King 1993; Slesser et al, 1994, 1997). It provides a broad-brush sketch of the entire economy which allowed us not only to calculate the direct impacts of renewables on the electricity-generating sector, but also the synergies that may exist between renewable generation of electricity and other technologies and economic activities. We were not primarily concerned with forecasting, but with representing the potential for change of the economy under a range of scenarios.

ECCO has a number of characteristic features, physical, dynamic and holistic:

A) Physical

ECCO is primarily a physical account of the economy. Energy analysis theory, as defined in the proceedings of the IFIAS workshop of 1975 (IFIAS, 1975) underpins the model, and is explained in the primer which follows this article. It explicitly recognises the importance of the second law of thermodynamics in limiting the options available to the economy. According to this law, any transformation to a system incurs a net dissipation of energy and an overall increase in the entropy (which can be thought of as a measure of disorder) of the system.

Within a system, the entropy of a local region can decrease if it is able to export the entropy increase elsewhere. In industrialised economies, we generally order our built environment by exporting huge volumes of disorder to natural ecosystems, as dissipation of energy resources and as pollution. This behaviour was first formally described in these terms by Ilya Prigogine and colleagues as 'open systems' (Prigogine & Stengers, 1984). National economies such as the Republic of Ireland are very much open systems, interacting not only with natural environments, but with the global political environment through trading goods, services and financial flows. (Financial flows have no direct physical presence themselves but determine the direction in which physical effort is expended).

By describing the economy in such physical terms we get a direct handle on some of the key interactions with nature, such as rates of fossil fuel extraction, use of materials and emission of atmospheric pollutants, as well as many interactions that occur within the economy. However, our concern with exact thermodynamics does not overshadow our desire to accurately describe aspects of the real world, and we do not try to superimpose a grand theory of energetics upon reality. Where appropriate, other units are used to measure specific variables (e.g. transport demand in passenger-km and tonne-km for freight).

B) Dynamic

ECCO is a dynamic model. It does not describe the state of the economy at a single point in time, but the unfolding of events in the economy over a period of decades. It is suited for describing long-term economic patterns over such timescales, but less suited for explaining short-term fluctuations over periods of months or quarters. The computational techniques used to describe these dynamic relationships are classical system dynamics, as developed by Jay Forrester & colleagues in the 1960s at MIT (Forrester 1968, 1971; Meadows et al, 1973).

The dynamic nature of the model is important in deeper ways than simply allowing us to describe key indicators as time series rather than snapshot values. A simple linear programming model can accomplish this. System dynamics, however, excels at describing complicated feedback interactions between many factors, and the ECCO model contains many feedback loops. These often lead to counterintuitive behaviour in the model, that is, behaviour that may seem to be unexpected at first glance, but, when its causes are traced back through the model structure, does make sense. When we engage with the model in this way, we are encountering questions about the way our economy operates, and gaining insights that are qualitative as much as they are quantitative.

As an example, a model may show that making a large reduction in energy demand for a sectoral activity at negligible capital cost causes the economy's overall energy demand to decrease initially, but increase in the longer term. This latter increase is counterintuitive, but can be explained by the mechanism that decreased energy demand either benefits balance of payments or reduces required domestic energy extraction investments, allowing the economy to grow at a faster rate than it otherwise would. This 'rebound effect' is discussed in greater detail in Slesser *et al*, 1997. The point is that formalising the structure of the economy in our model has brought to our attention an inherent outcome of the assumptions that we have fed into it that had previously not been noticed. Even if we recognise that the model is a very limited representation of reality, with many factors simplified or omitted (and this is true of any model, however detailed), we can take the insight about rebound effects away with us and consider its place in the real world. This qualitative insight is arguably more important than the numerical time series data that the model generates.

The world-view of the dynamics modeller informs our definition of sustainability too. We do not seek to describe sustainability as an endpoint, a goal that our model economy seeks and then steps into some sort of steady state once it reaches it. If we were to consider that an economy achieved sustainability by 2050, and was still sustainable in 2100, it is unlikely that the two economies would be identical. They might be radically different in some ways.

C) Holistic

ECCO is a holistic model. Rather than covering one part of the economy in fine detail, the entire economy is described in coarse detail. Specific sectors may be developed to a greater level of detail than others (in our case, electricity generation and energy conservation, for example), but all sectors are represented at some level of detail. Because the model determines its own growth rate (see below) it is important that we know the demands and supplies associated with all parts of the economy in order to assess the overall growth potential. A sector described at the lowest level of detail can be thought of as a placeholder. It is unlikely to do anything surprising during a simulation. When developing a model for specific purposes, we need to evaluate where we wish to apply detailed policy options, and from there, what level of detail is appropriate for the other major sectors. For example, if we were to develop a model with the aim of studying water usage, we would need a high level of detail in the industrial, domestic, agricultural and possibly electricity generation sectors. Services and transport sectors could be simpler, taking their cues from the ups and downs of the more detailed sectors.

In some studies, the broad overview offered by ECCO has been usefully combined with more detailed static analysis (Crane & Foran, 2000).

Where this has been done, much of the cross-talk between the models has been conducted through a sharing of insights, rather than an attempt to hitch the computational data streams together into a single super-model.

SELF-DETERMINING GROWTH RATE

The model will determine its own growth rate over time. Most dynamic economic models will feed in the average growth rate as a user-defined input. We allow the modelled economy to grow as fast as is possible under the policy options that are in place. User-defined policies may well affect growth rates, albeit indirectly, and these allow us to capture some of the more subtle long-term effects of policy options (such as the rebound effect described earlier).

The model's central 'growth loop' represents the key influences described by the model that lead

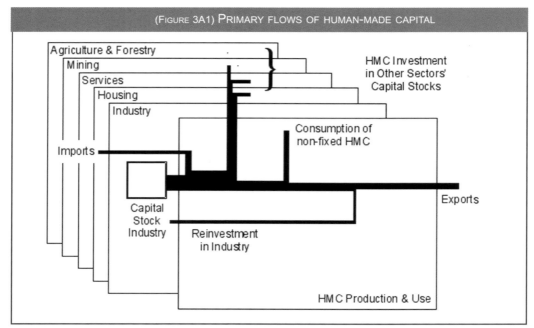

(FIGURE 3A1) PRIMARY FLOWS OF HUMAN-MADE CAPITAL

Agriculture & Forestry
Mining
Services
Housing
Industry

HMC Investment in Other Sectors' Capital Stocks

Imports

Consumption of non-fixed HMC

Capital Stock Industry

Exports

Reinvestment in Industry

HMC Production & Use

Human - made capital (HMC) produced by firms in the industrial sector flows to the other sectors of the Irish economy and is also exported.

to physical growth in an industrialised economy. All variables here are referred to in embodied energy terms. An 'industry' sector is defined as containing all those activities that produce physical goods. Other sectors are also defined, such as agriculture, services, housing, etc. These all contribute meaningfully to the economy, and all require a stock of fixed capital (buildings, machinery, etc.) through which to do so. Only the industrial sector is able to supply that capital - either the domestic industrial sector, or one overseas, at any rate. International trade complicates the picture a little, but can be adequately handled by the 'growth loop' model.

As shown in *Figure 3A1*, the aggregated flow of 'human-made capital' (HMC) from the industrial sector can be diverted to a number of purposes:
• consumption of non-fixed/disposable products
• reinvestment in and maintenance of the capital stocks of industry
• reinvestment in and maintenance of the capital stocks of other sectors
• exports of goods to other economies.

 Note that all capital stocks depreciate (an inevitable consequence of the second law of thermodynamics, and a practical fact), and maintaining a sector at a given size requires continual investment. The overall demands for reinvestment by all other sectors will be determined by the assumptions we make about them, and by policy options that we may set. For example:

• required investment in energy will be driven by market forces in most western economies. Ultimately, this will depend upon a diverse range of factors, such as energy costs of extracting the fuels, comparative energy costs of alternative fuels, and demands for the fuel by the domestic economy and export market. All of these factors can be represented in the model.

• required investment in housing will be driven by population in a very simple model, and possibly by a measure of affluence. In a more complex model, we may also wish to introduce average size of a household in capita terms. Many western economies have seen considerable decreases in average household size over the last few decades, with considerable consequences on per-capita consumption of energy and resources of a domestic nature (a six-person household does not generally own a house six times the size of a one-person household, nor a fridge or heating system consuming six times the energy). If we choose to consider the social dynamics of increasing divorce rates and decreasing family sizes, we can see implications for our physical growth loop.

We calibrate the rate of consumption of disposable goods based on short-term indicators of economic well-being, and, after factoring in balance of payment adjustments, allocate the remainder to industrial reinvestment. If this amount exceeds the rate of depreciation in industry, our industrial sector will grow over time, and hence the future production of human-made capital will increase, all other things being equal (and we can break that assumption and model effects of technological change within industry if we wish to). Conversely, if the reinvestment in industry is too small, future output of HMC will contract, to the detriment of the entire economy. Because this reinvestment term is sensitive to changes in consumption, in investment in every sector and to international trade in goods, services and financial flows, the growth of the model as a whole is sensitive to a wide range of policy options.

Figure 3A2 portrays the growth loop in terms of influences between terms, with the arrows pointed from influencer to influenced. A plus sign indicates that the variables will move in the

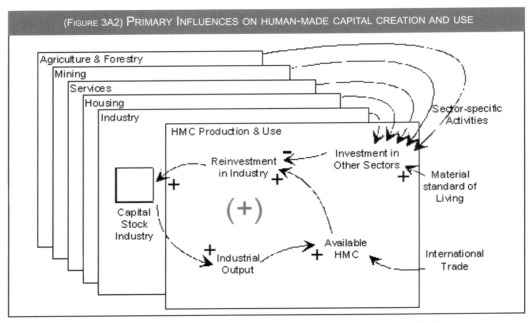

(FIGURE 3A2) PRIMARY INFLUENCES ON HUMAN-MADE CAPITAL CREATION AND USE

Feedback from the various sectors of the economy and from international trade influences the way that human-made capital (HMC) is allocated.

same direction (as x goes up, it will push y up, as x goes down, it will push y down), and a minus sign opposite directions.

Finally, it is worth elaborating a little on the balance of payments sector. In a national economy, there will be significant trades with the outside world, in physical goods, in services, and in financial flows. The physical flows can easily be incorporated into the above model, and in some cases (notably energy resources) will already be calculated by the model. In the case of intangible trades, we convert these to a nominal embodied energy value based upon the average energy intensity of the economy, a term that we calculate for internal accounting purposes anyway. An economy that exports significant intangibles (e.g. Switzerland) can, as a result, afford a much greater inflow of HMC than would otherwise be possible. The internal costs of generating such flows can be accounted for in our representation of the services sector, which would probably be quite detailed for

such an economy.

THE IRISH MODEL

The pilot model of the Republic of Ireland was developed over a period of approximately six months. We aimed to replicate the broad growth patterns of the Irish economy over the period 1990-2002 (or as recently as official time-series have allowed), and then simulate them out to 2050. This was successfully achieved, although inevitably some areas were sketched-in in relatively little detail. In describing the model, it is useful to note omissions as well as the detail that has been included, particularly for the sake of pointing to relationships between policies that we may have failed to capture in this first iteration of the model.

The model divides the economy into a number of broad sectors, following the sectoral divisions provided by the main data sources that we used to calibrate it. These are:

•**Agriculture, Forestry & Fishing**

This sector was sketched-in in terms of fixed capital stocks, and energy resource use. Future growth is driven by domestic requirements and export markets. No attempt was made to distinguish between types of agriculture, nor to assess land use. This latter would be required were we to factor in the land-use requirements of a large-scale biomass initiative (and, to a lesser extent, land-based wind generators, although it can be argued that these can happily coexist with many types of crops).

•**Mining, including gas and peat extraction**

Our primary focus here was on describing the reserves of natural gas and peat, and the fixed capital stocks employed to extract them. Investment in these sectors was driven by domestic demand and world export markets (significant only in the case of gas).

• **Industry & Manufacturing**

This sector was treated as a single entity, although in reality it covers a range of activities from heavy industry to food processing and the construction industry. (Even in much larger, more mature ECCO models we rarely disaggregate this sector.) The effects of investment in fuel-efficient technologies in this sector were characterised.

• **Utilities, primarily electricity generation**

Electricity generation was divided into a number of technologies, covering conventional fossil-fired plant, combined-cycle plant (a more modern technology with greater efficiency of use of fuel), conventional hydro-electricity, and renewables. Separate subsectors were drawn up to characterise wind generation, photovoltaics, biomass-generated ethanol and methanol plant, and wave energy, although our analyses here focussed primarily on wind power. User-defined policies for future uptake between existing technologies were developed, with

Business-As-Usual policy allocating 90% of new plant built beyond 2000 to combined-cycle fossil plant, and 10% to renewables. The differences between technologies were characterised primarily as:

1. **Load Factor** i.e. percentage of time a plant would typically be online
2. **Thermal efficiency of converting fuel to electricity** (where the plant is fuel-powered)

• **Fixed capital cost of building and maintaining plant**

We did not account for one potential benefit of wind power, that the technology could be developed indigenously, and potentially sold worldwide, whereas fossil-fired futures would be dependent upon foreign technology bases (and therefore represent a poorer situation for international balance of payments).

• **Services**

The services sector was characterised in terms of fixed capital and physical resource consumption (e.g. thermal fuels, electricity). Demand for services was limited to the three major consumer sectors, industry, domestic dwellings, and the services sector itself.

•**Domestic dwellings**

These again were characterised in terms of fixed capital and resource requirements. Effects of domestic energy efficiency technologies were taken into account (and here the payback could be significantly greater than in the industrial sector, owing to the poor starting position of the Irish housing stock in terms of simple energy efficiency 'quick wins' such as insulation), as well as potential for electricity-powered ground source heat pump technologies.

• **Transport**

The transport sector does not maintain its own capital stock, as national accounts data describes the fixed capital in transport machinery as belonging to the owning sector e.g. industry, services, domestic. Energy use by transport is defined separately, though, and we were able to calculate demand based on passenger and freight volumes. Policies describing potential future modal splits between transport sectors are in place, as well as future fuel mixes, including electrically-powered passenger vehicles utilising fuel cell technologies.

•**International Finance**

This sector defines the net impact upon the growth of the economy of international trade. Some parts of this can be characterised well by the model, such as the necessity of fuel imports, others are defined as user policies, such as future levels of international investment capital. Over the calibration period, Ireland enjoyed an

unusually high influx of international capital, which we have allowed to decrease somewhat in the Business-As-Usual profile for the model.

DEFINITION OF SUSTAINABILITY

Sustainability is an ill-defined and much-abused term. For the purposes of assessing the relative merits of the outcomes generated by our scenarios, it is useful to have one or more sustainability indicators to hand. For this study, we focus primarily on energy-based measures, because we are looking at energy-related scenarios.

Carbon-dioxide emissions are a good sustainability indicator, and can be readily compared against the agreed Kyoto targets for the Irish

(FIGURE 3A3) KEY ASSUMPTIONS DEFINING THE BUSINESS AS USUAL SCENARIO	
SECTOR	**FEATURES**
Agriculture	No change in diet, self-sufficiency of agriculture, or fuel, resource mixes between 2000 and 2050. Agriculture is a relatively small sector in terms of total resource demands.
Energy Extractor	No further discoveries of natural gas post 2000, allowing production of native resources to dwindle by 2010 to one-quarter its magnitude in 1990, and scarcely recover thereafter. Peat production declines slowly to zero by 2030, based on declining demand.
Industry	No changes in fuel mix, nor efficiency of use post-2000. No implementation of energy conservation options.
Services	No changes in fuel mix post-2000. Demand for services driven by growth of private consumer spending, industry and service sector itself in simple linear relationship to current rates of demand.
Dwellings	No changes in fuel mix, nor efficiency of use post-2000. No implementation of energy conservation options. Future growth driven only by population size, hence essentially static sector.
Electricity Generation	The majority of new generating capacity is gas-fired, with renewables continuing to play a small part. Existing coal fired plant is allowed to depreciate slowly, being phased out by around 2030.
Balance of payments	Credits and debits balances remain at 2000 levels out to 2050. Fuel imports driven by model, following the notes above regarding electricity generation and energy extraction in particular. Net 'invisibles' balance in 2000 was 18 billion euros, declining to 12 billion by 2030 and 8 billion by 2050.

Republic. If we define energy sustainability as receiving all energy requirements from renewable resources, we can compare our progress towards that goal by plotting fractions of energy derived from renewables, both for electrical energy and all primary energy. We also created a third variant for this study, in which we included indirect imports of primary energy in an attempt to reflect the energy expended elsewhere in the world. This would counter the 'accounting loophole' of the simpler indicator whereby an economy could simply shift energy-intensive activities overseas. In the case of the Irish model, it made only a slight difference in most cases.

In terms of security of energy supply, we could compare Irish demand for exported oil and gas against projected world outputs of oil and gas (using data from Campbell, 2002). Again, it is worth stressing that our assessment of the sustainability of each outcome does not end with the set of indicators outlined above, and that it is necessary to step back from the model and

consider the results in the light of the real world.

CALIBRATING THE MODEL

The model was initialised for the year 1990, and run over a ten-year period against real historical data in order to calibrate it. The primary data sources used to calibrate the model were:

• National accounts data from the Central Statistics Office of Ireland (http://www.eirestat.cso.ie), particularly for the purpose of getting Gross Domestic Fixed Capital Formation (GDFCF) data (series naaa04xx) upon which to base the model rates of capital formation. In this case, as no Fixed Capital Stock data was available from the CSO, the GDFCF data was also used to estimate initial capital stocks by using a simple spreadsheet model that tracked growth and depreciation of sectoral capital stocks over the calibration period. The CSO bpaa series data was also used to calibrate the international finance sector of the model.

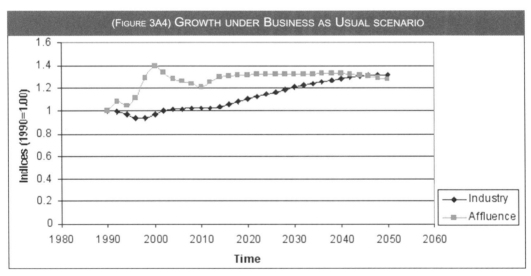

Growth Indicators under BAU scenario. Growth in both personal material affluence and manufacturing capacity is slow

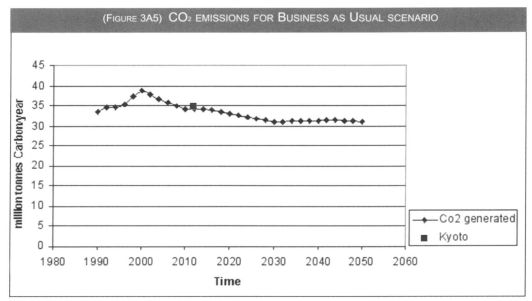

Projected CO₂ emissions under Business as Usual. The temporary decline in emission rates (which does not mean a decrease in atmospheric CO2 levels) can be explained by looking at the changing structure of the electricity generating sector. Note that the model underestimates CO₂ emissions for 2000 by roughly 5%, as the actual figure was around 41 million tonnes carbon/year.

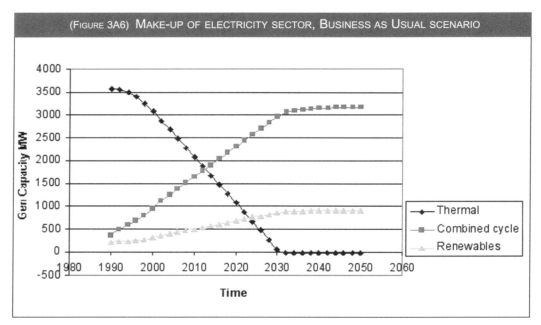

Make-up of electricity sector generating capacity under Business as Usual. Existing thermal capacity declines through to 2030, and the majority of new capacity is introduced as combined-cycle plant. Renewables play a minor but not inconsiderable role.

(FIGURE 3A7) KEY INPUTS DEFINING THE SCENARIOS DESCRIBED IN THIS REPORT

Scenario	Policy Inputs / Scenario Definition
Renewables 1	Mix of new generating capacity post-2000 is 30%: 70% cct: wind cct is combined cycle gas turbine
Renewables 2	Mix of new generating capacity post-2000 is 10%: 90% cct: wind
Transport	50% of passenger road transport runs on electric fuel cells by 2030, and 75% by 2050
Domestic Energy Conservation	Up to 20% additional investment in energy conversation in the domestic sector by 2050
Industrial Energy Conservation	Up to 20% additional investment in energy conversation in the industry sector by 2050
Domestic Heat Pumps	30% of domestic sector space heating is supplied by geothermal heat pumps by 2030, 50% by 2050
Sustainability 1	All of the above
Sustainability 2	All of the above but pursued more vigorously • *100% new generating plant is renewables* • *100% fuel cells for passenger road vehicles by 2050* • *100% domestic space heating from geothermal heat pumps by 2050*

•Energy balance data for Ireland, from the Department of Public Enterprise. The report *"Energy in Ireland"* provides data for the period 1980-1993. Energy balances for 1994-2000 were taken from the DPI website (http://www.irl.gov.ie/tec/energy/statistics/). These provide a detailed breakdown of energy resource production, imports and domestic usage by sector, as well as transformations into secondary fuels such as briquettes and electricity. Combining the energy balances over the calibration period, it was possible to develop detailed time-series data of sectoral energy usage by fuel type.

•The Electricity Supply Board Annual statements contained much detailed information on generating capacities and types of generator, from which a more detailed description of the electricity generation sector could be developed.

•The final report of the EU-funded ALTENER

report *"Total Renewable Energy Resource in Ireland"* provided helpful information when developing the renewable energy sector.

This calibration process led to the definition of a business-as-usual (hereafter BAU) scenario, in which current technologies and policies were extrapolated out over a further fifty-year period. This is not intended to provide for an accurate forecast of Ireland's future, but to develop a well-defined baseline against which we can compare the effects of the changes we introduce in our policy studies. In the electricity-generating sector, we assumed that the majority of new generating capacity would be gas-fired, with a small fraction (10%) being wind energy. We assumed a continued high level of investment in Ireland from overseas, although less than was seen in the 1990s, recognising this to be an unusual decade. Key assumptions of the business-as-usual scenario defined for the purposes of this report are outlined in *Figure 3A3*. Key features of the outcome of the Business-

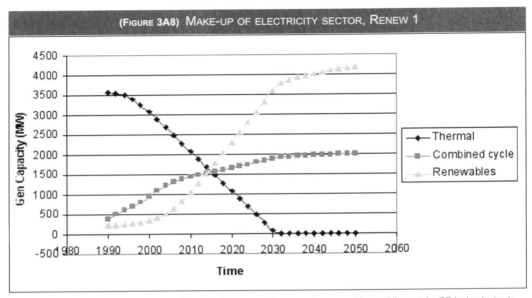

Make-up of electricity generating capacity under first renewables scenario: renewables rapidly ovetake CC technologies to become the dominant technology.

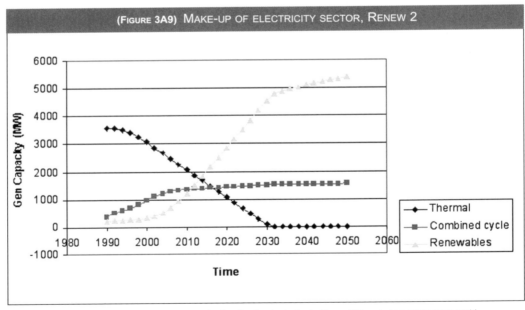

Under the second renewables scenario, the situation is similar to Figure 3A8, only somewhat more rapid.

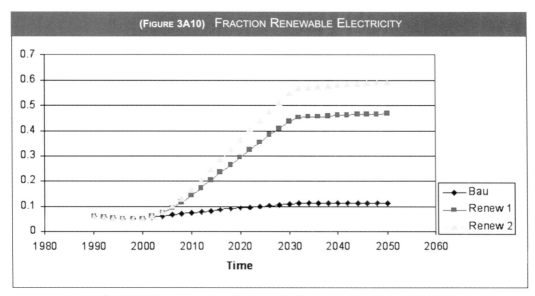

Fractions of electricity generated by renewable resources under the three scenarios

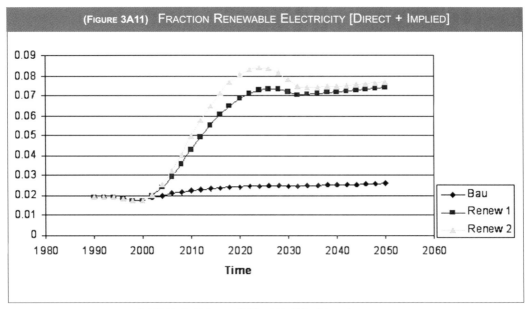

Fractions of energy supplied by renewable resources.

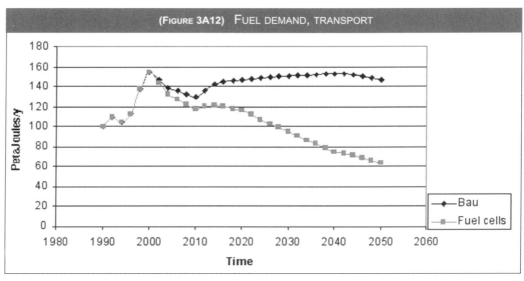

Fossil fuel demand by transport under Business as Usual and fuel cell scenarios

As-Usual scenario are outlined below:

•The economy continues to grow, but very slowly (figure 3A4). Our key indices of growth, for average per capita material affluence and manufacturing output, show less than a 50% increase over the 50 year period, equating to an average growth rate of less than 1%. This slow growth is in spite of the continued inward investment from overseas, and partly reflects the longer-term effect of this, as returns on the investment begin to leave the country.

•Carbon dioxide emissions show a decrease from through to 2030 (figure 3A5), owing to a combination of structural changes and economic decline. Beyond 2030 they remain essentially flat, in step with the negligible economic growth rates during the latter phases of simulation. The decrease from 2000-2030 can be explained by the phasing out of the current cohort of conventional fossil-fired electricity plant, and its replacement by more efficient combined cycle plant (figure 3A6). This in itself is enough to meet the Kyoto requirements for 2012, with no positive action required. In terms of energy policy, it is apparent that there

is a window of opportunity over the next thirty years within which alternative energy strategies can be developed while enjoying the benefits of the decline of this technology. Beyond 2030, achieving an active reduction in CO_2 emissions would not be so easy, particularly if other policies were brought into play during the next fifty years that resulted in positive economic growth. The lukewarm 'good news' of matching the Kyoto targets shown here would be better characterised as a combination of opportunism and economic doldrums, and shouldn't be mistaken for actively getting to grips with the required decoupling between economic activity and fossil fuel use. (It is also worth pointing out that a flat CO_2 profile is not particularly good news for the environment, as it simply represents a steadily increasing stock of CO_2 in the atmosphere rather than a rapidly increasing one.)

•Dependency on imported fuels remains very high. Native supplies of natural gas are already mostly exhausted apart from the recently discovered Corrib field off the coast of County Mayo. We decided to treat this field as a non-native resource as its owner, Shell, will find the capital for its exploitation outside Ireland and

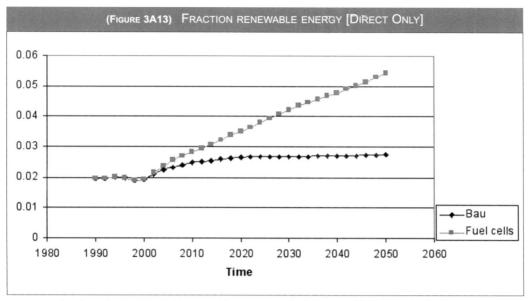

Fractions of energy supplied by renewable resources under Business as Usual and fuel cell scenarios.

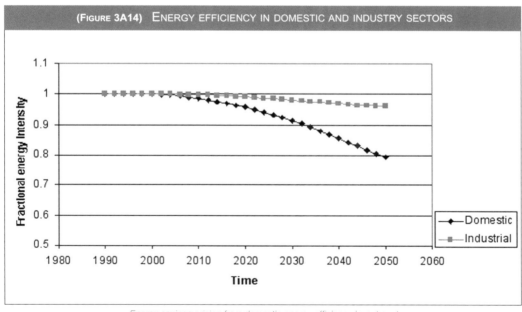

Energy savings arising from domestic energy efficiency investment

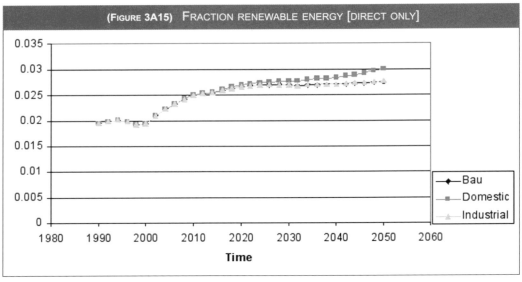

(FIGURE 3A15) FRACTION RENEWABLE ENERGY [DIRECT ONLY]

Domestic energy efficiency policy has a minor impact on the fraction of national energy demand met by renewables.

send almost all the money it receives for the gas outside Ireland too. As this makes gas from Corrib functionally identical to gas coming into Ireland across the interconnector, it allows it to be left out of the model. Ireland's only other indigenous fuel, peat is a small fraction of the total energy demand. Major fuel demands include natural gas for electricity (21% of total fuel demand by 2050), oil fuels for the transport sector (42% of total fuel demand by 2050) and domestic heating fuel (18% of total fuel demand by 2050). In terms of fuel supply security, the combination of declining native gas supplies and buying into a gas-dependent electricity future do not make for a good combination.

SIMULATION EXPERIMENTS

A number of simulation experiments were conducted to assess the viability of some proposed solutions to Ireland's (and the Western world in general's) current sustainability problems of reliance of depletable resources and increasing carbon dioxide output. The options assessed here are primarily technological. *Figure 3A7* contains a brief summary of the changes to the BAU profile made in defining all the scenarios undertaken in this report.

RENEWABLE ELECTRICITY

Ireland has significant potential for renewable electricity generation, primarily in the form of wind and wave. Bio-fuels are also an option, although not one that we examined in detail here, as doing so would require a more detailed model of land-use interactions between fuel crops and other forms of agriculture than we have currently developed. Compared to gas-fired combined cycle plant, wind power is roughly 3 times more expensive to build (the capital costs per megawatt of generating capacity are not widely divergent, but the load factor for CCGT is much higher, leading to a far greater return in terms of electricity generated). Potentially, a large-scale adoption of wind power would have a negative impact on economic growth as a result of this extra capital expenditure (in the BAU scenario, investment

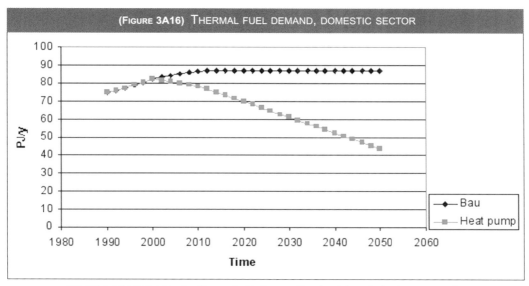

Thermal energy demand by dwellings under Business as Usual and domestic heat pump scenarios.

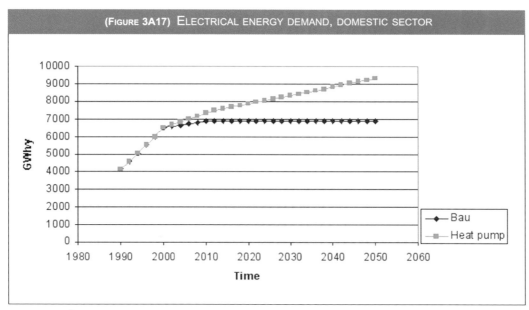

Electrical energy demand by dwellings under Business as Usual and domestic heat pump scenarios

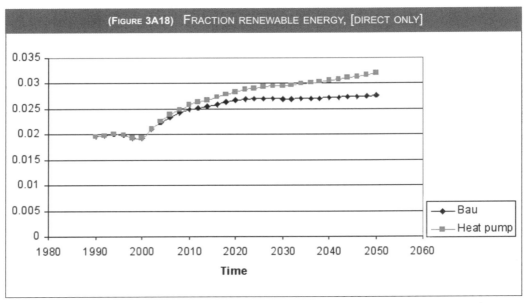

(FIGURE 3A18) FRACTION RENEWABLE ENERGY, [DIRECT ONLY]

Fraction of national energy demand met by renewables under Back At Work and domestic heat pump scenarios

in the electricity sector accounted for roughly 5% of total investment in fixed capital stocks). Although the economy can support the more extreme penetration of wind power, overall, this has a relatively minor impact on the sustainability of the nation. As we pointed out earlier, there are major direct demands for fossil fuels outside of the electricity sector. *Figure 3A10* plots the rather smaller share that renewable electricity gains of the economy's total energy usage. The 9-10% share achieved by the second renewables scenario is certainly an improvement on current arrangements, but is unlikely to make a long-term difference environmentally (the CO_2 profile for this scenario is only 5% lower than for the BAU scenario by 2050). If renewables-generated electricity is to have a serious impact, it must also begin to replace some of these other demands. The remaining scenarios look at some options for doing this.

RENEWABLES-POWERED TRANSPORT

Fuel cells represent one technology that may be used in the transportation sector as an alterna-

tive to continued fossil fuel dependency. We made a broad assumption that an electricity-powered car could convert energy to motive power with roughly twice the efficiency of a petrol engine. The conversion of fuel to electricity (the thermal efficiency) for conventional electricity generators is roughly 30-35%, with combined cycle plant achieving a somewhat higher value. Hence, from a system-wide perspective, the use of fossil-fired electricity to power transport makes little sense.

In the case of renewable electricity, of course, there is no initial fossil fuel input, and a clear case for sustainable transport through use of fuel cells can be made. We adopted the more extreme renewable energy policy at the same time as driving a significant substitution of conventional road transport with electrical vehicles, achieving 50% penetration by 2030 and a 75% penetration by 2040. This has a significant effect on the demand for thermal fuels by transport, as shown in *Figure 3A12*, and reduces the total energy demand of the economy by around 7% by 2050 when applied by itself, and has a

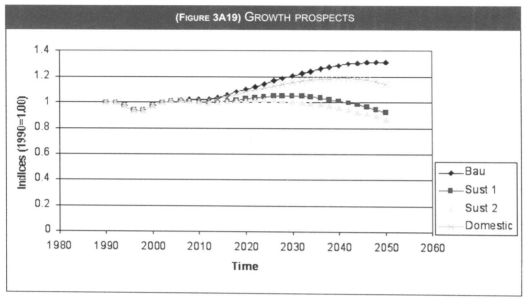

Sum effect of sustainability policies on growth

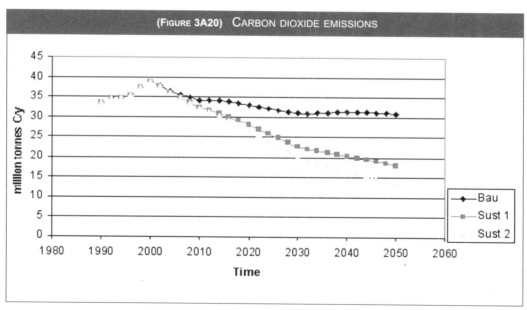

Sum effect of sustainability policies on CO₂ emissions

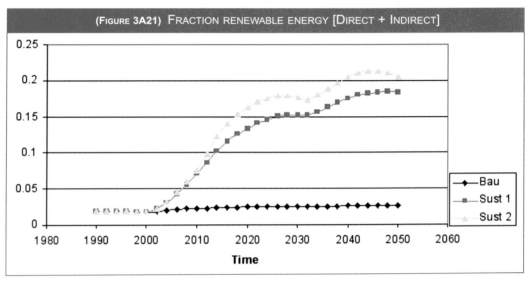

Fraction of total energy demand met by renewables under combined sustainability scenario

marginally positive effect on the fraction of renewable energy use indicator (*Figure 3A13*).

Domestic energy conservation

Ireland's housing stock generates a significant thermal energy demand, used almost entirely for space heating. The current housing stock can be characterised as poorly insulated, with even modern dwellings tending to opt only for simple cavity insulation. A number of quick wins could be made by insulating this housing stock. We characterise the impact of investment in domestic energy efficiency as one of diminishing returns, assuming that the first investments made are the most cost-effective. The data we use is based on a study by the TNO, Netherlands (Melman *et al.*, 1990), and probably under-represents the capacity of the Irish housing stock to benefit from such investments. Nonetheless, with sufficient investment, energy savings of up to 50% would be feasible, although this would require significant additional investment.

Under the domestic energy scenario, we invest additional resources in the housing stock with the express purpose of applying energy conservation technologies, matching the main investment in the domestic sector by 5% in 2010 through to 20% by 2030 onwards. The knock-on effect of this is to reduce energy consumption per household by 20% by 2050, as these investments trickle through the existing and new housing stocks (*Figure 3A14*). Overall effects on the fossil fuel dependency of the economy are very marginal (*Figure 3A15*).

Industrial energy conservation

Industry and manufacturing is also a large consumer of fossil fuels. Here, the fuels are used to provide a mixture of heating and motive power, as well as cogeneration of electricity. Following the TNO study data, we assume that the returns on energy efficiency investment in manufacturing would be less than with the housing sector, with a maximum reduction of around 10% being achievable. These figures are, again, probably rather cautious, but we present them here in the absence of any other hard data.

The scenario here was defined in an identical fashion to the domestic energy efficiency case, with a ramping up of additional investment to match 20% of the primary investment in the sector by 2030. *Figure 3A14* shows that the reduction per unit of operational stock is much less than for the domestic sector, and *Figure 3A15* confirms that the impact on the national renewables balance is negligible.

Domestic heat pump technologies

An alternative (or complement) to domestic energy efficiency is the use of electrical heating for homes. This makes very little sense when electricity is generated by fossil fuels (up to two thirds of the heat content of the fuels goes up the generator chimney and one third is delivered to the home), but under a predominately renewable energy regime it might make more sense. Rather than looking at systems that convert electrical energy directly into heat, however, we chose to examine heat pump technologies, in which the heat energy generated is extracted from ambient heat gradients in the ground, and the electricity is simply used to access this rather than being the primary source of the heat.

In characterising the technology, we assumed an average thermal efficiency of traditional domestic heating of 80%, and a coefficient of performance of the heat pumps of 25% (i.e. 4 units of electricity, measured in heat energy terms, are required to transfer one unit of heat energy). The example scenario pushes the technology quite aggressively, aiming at 10% penetration of the housing stock by 2010, through to a 50% penetration by 2050. Predictably, this roughly halves the domestic sector intake of fossil fuels (*Figure 3A16*), and increases electricity demand by dwellings significantly (but not by 50%, as a large fraction of this is required to power consumer goods of various sorts as well) - (*Figure 3A17*). Again, we see a mild improvement in the national renewable energy balance (*Figure 3A18*), and leads to an

increase in total renewable electricity generating capacity of 10%.

All of the above

Finally, we adopted all of the above measures at once.
- A large-scale substitution of renewable electricity technologies (wind-powered), with 80% of all new generating capacity being wind.
- Large-scale transition towards electric fuel-cell road transport
- Significant investment in domestic and industrial energy conservation
- Widespread adoption of heat pump technologies for domestic heating

As outlined in *Figure 3A8*, we introduced these both at the magnitudes already examined one-by-one, and then finally at a greater rate, simply in order to see how far we could achieve sustainability by the measures we had focussed upon.

CONCLUSIONS

The Republic of Ireland is capable of making a transition towards sustainability over the next fifty years, owing to a plentiful supply of renewable resources and modest growth prospects. Structural factors such as the decline of current 'dirty' generating technologies, and the quick wins available from a poorly insulated housing stock, also serve to play a part.

While renewable electricity generation can play a major part in this transition, a simple approach aimed only at replacing current fossil-fuel generation of electricity with renewables will have a limited effect. A much greater effect can be had by looking for synergies with other parts of the economy, where electricity-based technologies that would simply be inefficient (in system-wide energy terms) can be brought into play. The more high-tech options considered here, such as car fuel cells and heat transfer pumps, are wasteful of fossil fuel if fed on fossil-generated electricity alone, but can become very useful in widening the circle of influence of a renewable electricity technology. The renewable electricity industry would do well to seek partnerships with developers of such technologies, in our opinion.

The technologies that we have looked at in this study are by no means exhaustive, and a more thorough cataloguing could doubtless achieve even greater gains towards sustainability than we managed in our final scenario. There are other renewable energy technologies, such as wave power, solar-power systems (perhaps less of an opportunity in the Irish climate, but still offering some potential) and biofuels, which can be represented by the ECCO methodology (and have been in other studies). There are many other technologies that may substitute fossil fuel consumption for electricity use, developing fur-

ther synergies with an expanding renewables sector.

As with any modelling study, we have presented a greatly simplified picture of a real economy, and left out much detail. In balance of payments terms, the economy may benefit from technical leadership in renewable technologies, which it is far more likely to develop through early adoption than in the already-saturated market for combined cycle turbines. We have not examined in detail the land-use implications of our policies, what the spread of wind generators across the landscape would look like (and, were we to consider biofuels, this would be an even more important aspect to factor in). We have not discussed nuclear power as an option here, although the model is capable of representing the shorter-term costs and benefits of that technology at least.

Energy Analysis: a primer

Energy analysis is a technique for looking at physical activity within an economy. The main principles were developed in the 1970s following the 1974 oil crisis and a sudden awareness of the importance of fossil fuels in nearly every aspect of our lives (or, at least, our lifestyles). Similar issues look to be coming up again, with the recent debates in the US about whether to open up new oil reserves in environmentally-sensitive areas, and even a reconsideration of nuclear power, long out of favour, as a viable alternative.

The ECCO model uses energy analysis theory as one of its main tools, and many of the variables in the model are expressed in energy terms. This article lays out the fundamental concepts of energy analysis.

In discussing energy analysis, it is important first of all to define energy. Energy is an abstraction, designed to account for the outstanding difference between the initial and final state of a system to which some change has occurred. We call this difference the energy content of the system. Energy exists in several different forms, and, when effecting change to a physical system, will generally shift between these forms. Kinetic energy is energy as applied in moving physical objects. Electromagnetic energy is applied to the vibrating modes of sub-atomic particles, and can be experienced as radio waves, visible light, x-rays, electric current, etc. Potential energy refers to energy stored in some form, capable of being released. A nickel-cadmium battery possesses chemical potential energy, capable of being released as electricity. Finally, heat is a form of energy, the form to which all other types of energy eventually degrade. Energy is governed by a set of physical laws, expressed last century in the discipline of thermodynamics. These are discussed briefly below.

THE FIRST LAW OF THERMODYNAMICS

The First Law of Thermodynamics states that energy can neither be created nor destroyed, within a closed system (defined as a system in which no energy or mass may enter or leave). Energy cannot be thrown away. In applying this law to an economic analysis, we must determine the extent to which the system of study is closed.

For example, the global economy is far from a closed system. There is a significant exchange of both matter and energy between it and the natural world. Even if we treat the economy and environment as a single system, there is a size-able exchange of energy, mainly influx of solar radiation and re-emission of heat to space. Meteorites represent a small, arguably insignificant, transfer of matter between this system and its environment.

At a national level, the system is even more open. That is, the size of the matter and energy transfers is greater, relative to the overall system size. Nonetheless, the First Law contains important consequences for economic systems, providing an absolute physical limit on the availability of energy to a system, and the assimilation of "waste" energy and products. Of course, other more pressing limits, whether physical or social in origin, may impinge more directly on the system, meaning that those imposed by the First Law may not be reached.

THE SECOND LAW OF THERMODYNAMICS

The Second Law of Thermodynamics is more directly concerned with the process of transformation, rather than the natures of the initial and final states. As such, the consequences that it has upon an economic system are more pressing than those of the First Law.

The Second Law raises the question of energy quality. Energy cannot be created or destroyed, but it can be made more, or less, useful. That is, the work (in a rigorous physical sense) that can be done by that energy is more than simply a function of the energy content. In order to be able to discuss this, a second abstraction, called entropy, was developed.

Entropy is a measure of the degree of disorder in a system. For example, salt, with its highly regular lattice arrangement of atoms, has much less entropy than the same salt dissolved in water. A house has less entropy before the roof falls in than after. A marching band has less entropy when all dressed in uniform and marching in time than when relaxing in their homes afterwards. As a system's entropy increases, its degree of order, or information content, will decrease. This will not necessarily alter the energy content of the system, and hence a closed system may undergo changes in entropy content.

The Second Law states that, in effecting any change to a system, the overall level of entropy in the system will always increase. It is only possible to reduce the entropy of any part of a system by effecting a greater increase in the entropy elsewhere. For example, a rotting house may spontaneously collapse, but a reversal of the process (i.e. rebuilding the house) requires an external input of an energy resource, the entropy content of which is increased.

Some of the forms of energy discussed above are more entropic than others (that is, they are less ordered). Of these, heat has the highest entropy, and it is for this reason that all other forms of energy eventually disperse as heat. No transfer of energy is totally efficient, and the "lost" energy is usually dispersed as heat. Labelling the energy as "lost" is simply a value judgement. The energy is not destroyed, but is transformed into a form where it either cannot be, or simply is not, used by the economy. Of course, this distinction is essential in an economic analysis.

Examples of energy "loss" include the heating of machine parts through friction as they rub together, the heating up of electrical transmission wires, or the heat generated by a human, or animal, during physical exertion.

ENERGY QUALITY

It has been calculated that the energy required to heat a bathtub of water from room temperature to 60 Centigrade is equivalent to the work exerted by a lumberjack working for approximately 19.5 hours (Slesser 1978). This comparison is made here in order to highlight the notion of energy quality. The hot bathtub consists of high entropy energy, the lumberjack's work of low entropy energy. Although the lumberjack and bathtub have equivalent energy contents, the lumberjack may use his/her energy to effect a larger amount of work.

Energy quality is reflected in the perceived economic value of the energy. In rugged pioneer country, offering to pay a lumberjack for a long day's work with a bathtub full of hot water would be poorly appreciated. To look at the situation the other way around, though, if one desired a hot bath, one would hardly go about it by hiring a lumberjack to stir the water for 19.5 hours. High quality energy is not necessarily more valuable than low quality energy in the economic context, but, in general, low quality energy is suited to a smaller number of uses.

In all modern economies, the energy exerted by the human workforce is negligible (Slesser 1978). The work equivalent of a lumberjack working for a full day can be purchased in the very high quality form of electricity for about 6 pence. The human workforce, even in "manual" labour, is employed primarily to make decisions rather than for the physical work it actually does.

The bulk of energy utilised by the global economy at present is in the form of three fossil fuels, namely oil, coal and natural gas. The energy qualities (thermodynamic availability) of these three are all very similar. Hence, substitution between them can be calculated accurately with reference only to the energy content. In ECCO this is the "reference energy quality", by which all other energies like electricity (higher quality) or biomass (lower quality) are measured.

For these reasons, a number of practical decisions have been made in the construction of the Irish ECCO model (and other ECCO models). Firstly, fossil fuels are measured solely in terms of energy content, and are assumed to be substitutable (unless explicitly stated otherwise in the model structure). Where we look at substituting fossil fuels and electricity, as in the heat pump or vehicular fuel cell technologies, explicit coefficients for commensurating the two are developed, generally from first principles or the engineering literature.

Secondly, electrical energy is measured separately, and any assumptions made about the substitution between thermal and electrical energy are based on empirical observations, not an equivalence between energy contents. Thirdly, other energy sources, such as nuclear fuels and renewable sources, are treated in terms of fossil fuel equivalents. As these sources are currently used only to generate electricity, that measure is made by equivalencing the inputs required per unit electrical output. These inputs are based on empirical data, i.e. current technological practice. All forms of electricity, generated from whatever source, are, of course, fully substitutable once entered onto the national grid.

These simplifying assumptions present no problem when examining the current technology of energy supply and demand. However, were radical energy policies, involving different qualities of energy carrier, to be explored by the model, the question of energy quality would have to be compiled in terms of the chosen reference qualities mentioned above.

ENERGY VERSUS MONEY AS A NUMERAIRE

Having provided a definition of energy, it is necessary to establish the reasons for adopting it as the numeraire for the ECCO model. After all, most economic statistics use money, and the adoption of an alternative involves a lot of extra work and inconvenience to the model builder.

Money, like energy, is a human invention, an abstraction designed to represent transactions in the messy real world in a neat, symbolic way. Money is an opinion. Or rather two opinions, that of the seller, and that of the buyer. The price of the good is arrived at by a process that "evenly distributes the disappointment", in the language of traditional economics.

Being an opinion, money has two disadvantages. Firstly, it is subject to change over time as a result of different perceptions of the world, which may or may not be grounded in reality. If they are not, then prediction of these perceptions is very difficult, if only because the cultural world is capable of changing much more rapidly than the physical world, and is harder to quantify.

The second disadvantage of money, as an opinion, is that it has no international standard. Each nation sets up its own currency, and the coefficients relating these (the exchange rates) vary considerably, and quickly. Further, money is applied somewhat arbitrarily to work in most modern economies. In an economic model using money as a numeraire, there is no method for accounting for voluntary or unpaid work, such as child-raising and housework, or for work paid in kind (ie work paid for by other work).

Energy is also an abstraction, but one grounded in a more rigorous school of thought. Certainly, more than one unit for energy has enjoyed passing fashion; the calorie has been superseded by the joule over the last twenty or so years. The important distinction, though, is that there are international standards for energy units, due to the precise first-principles methods by which they are defined. Anywhere, at any time, one joule is capable of moving a weight of one Newton by a distance of one metre.

So, the "cost" of goods can be measured by considering the energy that went into their making. Note that this is not a valuation of the good, in that it does not consider the utility of that good to the system. It is simply a measure of the inconvenience that was undergone in the past to create that good, or, more generally, the inconvenience involved in replacing it.

This distinction is perhaps best clarified by illustration. To build an ocean liner would require an energy input of approximately 1.2 PetaJoules using current shipbuilding technologies. In other words, the embodied energy content of the liner would be 1.2 PJ. As a simplifying assumption, let us assume that shipbuilding technology has not altered greatly in the last thirty years, and the estimate of embodied energy is valid over that period.

During the last thirty years, however, air transport has increased in volume, and partially replaced sea transport. Hence, the demand for ocean liners has dropped, and the money-value of the liner has probably dropped too. This decline has not resulted directly from changes in shipbuilding technology, but from wider interactions within the transport sector and in social behaviour.

Hence, the money-value of a good is subject to a wide number of influences. Further, some of these are extremely difficult to quantify. The embodied energy numeraire, in contrast, is relatively unchanging. Thus, for the purposes of the ECCO study, the money numeraire is too unpredictable. For other types of economic analysis, however, this compaction of multiple unknowns into a single value, even through an imperfect market mechanism, may be highly attractive.

Energy, then, is not subject to the wild fluctuations that money experiences. Then again, neither is mass. Why not set up an accounting system based on the mass of goods? The answer lies with the second law of thermodynamics, and a concept known as substitutability. Only through energy can one material be substituted for another. From the second law of thermodynamics it can be seen that as energy is used in the manufacturing process, in other words making something with a lesser degree of entropy than its constituent parts, the entropy of the energy used increases. Thus it cannot be used again: it is non-renewable.

This is not to say that energy is scarce - the solar flux impinging on the Earth's surface currently provides ten thousand times the energy used by all human activities. Were sufficient suitable human-made capital present to exploit this energy, then it would be capable of supplying human needs (or wants) practically indefinitely.

However, because energy use is irreversible, it places a real physical limit on the growth of economic systems, and in using energy as a numeraire we are explicitly facing this. In money-based economics, there is no such limit applied; money can be created by any government capable of operating a printing press. Thus money-based economics fails us in not recognising important, insurmountable limits to economic growth, and energy-based economics does not.

The other important property of energy is that it is unsubstitutable, meaning that no other physical resource is capable of performing the functions currently effected by energy. In this it is unique. Metals can be substituted by plastics or wood, ceramics by glass, etc. And, provided that sufficient energy is available, no other natural resource is ever depleted, it simply increases in entropy. The factors limiting the accessibility of high-entropy resources lie with the ability of the economy to provide the capital and energy supplies needed to access them, not with an insuperable physical limit deriving directly from thermodynamic principles. In other words, the problem lies with distribution of finite capital and energy supply capacity within the economy.

In concluding this section, then, the ECCO methodology is concerned with addressing a particular economic issue, namely how a national or large-scale economy's growth rate is constrained by the physical limitations of its production processes, and how these physical processes underlie much of what we would normally classify as 'economic' factors. The methodology can be usefully applied in a wide variety of contexts, and works best when a narrow sectoral analysis is subsequently broadened out to incorporate linkages with other sectors, as in the case of the renewable energy study presented in this paper. In performing an analysis of these underlying processes, the choice of numeraire is important, as energy-based accounting provides an absolute yardstick that monetary numeraires cannot.

Two numeraires, money and embodied energy, have been examined here, in terms of their ability to express the nature of this problem. The money numeraire is discarded, because of its sensitivity to too many unquantifiable parameters, and its non-conservative nature. Embodied energy, in contrast, is shown to be well suited to this task, given the caveat that energy quality may need to be explicitly introduced in some unusual circumstances.

MODELLING DEPLETABLE RESOURCES

It might be useful to illustrate the application of energy analysis principles to the extraction of depletable energy resources namely oil, gas and coal. The ECCO model uses the same approach to all three. Firstly, it is assumed that a variety of grades of any particular resource exists and that the distribution of grades is log-normal, tailing off at the lower end towards the background level found in the Earth's crust. (With a log-normal distribution, if the cumulative amount of the resource already extracted is plotted on the x-axis of a graph using a linear scale, and the energy input required to extract one unit of the resource is plotted on the y-axis, using a logarithmic scale, a straight line results. This assumes that extraction takes place with the easiest resource first, progressing to the more difficult. Real life isn't always quite so logical, of course, but on the large scale the pattern has been shown to hold up quite well.)

The important characteristic of a natural resource reserve, in terms of the ECCO methodology, is the amount of energy, direct and indirect, that must be expended in extracting the resource from the ground. This aggregate value covers fuel and electricity demands, non-energy resource demands, and fixed capital consumption. In the case of an energy resource, this is known as the Energy Requirement for Energy, or ERE for short. It is expressed in units of energy input per unit energy extracted.

Obviously, the ERE of a resource reserve will depend upon the grade of the resource, in addition to other geological features, such as depth and hardness of covering rock. Because the grade of the reserve is variable, the ERE will also vary. This holds at any scale, from a single oil well to an entire set of fields, to global reserves of a resource. The exact relationship between resource grade and ERE is discussed more fully in Chapman (1983) but, as a simple assumption, we can assume an inverse relationship of some sort. In other words, as resource grade declines, the ERE will rise.

The final assumption made about the process of resource depletion is that the reserve is depleted in strict order of decreasing grade, i.e. highest grade first. This assumes perfect knowledge of the entire resource reserve before depletion commences, which is obviously fallacious. However, any individual discovery of a new high-grade pocket of resources will simply create a kink in the smooth log-normal decrease in grade observed under a "perfect" model, and will not upset the underlying behaviour of the model. The work of Peckham & Klitz (1978 & 1979) does show that the long-term trends described here operate in reality at a national level.

Because the resource grade declines log-normally, we can expect a log-normal increase in the ERE of the reserve, in the absence of technological change. The ERE of reserves can then be set as functions of cumulative extraction, and so will rise over time at a rate dependent on the rate of extraction from the reserve, which will itself depend on the economic policies being enacted.

Note that the above model does not postulate a cut-off point, at which the reserve runs out. Given suitable energy supplies, the reserve can be depleted down to the grade of the base rock. Of course, the economic consequences of securing such a large energy supply may well provide a cut-off point based on economic, rather than geological, constraints.

The above model structure has been compared to the model for land prices postulated by Ricardo, and, indeed, there is a degree of structural similarity. It is important to note the difference, however: Ricardo's increasing price with scarcity of the commodity arose from an increased valuation being placed upon remaining resources by the market, whereas the driver in the depletable resource model is based on physical variations in the Earth's crust.

Technological change, will, of course, alter the ERE of a given reserve, and, conversely, rising ERE may often provide a spur to developing new technologies. An example of this inter-relationship is the development of sub-sea satellite wells in the UK Continental Shelf, which allow small, high-ERE fields adjacent to large, well-developed fields, to be extracted with a significantly reduced capital input. To state things very broadly, technological change will tend to have a similar effect to the discovery of a new reserve pocket; it will create an anomaly in the smooth rise of the ERE curve, but will not alter the underlying behaviour.

Finally, it is worth mentioning the approach taken in the Irish ECCO model to imports of depletable reserves, such as fossil fuels and metals. The above model cannot be applied to global reserves in a national model, because the overall rate of extraction is not calculated at a global level. In this case, time-series data from a global ECCO model, GlobEcco, has been imported into the Irish ECCO model, using a business-as-usual scenario. Hence, it is assumed that domestic activities have no direct effect upon the world "energy price" of depletable resources.

OILWELL EXAMPLE

Suppose that a large reserve of oil is discovered under a house, say 8634 barrels of crude oil. At $20 a barrel, the gross income anticipated is $172,000. Having taken some initial seismic readings, the owners discover that their oil reserve is perfectly cylindrical, with one metre diameter, and is located between 200 and 2200 metres below the ground. There is no gas associated with the oil, so it will be necessary to pump it out of the ground mechanically. This process will require energy. In addition, there will be the cost of buying the pump in the first place, and then the cost of refining the crude output.

Pumping begins, and everything goes well for a few days, then the oil stops coming. As oil is extracted, the level remaining in the well drops, until the remaining oil is too low down for the pump to be able to bring it to the surface. This is remedied by buying a larger, more powerful pump. A side effect of this is that the fuel bill increases; the larger pump requires more energy to bring each barrel of oil to the surface. Say, the small pump required one-fortieth of a barrel of oil per barrel extracted, the larger pump requires one twentieth. It is realised that this larger pump will fail in the future, as the level of oil in the well decreases further. To summarize, there is an energy gain in the form of extracted oil. Energy is spent by the pumps in terms of the fuel required to power them, and the devices for refining the oil. Furthermore, new capital is constantly required, in the form of larger pumps, as the reserves deplete. The manufacture of these pumps required energy; this is the embodied energy content of the machinery. Using the principles of process analysis exact figures can be calculated for the embodied energy, and primary energy (i.e. pump fuel) requirements of the extraction, as a function of the cumulative removal of the oil. By comparing this with the amount of energy extracted, the ERE can be calculated.

As demonstrated above, the ERE of the oil rises as more is extracted. Ultimately the ERE will reach 100%, and the net energy gain from the extraction process will be negative. At this point, the oil well will be physically uneconomic.

In a market economy, of course, the point at which the process becomes uneconomic may arrive earlier. With several wells in operation, all of different shapes, size and levels of extraction, the ones with lower ERE values will be at a competitive advantage, being able to produce their goods at a cheaper energy price. Given sufficient reliable data to calculate the ERE values of different oil-wells or fields it would be possible to predict the economic fates of oil producers without having to discuss (monetary) oil prices, which are subject to considerable fluctuations and uncertainties.

David Crane

REFERENCES

Campbell C (2002) "Limits on Supplies of Conventional Oil" talk given at the Conference Ireland's Transition to Renewable Energy, organised by FEASTA, October 2002

Chapman (1983) *Energy Resources*, London: Heinemann

Crane DC (1996) "Balancing Pollutant Emissions and Economic Growth in a Physically Conservative World" *Ecological Economics* 16: 257-68

Crane DC & Foran B (2000) "Modelling the Transition to a Biofuel Economy in Australia" Proceedings of second international workshop, Advances in Energy Studies: Exploring Supplies, Constraints and Strategies, Porto Venere, May 23-27, 2000: pp.23-39

Forrester JW (1971) *World Dynamics*, Massachusetts: Wright Allen Press.

Forrester JW (1968) *Principles of Systems*, Massachusetts: Wright Allen Press.

IFIAS (1975) Energy Analysis, Report #6 of the International Federation of Institutes for Advanced Studies

Meadows DL & Meadows DH, eds. (1973) *Toward Global Equilibrium: Collected Papers*,
        Massachusetts: Wright Allen Press.

Melman AG, Boot H & Gerritse G (1990) *Energiebesparungspotentielen* – 2015, TNO Eindrapport 90-258, 2nd. edition
        April 1991, Institut voor Milieu- en Energietechnologie (IMET)TNO

Peckham, R. & Klitz, K.,(1978) *Energy Requirement of Scottish Offshore Oil*,
    Research Paper EUR 6062 EN, EU Joint Research Centre, Ispra.

Prigogine N & Stengers I (1984) *Order out of Chaos: Man's New Dialogue with Nature,* London: Heinemann

Slesser, M. (1978) *Energy in the economy*, London: Macmillan.

Slesser M & King J (1993) "Can Solar Energy substitute for Oil? A natural capital accounting approach"
    Opec Review XVII, 3: 377-98

Slesser M., King J. & Crane D.C. (1997) *The Management of Greed: A Bio-Physical Appraisal of Environmental and
    Economic Potential*, Edinburgh: RUI Publishing

Slesser, M. King, J., Revie, C and Crane, D. (1994) Non-monetary indicators for managing sustainability. Contract report
    to DG XII of the European Community, Centre for Human Ecology, University of Edinburgh, Scotland

WEB SITES & SIMULATION SOFTWARE

In addition to the conventional citations above, some resources used to develop the model, and pertaining to the model, are located on the internet. These are listed separately below.

http://www.eirestat.cso.ie Central Statistics Office, Ireland website, from which a wide range of economic data can be downloaded in spreadsheet-readable format

http://www.irl.gov.ie/tec/energy/statistics/ Dept. of Public Enterprise website, from which most of the energy data used to calibrate the model was originated.

http://www.eccosim.org.uk ECCO model website, containing further essays and resources regarding the ECCO model, and an experimental online simulator for a model of the UK. The simulation software is in active development as part of the 'Uncle Unc' software project at http://uncleunc.sourceforge.net. (The main purpose of Uncle Unc has relatively little to do with simulation models, and the connection to the ECCO models might not be obvious at first glance. Contact Dave Crane <dave@cranefamily.f9.co.uk> if clarification is required.

ECCO model available

Those readers who would like to project Ireland's energy future on different assumptions to tho used here may purchase the complete software from the Feasta office, 159, Lower Rathmir Road, Dublin 6. The price is 20 euros or £15 sterling. A user-group has been set up and purchase will be able to download improvements to the software from the internet.

ECCO models used around the world

The early roots of the ECCO model lie in the energy crises of the 1970s and the growth of energy analysis as a discipline. The first simple computer model was developed in 1978 by Ian Hounam and Malcolm Slesser at the Systems Analysis Division of Euratom, Italy. Slesser continued to develop the methodology at Edinburgh University's Centre for Human Ecology with Jane King, collaborating with local researchers on small-scale models of Kenya and Mauritius.

In the 1990s, the EU funded a small team at Edinburgh to build models of the UK and the European Union in collaboration with partner institutes in France, Spain, Germany and Finland. At the same time, the University of Groningen's Centre for Energy and the Environment adopted the modelling approach, as did the University of Canterbury in New Zealand, and doctoral theses on the model were completed at Groningen, Canterbury and Edinburgh.

In 1995, Barney Foran of the Australian organisation CSIRO undertook a study tour in Europe and America in preparation for a large 'Resource Futures' research programme. After meeting the Edinburgh ECCO team, he opted to use ECCO as one of the key modelling techniques for his programme and the Australian ECCO model has continued to be developed over the last eight years, initially with the University of Edinburgh, and latterly with Dr. Crane's Sunwheel Technologies Ltd.

As a result, the Australian model has expanded to cover an increasing range of issues, as the Irish model may do over future iterations. The model was able to examine the broader consequences of sectoral policy issues, providing deeper insights than a static or linear analytical exercise could offer. Recent enhancements to 'OzEcco' include a comprehensive transport fuels module covering ethanol-and methanol-powered vehicles. According to a study [1] Crane and Foran carried out in 2000:

• Within 50 years the Australian demand for transport fuel could be met by covering 30 million hectares (74.1 million acres) of the country's cropland and high rainfall pasture zones with tree plantations.

• Using methanol would reduce carbon dioxide emissions by 400 million tonnes a year compared to continuing 'business as usual' scenario

• Planting deep-rooted trees would also help control problems such as dryland salinity, create employment in rural Australia and help replace future energy imports

• A 'methanol economy' would lead to the generation of 100,000 direct jobs by 2020 and more than 400,000 by 2050. Most of these jobs would be in rural areas of Australia

• Total savings on energy imports by 2050 were estimated at $18 billion in today's currency, if oil is priced at US$25 a barrel

Methanol would be produced from the biomass of forests growing under a 20-year rotation at a rate of 20 cubic meters a year. Plantations would need to be established at the rate of 400,000 hectares (988,000 acres) a year costing about $2,500 a hectare. The cost of a biomass electricity plant was assumed to be about one and half times the cost of a traditional electricity plant on a megawatt basis. Overall, the study showed that a methanol economy would 'decarbonize' economic growth in Australia while simultaneously helping restore its degraded land and its marginalised local economies.

The model's business-as-usual scenario assumed that the Australian population grew to 25 million by 2050, that food exports were maintained at current levels, and that renewable energy and more efficient electricity production continued to be implemented to reflect government policies on greenhouse gas emissions.

David Crane writes: "The ECCO model offers a cross-sectoral analysis which is vital to identify synergies and the potential for 'win-win' policy options. It can't tell us whether we are ready for radical social, political and microeconomic changes. Nonetheless, by validating visions from a 'top-down' perspective, the model can play a vital role in the process of effecting real change towards sustainability."

1] Foran BD & Crane DC (2000) "Modelling the Transition to a Biofuel Economy in Australia" in Ulgiati S et al. (eds) Proceedings of the 2nd International Workshop on Advances in Energy Studies: Exploring Supplies, Constraints and Strategies, Porto Venere, Italy, May 23-27 2000, pp 423-439.

Part Four
EU policies and energy security

EU policies are likely to play the key role in determining the pace and extent of Ireland's transition to renewable energy and the technologies used. However, the next Irish presidency could help shape those policies, particularly on transport fuel.

A. The European Union's support for renewable energy
   by **Nuala Ahern**

B. EU policy and the development of renewable energy technologies
   by **Andrew Gouldson**

C. The risks of oil supply disruption for the transport sector
   by **Dan Plesch**

The European Union's support for renewable energy

by Nuala Ahern MEP

*Although the EU has promoted renewable energy sources, it has failed
so far to ensure that energy markets take into account the cost of the
environmental damage caused by the use of fossil fuels and nuclear
energy. Renewables would be fully competitive if this was done.*

The European Union doesn't have a single
energy policy, but rather a series of communications, white and green papers and directives
which when patched together form a less-than-
coherent series of policy measures in the energy field. This is somewhat ironic as the EU was
largely formed out of the desire by countries to
support their energy industries. Of the three
founding treaties of the EU, two related to supporting energy industries. In 1952, the
European Coal and Steel Community agreement was signed to support the development of
these two industries for fifty years - and in July
2002 ceased to exist. In 1957 the treaty establishing the European Atomic Energy
Community (Euratom) was signed, which will
run indefinitely, explicitly promoting nuclear
technology.

Following the 1997 Amsterdam Treaty that
established the requirement for Community
policy to 'contribute to sustainable development' the EU's energy policy is said to be based
on three core objectives. These are[1]

• **Security of supply.** This aims to minimise the
risks and impacts of possible supply disruptions
on the EU economy and society.

• **Competitive energy systems** - to ensure low
cost energy for producers and consumers to
contribute to industrial competitiveness and
wider social policy objectives.

• **Environmental protection.** This is integrated

in both energy production and energy use to
maintain ecological and geophysical balances
in nature.

Let's look at the way renewables are treated in
relation to each of these core objectives.

1. SECURITY OF SUPPLY

In November 2000 the Commission published
its Green Paper on Security of Supply[2]. A public consultation process followed its release and
lasted until February 2002. The Commission
was initially expected to prepare a white paper
or a directive based on the original documentation and the comments received but in mid-
September 2002 it published two new directives
designed to reduce the insecurities for energy
supplies in the oil and gas industries.[3] The purpose of these directives is to propose specific
measures in the framework of a liberalised
energy market, particularly by increasing the
quantity of fuel mandated to be kept in stocks.
In the case of oil this will increase from 90 to
120 days, for natural gas to set a new requirement of 60 days supply for an average bad
weather period.

The November 2000 Green Paper states clearly
that renewable energy has a vital role to play in
reducing the EU's dependency on third countries for their energy. It says:

*With regard to supply, priority must be given to
the fight against global warming. The develop-*

ment of new and renewable energies (including biofuels) is the key to change.[4] *Only technology-intensive renewable sources can help mitigate the present trend towards increasing energy dependency.* [5]

Despite this, the Green Paper merely calls for member states to give a 'firm commitment'[6] to achieve the 'realistic' objectives of the 1997 White Paper on Renewable Energies. It is important to note that the Green Paper was published before a final decision was taken on the 2001 Directive on Renewable Energy and thus undermined attempts to have the White Paper targets made mandatory. At the request of the Council, but clearly with the support of the Commission and against the desires of the Parliament, the White Paper targets were not mandatory in the Directive on Renewable Energy. So, while the Green Paper points out renewables are fundamental for the future energy supply of the Union, it fails to call for these targets to be mandatory.

2. COMPETITION

In January 2003 the Council came to a Common Position for the two security of supply directives. The European Parliament has begun discussions on these and is expected to conclude its work in May 2003.

When the draft directive were read for the first time in the Parliament, the Green/EFA group made a number of key recommendations. These were intended to accelerate the introduction of renewables by creating a level playing field for generators. The key recommendations were:

• **Priority access for renewables:** The current Directive on renewable energy states that priority access may be given to electricity produced by renewable energy sources. This must be changed to *require* priority access for renewables.

• **Electricity Labelling:** Companies should be required to include information about the mix of fuels they use to produce the electricity they sell and the environmental impact of these fuels on their advertising and all bills to their customers.

• **Planning Applications:** Smaller power plants should not be subject to the same planning applications as much larger stations. The environmental impact, actual and potential, of a 1000 MW nuclear power stations is clearly larger than the installation of a handful of wind turbines. The Group therefore proposed that generators under 50 MW should have access to an accelerated planning process.

• **Grid Pricing:** Because there is excess generating capacity in the EU, long-established conventional generators often see renewables and cogeneration projects as being in competition with their existing or planned production. These generators often influence grid companies with whom they may be linked financially to discriminate against the new players. For example in France even producers of low voltage electricity which is not passed through the grid at all have to pay a standard fee as if it were.

The Group's rapporteur therefore proposed that all financial links between grid operators and generators should be prohibited, that statutory regulators should have greater powers to set prices for the use of the grid and that grid system operators should be required to take account of the economic advantages of embedded generators.

Many of these proposals were accepted by the Parliament but we now have to wait and see the extent to which the Council will adopt them too. However, even at this stage it is clear that most of the Parliament's language will be dropped or significantly watered down.

3. ENVIRONMENTAL PROTECTION.

In 2001 the Community finally adopted the Electricity Production from Renewable Energy Sources (RES) Directive. The primary justification for the directive is the need to promote renewable energy sources as a priority measure given that their exploitation contributes to environmental protection and sustainable development. However, rather than the mandatory targets requested by the Parliament and NGOs, the directive only has indicative targets of 12% of energy to be produced by renewable sources by 2010 -including a target of 22% of electricity. These targets translate into the indicative national requirements shown in figure 4A1, which were determined by the present level of renewable energy sources within each country's current energy mix.

Besides the lack of binding targets, critics point to the inclusion of incineration of wastes as a renewable energy source as a major loophole and an environmental problem in the directive. Member states have to transpose the directive into national legislation during 2003.

ENERGY FUNDING

The major mechanism for EU funded research and development is through the Framework programme. Figure 4A2 shows that nuclear, fission and fusion, research has remained relatively constant in recent programmes, while conventional energy has seen a decline of 20%. As a result, *nuclear technology receives 50% more research funding that all other energy sources combined.*

(FIGURE 4A1) GREEN ELECTRICITY PRODUCTION AND TARGETS IN EU			
	RES-Electricity TWh 1997	RES-Electricity % 1997	RES-Electricity % 2010
Austria	39.05	70.0	78.1
Belgium	0.86	1.1	6.0
Denmark	3.21	8.7	29.0
Finland	19.03	24.7	31.5
France	66.00	15.0	21.0
Germany	24.91	4.5	12.5
Greece	3.94	8.6	20.1
Ireland	0.84	3.6	13.2
Italy	46.46	16.0	25.0
Luxembourg	0.14	2.1	5.7
Netherlands	3.45	3.5	9.0
Portugal	14.30	38.5	39.0
Spain	37.15	19.9	29.4
Sweden	72.03	49.1	60.0
United Kingdom	7.04	1.7	10.0
European Union	338.41	13.9%	22%

Ireland's below-average target for Energy Electricity from Renewable Sources (RES)

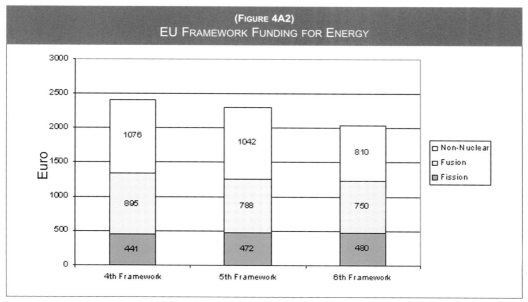

The shrinking amount of funds for non-nuclear energy research

The €810 million provided for non-nuclear research in the 6th Framework Programme covers:

1. In the short and medium term:

• The main new and renewable energy sources and their connection into the grid system
• Alternative motor fuels
• Energy saving and energy efficiency, particularly in buildings

2. For the medium and longer term:

• Fuel cells including applications for transport and for stationary use
• Technologies for hydrogen as an energy carrier and storage system
• New and advanced concepts for photovoltaic energy and the advanced use of biomass
• Disposal of the CO_2 produced by fossil fuel plants.
The framework programme is not the only mechanism for EU financial support for energy

research. The figure 4A2 above is a snapshot of funding in 1996 for energy research. From this it is clear to see how little funding renewables actually get in relation to all other programmes. The only line dedicated to the development of renewable energy is the Altener programme, while the Synergy, Joule and JRC have also co-funded some research. Furthermore, Phare and Tacis programmes have also funded some research into renewables, but only as a small percentage of their total work, with most once again going to nuclear technology.

ONGOING SUBSIDIES FOR THE NUCLEAR INDUSTRY

Despite the European Commission and Council both stating that they want to create a level playing field in the energy sector, nuclear power continues to get significant state subsidies that distort the electricity market. Apart from tax exemptions on the cost of nuclear fuel, these are in two main areas:

	(Figure 4A3) Total European Union Energy Programme Funds for 1996 (MECU)				
Area	Programme	Grants	Loan	Credit Guarantees	
Policy Action	THERMIE	141			
	SAVE	9			
	ALTENER	8			
	SYNERGY	9			
Research and Development	JOULE	116			
	Nuclear fission	43			
	Nuclear Fusion	212			
	Joint Research Centre	78			
	INCO	7			
International Co-operation	PHARE	53			
	TACIS	138			
	Asia	7			
	Latin America	8			
Trans-European Networks	TENS	22			
Structural Operations	Community Support Frameworks	416			
	Community Initiatives (REGEN/REGIS)	89			
ECSC Support	Research, Readjustment, social measures	112			
European Investment Bank	European Union		4975		
	Third Countries		702.4		
ECSC			97.3		
European Investment Fund Guarantees	European Union			88	
	Third Countries			182	
Total		1468	5774.7	270	

1. **Nuclear liability:** Operators of nuclear plants have their maximum liability for the damage done by nuclear accidents limited under the Paris and Vienna Conventions. In some cases the nuclear facilities are insured for more than the operator would ever have to pay out. As the cost of a large-scale release of radiation in Western Europe could run into trillions of Euro, not having to insure against such an eventuality is a considerable saving. It has been calculated that the liability ceiling saves German operators between 0.0003 and 0.022 EUR/kWh.

2. **Nuclear waste:** Although nuclear power companies are required to put aside funds to pay for the decommissioning of their reactors and the management of the waste from them, many are failing to put aside enough. For example British Energy, a private company, puts aside nothing to cover the first and second stages of decommissioning, the shutting down of the reactors, the removal of the fuel and making safety the facility for 70-100 years. Only the third stage, the dismantling of its reactors is funded. In other member states including Germany the nuclear industry receives special tax exemptions - or a reduction in the level of tax - for their nuclear waste and decommissioning funds.

LEGAL CHANGES

The scope that governments have for supporting the greater use of renewables has recently been increased by two rulings from the European Court of Justice. These were:

Decision on Environmental Protection: On 18 March 2001 the European Court of Justice stated that the protection of the environment is a valid reason for taking action within the market. This decision has been used to justify the laws allowing renewable energy to be fed into the grid on favourable terms in some member states.

Decision on Public Procurement: On 17 September 2002, the European Court confirmed the need for the EU to amend its public procurement directive to take into account the Amsterdam Treaty and allow public authorities

to take social, environmental and fair trade criteria into consideration when awarding public procurement contracts. This decision opens the door for public bodies to choose energy suppliers on criteria other than price, thus allowing them to purchase more renewable energy.

CONSEQUENCES

The growth of wind power has been constantly increasing in the EU over the last decade, with the installed capacity rising from 629 MW in 1991 to 17,319MW in 2001. The graph 4A4 demonstrates this increase.

Other renewables, especially biomass, have not fared nearly so well while solar and wave power have yet to compete commercially with conventional power sources, particularly natural gas. The graph 4A5 shows the extent to which natural gas dominates new construction .

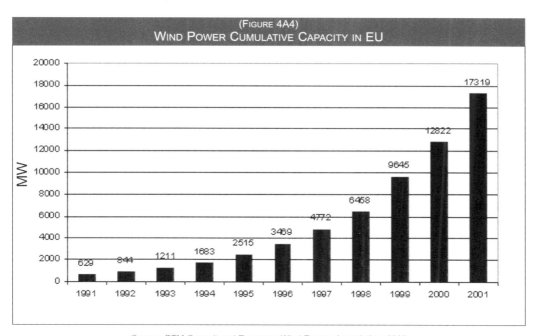

(FIGURE 4A4)
WIND POWER CUMULATIVE CAPACITY IN EU

Source: BTM Consult and European Wind Energy Association, 2002

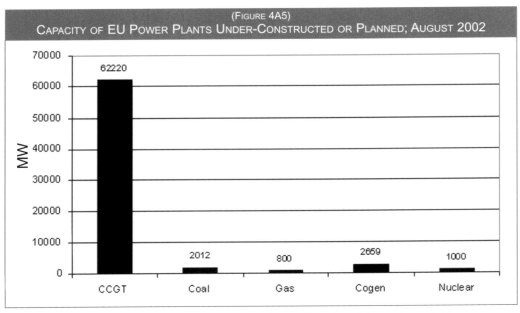

CCGT stands for Combined Cycle Gas Turbine. Source: Platts; Power in Europe August 2002.

There is currently 62 GW of new combined cycle gas turbine power plants being built or under active consideration.

Wind power is runner-up to CCGT with approximately 4500 MW of capacity being built each year. It is hard to compare this figure with those in the graph as the graph shows stations on order or under construction, a process which can take between two and ten years. Even so, wind power is now the second most important choice for new electricity capacity and given the ever-increasing dominance of natural gas power stations, it is essential to try and increase the diversity of electricity sources

WHAT NEEDS TO BE DONE?

Step 1: Member states need to transcribe the Renewable Energy Sources Directive into national law as quickly as possible.

Step 2: The Commission and member states must act to ensure that all member states meet the targets included in the Renewable Energy Sources Directive.

Step 3: Assessments must be taken on how the EU can meet medium and long-term targets for the widespread introduction of renewables, and targets set for renewable energy in 2020 and 2030, especially for the transport sector.

Step 4: The research priorities and their associated budgets laid down in the 6th Framework Programme must not be repeated. In particular, funds earmarked for fission and fusion research should be dramatically cut and the savings switched to renewable energy sources and energy efficiency. This would require the abandonment of Euratom's own Framework programme, but this, along with the general reform of Euratom, is long overdue and should be carried out by 2007, the 50th anniversary of the founding of the Euratom Treaty, at the latest.

Step 5: Widespread support should be given to the EU's campaign to enable renewable energy technologies to take off by promoting the installation of 1,000,000 photovoltaic systems; 15,000,000 square metres of solar collectors; 10,000 MW of wind turbine generators; 10,000 MWth of combined heat and power biomass installations; 1,000,000 dwellings heated by biomass; 1,000 MW of biogas installations; 5 million tonnes of liquid biofuels per year and a hundred communities aiming to meet all their energy needs from renewable sources.

Step 6: 'Green' the Electricity Directive to provide priority market access for renewable energy sources generated electricity, accelerated authorisation for small power stations and a level playing field for embedded generators.

Step 7: Ensure that electricity bills specify the source of the electricity supplied so that consumers can choose their electricity supplier on factors other than cost.

THE WAY FORWARD FOR THE EU AND SUSTAINABLE ENERGY

Fossil fuel use has to be reduced drastically over the next fifty years and nuclear power cannot take up the slack as it is not sustainable. A bad accident would have a devastating effect on the environment and human life and more reactors would create an insoluable waste problem for future generations. Renewable energy therefore needs at least as much investment as the nuclear industry has had over the past fifty years, which amounts to billions of Euro. This level of investment is not happening and yet nuclear energy continues to be heavily - even covertly - subsidised.

Although the EU has promoted renewable ener-

gy sources, their present use is limited because energy markets do not take into account the cost of the environmental damage caused by the use of fossil fuels and nuclear energy. The cost of this damage should be reflected in the price of power and this internalisation of external costs should also extend to the transport system. Currently transport is relatively cheap because the environmental costs it imposes are not included in the price the customer pays. As a result, too many goods are being carried about. People in the alpine regions have strongly objected to the environmental damage caused by trucks carrying goods through their region from south to north Europe and *vice versa*.

If we internalise external costs we can develop renewables through market mechanisms and they will be competitive - particularly wind energy in Ireland. Global warming is already the probable cause of very substantial damage such as the floods in central Europe this summer. In Prague alone transport infrastructure was destroyed and will need to be rebuilt, and the UK is experiencing increased wind and flood damage. All this leads to huge insurance costs.

CREATING A SUSTAINABLE IRELAND

In Ireland we have had rapid growth in the last decade. Car use has risen by over 50%, there has been a huge increase in electricity demand and CO_2 emissions are up by more than 30%. We are not a sustainable society and we cannot continue in this mode. Already Dublin is spreading out into Meath, Kildare, Wicklow and Louth and we look like having all the problems of the city the size of Los Angeles without its benefits.

It is not sustainable to keep moving people further and further from their work place in order to find an affordable place to live and at the same time provide no public transport infrastructure. All this apart from the level of growth was foreseen in the early 90s and yet very little was done. Indeed, the Dublin Transport Initiative was stifled by vested interests in the Dublin Chamber of Commerce for more than five years. If the Luas had been given the go-ahead five years earlier we would have had it by now.

Ireland can move towards sustainability if we take decisions and implement them. We need to use massively more renewable energy, stop using peat-fired power stations, transform the public transport system, and implement the hydrogen economy.

ENDNOTES

1. Energy in Europe, Economic Foundations for Energy Policy, The Shared Analysis Project, December 1999, European Commission, ISBN 92-828-7529-6, page 8.

2. Towards a European Strategy for the Security of Energy Supply, Green Paper, 29th November 2000, Com (2000) 769.

3. http://www.europa.eu.int/comm/energy/home/internal_market/oil_gaz/index_en.htm

4. Green Paper, page 5

5. Green Paper, page 22

6. Green Paper page 49

Europe Reaches Agreement on Energy Tax Framework

BRUSSELS, Belgium, March 21, 2003 (ENS) - Finance ministers from across the European Union have finally reached political agreement on a proposed common framework for energy taxation, six years almost to the day after the plan was first put forward by the European Commission, the EU's legislative branch.

The framework is seen as a key element in the EU's climate change policies. But its influence will be felt only in the medium to long term as minimum EU tax rates have been watered down in the six years since the Commission's initial proposal. In addition the draft law is now larded with derogations and transition periods for various countries and economic sectors.

Under current European Union law, only petroleum derived products are subject to minimum tax rates across the bloc, and these have not been upgraded since 1992. The draft energy taxation law will extend this framework to include coal, natural gas and electricity while raising existing minimum rates for oil products.

Harmonized minimum tax rates should reduce distortions of competition between European Union states and between energy products.

The proposal's environmental policy significance is that it provides a basis for the European Union collectively to raise energy prices over time, thus increasing incentives for more efficient usage.

An agreement on EU wide minimum energy tax levels was originally scheduled to be reached by the end of 2002. But conflicting demands from a number of countries caused a series of postponements in the early weeks of this year.

Earlier this month, Italy emerged as a final hurdle to overcome, as it blocked the agreement on the grounds that it would harm its truckers' competitiveness and sought tax breaks on fuel for Italian truckers. Yesterday, Italy rallied to the agreement by accepting a phase out of special consideration for truckers by 2005.

At last, ministers reached agreement after Austria withdrew a last minute attempt to prevent energy intensive industries from being exempted from minimum tax rates.

Despite repeated haggling by ministers in recent months, the eventual agreement is very similar to proposals made by the then Spanish EU presidency in May 2002.

At that time, EU Internal Market Commissioner Frits Bolkestein compared the proposals to cheese "with too many holes." Though the number is now even larger, Bolkestein today bowed to political reality and declared himself "delighted" with the agreement, which he said would have "immeasurable" benefits for the environment and transport.

The ministerial deal must be scrutinized by the European Parliament before it can be formally adopted. However, Members of the European Parliament have only consultative powers on the law, as with all tax measures, making the agreement virtually final.

EU policy and the development of renewable energy technologies

by Andy Gouldson

*Ideal policies to promote renewable energy development in the EU
are not yet in place. The Renewables Directive was only agreed
after many compromises and national interests might blunt its
effect. It is, however, a significant achievement*

In practice, policymaking rarely, if ever, conforms to the rational ideal. One of the many reasons for this is that there are often competing rationalities that make it difficult or even impossible to identify what the 'ideal' would be. Different actors with competing objectives have contrasting views. What is good for society at large need not be good for each of the individual actors within that society. Although in theory governments should act on behalf of the wider public interest, in many instances if they wish to adopt new policies they must either confront or compensate those actors that benefit from the *status quo.*

Even when there are a relatively small number of competing interests, policymaking necessarily involves contestation and compromise and the nature of these compromises depends on the relative power of the winners and losers. When the definite costs of change are imposed on actors who are powerful in the here and now, while the prospective benefits will be secured by actors who might become powerful in the future, there is an in-built bias towards the *status quo.* In the case of environmental policy there is the extra issue that while many of the costs associated with environmental policy are relatively easy to measure in monetary terms, many of the diffuse and often rather intangible social and environmental benefits are not easily monetised.

A second reason for departures from the ideal is that governments commonly operate under conditions of 'bounded rationality'. When surveying the options that are open to them, they rarely have the time, the resources or the expertise needed to conduct a comprehensive analysis of the numerous ways with which they could achieve their objectives. Instead, they have to muddle through, often taking satisfactory rather than optimal decisions. Furthermore, when deciding how to progress, they very rarely start with a blank sheet of paper. Instead, they normally inherit various habits and traditions, as well as the institutions that emerged to support previous policies. Because decision makers are often risk-averse, they may stick with an approach that has worked (or at least not failed) in the past instead of trying to adopt something that might be better but that also might fail. As a result, many of the more radical opportunities that could only work if policy-makers were able to create new institutions and if they took a risk are commonly overlooked. Instead, policy tends to evolve gradually, often through a series of small and frustratingly slow steps.

A third reason is that while some issues can be addressed within a single sphere of policy, many issues can only be addressed through a complex multi-sectoral and multi-level approach that is inherently difficult to coordinate. The need for a multi-sectoral approach is particularly evident in the environmental field as environmental policymakers are commonly required to respond to the negative after effects of other policies (c.f. agriculture, transport etc.). Joined-up thinking is therefore required; but this would require increased environmental awareness and a change of culture across the different spheres of government.

Fourthly, despite the focus on governments making policy, it is probably more accurate to say that while policies are *designed* by governments, they are not really *made* until they are interpreted and applied by implementing agencies. Particularly in the context of the EU where subsidiarity is such an important principle, this means that all of the organisations and individuals that are involved in the transposition, implementation and enforcement processes are able to influence the practical substance of policy. These actors may or may not subscribe to the central objectives of the policy in question, and even if they do they have a considerable amount of discretionary room for manoeuvre. Furthermore, there is an obvious and critically important role for local and national inputs to the policy process. Bottom-up approaches to policy development with all of the diversity that they bring are at least as important as top-down approaches, and as a consequence harmonisation on paper does not necessarily equate to harmonisation in practice.

Finally, many policies have a long shelf life, information on their performance is often scarce and the opportunities for policy learning are commonly limited. *Ex-post* evaluations of policy performance are quite difficult to conduct, not least because it is difficult to isolate the influence of the policy in question from that of the wide range of other factors that combine to shape behaviour or performance on the ground. As a result, sub-optimal policies often remain in place for some time, especially if they are not so much failing as mildly under-per-

forming. The maxim of if it's not broke, don't fix it is as true for policy-makers with limited time and attention as it is for everyone else.

THE INFLUENCE OF POLICY ON TECHNOLOGICAL CHANGE

To compound these problems, there are real questions about the ability of government to influence technological change processes. Two contrasting viewpoints are significant here. One very economic perspective is that if governments and markets get the costs and benefits right, rational and responsive actors will quickly change their behaviour to suit. The other more institutional perspective suggests that actors are nowhere near as responsive as the economic perspective implies. Instead, they are deeply embedded in existing trajectories, and while there may be moments when they are open to influence, for long periods they are actually quite resistant to change.

More fundamentally, the institutional perspective suggests that technological change processes are unpredictable and often unmanageable. Instead of being omnipotent, therefore, governments are often confined to a role where they can only react to the technological changes brought about, for example, through globalisation. As a result, in many instances governments can exert only a marginal rather than a defining influence on the pace or the direction of technological change.

Again the reasons for such observations are manifold. However, two or three theoretical observations can help us to understand the reasons why technological processes may be resistant to government influence.

Firstly, the right conditions have to be in place if policy is to trigger an innovative response. As in every market, successful outcomes only emerge where the supply of new technologies is matched by demand for those technologies. The supply of innovation is dependent upon the technological opportunities, market structure and the ability of the innovator to appropriate a proportion of the benefits associated with the innovation (see Dosi, 1988). Similarly, the demand for innovation is dependent upon the price and quality of the innovation, the transfer of knowledge and information relating to an innovation and the perceptions of economic risk and uncertainty associated with the application of that innovation (see Kemp and Soete, 1992). In order for supply to meet demand, we need networks that facilitate the transfer of information and understanding between the actors at various stages of the innovation process. Where information flows freely, interactive learning between actors at different stages can facilitate a cumulative and self-reinforcing process of innovation. The consequence of this is that systems that have been innovative in the past are more likely to be innovative in the future. While this can be good for some sectors or regions, it can be very difficult to encourage technological change in contexts that have not been innovative in the past. Overcoming this threshold can require substantial and sustained investment.

Secondly, new innovations depend upon a system or network of relations without which their adoption would be impossible. The introduction of a new innovation into one part of an existing system may require changes to be made to other parts of the system. Considerable resistance and inertia may be apparent in this respect. For example, firms (and indeed sectors, regions and countries) that have successfully mastered the operation of old technologies and techniques commonly face difficulties in acquiring the new skills and knowledge needed to successfully apply new technologies and techniques (OECD, 1992). Consequently, innovations that require only incremental change to existing systems are

more likely to be adopted than those that require more radical change. As a result, change becomes path-dependent and significant barriers to radical change emerge even where there is both a supply of raw technologies and a latent demand for them.

Thirdly, there is an inherent paradox that lies at the heart of the technological change process: in their early stages, new technologies will not be adopted because they are costly to produce and risky to use, but the only way in which their costs of production and the risks of their adoption fall is if they are more widely adopted (OECD, 1992). However, where initial reluctance can be overcome, there can be increasing returns to adoption (see Kemp, 1993; Soete and Arundel, 1995). On the supply-side, the diffusion of a new technology is normally associated with improvements in its quality as experience with its production accumulates and reductions in its cost as economies of scale are exploited. On the demand side, as the innovation is adopted, users learn to apply it more efficiently and effectively and establish or adapt an appropriate system to surround the innovation. Over time therefore, the cost of the innovation drops and the quality increases. Furthermore, the information and knowledge gathered by actual users can be transferred to potential users so that the risks of adoption decrease. An increased community of users can also facilitate joint problem solving, cumulative learning and the establishment of a supporting infrastructure. In combination, these factors mean that first-movers need to be encouraged to adopt new technologies as second and third movers will then benefit from lower costs, reduced risk and higher quality.

Thus, we can see that if new technologies are to be adopted, the right conditions have to be in place on the ground and the incentives have to be strong enough to overcome initial inertia. These factors become more and more significant where the technologies to be adopted are radically different from their predecessors. However, as has been established, as policy makers may not be in a position to put the best policy framework in place to enable this to happen, significant barriers to change may remain.

THE IDEAL POLICY FRAMEWORK

In view of all this, if someone were to design the optimal policy framework to promote the development and diffusion of renewable energy technologies, what would it look like? Within the EU there are clearly different perspectives, and policy must be developed and enacted at levels ranging from the EU to the local. However, in theory at least, most would agree that an optimal policy framework would include some common components:

1) Where they needed to intervene, policy makers could do so safe in the knowledge that the competitive implications of their interventions would be minimal as their major competitors would adopt similar goals.

2) There would be ready access to investment resources at both the macro- and the micro-levels that would allow any short-term costs to be more than offset by medium-term benefits. The overall level of the benefits would also be enough to compensate any losers whilst still leaving society as a whole better off.

3) There would be a broad and stable consensus amongst different actors and at different levels (EU, member state, regional, local) both on the ultimate objectives for policy and on the ways in which these would be achieved. Unambiguous goals would be clearly communicated to give consistent and predictable long-term signals to the market place.

4) There would be an integrated or joined-up approach that spanned the boundaries between different areas of policy. Policies in areas as diverse as energy, environment, agriculture, transport, tax and competition would all be pulling in the same direction.

5) Different policy instruments would be applied which would both encourage and enable change. These instruments, which would include mandatory targets, economic instruments, information-based approaches, capacity building measures and support for basic R&D, would be applied in concert within a complementary policy mix.

6) There would be perfect implementation so that the range of policies and instruments adopted were applied as intended at the national, regional and local levels.

7) There would be enough flexibility in the system to allow implementing agencies to take into account the variable conditions encountered by different technologies and by diverse actors operating in contexts that change over time and space.

8) Markets would serve to reinforce government policies. External costs and benefits would be internalised so that social and environmental impacts were accurately reflected in economic transactions and there would be perfect information to inform voter and consumer behaviour.

9) Actors on the ground would understand, support and have the capacity to respond to the wide range of signals from government, from the market and from society at large.

10) Infrastructure would also be flexible enough to accommodate the needs of new renewable energy technologies.

Even a basic understanding of the political realities of life in the EU, as well as of the administrative contexts within which policies are made and implemented and of the economic contexts within which target actors must respond, suggests that such a 'rational ideal' is unlikely to be grounded in reality. Of course this is not to say that policy makers should not seek to identify the ideal and then work towards it, merely to point out that in practice there are lots of barriers to be overcome before this can happen. In an acknowledgement of these barriers, more and more commentators are emphasising the significance of 'multi-level governance' in the EU, where action depends on not on the top-down imposition of policy but on diverse actors at different levels actively 'buying-in' to the objectives of policy.

EU POLICIES ON RENEWABLES

Now that we have set up an ideal and explored the reasons why it may not be realised in practice, we are in a position to examine the extent to which EU policies are likely to promote the further development and diffusion of renewable energy technologies. While many other policies also play an important role, two key policy documents will be assessed here: first, the EU White Paper for a Community Strategy and Action Plan on Renewable Energy Sources which was published in 1997, second, the EU directive on the Promotion of Electricity Produced from Renewable Sources which was adopted in 2001. By examining these policy documents, the paper will be able to review the factors shaping the evolution of EU policies on renewables over the last five years or so. By examining the European Environment Agency's report on 'Renewable Energies: Success Stories' (2001) the paper can also speculate about the future of EU support for renewables.

In 1996, the European Commission first mooted its intention to double the contribution that renewables made to energy generation to 12% by 2010. As the 'business as normal' scenario was predicted to lead to renewables growing from 6% to 7.7% of the market, the Commission surveyed best practice in the member states and predicted that if these national examples of good policy were applied across the EU, renewables would attain a market share of 12.5% by 2010. Policy learning and the diffusion of good practice were therefore built into the policy process from the start.

The European Commission's initial soundings led to mixed reactions. The European Parliament, a range of environmental groups and the renewables lobby called for higher targets and more support. However, there was opposition from some member states, as well as from some trade associations and conventional energy generators, who claimed that the targets were over-ambitious and would be expensive to meet. Nonetheless, in 1997 the European Commission proceeded to publish its White Paper on Renewables that maintained the 12% target and set out a range of measures that would need to be adopted if the target was to be met. Recognising that there was a need for a 'concerted and coordinated effort by the various players over time', the measures proposed included:

• Measures designed to ensure that renewable energy sources had fair access to electricity markets;

• A range of fiscal and financial measures designed to establish incentives and enhance access to investment resources;

• Measures to raise the priority awarded to renewables in other EU policies - including environment, economic development, research and development, regional policy, agriculture and competition;

• Measures to build networks and to promote cooperation between the member states;

• Targeted financial support for renewables through the ALTENER II scheme;

• Specific programmes designed to lead to the adoption of one million PV systems, 10,000MW of large wind farms, 10,000 MWth of new biomass installations and the integration of renewables into 100 communities;

• Mechanisms designed to monitor implementation by the member states and to monitor progress towards the objectives of the strategy.

Again the White Paper received a mixed response, and the debate rumbled on for nearly three years before the European Commission translated the broad statements of intent that were included in the White Paper into a draft directive which, if adopted, would introduce legally binding obligations. In the period between the publication of the draft directive in May 2000 and its adoption in October 2001, some of the proposals were watered down in a number of ways whilst a number of others were retained despite some opposition.

Firstly, the binding targets that were originally proposed by the Commission became merely 'indicative' targets that the member states were obliged to work towards but that they were not legally obliged to meet. While the Commission is obliged to review progress and to consider the need for mandatory targets after three years, opposition to such mandatory targets amongst the member states is likely to remain and unless the position changes they are unlikely to be adopted.

Similarly, although the directive initially sought to harmonise the ways in which the various member states supported the development of renewables, these proposals were rejected fol-

lowing opposition from some countries. Instead, a diversity of national schemes will continue to be applied across the EU for a further five years, although once more the Commission has the right to review these schemes and to propose an EU wide scheme if necessary. However, as with the question of whether targets should be made mandatory, there is no guarantee that any future proposals for harmonised support for renewables will actually be approved.

Despite some significant opposition, the directive also established a basis for financial support to be given to renewables. Although the Energy and Environment Directorates of the European Commission clearly saw the need for financial support to be provided to renewables, the Competition Directorate of the European Commission argued for such financial aid to be phased out as quickly as possible as it distorted markets. Countering this view, a consortium of environmental groups argued that:

In the European Union at present the electricity market is significantly distorted to the detriment of renewable energy generators: access to grids is restricted, excessive transmissions costs are applied to renewables; there is still no internalisation of environmental and social costs; embedded generators do not receive remuneration for the savings they create. These factors and the use of nearly 15 billion ECU in direct subsidies to the conventional generation sector all contribute a market distortion that continues to hold back the harnessing of renewable energy in the European Union (Greenpeace et al, 1999).

Thus, provisions within the directive for financial support for renewables are retained, although as the ALTENER II scheme offered on €22 million over a 5 year period, the level of support is likely be comparatively modest.

Otherwise, the directive also introduced an obligation for member states to establish mechanisms that would guarantee the origin of energy generated through renewables. In the future, certificates might then be issued which could be used as the basis for the trading of green electricity as countries buy or sell certificates depending on whether they fall short of or exceed their targets for renewables or their climate-change obligations. This would incentivise renewables generation and lead to greater investment and more efficient outcomes across the EU. However, there has been some reluctance to see the EU pioneering this form of marketable permit as it is seen by some to be untried and untested.

For the member states, the directive includes a requirement that they prepare a report on how they plan to reduce regulatory and other barriers to renewables and on how they might streamline planning procedures to allow for quicker approval of site-applications relating renewables. Finally, the directive introduces an obligation for the operators of transmission and distribution networks to give priority access to electricity from renewable sources, although 'these provisions are couched in such general terms that their impact may be limited' (ENDS, 2000).

While the Renewables Directive is not as strong as was originally proposed, or as ambitious as the European Parliament, the renewables lobby or the environmentalists had hoped, it remains a significant piece of policy. However, it does not exist in isolation. As the European Environment Agency points out (EEA, 2001), member states can do a lot to create the conditions needed to allow actors on the ground to respond effectively to the directive. As stated above, within the Renewables Directive there is an obligation for the Commission to review these national mechanisms and to consider the need for an EU-wide support scheme. The EEA's review of national

'success stories' may therefore offer some insight into the EU policies of the future.

In seeking to identify those factors which would allow the successful introduction of renewable energy technologies, the EEA (2001, p8) states 'no single factor was identified as being of over-whelming significance. It is the cumulative benefits of a series of supportive measures that determine the extent to which a renewable technology is successfully exploited'. However, seven essential factors were identified which help to create an environment within which renewable energy exploitation can succeed, namely:

• Political support, i.e. through long-established policies in support of renewables.

• Legislative support, i.e. in the form of feed-in systems that combine favourable tariffs for energy from new renewables with an obligation on utilities to purchase renewable energy at these tariffs. Such support can also come in the form of guaranteed prices for renewable energy generators that win a competitive tendering process. Legal mechanisms can also be used to enhance grid-access.

• Fiscal support, i.e. through measures designed to penalise fossil-fuel based energy sources or give tax exemptions to renewable sources.

• Financial support, i.e. in the form of favourable loans to actors developing new renewables technologies.

• Administrative support, i.e. in the form of planning guidance or altered planning or building regulations.

• Technological development, i.e. with financial support given to particular technologies and at different stages of the innovation process.

• Information, education and training, i.e. to raise awareness amongst the general public and particularly amongst the communities where renewables might be adopted.

Thus, the EU has adopted a Renewables Directive that is backed up by a range of national support mechanisms. Although the directive is not as strong as was originally proposed or as ambitious as some groups had hoped, it is leading to the development and diffusion of new renewables technologies in some contexts. Furthermore, although further changes may not take place for some years, it seems likely that EU policy will continue to develop, for example if the various support schemes that have been successful at the national level are adopted in a harmonised framework applicable across the EU.

CONCLUSIONS: HOW CLOSELY DOES EU POLICY REFLECT THE IDEAL?

Having considered the nature of EU policy on renewables, and examined the reasons why their design may be sub-optimal and their influence rather limited, we are now in a position to return to the ideal policy model to see how it compares with the real world.

1) Where they needed to intervene, policy makers could do so secure in the knowledge that the competitive implications of their interventions would be minimal as their major competitors would adopt similar goals.

Clearly this is not yet the case. As with the Kyoto Protocol, the lack of parallel commitments from other countries raises the prospect that in the short-term at least the EU will be put at a competitive disadvantage if it raises taxes on conventional energy sources. Consequently, renewables are put at a relative disadvantage.

2) There would be ready access to investment resources that would allow action to be taken, as any short-term costs associated with transition could be more than offset by the medium-term benefits. The level of the social benefits would be enough to compensate any losers whilst still leaving society as a whole better off.

Despite some support for renewables, the amount of money made available through the EU is really very modest. However, the indicative targets introduced by the EU suggest that the renewables market will grow significantly in future years. Even in the absence of significant incentives or subsidies from the EU, this is likely to build support at the national level and to encourage private sector investment.

3) There would be a broad and stable consensus both on the ultimate objectives for policy and on the ways in which these would be achieved. Unambiguous goals would be clearly communicated to give consistent and predictable long-term signals to the market place.

Clearly this has not been realised. Despite some loose alliances between the Energy and Environment Directorates of the European Commission, the European Parliament, some environmental groups and the renewables lobby, these actors have not been powerful enough to prevent policy targets being watered down. Actors on the ground therefore receive mixed messages from different sectors of government and from the market.

4) There would be an integrated or joined-up approach that spanned the boundaries between different areas of policy. Policies in areas as diverse as energy, environment, agriculture, transport, tax and competition would all be pulling in the same direction.

As above, there has been only a limited amount of 'buy-in' from some other sectors, most notably in fiscal policy and competition, where policies that contradict the goals for renewables remain in place.

5) Different policy instruments would be applied which would both encourage and enable change. These instruments, which would include mandatory targets, economic instruments, information-based approaches, capacity building measures and support for basic R&D, would be applied in concert within a complementary policy mix.

A range of policy instruments have been applied which should complement each other to some extent. However, the links between the different instruments could be better developed so that the framework as a whole was more cohesive.

6) There would be perfect implementation so that the range of policies and instruments adopted were applied as intended at the EU, national, regional and local levels.

As the targets set out by the EU Renewables Directive are only indicative, its success depends very much on the commitment of the member states. While the indicative targets will be taken seriously in some settings, some states remain less than fully committed to the national targets whilst others have resisted the adoption of a harmonised approach, seemingly preferring to go their own way. Again this means that the framework could be more coherent/consistent.

7) There would be enough flexibility in the system to allow implementing agencies to take into account the variable conditions encountered by different technologies and by diverse actors

operating in contexts that change over time and space.

The Renewables Directive does give some scope for flexibility as to how the different targets are to be met at the national level. It also builds in an obligation for a review of progress that creates an opportunity for further policy development at the EU level and policy learning at the national level in the near future.

8) Market mechanisms would serve to reinforce government policies. External costs and benefits would be internalised so that social and environmental impacts were accurately reflected in economic transactions and there would be perfect information to inform voter and consumer behaviour.

The external costs and benefits of the different forms of energy generation have yet to be internalised. This puts renewables at a clear competitive disadvantage. Furthermore, liberalisation has meant that the overall market for energy has become much more competitive. Nonetheless, market-pull backed up by government support will probably be sufficient to lead to the commercialisation of some renewable technologies. As they are more widely adopted, their quality will improve and their costs will drop. However, market-pull will be insufficient to stimulate investments in blue-sky research for other technologies. Government support to overcome some of the most important barriers to innovation therefore remains necessary.

9) Actors on the ground would understand, support and have the capacity to respond to the wide range of signals from government, from the market and from society at large.

Capacities are developing in many settings - however it is clear that those regions/sectors that are most likely to be innovative in the future are those that have been innovative in the past. In those contexts where there is no history of innovation relating to renewables, significant and sustained investments will be necessary not only in the technologies themselves but also in the networks that underpin the innovation process.

10) Infrastructure would also be flexible enough to accommodate the needs of new renewable energy technologies.

Despite calls for greater access to the grid, the infrastructure continues to reflect the fact that it was designed to meet the needs of large-scale conventional generators rather than smaller scale renewables. Grid access therefore remains a major barrier to the development of renewable energies.

As a consequence, it is clear that the ideal policies have yet to be put in place to promote the wider development and diffusion of renewable energy sources in the EU. The negotiation and compromise needed to secure support for the Renewables Directive from other departments of the EU and from various member states meant that the policies departed from the original ideal in quite a number of ways. Furthermore, diverse national approaches and competing interests in the member states mean that the policies may not be implemented whole-heartedly or in the intended way. And finally, conditions on the ground may restrict the ability of actors to respond to the policies in the ways that are hoped.

Nonetheless, the Renewables Directive represents a significant achievement, and with scope for learning, EU policy design can develop further over time. Ultimate success depends upon the member states' capacity and commitment, both to deliver these policies and to create the conditions that will allow actors to respond to them in efficient and effective ways.

REFERENCES

Dosi, G. (1988) The nature of the innovative process, In: *Technical Change and Economic Theory*, pp. 221-237, G. Dosi, C. Freeman, R. Nelson, G. Silverberg, L. Soete, (Eds). Pinter Publishers, London

European Commission (1997) *Energy for the Future: Renewable Sources of Energy* - White Paper for a Community Strategy and Action Plan, COM(97) 599, 26.11.1997.

European Commission (2001) "Directive 2001/77/EC on the Promotion of Electricity Produced from Renewable Energy Sources in the Internal Electricity Market", Official Journal of the European Communities, L283/33, 27.10.2001.

European Environment Agency (2001) *Renewable Energies: success stories*, Environmental Issue Report 27, EEA, Copenhagen.

Kemp, R. (1993) An economic analysis of cleaner technology: theory and evidence, In: *Environmental Strategies for Industry: International Perspectives on Research Needs and Policy Implications*, pp. 79-116, K. Fischer and J. Schot, (Eds). Island Press, Washington.

Kemp, R. and Soete, L. (1992) "The Greening of Technological Progress" *Futures*, June pp. 437-457

OECD - Organisation for Economic Cooperation and Development (1992) *Technology and the Economy: The Key Relationship*. OECD, Paris.

Soete, L. and Arundel, A. (1995) European innovation policy for environmentally sustainable development: application of a systems model of technical change, *Journal of Public Policy*, 2, 2, pp.285-385.

The risks of oil supply disruption for the transport sector

by Dan Plesch

No country could survive economically if its goods and people could not move from place to place. Highest priority should be given to replacing oil as the main transport fuel in view of the unstable nature of the regions where most of the world's supplies are found.

If oil, the *raison d'être* of a large part of the Western military complex since the Soviet Union collapsed, could be removed from its central role in economic life, then that would have a very significant positive political effect on the international situation. At present, half the United States' military is devoted to and justified by potential wars to do with oil in North-West Asia.

To bring about a reduction in oil's importance, we need to establish a new set of coalitions and alliances between the security community, the traditional disarmament community, which hasn't quite got the message yet, and the green community that is downloading it rapidly. As these alliances can only be successful if there is a powerful, objective, real case for energy security, that is what this paper will discuss, focussing on oil and transportation.

The energy security issue as it confronts us today is a very old one. It probably stretches back beyond the eighteenth century, but just as an illustration, Frederick the Great, as part of what led to the destruction of Poland, moved in to occupy Polish Silesia to gain access to its coal. By World War Two, oil had become a strategic issue, not least because Winston Churchill had decided that the Royal Navy should not rely on coal because of the difficulties of maintaining coaling stations and supply-

Editor's Note: this paper was written in October 2002, before the Anglo - American invasion of Iraq.

ing them. Accordingly, in the late nineteenth and early twentieth century, he moved the Royal Navy to oil.

A quick few points to illustrate our vulnerability. The tax on oil is very high in Western Europe - between $50 and $100 a barrel on top of the purchase price, which is currently $25-$30 a barrel. These exact numbers may be wrong, but the scale is not. In addition to this there is the continuing high cost of securing, or that is to say, not securing, the oil in the Gulf right now. Plus or minus, I think that around 150 plus billion dollars a year are spent by the US and the West and the western-orientated Gulf states themselves to try to secure the production of some 6 or 7 billion barrels a year. This gives us a per-barrel price of policing the petrol supply of between 15 and 25 dollars a barrel. On top of this, of course, is the cost in democratic values of deciding to prop up all sorts of extremely unsavoury regimes that we wouldn't otherwise particularly care for. That's a year-on-year cost, and it doesn't actually secure the supply.

Some right-wing commentators, notably Samuel Huntingdon, have long proposed that we are faced with a clash of civilizations between the West and Islam. Personally I don't subscribe to that view but with people like Samuel Huntingdon in charge, we may yet experience such a conflict despite its lack of inevitability. At the other end of the spectrum we have the radical Islamists who have launched some kind of global guerrilla war - probably the first we have seen historically. Their intention is clearly to try to incite a global civil war. They look at Islam's high point in the ninth and tenth centuries, see that it hasn't come much further since the early Middle Ages, and would like to see that go very much further. So there are plenty of people out for a scrap.

Whether or not we are able to contain the situation is an open question. What we do know is that if we get it wrong, we are enormously vulnerable and there are groups with the capability to exploit our vulnerabilities. Look at this nice little Landsat image of the Kuwaiti oil-field

Kuwaiti oil-field fires

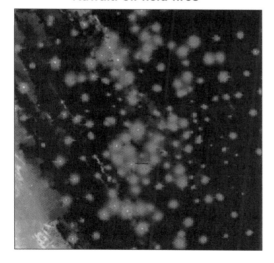

fires. One or two nuclear weapons, perhaps from the Pakistani nuclear programme, loosed off in those fields might make our future slightly more complicated.

Is this risk small enough to ignore? Well, we're all accustomed to risks of one sort of another and the conventional wisdom plays down the risks both from those that dream of the seventh century and those from Bush and Sharon. But we downplayed other risks in the past and were proved to be quite wrong. So far, the best we can say is that the doom-mongers have not been proved right, yet.

Coming to Iraq, well, the war might be a push-over like the last one in the Gulf, and I think it probably will be, but the political and longer-term ramifications, particularly of an American general managing a US oil cartel on the Basra and Mosul oil fields, may have further knock-on effects beyond that of those who carry out the action.

The risk from the West's perspective is regime change. We have, I think, quite short memories. Remember that in the fifties, sixties, and into the seventies, military coups were very frequent in many parts of the world and certainly in the Arab part. I find it interesting that much of the discussion is in terms of Muslim public opinion, but I would be more concerned about a group of junior officers carrying out a Ghadaffi- or Nasser-ite style coup. And while we look with great complacency at the fall of the Warsaw Pact over the course of not much more than a year at the end of the 1980s, we may face a situation in which from Ankara through to Jakarta we see a similar collapse of western-orientated, police-state-reliant regimes.

Now, I haven't got much time for those regimes, and I haven't got much time for a policy that supports them, but without a more enlightened policy, the risk of such a major change seems to me a bit too real to set aside. I was a journalist at NATO when the NATO Secretary General came out one day, about twelve years ago, in the middle of a defence ministers' meeting and said, 'Well we've got news today, we got a fax from Boris Yeltsin. He just sent us a fax to say the Soviet Union no longer exists.' That would have been quite unthinkable a few years previously. So can anyone guarantee that we are not going to get an e-mail one day from Tehran, Baghdad or Riyadh saying 'Well actually we are going back to the desert, we have a Cambodian Pol Pot approach to the middle class, we don't care about selling the oil to sustain our national economy, what we do care about is completely messing your societies and destroying them.'

Now, I think that's very unlikely. But the point is that our existing response to that risk is simply more investment in the current approach. At various points around the world, where people on the receiving end aren't stupid, they see the signs of our desperation to diversify our oil sources. You only have to open a copy of *The Financial Times* to find out how we are busily

A 747 prototype for an American airborne laser system

trying to extract more oil from Africa or Central Asia, or some other far-flung place where it's very difficult to get the oil out for technical and strategic reasons. Or ponder this nice little picture of a beefed-up 747 which is a prototype for an American airborne laser system. Well, they are shelling out $1.3 billion just for programme definition on that.

Now think about what that sort of money could achieve if military-style resourcing was applied to developing renewable energy sources in order to remove our strategic oil dependency. Where could that leave us strategically in ten or fifteen years' time? We simply have no Plan B at present, which from the perspective of elementary military strategy is not a good position to be in. If you are having to fight wars in the petrol station you have to be very careful because if things go seriously wrong, then things go wrong at home very quickly too.

Of course there are some strategic petrol reserves but these are all extremely short-term measures. None of them has the prospect of lasting more than a year on the most generous of estimates. And we, I think, need to learn how different our societies are today compared with, let us say, the societies that faced the oil crisis of '73 or indeed that of '56. Seventy-three feels almost moderately recent but remember we've become a just-in-time economy since then. As a result, the tanker-driver dispute in the UK two years ago brought the country close to a very serious national emergency.

The drivers weren't unionised so there was no one to talk to. The managers were in Milan - what do you do? We had no surplus capacity, no infrastructure to enable us to cope. And, as one of my colleagues in government pointed out, there's no point in giving petrol coupons to the doctor to get to the hospital if the boiler man is a forty-minute car drive away. Railway men no longer live in railway cottages now, other people do and commute to some other city while the railway men live somewhere else again. And they're all using cars. The vulnerability is vastly greater even than in the 1970s.

So, while we don't have a Plan B, we do know that there is a risk of unquantifiable size that Plan A will fail because some people have a very great capability to exploit our very great vulnerability at a very high cost to us.

If you open up any car magazine you'll see that a whole range of hybrids and alternative-fuel vehicles are now becoming commercially available because of the environmental concern, the environmental push. What this means is that there is a technology that is in a state to be picked up and brought into service. It isn't a question of the position we were in, in the 1970s. And if we decided to switch our resources from the airborne-laser simulation preparation budget into fuel cells we might see things happen a little bit faster.

The prize for us in Europe is not just to greatly reduce our strategic risk and our dependence on the United States, but also to create greater freedom to choose where to send what troops we have. I'll ask you to start thinking about the role that Ireland might play when, in a year or so, it takes the presidency of the European Union again, and what possibilities might be taken up by a very well-organised internationalised civil society focussed on that presidency, because Ireland's presidencies in the past have achieved a fair amount. We shouldn't think that a rapid transition to renewable energy sources is without precedent. The history of technology is full of very rapid transitions and developments, unfortunately mostly during times of war. To pick some at random - the landing craft used by the Americans to liberate Europe was essentially an obscure oilrig tender from the Gulf of Mexico. Commercial long-range air travel came out of the World War II bomber. The advantages of satellite technology came first of all from a military use and of course in peacetime we have brought about the stagecoach/canal/rail/private car transition.

I would argue that one can take to established politics a very hardcore security argument that in traditional military strategic terms there is an imperative to develop renewable energy for transportation. We could build on that strategic imperative by using the technical resources and lobbying power of the green movement along with those of people in the political/military world who aren't really aware of the technological possibilities. I think it would be a nice idea if Feasta could do it. I jumped at the invitation to this conference because the construction of the alliance I spoke about ealier should perhaps the focus on the EU (and Mr Prodi, the President of the European Commission who has just created a hydrogen advisory group, with which we should become rather more closely associated, I think).

The European Union as such does not have an energy policy but nevertheless the development of a presidency agenda could move the security issue forward far more rapidly than it might otherwise happen. After all, there are plenty of people sipping espressos in Europe who have great distaste for the current American administration but can't see a way out of the current strategic dependency. We are offering one, vastly more practical than establishing a European army, of which the least said the better, I think. It is also, I have to say, a more realistic, *realpolitik*, approach to the security problem, because a European army is not going to make this problem go away, it just adds competition between a European military and an American military to the equation. And draws a hell of a lot more money into the trap that perhaps Mr Bin Laden and his friends are setting for us. The present response is no more a strategy than the bull charging the red rag is a strategy. I think we can offer to produce a good deal more security for an awful lot less money.

I'll close with one final point. It is not about the fact that there isn't enough oil in the ground. There is, and there is going to be enough oil in the ground for quite a long time to come. The price may get higher, we may find more, though we probably won't find very much more, but for twenty, thirty years from now, we will probably have enough oil. Now, planning long term, of course we need to be thinking about the transition to renewables. The point is, the risk of an oil supply disruption makes the need for that transition much more immediate. Of course, if oil was as available as water, then we wouldn't be shelling out all this cash to try and secure it. Clearly, shortage of supply and concentration of supply are already critical issues, and will get worse, particularly with the growth of Chinese demand coming on stream. But, being entirely shameless about it, the security issue provides environmentalists with another powerful argument for getting to where they already want to go.

Grim energy security scenario developed for the US

US Energy Scenarios for the 21st Century, a report published in July 2003 by the Pew Center on Global Climate Change, looks at three possible energy futures for the US and the effects that each would have on greenhouse gas emissions up to 2035. Perhaps the most convincing scenario is *Turbulent World* in which 'constant dislocations, ubiquitous conflicts, and historically low levels of global cooperation shake the US economy and disrupt the energy sector.' The report sets the scene thus:

Outside the United States, nationalistic and geopolitical forces undermine stability in several important oil-producing states. Venezuela loses half of its export capacity due to conflicts between a populist government and an entrenched management bureaucracy. Iraq is invaded by an international coalition, with the next ten years spent rehabilitating and modernizing Iraqi oil fields. Fundamentalist challenges to reigning national governments lead to major economic and political dislocations on both sides of the Persian Gulf. Hostility to US presence in the region and to sustained US support for Israel continues to grow during 2000 to 2010. Political challenges to regimes in Saudi Arabia, Kuwait, and the United Arab Emirates boil over, with major disruptions of petroleum output occurring from 2005 to 2010.

The resulting series of price shocks and supply interruptions culminates in 2010 with fundamentalist radicals overthrowing the House of Al-Saud, destroying the production infrastructure in the Eastern Provinces of Saudi

Arabia, and torching large oil shipping terminals in the Gulf. A wave of attacks on oil tankers in the Gulf and sporadic terrorist attacks on energy facilities within the United States follow the fall of the Saudi regime. These events lead to a series of price spikes and a major disruption of oil supply. As a consequence, world oil prices more than double from year-2000 levels by 2010...

[The] price spikes and supply disruptions in the energy sector combine with terrorist incidents, accidents, and domestic weather-related disasters to unsettle the confidence of US investors and consumers in large-scale, conventional, centralized technologies.... The principal driving force for policy is concern about energy security. The emphasis of domestic energy policy shifts abruptly from one technology to another, but one by one, each "solution" is revealed to have a major flaw. There is one exception: to reduce dependence on imported oil, the federal government initiates a "crash" program designed to accelerate the commercialization of fuel cells that burn hydrogen derived from coal. This program, implemented on the scale of the Apollo "moonshot," proves successful.

As a result, and despite slow economic growth, carbon emissions rise 20 percent above the year 2000 level by 2035.

In another scenario, *Technology Triumphs*, US firms successfully commercialize technologies to improve energy efficiency and lower carbon emissions and then develop an international market

for them. Even so, because of economic growth and an increase in energy consumption, carbon emissions rise 15 percent above their 2000 level by 2035;

The least likely scenario seems to be *Awash in Oil and Gas*, in which abundant supplies of oil and natural gas remain available to US consumers at low prices. Energy consumption rises considerably and conventional technologies dominate the energy sector. With few incentives to improve energy efficiency and little concern for energy issues, carbon emissions rise 50 percent above the 2000 level by 2035.

Not surprisingly, the report concludes that without a mandatory limit on fossil fuel consumption, US carbon emissions will continue to increase over the next thirty years. It says that "early and sustained investment, engineering success, and consumer acceptance of innovative low-carbon and efficiency-improving technologies would make the task of reducing emissions easier, as would energy security policies that reduced oil import dependence." On the other hand, low fossil fuel prices would make emissions reduction harder by encouraging high-carbon and energy-inefficient investments.

The report, written by Peter Schwartz of Global Business Network who was originally responsible for developing the use of scenarios at Shell, Irving Mintzer and J. Amber Leonard, can be downloaded from http://www.pewclimate.org/global_warming_in_depth/all_reports/energy_scenarios/index.cfm

Part Five

The attitude of the electricity companies to renewable energy

Major changes will be needed if an electricity supply system built on the basis that a few big plants will supply the power is to cope instead with smaller, scattered, less-constant renewable energy producers. Political and public support is required.

A   Towards a sustainable energy system
by **Owen Wilson**

B   The challenge to the National Grid in coping with renewable power
by **Anne Trotter**

C   Selling green electricity – a wind farmer's view
by **Declan Flanagan**

Towards a sustainable energy system

by Owen Wilson

The Irish state electricity company believes that global climate change rather than oil and gas depletion will force Ireland to move to a sustainable energy system. Building the latter, it says, will be a political and ideological exercise as much as a technical and economic one.

The social and economic development of human societies is inextricably linked to energy use. However, in developed countries today the linkage between growth in energy consumption and economic growth shows signs of de-coupling. Nonetheless it is doing so at a level (4.7 toe/capita in the OECD) that is significantly above the current energy consumption levels of the least developed countries (0.6 toe/capita in Africa). The continued growth in global population and the justifiable demand for all humans to have access to energy will ensure that total annual global energy consumption will continue to increase well into the future (from approximately 10 Gtoe p.a. in 2000 to 25 Gtoe p.a. in 2050) under business-as-usual conditions. In this context, the recent World Summit on Sustainable Development (WSSD) in Johannesburg placed heavy emphasis on the need for developing countries, with the support of developed countries, to create energy systems that are 'reliable, affordable, economically viable, socially acceptable and environmentally sound' as an essential element in eliminating poverty.

These five requirements essentially define the basis for the sustainable energy systems that will be put in place to serve the majority of humanity for the next 40-50 years. While emphasising a strong role for energy efficiency, conservation and renewables, the WSSD recognised the continuing dominant role that fossil fuels will play. In terms of energy supply, even under high growth scenarios, no shortfall in coal, oil or gas supplies is anticipated given current estimates of proven reserves and projected resources (e.g. WEC/IIASA, Shell forecasts). However, sustainability addresses more than energy supply and it is recognised that the limiting resource in the future will be the capacity of the biosphere to absorb emissions from the extraction, transformation, distribution and use of fuels.

The requirements for sustainable energy applied by the WSSD reflect substantively the three pillars of Ireland's domestic energy policy – competitiveness, security and environmental protection. The issue today is what pressures apply in the developed world that will drive the shape of global energy systems up to and beyond the 2050 period. Assuming reserves of fossil fuels are not a critical factor then it is supply security, cost and, above all, environmental factors which will mould future global energy systems.

SUPPLY SECURITY

The goal of the UN, individual governments and consumers is to have available a reliable supply of energy to meet the current needs of individuals for heat, light, power, transport and electrical energy. No international agency is suggesting that any other societal imperative justifies measures to ration energy supplies by curtailing their availability or reliability. The availability and reliability of energy services are satisfied through functioning distribution infrastructures with fuel and source diversity supporting transparent energy markets.

Significant investments are required to keep in place the various infrastructures needed for energy delivery including extraction, transformation (electricity generation), transportation, distribution and use. The recognised concerns affecting security of supply relate to geo-political instability and, in those sectors where market structures have not been well established, regulatory risk. Concerns in relation to Middle East oil or North African or Russian gas are well recognised and, to the extent political events in these regions affect the continuity of supplies (and fuel prices), they drive the exploration cycle in more stable regions of the globe. More interesting in the short-term will be the effectiveness of new energy regulatory regimes in providing the necessary stability and incentives for investment in the recently liberalised energy sectors (gas and electricity). Significant teething problems are being encountered in these two areas which have important contributions to make in moving towards and facilitating sustainable energy supplies.

Additionally, supply security must be subject to societal expectations. In this context, nuclear energy is not considered a desirable component of the energy mix in certain countries. Equally, some societies may place greater value on other objectives (e.g. the preservation of unspoilt landscapes) above the exploitation of available renewable resources (wind, monoculture biomass).

ENERGY COST

Affordable energy is a key goal of policy-makers. In more developed countries affordability relates primarily to industrial/commercial consumers with the objective of maintaining national economic competitiveness. However, affordable energy for consumers must also be economically viable from an investor perspective if affordability is to be sustained over the long-term and sufficient support for research and development of new technologies is to be provided. As with energy security, the primary risks to affordable energy relate to supply and/or market failures.

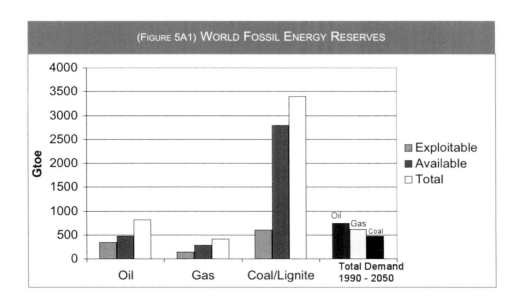

(FIGURE 5A1) WORLD FOSSIL ENERGY RESERVES

ENVIRONMENT

As noted above, the impact of energy extraction, transport, transformation and use on the environment is the main driver for change in an energy system that effectively meets the current economic and social needs of developed countries. The global issue of climate change (the capacity of the atmosphere to absorb increasing amounts of CO_2) and policy responses in this area will provide the major impetus towards long-term energy sustainability, moderated by the need to maintain security and affordability. The Kyoto Protocol to the UNFCCC establishes, to a degree, a carbon constrained future well ahead of any physical shortages of fossil fuels. For the developed world the Kyoto Protocol will require progressive reductions in the carbon intensity ($tCO_2/\$GDP$) and energy intensity ($GJ/\$GDP$) of national economies to sustain economic growth into the future. In the longer term all economies will face an environmental carbon constraint. In essence this means greater efficiency will be required in the patterns and systems of fossil energy transformation and end use. It will require progressive reduction in the reliance on fossil fuels and their substitution by renewable energies, hydrogen and, in countries where it is deemed acceptable, nuclear power. In the interim it will involve a greater dependence on gas.

The key issues facing developed economies are the related factors of the speed and cost of transition to an environmentally driven sustainable energy system given the current distance from the desired objective of stabilisation of CO_2 in the atmosphere at a level that will not cause irreparable damage to the planet. Because policy responses will impact on individuals, most notably in terms of increased energy cost, building the basis for a sustainable energy system will be as much a political and ideological exercise as it is a technical and economic one. Recent experience with the Nice Referendum is hopeful, suggesting that debate can facilitate the public in ordering priorities on complex issues such as this.

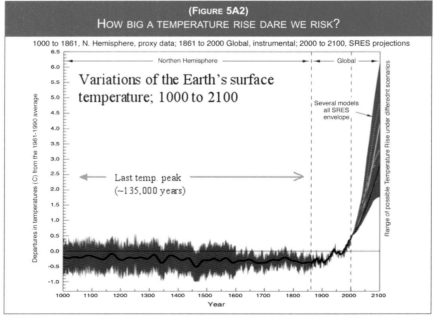

(FIGURE 5A2)
HOW BIG A TEMPERATURE RISE DARE WE RISK?

1000 to 1861, N. Hemisphere, proxy data; 1861 to 2000 Global, instrumental; 2000 to 2100, SRES projections

By the end of the current century, the average surface temperature of the Earth could be between 1.5 °c to 6 °c higher according to Intergovernmental Panel on Climate Change scenarios
Source: IPCC, Third Assessment Peport, 2002

However, by placing a price on CO_2 the Kyoto Protocol provides the most significant step at present towards developing a sustainable system. Kyoto provides the necessary conditions to promote energy efficiency, conservation, renewable energy and technological research and development by requiring that the externality cost associated with climate change be included in energy prices and providing for this to be addressed in a market-based framework. It is therefore critical that the Kyoto Protocol be seen to succeed as its collapse will stall the political drive necessary to achieve a sustainable energy future.

The key risk in implementing measures to comply with the Kyoto Protocol is the scale and timing of the impact they will have on energy prices. Sudden, large-scale increases in energy prices brought about by rapid stranding of energy infrastructure assets (e.g. electricity generation, distribution systems) will cause social and economic difficulties and, possibly, the collapse of the Kyoto Protocol. The main restraint on this is the linkage of the Protocol requirements with market mechanisms that will facilitate the transition to an environmentally sustainable energy system in an economically logical fashion. Nonetheless, care is required in designing the market systems necessary to implement the Protocol in order to avoid market failures. Despite major progress to date in the development of the proposed emissions trading Directive, which will provide the main vehicle for implementing Kyoto in the EU, significant weaknesses remain in relation to the proposals for market management that could yet result in its collapse.

PATHWAY

Ireland will not determine the technological global pathway to sustainable energy. It is a technology taker rather than an innovator due to the scale of investment in research and develop-

ment required to radically restructure its energy systems compared to the size of its economy and its openness to global forces. Ireland can shape the path internally to one that best suits its economy and society. A number of elements will be required in order to do so including the following:

• Educate and build consensus around problem definition and solutions. Work has been progressing on sustainable development and climate change at a technical and institutional level for some time. There must be more general acceptance of the need to radically reduce the use of fossil fuels and replace them with renewable forms of energy. However, is the public really engaged in this debate other than to complain that global warming isn't working?

• Use markets and policy measures that integrate with markets to the extent possible. Properly functioning, transparent markets provide the best opportunity to achieve environmental sustainability goals at least economic cost. Nonetheless, markets may not provide solutions to all issues aimed at promoting behaviour supportive of sustainability or discouraging contradictory behaviour and other policy instruments may be required (e.g. building standards). Do we posses the perfect foresight now to predict the structure of a sustainable energy system and the least cost way to get there?

• Put in place stable regulatory frameworks for the new energy markets. Regulatory certainty is a critical element of investment decisions in energy infrastructure given the scale of individual investments. Certainty applies equally to measures aimed at modifying the markets to support other specific policy objectives such as security, accessibility and affordability. Why would investors risk their money in conditions of uncertainty?

• Establish frameworks to support and reward technological research, development and dissemination (RD&D) that deliver improvements in sustainability. However, economic sustainability dictates that Ireland must maintain the competitiveness of its energy infrastructure in line with that of its trading partners – in reality RD&D investment resources are limited. In this context, facilitating uptake of new technologies at the same rate as national competitors may be the most appropriate response in many cases.

• Develop and strengthen the national infrastructure for gas and electricity. Natural gas will act as the main transition fuel to a lower carbon intensive economy. Electricity is the means by which most renewable forms of energy are delivered.

• Address the social issues arising form higher energy costs, including responses to fuel poverty. Sustainability will not be achieved if it means high costs, lower living standards and no alternatives.

In the end we must all accept and respond to the fact that the global environment must be capable of sustaining the world the global economic game is creating.

The challenge to the National Grid in coping with renewable power

Anne Trotter

The fact that wind turbines trip out if the supply from conventional generators fails coupled with the intermittent nature of wind energy make it difficult for the national grid to take much power from them. Efforts are being made to beat these problems.

The ESB National Grid is Ireland's Transmission System Operator and this paper about renewable energy is written from that perspective. First, I will introduce the role and responsibilites of a Transmission System Operator (TSO); I will then discuss the impact of changes in the way electricity is generated on the system's development; and finally look at some TSO initiatives. I will use the three-letter acronym TSO because it makes my presentation a little easier.

(FIGURE 5B1) IRISH TRANSMISSION SYSTEM

───────	400 kV Lines
───────	220 kV Lines
───────	110 kV Lines
○	400 kV Transformer Stations
○	220 kV Transformer Stations
●	110 kV Transformer Stations
●	Hydro Generation
■	Steam Generation
▲	Pumped Storage Generation
-------	220 kV Cable
-------	110 kV Cable

The TSO is responsible for the development, operation, and maintenance of the transmission system. Although the role of the TSO role is currently filled by ESB National Grid, it will be performed by EirGrid when the infrastructure agreement and transfer agreement between ESB and EirGrid are complete.

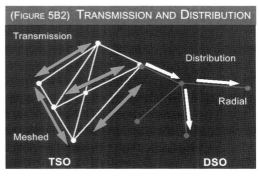

(FIGURE 5B2) TRANSMISSION AND DISTRIBUTION

Transmission

Distribution

Radial

Meshed

TSO   DSO

Figure 5B1 shows the Irish transmission system: it is made up of the 400KV system. the 220KV system; and the 110KV system. It is distinct from the distribution system as Figure 5B2 shows.

A transmission system is a mesh or a network which means in electrical terms it is normally closed and it is designed to withstand the loss of any single item of plant without the system going outside set standards. Flows can go in either direction along the lines and it is normally used for the delivery of bulk supply to the distribution network which is shown in Figure 5B2 as a radial or normally open system. Normally, electricity flows from the transmission system to the distribution system, and on to the local customers. However, if a generator is embedded in the distribution system, the flows can also go in either direction.

One of the advantages of the network aspect of the transmission system is the high level of security and continuity it gives. Both of these are very important, obviously, for our major industrial customers. Indeed one of their main issues when they meet us is the levels of quality and continuity that they can expect. The disadvantage is that a connection, be it an increased demand, or increased generation, at one node can cause changes throughout the network and at quite remote points, which makes the system more complicated to operate and control, whereas with a radial system the loads and demands and generation on any branch can be calculated by a simple arithmetic sum. Basically, though, in the Irish system, the Transmission System Operator looks after the transmission system and the Distribution System Operator looks after the distribution system.

Another comment on our system: it is a small island system. I read something recently by an academic in the UK who had described the UK system as an island electricity system, so certainly I think we could regard Ireland as a small island system. Our generated system peak is just over 4000 megawatts with a summer night valley or minimum load at just less than 1500 megawatts. We are lightly interconnected with Northern Ireland, which is lightly interconnected with the UK. As a result, a small amount of generation in European terms, say, 400 megawatts, has a big impact on our system.

The TSO's responsibility is to maintain, operate and, if necessary, develop a safe, secure, reliable, economic and efficient electricity transmission system and to explore and develop opportunities for interconnecting that system with other systems so that all reasonable

demands for electricity are met while having due regard to the environment. That is the context in which we are operating.

So what impact will the development of many more electricity sources have on system development for the TSO in Ireland? What changes are we seeing? On the traditional thermal side, we are certainly seeing an increase in unit size, up to 600 megawatts now being typical and possibly even larger for nuclear stations. This has transmission system and reserve implications for the Transmission System Operator. On reserve requirements, our current standard is that we must have the ability to withstand the loss of our largest generator, so as the single largest unit increases, that has implications for us.

RENEWABLES IN THE SUPPLY MIX

There is now an increasing proportion of renewables in the overall generation mix. Small synchronous generators using predictable fuel sources create no new issues for a Transmission System Operator. If they act very much the same as any other generator, they really make no difference from the point of view of a system planner. But of all the renewable generation sources, wind, a very large natural resource in Ireland, does pose a great challenge for TSO, for two main reasons. One is the operating characteristics of wind turbine generation. Intermittence is one everyone is familiar with. The other is fault ride-through, the ability of the generator to stay connected when there is a fault on the system. I'll go into that in a little more detail. As I explained earlier, we have to be able to withstand the loss of our largest generator but, with current wind turbine technology, our dynamic models tell us that whenever we have, say, a cable fault close to, for example, our largest 400-megawatt generator on the system, Synergen, in Dublin, that would also trip every wind farm connected to the system for quite a large radius. This therefore means that not only do we have to be able to withstand the loss of Synergen but also every transmission-connected wind farm within a large radius as well. That is serious since the size of wind farms is increasing. We have recently signed a connection agreement for an 82.5 megawatt wind farm.

These are the challenges we are facing. On top of those, there are legislation issues and a lot of uncertainties about where our generation and our demand will come from, which is why we do scenario planning and construct models. It takes time to build in any reinforcements

demand customer signs a connection agreement. We operate that policy to avoid having plant built which will subsequently be stranded. Typical lead times for significant transmission projects are currently from four to eight years. This is much longer than in the past while the typical lead-time for generation plant is about one to three years, much shorter than in the past. There is a mismatch here. From an economic point of view, someone is losing if there is too much generation in a particular location, be it the generator or the system or the public.

Another issue for us is the reducing capacity benefit of increasing wind power installation.

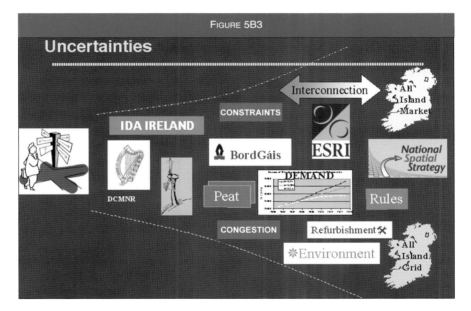

FIGURE 5B3

required to handle these various different uncertainties.

So, as I said, even a small amount of generation in some locations could result in a major transmission project. It just depends what the existing capacity is at that location and what impact it has on the overall network. Transmission projects to facilitate additional generation can only begin when a relevant generator or

As the level of wind power generation on the system increases, the plant margin required to maintain system adequacy rises as well. As an example, we have currently 150 megawatts of wind connected to the system. Most of this is connected to the distribution side - only about 15 megawatts is connected to transmission. Recently we had a high load period and we required generation and we had only 3 megawatts available at that point in time as the wind farms had too little wind to produce.

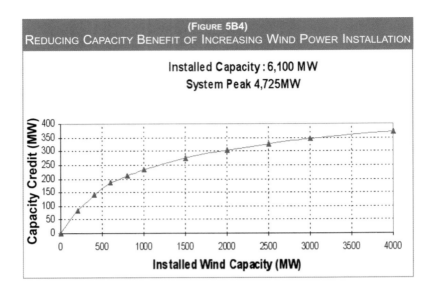

(FIGURE 5B4)
REDUCING CAPACITY BENEFIT OF INCREASING WIND POWER INSTALLATION

Installed Capacity: 6,100 MW
System Peak 4,725MW

Figure 5B4 shows this issue. It is an input that ESB National Grid made to the Renewable Energy Strategy Group. It looks at a system peak of over 4000 megawatts which is not too dissimilar from where we are at the moment with only around 150 megawatts of wind installed. We do get some capacity benefits from that but as the windpower capacity increases, we get less and less benefit from each unit of wind capacity installed because we have

(FIGURE 5B5) IRELAND S ELECTRICITY INTERCONNECTORS - EXISTING AND POTENTIAL

to provide a back-up for it in case it is not available.

INTERCONNECTORS

An interconnector with another country's grid can facilitate power flow in both directions. Currently, as I said, we have interconnection with Northern Ireland, which has interconnection to the UK, into Scotland and down through England and indeed England is interconnected to Europe. I have drawn a double-headed arrow between Wexford and Wales to represent possible interconnection between the Republic of Ireland and the UK. This is a proposal which has been discussed for some time and it is currently being reviewed again. The EU would like to see greater interconnection and it has been specified as 10% of installed capacity.

An interconnector would certainly be a significant intrastructural project. It would bring Ireland closer to the markets in the UK and it would facilitate more competition in the Irish market. Whether there would be cheaper imports from the UK is questionable, however, but it would give us energy-source diversity. Imports through it could be seen as equivalent to extra generation on the east coast; but, equally, since the arrow goes the other way as well, it could facilitate the export of power from there. The various pros and cons and different impacts are going to have to be taken into consideration when interconnection is being assessed.

We have put up a number of different information documents on our website "http://www.eirgrid.com"
These mostly fall into the following categories: system, charges, connection and market, and one of the main pieces of information which will be useful to people in the generation area, is the forecast statement, which more or less shows the network currently, the reinforcements we intend to make, those for which we have capital approval to complete, and what capacity is available in the network for increased generation etc.

We are involved in the British Isles Wind Technical Panel, a group of TSOs and others who want to be able to model power supplies from wind farms just as they would model those from any other large generator. We are also a technical advisor to the Grid Investment Steering Group and have submitted discussion documents to the Commission for Electricity Regulation (CER) on the implications of large wind farms connecting to the grid and the specific requirements of the grid for that. We've been analysing various wind forecasting simulation systems such as Prediktor, which is used by one of the Danish utilities. We are involved in an EU group called More Care, again to do with wind forecasting, involving academics, TSOs and industry people. We are also part of another study on the impact of large amounts of wind generation on the performance of other generators if wind can't provide the generation at a given point in time and other generators have to. We have also made inputs into the joint

British Office of the Regulator of Electricity Generation (OFREG) and CER wind study, which is being carried out at present.

Technical advances could help increase the amount of wind-generated energy that can be connected to the transmission system without diminishing the quality and continuity of supply. For example, a number of turbine manufacturers are working to improve the fault ride-through capability I mentioned earlier because the ESB is obviously not the only transmission system operator to raise this issue with them. The provision of frequency support and ancillary services, currently available from the thermal generators, is also important as the more that large wind farms can act like traditional power suppliers, the more people will be able to enjoy the same quality of supply from the transmission grid and yet have green energy.

ENERGY STORAGE

Accuracy of wind forecasting is obviously a major issue, and as I have said, we're doing a significant amount of work on that at the moment. Dispatchability, that is central control for larger wind farms, is highly desirable as it enables the TSO to actually instruct the wind farms to switch on or off their banks of turbines. And energy storage is obviously a key issue because a wind farm with energy storage provides the TSO with a lot of the advantages of the traditional thermal generator.

A final comment. As Transmission System Operator, as I have outlined, our main duty is maintaining the integrity of the main grid. We are currently working with a lot of wind farm developers and a huge effort has been put in by them and their manufacturers and consultants to try to accommodate our needs when they are discussing generator connections with us. That is part of the way forward just as here today we are trying to understand each others' needs and establish a collaborative process for the future.

Selling green electricity: a wind farmer's view

by Declan Flanagan

If wind energy is ever to provide a significant amount of electricity in Ireland, the present method of giving supply contracts to generators has to be abandoned. But that would mean the industry becoming dominated by big companies and big banks.

This paper is about the realities of operating a renewable energy company selling electricity. It looks at the commercial practicalities of policy decisions and their implications. The title it was suggested I use - 'Should Ireland export green electricity or just sell green credits?' - reminded me of a story I heard from an official in the Department of Trade and Industry in the UK some time back. When the UK was introducing its green credit scheme (which I'll touch on a little later), he got a call from a guy in the Caribbean island of Montserrat, which is under British administration, who wanted to know if he could get renewable green credit value for a scheme he was planning, a 50 megawatt geothermal scheme on the island. Now, the official just happened to know a little about Montserrat, and asked him 'What's the peak electricity demand on the island?' 'Five megawatts.' 'And what are you going to do with a 50 megawatt geo-thermal scheme?' 'That's not important, I'm going to produce all this greenness that I want to sell.'

The man in Montserrat thought that the fact that there was no outlet for the electricity was somewhat irrelevant. I think that is an important point, because we're talking about the electricity market, the energy market, and I think people need to focus on exactly what is meant by green credits and to understand the implications they will have for the market and for the renewable power generation industry.

First, though, a brief introduction to airtricity. We are an integrated renewable energy company, active currently in the Republic of Ireland, Northern Ireland and Scotland. We have in excess of 2000 megawatts of onshore wind power in development, and we are active offshore in the Arklow Banks project. We have four wind farms currently under contract in the Republic of Ireland, the latest one being with Hibernian Wind Energy which began production in October, 2002. We have a further two under construction. One on King's Mountain, Co. Sligo, is the first transmission-connected wind farm under the new market rules.

The wind farms we own and have constructed have been financed solely on the electricity retail value. This means that they are inherently based on a market risk scenario rather than Alternative Energy Requirement (AER)-type contracts which are supported by a public service obligation framework. This has given us experience in the practicalities of trying to finance long-term, extremely capital-intensive pieces of plant in a market risk scenario where you are talking about a view of the market over the next fifteen years. The implications of EU and government policies are of more than passing interest when you are trying to secure debt for that type of project.

Airtricity is, at least in customer number terms, the largest independent supplier in the all-island market. I use the all-island term because we are active in the North and in the Republic of Ireland; we've been supplying Northern Ireland since July, and in part supplying those customers with renewable energy generated in the Republic. And we also have a track record in the area of green certificates emissions trading. We have done trades into the Dutch and German markets. We are currently developing and are in process of hammering out an innovative renewable obligations certificate with contract in the UK for our first UK farm which should come on stream in the middle of next year. (2003) We also have had some experience in derivative products such as calls and quote options.

Airtricity's first wind farm in Co. Donegal

Here's a picture of Airtricity's first wind farm in Co. Donegal because I think it helps to give some perspective on trying to build more farms, particularly because each turbine in the picture cost a little over a million euros. The next picture is of the first offshore measuring mast in Ireland or the UK which is located 10 kilometres off the coast of Arklow, on the Arklow Bank. It's been there since December 2000.

I think it's important to start by getting clear what we mean when we talk about green credits. It's a term that is bounced around a lot, the saviour and major driver of growth in the renewable energy industry, but it's quite a complex area. Then I'll look at the question should

Ireland adopt the green credit approach to RES, to use the acronym for renewable energy systems. The implications of green credits are

First offshore measuring mast in Ireland or the UK: 10 km off the coast of Arklow, Co. Wicklow installed December 2000

actually quite profound when you adopt a fully market-based approach to the development of the renewable energy industry. And then I will deal with the possibility of Ireland becoming a net exporter of electricity and/or greenness and the commercial risks involved. Airtricity does export but Ireland is not a net exporter of electricity. I think there are lots of practical commercial issues.

The map on the next page is important because it sets out where the wind resources in Europe are, an important consideration when you move to a fully market-based scheme. As it shows, the best resources are in the Republic of Ireland, Northern Ireland and Scotland, and that's where Airtricity is active.

Various support schemes for renewable energy are being used in Europe at present. There is the Refit scheme in Germany, a fixed feed-in tariff available to anyone who connects onto the system. It is quite attractive but it needs to be because of the low wind speeds in Germany. Ireland's AER scheme is a competitive tendering process, similar to the Non Fossil Fuel Obligation (NFFO) one the UK used until recently. And then you have two very different types of green certificate schemes. One type is obligation-based and is now used in the UK. This basically puts an obligation on suppliers of energy to source a certain amount of their energy from renewable schemes and, very importantly, imposes a penalty if they fail. It's a market-based scheme, and with good long-term security: you have the British Government saying that they are committed to this obligation for twenty-six years and so it gives good security to the bank, to the debt-providers, and to us, the commercial operators which is very important.

The other approach to green credits is used in Holland. It involves making qualifying energy exempt from an energy tax. The main problem with that is that the long-term security is not there. Taxes can be changed very quickly at the whim of an incoming government. In fact, the right-wing government in Holland cut it in half, so it doesn't present the type of long-term secu-

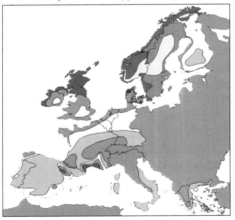

The darker areas are those with the best wind energy resources. Source European Wind Atlas.

rity needed to finance new turbines.

Are market-based obligation schemes better than non-market-based ones such as the Refit type or the NFFO type? Well, non-market-based supports have had their good aspects. The Refit system in Germany created the European wind energy industry which, you could argue, might never have got off the ground otherwise. It also promoted the advancement of technology. But their time, in my view, has now ended. Wind energy cannot move beyond being more than a niche player in the electricity market if it depends on high feed-in tariffs that come under increasing scrutiny as the percentage of energy coming into the system at the perceived high prices goes up. Look what has happened in Denmark where the perceived cost or extra expense of wind energy eventually led to the scrapping of a lot of schemes.

Non market-based schemes do not drive efficiency and do not give the incentive to the industry to strive to become the dominant technology in the world energy market. So, for the reasons I mentioned, market-based obligation schemes are the best way to move the industry forward. The impact, though, of a move from a type of Refit or NFFO system which is perhaps more favourable to small-scale operators than to large-scale ones, to a fully market-based green credit type scheme has very profound implications for the structure of the industry.

In the major Central European markets and Germany in particular, the focus to date has been on the best price supports and not on the best sites. Wind farms have been located not

Wind resources at 50 metres above ground level for five different topographic conditions									
Sheltered terrain		Open plain		At a sea coast		Open sea		Hills and ridges	
ms⁻¹	Wm⁻²	ms⁻¹	Wm⁻²	ms⁻¹	Wm⁻²	ms⁻¹	Wm⁻²	ms⁻¹	Wm⁻²
>6.0	>250	>7.5	>500	>8.5	>700	>9.0	>800	>11.5	>1800
5.0-6.0	150-250	6.5-7.5	300-500	7.0-8.5	400-700	8.0-9.0	600-800	10.0-11.5	1200-1800
4.5-5.0	100-150	5.5-6.5	200-300	6.0-7.0	250-400	7.0-8.0	400-600	8.5-10.0	700-1200
3.6-4.5	50-100	4.5-5.5	100-200	5.0-6.0	150-250	5.5-7.0	200-400	7.0-8.5	400-700
<3.5	<50	<4.5	<100	<5.0	<150	<5.5	<200	<7.0	<400

ms⁻¹ is metres/second   Wm⁻² is watts/square metre

where wind farms should best be located because of the characteristics of the site, but where the best supports were available. That is fine to get an industry started, but it is not the right way for the industry to develop in the long term. As the market outside the meter was of limited importance, operators could just sit back and wait for their Refit, AER or NFFO cheque to arrive. There was limited market risk. But in the future if you go for a green credit type scheme you will be trading a commodity whose price changes, half hour by half hour. Moreover, the green credits themselves will also be tradable and the price will be volatile although maybe not half hour by half hour.

With green credits, future development focuses on the best, highest-yielding sites so you have the most commodity to trade in the market for the lowest production price. The market for things beside electricity now is of absolutely crucial importance. If you don't understand in detail how that market functions, then you are not going to survive. At worst you'll just get ripped off by people in the market because you don't understand the full value of what you have to sell. This is quite common in the UK where people are paid ridiculously low, or offered ridiculously low prices, for wind output energy because of what the supplier says is the discount due to variability. Market risk is greatly increased and this fundamentally changes the debt-raising capacity of operators in the industry as they move from very low risk AER, Refit or NFFO contracts to quite high risk ones under a renewable obligation or a green certificate scheme.

BANKABLE AGREEMENTS

All wind farm developers require bankable power purchase agreements giving security over fifteen years if they are to raise funds. A long-term contract is required. When you move to a green credit type scheme, now your wind farm is not just producing electricity, it is producing electricity and greenness, both of which have different markets, potentially different customers, different contract structures, different characteristics that will drive their price and their value related to the detail of the market rules that exist. The UK is quite an advanced market in terms how far it has gone down the road of market solutions - not all of which have worked, and some of which have been a disaster. A wind farm in the UK now produces five products: electricity; embedded benefit, [if the grid operator benefits from reduced system losses or not having to spend on strengthening the system because a wind farm begins to supply power, the operator will pay the farm for that benefit]; tax benefit, climate change levy; and then the greenness, which has further associated complexity. The complexity of the contractual frameworks involved in financing such a project changes the nature of the industry; it is not a small-time operator's industry any more. You now aim to build, not one or two farms but hundreds of them producing thousands of megawatts because, quite simply, complexity equals risk equals increased cost of capital. It is an unfortunate fact of life that when we consider transition to renewable energy the views of the bankers are absolutely crucial.

Moving to a green certificate market introduces a lot of regulatory risk and this affects the cost of capital. In order to deal with all these complexities and keep the cost of capital down you need to think about derivative products and other ways of securing your cash flows. And so, from an industry dominated by enthusiasts and by small companies, you move to one dominated by large banks and large energy companies. If you go now to renewable energy conferences in the UK, they are dominated by investment banks, something which would not have been the case ten years ago.

So, if we move to green credits, a major consolidation within the renewable energy industry is inevitable. The reason I labour this point is because when we talk about Ireland being a net exporter of renewable energy it is important first of all to think who will actually be generating it? Who will own it? Who will control it? We need to make our decisions on that basis. Airtricity is in the electricity business first and foremost and it is dangerous to think, like our friend in Montserrat, that electricity is just a pesky by-product of the production of this greenness.

In the UK, having introduced the renewable obligation they effectively said 'well, that's renewable sorted, let's forget about them' As a result they introduced an electricity trading regime, connection policy, grid rules, embedded benefit rules and so forth that completely act against renewables, so generators got value for their agreements but lost on all other fronts. Ireland must avoid that trap and focus on renewable energy as an electricity industry first, and develop the market and the physical infrastructure accordingly, to maximise everyone's opportunities.

Should Ireland export renewable energy? I've had some experience of this with Airtricity trades into Ireland and out of the Republic and since six o'clock this morning (November 1, 2002) we have been exporting wind energy into Northern Ireland. Interconnection is obviously the key to the long-term development of renewables but it can work in both ways so it is not that straightforward. Key issues are the availability of capacity, how it is allocated to people in the market, the costs and the rules. This is because as with everything in the electricity system, interconnector rules demand predictability and controllability; and the cheapest renewable wind has neither of these characteristics. So you have to rewrite the rulebook in order to introduce a regime that would allow exports of intermittent renewables. But to do it on a large scale, the type of scale that we are aspiring towards, requires quite a lot of work, not just on the physical issues, but on the commercial practicalities of how much it costs, and how you deal with your risks and exposures in the market.

Despite the warnings I sound, if we want to get a renewable industry that is more than a niche player, then we have to have a market-based regime. This would be extremely complex and the ability to deal with market risks would be crucial. The sector would change utterly but huge opportunities would be created for Ireland because we have the best resource. It is therefore up to us to make sure that we set the rules so that we can exploit it while minimising the potential downsides.

Commission for Energy Regulation

At the end of July 2003, just as this book was going to press, the Commission for Energy Regulation, the body set up to introduce competition to the Irish electricity market, issued a press release outlining the way that electricity would be sold by producers from 2005 onwards. This is the text of the release:

'The Commission for Energy Regulation has announced the new wholesale trading arrangements for electricity market in Ireland, which will come into effect in 2005. According to the Commissioner for Energy Regulation, Mr Tom Reeves: "the finalisation of the new market arrangements for the buying and selling of electricity represent a fundamental change in the way electricity will be traded in Ireland and is one of the most significant milestones to date as we progress towards the full opening of the electricity market to competition in 2005"

The new system of trading in electricity will replace the transitional trading arrangements, which were put in place to open the electricity market in 2000. As electricity cannot be stored, it is bought or sold at half hourly intervals throughout the day, for each day of the year. Under the new arrangements, all generators and suppliers of electricity will be required to buy and sell electricity from a centralised wholesale electricity market, operated by EirGrid. Generators will offer their output into this market, allowing EirGrid to select the lowest offers in each period. EirGrid will also contract, on a half-hourly basis, for spare reserve capacity to maintain a secure supply.

The new market arrangements will encourage new market entrants to build new power stations in locations where generation is most

needed. The prices generators will receive for electricity may vary depending on location. On the other hand, suppliers will pay a uniform wholesale price for electricity. This means that the price final customers pay will not be dependent on where they are located in the country.

These new arrangements will also facilitate a move towards an All-Island and Single European electricity market over the coming years.

Since its establishment in 1927, the ESB has been a de facto monopoly in relation to the generation, distribution, transmission and supply of electricity in Ireland. The adoption of the European Community Electricity Directive (96/92/EC) in 1996 established the legal framework for a Single European Market for Electricity and introduced competition in the Generation and Supply of electricity throughout member states for the first time. The Directive also guaranteed fair and equal access of all parties to the Electricity Networks throughout the country. In 1999, the Commission for Energy Regulation (CER) was established to introduce competition into the Irish electricity market.

Shortly after the CER was established, 28% of the electricity market here was opened to competition, which meant that the top 400 consumers of electricity were free to move from ESB and be supplied

by independent suppliers. In February 2002, an additional 1,200 customers were able to choose their electricity supplier as 40% of the market was opened to competition. In February of next year, SMEs will be free to shop around for electricity when the market opens to 56%. Finally, in 2005, all customers – both domestic and commercial – will be free to choose their electricity supplier.

In tandem with this phased market opening, the markets for "green" electricity or energy generated from renewable sources such as wind and hydro, together with electricity generated by Combined Heat and Power (CHP) are currently fully open to competition. This means that every domestic and commercial customer can currently choose a green or CHP supplier.

Further information on the Trading Arrangements, including a detailed briefing note, is available on the homepage of the CER www.cer.ie'

In another document explaining the arrangements, the CER said that generators would be able to enter the market without having a contract with a distributor. "This will ensure, in particular, that wind generators will not be disadvantaged by the inherent variability of wind generation. Prices will be high in this market at times of peak demand and renewables will get these prices if they are generating."

How the farmers' world will change - new problems, new crops, new opportunities

by Bernard Rice

Although the scope for replacing oil with plant-derived fuels is limited, energy crops could readily produce a tenth of Ireland's total energy demand without seriously curtailing other types of agricultural production. But financial incentives will be needed to make this happen

1. INTRODUCTION

Although farm-based renewable energy production is the main theme of this paper, three other energy-related issues need to be addressed too. First, the agricultural sector is a major source of greenhouse gas and acid-precursor emissions, and it must expect to come under increasing pressure to reduce these. Second, the cost of the energy input on farms is increasing rapidly, with consequent financial problems for an industry in which profit margins are already tight. Finally, the need to abate national greenhouse emissions may open up opportunities for the use of crops, by-products and wastes for renewable energy production.

This paper will therefore review the position under three headings:

• The energy input to agriculture, and possibilities for reduction
• Options for the reduction of greenhouse gas and acid-precursor emissions from present-day agriculture.
• Possibilities for the development of renewable energy from agricultural crops, by-products and wastes.

The new millennium brought a number of forecasts of the changes that might be expected in Irish agriculture over the next 10 to 15 years. These forecasts reflect the likely impact of fac-

tors such as input costs, production technologies, labour cost and availability, market forces, environmental constraints and expected EU agricultural policy. Major changes in the structure of the industry have been forecast, with a much reduced number of much bigger holdings engaged in intensive farming alongside an increased number of small extensive units farmed part-time or in niche activities. However, to date no major changes in the enterprise mix have been predicted (Downey 2000, Donnelly & Crosse 2000). Adjustments to the Common Agricultural Policy may eventually provide the impetus for a move from livestock to non-food production.

The expectation of major structural change, along with the problems caused by BSE and foot-and-mouth disease and the lack of profitability in many enterprises, have led to a fall in morale among farmers. While there is a widespread recognition of the need for new enterprises, the finance and commitment needed to make the transition may be in limited supply.

Of Ireland's total land area of 6.9 Mha, at present almost 5 Mha is used for agriculture and forestry. Of this, about 0.5 Mha is rough pasture suitable only for low-intensity grazing. The current use of the remaining land is grassland 3.5 Mha, forestry 0.65 Mha and arable crops 0.4 Mha.

2. ENERGY INPUT TO AGRICULTURE

The total energy input to agriculture can be divided into that which is used directly (i.e fuel, electricity) and that which is used indirectly to produce farm inputs (e.g. feedstuffs, fertilisers, plant protection products).

2.1 Direct energy use: Data from the Teagasc Irish Farm Survey indicate that Irish farmers purchased about 258 kt (258,000 tonnes) of oil in 2001 at a total cost of about €140M

The Teagasc survey does not include the fuel that was used by farm contractors. An approximate breakdown of on-farm energy consumption by operation, based on estimates of agricultural production and fuel consumption from various sources as well as Oak Park experience, is given in Figure 6A1 (O'Kiely et al 2000, Pellizi et al 1995, Postoven & van Daspelaar 1994, Wegener et al 2002). Since most silage-making as well as some arable crop operations and slurry spreading are carried out by contractors (Figure 6A2), this could bring the total fuel

(FIGURE 6A1) FUEL OIL USE FOR ON-FARM AND TRANSPORT OPERATIONS, 2001 (FROM IRISH FARM SURVEY, TEAGASC)							
System	Dairy	Dairy +other	Cattle	Cattle +other	Mainly sheep	Mainly tillage	All
On-farm oil use per sector (kt)	71.3	43.7	45.5	38.0	23.1	36.7	258.4
On-farm oil cost (M)	38.6	24.2	23.9	19.2	13.0	21.2	140.0
Transport fuel cost (M)	11.9	6.1	12.2	8.4	5.7	1.6	45.9

(Figure 6A1). Apart from a small amount (possibly 5 kt) used for grain drying, this was used predominantly in the engines of tractors and self-propelled machines. Of an additional €126M spent on road vehicle fuel (mainly petrol), €46M was attributed to farming operations. This is equivalent to about 50 kt of fuel.

use on farms up to between 370 and 400 kt at a cost of €220-€240M.

In the National Energy Balance (Dept of Public Enterprise website), 278 ktoe (kt of oil equivalent) was attributed to agriculture in 2001. This equates to 269 kt of diesel oil. The Central

(FIGURE 6A2) ESTIMATE OF ENERGY CONSUMED IN SOME ON-FARM OPERATIONS				
Operation	Area/ tonnage	Energy use	Energy input	
		GJ/ha (t)	PJ/year	kt/year
Forage conservation	1.2 Mha	2.5	2.8	80
Cereals - field operations	0.4 Mha	3.2	1.3	30
Slurry handling/spreading	30 Mt	.04	1.3	29
Other arable crop field operations	0.07 Mha	4	0.3	8
On-farm grain drying	0.1 Mt	0.4	0.4	9

BEFORE THE WELLS RUN DRY

PART 6: HOW A RENEWABLE ENERGY ECONOMY WILL AFFECT RURAL LIFE.

Statistics Office (CSO) website included in its estimates of inputs to agriculture a total of €298M spent on energy and lubricants. Excluding the expenditure on electricity (€74M) and lubricants (€7M), it is estimated that a total of €217M was spent on fuel oils. Both these estimates are in reasonable agreement with the Teagasc survey results.

Apart from fuel oil, the other significant direct energy use on farms is electricity. This is estimated at 52 ktoe in the National Energy Balance for 2001 and €74M in the CSO input estimates. In the Teagasc survey, farmers indicated that €38M (equivalent to about 30 ktoe) of their expenditure on electricity should be attributed to their farming operations. The discrepancy between these estimates stems from the difficulty in separating farm from domestic use.

The total direct energy input on farms is therefore between 400 and 450 ktoe, or between 18 and 20 PJ. This is about 3% of total final consumption in Ireland, so any reductions that might be achieved in agriculture would have little impact on the total consumption figure. Nevertheless an effort to achieve some reduction in on-farm energy consumption is worthwhile, to improve the profitability of operations that are under severe financial pressure as well as to reduce the contribution from agriculture to greenhouse gas and acid-precursor emissions.

According to the estimates in Figure 6A2, silage-making, tillage operations and slurry handling/spreading are the operations requiring most of the direct energy input. Efforts to reduce the use of energy in field operations can be tackled under the following headings:

• **Using the most efficient tractor-implement set-up:** good matching of tractor to machine, appropriate ballasting for high tractive efficiency, use of high-speed pto and high gears for low-power operations, using non-powered implements where possible, increasing working widths to maximum feasible, combining field operations etc

• **Modification of husbandry practices:** extending grazing season to reduce fodder conservation, wilting silage, minimising slurry volumes that require storage and land-spreading, elimination of ploughing, adopting non-drying preservation systems for moist grain etc.

• **Good routine maintenance of tractors and other machines.**

While research and advice can contribute to some efficiency improvements, it has to be acknowledged that the likelihood of achieving large improvements in the present economic climate is not great. At present, farmers' machinery management decisions are primarily concerned with reducing overhead costs and labour. In some cases this may lead to more efficient fuel use e.g. the hire of a contractor with new, efficient equipment. In other cases it may have a negative effect e.g. extension of machine replacement intervals.

Given that there is likely to be a slight reduction in animal numbers, and some diversion of land out of agriculture into forestry, amenity and building development, as well as some improvement in energy efficiency, a reduction of 15-20% in direct energy input to agriculture would appear to be a reasonable target for the next 5 years. In the longer term, a continued gradual reduction is the most that could be expected.

2.2 Indirect energy use: The major indirect inputs of energy into farming are in the form of animal feeds (mainly imported protein), mineral fertiliser, crop protection products and veterinary products. From an energy viewpoint, fertiliser use is the most interesting. Figure 6A3 shows that nitrogen (N) is the dominant factor linked to energy, and that fertiliser energy input is similar in magnitude to direct energy use (Postoven & van Daspelaar 1994). In addition to this energy input, N application also contributes to ammonia and N_2O emissions from the soil, as well as to the leaching of nitrates to watercourses. So a reduction of N use would have significant benefits for agriculture, provided it could be achieved without loss of crop

the next five years, with a further reduction at a similar rate in subsequent years.

Another approach to the reduction of mineral fertiliser input is to achieve a greater substitution of mineral nutrients by animal manure. At present about 400 kt of N is applied in mineral form in Ireland; about half that amount is present in the animal slurry collected on farms (Dept of Agriculture web-site). When farmers

(Figure 6A3) Energy used in fertiliser production			
Fertiliser type	Fertiliser used (kt/year)	Energy used (GJ/t)	Energy used (PJ/year)
N	400	39	15.6
P	50	4.3	0.22
K	150	2.6	0.39
Total			16.2

yield. Possibilities for achieving this will be discussed later.

In relation to current farming, input reduction is the most direct way of reducing emissions. In particular the reduction of N fertiliser would reduce N_2O emission as well as energy input. Farmers need to be persuaded not to exceed recommended fertiliser rates. REPS-type programmes and legislative controls will make a contribution in this direction. In the medium term, research will be directed at improving the precision of recommended rates and timings, backed up by the use of decision-support systems. Looking further ahead, techniques for variable-rate application in response to yield maps and soil analysis, will help to make more effective use of reduced amounts of fertiliser.

Taking all the above into account, a reduction of 10% in the total amount of fertiliser used might be considered an achievable target for

are choosing fertiliser application rates, they make little allowance for the N that is present in the slurry, for two reasons. First, an unknown amount of it is lost in conventional splash-plate spreading. Second, the rate at which the slurry N becomes available to the growing crop is less certain than that of mineral N. The first problem could be greatly eased by the use of a low-emission spreading technique, the second could be improved by anaerobic digestion which would make slurry N availability faster and more predictable.

If some progress can be made in the introduction of these technologies, a 10% increase in the substitution of mineral N by slurry N over the next five years should be attainable.

3. Greenhouse gas and acid-precursor emissions

3.1 Greenhouse gases Global warming is set to become a major international issue over the next

BEFORE THE WELLS RUN DRY

PART 6: HOW A RENEWABLE ENERGY ECONOMY WILL AFFECT RURAL LIFE.

ten years. Ireland's allocation of a 13% increase in GHG in the period from 1990 to 2008-12 was reached in 1998, and an increase close to 30% is feared unless corrective action is taken. The achievement of the 13% target will require that every possibility for CO_2 abatement be fully exploited.

With regard to agriculture, it is reasonable to ask:

1. How can the emissions from current farming practices be curtailed?

2. Can agriculture make a contribution to emission reduction, by creating additional carbon sinks or producing biofuels?

The agricultural sector accounts for 35% of greenhouse gas emissions (Figure 6A4, Convery & Roberts 2000, Environmental Resource Management 1998). This high ratio arises from our big livestock industry, most of whose production is exported. Whatever the reason, efforts to reduce emissions will inevitably focus on the farming sector. Agriculture differs from the other sectors in that it also affects the amount of CO_2 that is recycled by growing crops, and the amount that is stored in soil and over-ground biomass.

Of the approximately 24 Mt of CO_2 equivalent emissions attributed to agriculture, the major contributors are as in Figure 6A5. These figures are taken from the ERM report (Environmental

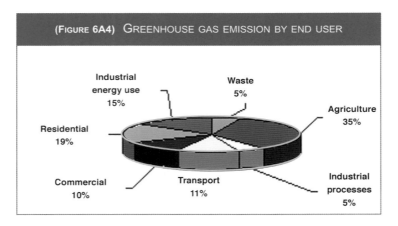

(FIGURE 6A4) GREENHOUSE GAS EMISSION BY END USER

Industrial energy use 15%
Waste 5%
Agriculture 35%
Residential 19%
Commercial 10%
Transport 11%
Industrial processes 5%

(FIGURE 6A5) SOURCES OF GREENHOUSE GAS EMISSIONS FROM AGRICULTURE

Source	Mt CO_2 equiv.	% of total
Methane from in-rumen fermentaion	12.0	49.6
N₂0 from soils	7.6	31.4
Methane from animal wastes	1.3	5.4
N₂0 from animal wastes	.9	3.7
Direct energy use	1.4	5.8
Energy in fertiliser production	1.0	4.1
Total	24.2	100

Resources Management 1998), with the addition of the CO_2 estimated to be associated with direct and indirect energy use on farms.

Methane from in-rumen fermentation can only be tackled by reducing animal numbers or altering their diet. While some reduction in animal numbers may be expected, a large reduction would have serious economic consequences. Diet adjustment would be very difficult to achieve in a largely grass-based industry.

N_2O from soils is very difficult to estimate. It would be reasonable to assume that a reduction

The Gothenberg Protocol requires a 9% reduction of national ammonia emissions (United nations, 1999). Of the total of about 120 kt of ammonia emitted from farms, that from pasture would be almost impossible to reduce by any means other than a reduction of animal numbers (Figure 6A6). Emissions from animal buildings and manure stores would be difficult and expensive to control. The main targets for reduction should be those from the application of mineral fertiliser and from the spreading of animal manure, which account for about 44% of the total.

(Figure 6A6) Sources of ammonia emissions on farms (Convery & Roberts 2000).

Source of ammonia emission	Amount (kt)	% of total
Land-spreading manure	33	27.5
Animal housing	32	26.9
Pasture	30	25.0
Land-spreading mineral N	20	16.7
Manure storage	5	4.2
Total	120	100

of N fertiliser would lead to a reduction of N_2O emissions, though the extent of the reduction is difficult to predict. This leaves us with the lesser items; N_2O and methane from animal wastes, as well as direct energy use and N fertiliser.

3.2 Acid-precursor emissions: In parallel with the Kyoto agreement on greenhouse gases, the Gothenburg Protocol binds Ireland to reductions in acid-precursor emissions over the same 1990-2010 period (United Nations 1999). From the viewpoint of agriculture, ammonia is the main concern, since 90% of ammonia emissions come from agriculture. Agriculture accounts for a much smaller proportion of NOx emissions, but some reduction of the agricultural c ontribution would still be of value.

Of the other acid-precursor emissions, NOx is directly related to combustion. NOx emissions from new and lightly-used tractors in Sweden and Switzerland have been reported at 5 to 15 g/kW h, or 0.42 to 1.27 kg/GJ at 30% engine thermal efficiency (Hannson et al 2001, Rinaldi & Stadler 2002). The US EPA has reported on its web-site average NOx measurements in a tractor fleet of 8.4 g/hp h (equivalent to 11 g/kW h or 0.93 kg/GJ). The Danish RISO National laboratory website lists a NOx emission factor of 1.28 kg/GJ for use with off-road diesel vehicles. This is somewhat higher than the other estimates, possibly because it includes off-road vehicles other than farm tractors which may have longer idling periods. McGettigan & Duffy (2000) have quoted an emission factor for

BEFORE THE WELLS RUN DRY

PART 6: HOW A RENEWABLE ENERGY ECONOMY WILL AFFECT RURAL LIFE.

off-road vehicles of 1.15 kg/GJ. If this is applied to an annual fuel consumption of 320-350 kt, NOX emissions would be about 18 kt. The emissions from the small amount of fuel used in heating/drying would be insignificant. For road vehicles, applying a lower emission factor (0.5 kg/GJ) to the combustion of 50 kt of fuel would give about 1 kt of NOx emissions. This suggests that the total emission of NOx from on-farm fuel use is about 19 kt.

This estimate is considerably higher than the 4.5-5 kt published elsewhere (Curtis 2001, Environment Protection Agency 2001). The difference arises mainly from confusion about the proportion of farm fuel purchases that is used in engines.

Potential for emission reduction:

Anaerobic digestion of slurry would allow the methane to be harnessed for energy use, and thus achieve a double benefit. A recent UK life-cycle analysis has estimated that anaerobic digestion of pig slurry has the potential to reduce emissions by the equivalent of 144 kg of CO_2 per tonne of pig-meat produced (Cumby et al 2000). On this basis, 75% adoption by the pig sector in Ireland would reduce emissions by 16 kt CO_2 per year. A high adoption rate may be achievable in this sector as the technology would fit in easily on the large centralised units that now make up most of the industry. Also these units are having increasing difficulty finding land nearby for land-spreading, and the smells from slurry transport and spreading are becoming an increasing problem.

The technology would also be applicable to the dairy industry, but is likely to have a much slower uptake. Units are smaller, smells are less of a problem, and to date on most farms the land bank is adequate to take all the slurry. A 10% adoption would abate about 60 kt CO_2 per year. The beef sector has had so many recent prob-

lems and is generally so unprofitable that it is difficult to envisage investment in anything but the most essential items in the near future.

If digestion could be introduced at the above projected levels over the next five years, a total of about 80 kt/year of CO_2 could be abated. An Irish Bio-energy Association report estimates that the total potential for CO_2 abatement by digesting all animal manures is 5Mt/year (Irish Bio-energy Association 2000).

A reduction of mineral N usage, or a transfer from urea to ammonium nitrate, would bring about some reduction in the associated ammonia emission. But the main possibility to achieve a substantial emission reduction is to use a low-emission slurry spreading system. Reductions of up to 50% could be achieved with a simple band-spreading technique. If 50% of animal manure were spread with this system, most of the required 9% reduction of ammonia emissions could be achieved.

The main limitation to the adoption of low-emission spreading techniques is the need to improve machine design and all stages of slurry collection and storage and agitation to avoid blockages. The extra cost of spreading would also be a deterrent, and farmers may be expected to continue with the present splash-plate system until they perceive some financial advantage in changing.

In summary, a combination of low-emission slurry spreading systems and slurry digestion could achieve a combination of useful objectives:

• Digestion would ease the blockage problems that are limiting the uptake of low-emission spreading
• Both would contribute to a reduction of slurry smells during spreading.
• The required 9% reduction in ammonia

emissions would be achieved.

• Methane emissions from animal wastes would be reduced by the equivalent of about 80 kt of CO_2.

• Crop utilisation of slurry N would be quicker and more predictable, so the opportunity to substitute slurry N for mineral N would be increased.

On this basis, a substitution of 10% of the applied mineral N by slurry N might be achievable over a five-year period.

A quick reduction of NOx emissions from agriculture would be difficult to achieve. The fall in fuel use projected in Section 2.1 would bring a corresponding reduction in NOx emissions. In the long-term, a 3-tier schedule of regulatory emission controls aims to halve

NOx emissions on new off-road engines by 2010. In the interim, the methods that might be considered to achieve a more immediate reduction of NOx emissions would be:

• Retro-fit catalytic converters, while tightening fuel specifications to prolong converter life

• Persuade users to reduce idle and low-load running of tractor engines, when NOx emissions are highest.

Many difficulties could be foreseen in the implementation of either action.

4. OPPORTUNITIES FOR ENERGY PRODUCTION FROM AGRICULTURAL CROPS AND BY-PRODUCTS

4.1 Overall potential: The total potential for energy production from agriculture can be esti-

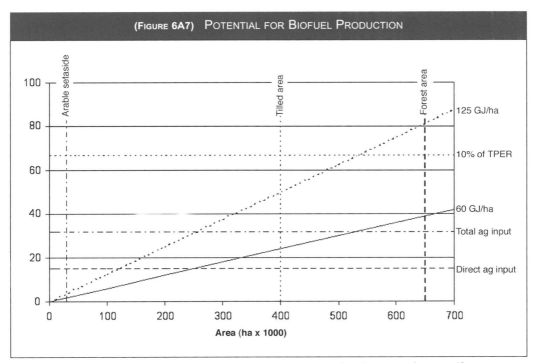

Figure 6A7: Potential for energy production from crops grown for direct combustion (forestry, coppice, hemp, miscanthus, whole-crop cereals etc) and for liquid biofuel production (rape-seed, cereals, sugar-beet etc). TPER stands for Ireland's Total Primary Energy Requirement.

BEFORE THE WELLS RUN DRY

PART 6: HOW A RENEWABLE ENERGY ECONOMY WILL AFFECT RURAL LIFE.

(FIGURE 6A8) POTENTIAL FOR ENERGY PRODUCTION FROM RESIDUE MATERIALS				
Material	Potential volume (kt)	Calorific value MJ/kg	Energy form	Total energy production PJ
Forest residues	300	13	Heat or ethanol	4
Cereal straw	300	13	Heat or ethanol	4
Manures	30000	0.07	Methane	2
Oils/fats	90	35	Liquid biofuel	3
Molasses			Ethanol	
Total				23

mated by adding the potential from energy crops to that from by-products of existing enterprises. From crops converted by some form of combustion to heat, an energy yield from 100 to 200 GJ/ha might be achieved, depending on the crop selection, land quality etc. Assuming that an average energy yield of 125 GJ/ha could be achieved, the current set-aside area could produce about 4 PJ, or 11% of the total agricultural energy demand. To achieve, say, 10% of national primary energy requirement from biomass crops, an area of over 0.5Mha would be required, i.e. more than the current arable area (Fig. 6A7). At the extreme, the total Irish land resource could just about produce our national primary energy requirement.

Crops grown for liquid biofuel production (e.g. rape-seed for biodiesel, cereals or beet for ethanol) would produce a lower amount of energy, probably about 60 GJ/ha. Crops for these purposes are more likely to be annual arable crops. If the full arable set-aside area were devoted to them, it would produce about 1.8 PJ, or 40 ktoe, i.e. about 15% of the agricultural fuel requirement. To supply the full agricultural fuel oil need would require almost all the current arable area to be devoted to it.

The main by-product materials that could make a contribution are as in Figure 6A8. Some of

these materials (e.g. molasses, some straw) have existing markets which underpin their price; others have more limited outlets. Also materials such as slurry from small dry-stock units could hardly be utilised economically, and forest residues would be better left in situ on many sites. A rough estimate of the volumes that might be available at a reasonable price and the amount of energy they might produce is also given in Figure 6A8.

4.2 Biofuel technologies: Of the many possibilities for producing biofuels from farm produce, three of the more likely possibilities for Ireland are considered here:
- biogas from animal slurry
- heating or diesel engine fuel from vegetable oils or animal fats
- ethanol from sugar beet, cereals or cellulosic materials.

4.2.1 Biogas from animal slurry: This has already been discussed in detail. If the targets mentioned for slurry digestion were achieved (i.e 10% of dairy slurry and 75% of pig slurry digested), about 10 MWe of electricity could be generated from the biogas produced. This is a much more conservative estimate than that of the Irish Bio-energy Association (IrBEA), who suggest that 250 MWe could be produced from biogas (IrBEA, 2000).

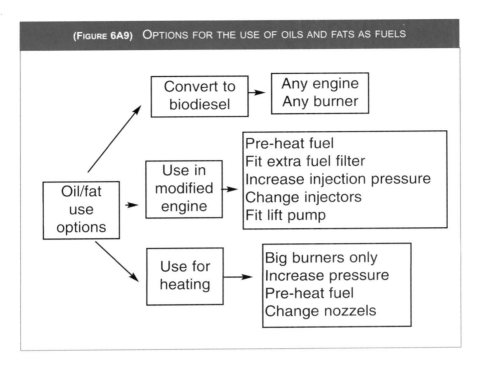

(FIGURE 6A9) OPTIONS FOR THE USE OF OILS AND FATS AS FUELS

4.2.2 Oils and fats as heating or diesel engine fuels: Vegetable oils and animal fats can provide a source of renewable fuel, either for diesel engines or heating systems. Some of these uses are already well developed, others are still under development (Fig. 6A9).

Any of these uses would reduce CO_2 emissions by over 3 tonnes per tonne of fuel used. Also these fuels have no sulphur, which improves exhaust emissions, and they are biodegradable, which reduces pollution risks from spillages.

These materials could never replace more than a small fraction of the mineral diesel requirement. They should be seen instead as premium fuels whose use should be directed to applications that make best use of their health and environmental advantages.

Oils and fats can be used as engine fuels in two ways:

1. In unprocessed form, with some peripheral modifications to the engine. This use is relatively new but developing rapidly in Germany; engine conversion kits are on sale and are working very well. The conversion consists of some combination of fuel pre-heating, extra filtration, increased injection pressure and replacement injectors. More information on exhaust emissions is needed. Fuel processing cost and industry start-up costs are kept to a minimum. This approach would have particular relevance in Ireland; it needs a low capital investment, the by-product cake can be used locally, and it is possible to start small and expand later.

2. Converted into biodiesel and used in any engine without modification. This use is widely accepted and supported by the vehicle industry. Also the fuel has been proven to emit less particulates and smoke than mineral diesel. This reduces the harmful effects of exhaust emissions in cities. About 1Mt/yr is produced and used in the EU. It requires substantial plant investment, and processing adds about 5-10

BEFORE THE WELLS RUN DRY

PART 6: HOW A RENEWABLE ENERGY ECONOMY WILL AFFECT RURAL LIFE.

cents/litre to the final cost of the fuel.

The use of these fuels for heating in large-scale burners is technically feasible, but economic viability depends on a very low raw material price, competitive with heavy-grade mineral oil. Use in domestic-scale heating units would be more economical, but the availability of suitable burners at a reasonable price remains a problem.

Currently, the main fuel use of oils/fats in the EU is biodiesel produced from crops grown on set-aside land: mainly rape in N. Europe, with some sunflower in the south. Oil-seed crops grown on set-aside in Ireland would also provide as a by-product a native source of GM-free animal feed protein, which would find a ready market. Ireland has about 30,000ha of set-aside; if two-thirds of this could be brought into oil-seed production, it would provide about 20 kt of fuel oil and 40 kt of oil-seed cake.

A cheaper raw material is recycled vegetable oil (RVO) oil from caterers. The use of this material in animal feeds has been disrupted since the 1999 Belgian dioxin-in-chickens incident, which was traced to RVO. If no alternative use is found in the Republic, two possibilities arise:

• Collection will shrink, and more will be dumped into sewers and land-fills.
• It will be exported for biodiesel production to Northern Ireland, which will benefit from the introduction of a 20p/litre excise remission announced in their 2002 budget.

Up to 10 kt/year could be collected. Oak Park research, together with research and practical experience in Austria, is showing that it can be used to make good quality biodiesel.

Beef tallow, whose market as an animal feed has been disrupted by BSE, is another possibility. The disposal of tallow from the rendering of BSE-risk offals (ca. 3000t) has been resolved

by its use in boilers in rendering plants. Total tallow production is about 60 kt, two-thirds of which goes to animal feed. The long-term future of tallow as animal feed is in some doubt, and alternative outlets are very desirable. Its use for heating is already being demonstrated, but a transport use would have a higher value.

Biofuel technologies are still relatively new. While the price difference between them and fossil fuels has narrowed significantly in recent years, they still need some pump-priming support in the early stages of competition with fossil fuels. Present costs vary from about 30 cents/litre for clean RVO used unprocessed to 55-65 cents/litre for biodiesel from fresh rapeseed oil. This compares with about 30-40 cents/litre for mineral diesel before excise, VAT and distribution costs.

Subsidy for biofuels could be justified on many grounds:
• Reduction of greenhouse gas emissions
• Reduction of harmful exhaust emissions from diesel engines
• Recycling of organic materials currently in or heading for the waste stream
• Provision of native, renewable fuel supply with associated economic activity
• Development of renewable fuel technologies that will be needed in the future
• Compliance with substitution obligations in upcoming EU Directive proposals

Some EU member states (e.g France, Germany, Italy, Austria and Spain) promote vehicle biofuel production by reducing road excise. This support mechanism is permitted by the EU. The Scandinavian countries promote all forms of biofuel use by means of their carbon tax regimes. In the UK, a remission of 20p/litre on biodiesel was introduced in 2002. At this stage, virtually all of Europe except Ireland has some form of support for vehicle biofuels. The UK measure is likely to stimulate considerable biodiesel production, and in the absence of similar action here, a cross-border traffic in feed-stocks is likely to develop.

The EU is now considering proposals from the Transport Directorate to oblige member states to achieve target substitution rates of mineral fuels by their equivalent biofuels. The targets proposed begin with 2% by December 2005, extending to 5.75% by 2010. To meet the 2% target on the diesel side, Ireland would need to use 70kt of oils/fats as vehicle fuel. This would be very difficult to achieve. A possible combination of feedstocks would be as follows:

- 20 kt rapeseed oil from 20,000ha set-aside
- 40 kt tallow
- 8 kt Recycled Vegetable Oil (RVO)

This would supply most of the buses and taxis in Dublin. If the fuel were used in this way it would achieve the following:

- *Halve the amount of particulates emitted by these vehicles*

- *Reduce CO₂ emissions by about 200 kt: Reduce sulphur emissions, and consequent acid rain damage to buildings*

- *Maintain the viability of rendering plants.*

- *Sustain jobs in RVO collection services and farms.*

- *Achieve the mineral diesel substitution tar get contained in the EU's proposed directive*

At a similar level of support to the proposed UK excise remission, the maximum cost to the exchequer would be 15M euro/yr. The combination of all the benefits from the project would well out-weigh this cost. Unlike the UK proposal, the support should be provided for any use of vegetable oils or animal fats as vehicle fuels. The market could then dictate which technologies are most appropriate in Ireland.

4.2.3 Ethanol as vehicle fuel There are two likely ways in which ethanol could be used as fuel for spark-ignition engines in Ireland:

(i) Petrol-ethanol blends may be used in conventional unmodified spark-ignition engines. An EU directive permits the use of up to 5% ethanol in blends with petrol (Commission of European Communities, 1985). This approach is widely used in the US, but has not been

(FIGURE 6A10) PRODUCTION COSTS OF ETHANOL FROM CONVENTIONAL FEED-STOCKS				
Feed-stock	Feed-stock cost less by-product value	Processing	Transport	Total
	Cost (cents/litre)			
Sugar beet	24	24	5	53
Wheat	22	29	1	52
Barley	22	29	1	51

BEFORE THE WELLS RUN DRY

PART 6: HOW A RENEWABLE ENERGY ECONOMY WILL AFFECT RURAL LIFE.

(FIGURE 6A11) PRODUCTION COSTS OF ETHANOL FROM LIGNO-CELLULOSE FEED-STOCKS				
Feed-stock	Feed-stock cost less by-product value	Processing	Transport	Total
	(cents/litre)			
Grass	18-24	25-32	7-17	50-73
Straw	20	36	5	61
Wood-chips	10-14	36	1-2	47-52

favoured in the EU, due to technical problems with the handling and storage of the fuel, caused by its solubility in water and high vapour pressure.

(ii) Blends of the ethanol derivative ETBE (ethyl tertiary butyl ether) and petrol may also be used in unmodified engines. The 1985 directive authorises up to 15% ETBE in blends. This has been the most favoured approach to ethanol use in the EU. ETBE can replace MTBE as an octane enhancer in lead-free petrol. MTBE is in the process of being banned from this use in California, due to the contamination of water supplies by exhaust emissions. If this trend becomes widespread, it would stimulate the demand for ETBE. A problem in Ireland would be the additional plant requirement for the conversion of ethanol to ETBE.

A Teagasc review has dealt with this subject in detail (Rice et al 1997). Total production costs have been estimated for conventional and ligno-cellulosic materials in tables 6A10 and 6A11 which show a range of production costs from 47 to 73 cents/litre, depending on the feed-stock materials, feed-stock price and transformation process.

Ethanol has a calorific value about two-thirds that of petrol. On this basis, its value as a petrol replacement, before tax or distribution cost, is less than 25 cents/litre. A comparison with the price of methanol, based on its octane-enhancing properties, would give it a similar value. Even a full remission of road excise would make only the lowest-cost wood-chip scenario competitive; further economies would have to be achieved to reduce costs with all the conventional conversion systems.

The main advantage of ethanol production as an outlet for arable crops is that it can be produced from such a wide range of feed-stocks, many of which are already being grown, so the technology for production, harvesting, drying and storage is already in place. If used as an additive to petrol, a distribution and marketing system is also in place, so the process plant is the only additional requirement.

In spite of the apparently unfavourable economics of bio-ethanol production to date, it has become well established in the US, where production is stimulated by the need to oxygenate mineral fuels to comply with clean air legislation. Current US long-term projections are for an industry producing large volumes of bio-ethanol from low-cost by-product or residue ligno-cellulose materials at a cost approaching that of petrol. The long-term availability of suitable raw materials in Ireland, and the benefit of a low-value outlet for by-product or residue ligno-cellulose materials, needs to be further evaluated.

Ethanol production from sugar beet merits special consideration because of its potential synergistic relationship with the existing sugar industry. Facilities are already in place for the organisation of crop production under contract, and for transport, reception, pre-cleaning and juice extraction; only the fermentation and distillation plant would need to be added.

Ireland currently plants about 35,000 ha of sugar beet. Land for the production of extra beet would be available; with sugar yields continuing to increase and at best a constant sugar quota, it would at least ensure that the area under beet would be maintained at current levels for the medium-term future. Sugar beet is a high-input crop; as well as creating a demand for farm labour and other inputs for the production of the crop, it also generates many spin-off benefits, such as animal feed supply, labour for haulage and processing, and local farm machinery production.

Beet for ethanol production would not be grown on set-aside land, so it would not compete for land with a vegetable oil industry. Teagasc estimates the variable costs of sugar-beet production for 2002 at 1462 Euro/ha (O'Mahoney, 2001). At the B-quota price of about 35 Euro/t, a yield of 42 t/ha would be required to recoup these costs. Given that this is close to the average yield, beet production at this price might be expected to have limited attraction for growers. However, other issues, such as the avoidance of outside-quota prices in high-yield years, would also play a part in farmers' decision-making.

A bio-ethanol industry would make only a small contribution to the reduction of CO_2 emissions, as a result of the relatively large amount of energy used in processing.

The main advantages of bio-ethanol as an additive to petrol are:

(i) its oxygenating effect, leading to a reduction of CO in vehicle emissions and a reduced potential for ozone formation in the atmosphere.
(ii) its effect as an octane enhancer, as an alternative to lead compounds or MTBE.
(iii) the absence of sulphur.
(iv) reduction of hydrocarbons in the emissions.

(FIGURE 6A12) A SCENARIO FOR AN 8% REDUCTION IN GREENHOUSE GAS EMISSIONS FROM AGRICULTURE		
Source	Mt CO_2 equivalent	
	Now	+ 5 years
Methane from animals	12.0	11.2
N_2O from soils	7.6	7.2
Methane from animal waste	1.3	1.1
N_2O from animal wastes	0.9	0.8
Direct energy use	1.5	1.3
Energy in fertiliser	1.0	0.9
Less oil/fat energy	0	-0.3
Total	24.3	22.2

BEFORE THE WELLS RUN DRY

PART 6: HOW A RENEWABLE ENERGY ECONOMY WILL AFFECT RURAL LIFE.

5. CONCLUSIONS

Given that there is likely to be a slight reduction in animal numbers, and some diversion of land out of agriculture into forestry, amenity and building development, as well as some improvement in energy efficiency, a reduction of 15-20% in direct energy input to agriculture would appear to be a reasonable target for the next five years. In the longer term, a continued gradual reduction is the most that could be expected. A reduction of 10% in the N fertiliser input, with a corresponding reduction of indirect energy input, might also be considered an achievable target.

Since much of the greenhouse gas emissions from agriculture are very difficult to control, the scope for reduction is limited. Nevertheless, some reduction is attainable. Figure 6A12 indicates how a reduction of over 9% could be achieved over the next five years.

The reduction in methane from animals is projected on the basis of a small reduction in animal numbers. The reduction in N_2O from soils and in fertiliser energy would be achieved by a reduction in mineral fertiliser use, which in turn would be partly due to a fall in overall N application and partly due to an increased substitution of slurry N. The fall in direct energy input would be mainly achieved by greater efficiencies in machinery use. Finally, the production of methane and the use of oils and fats as fuels could contribute an abatement of up to 300 kt. The reduction of N use in urea form and the adoption of low-emission manure spreading techniques could make up the required 9% reduction in ammonia emissions. There would be a synergistic effect from the simultaneous introduction of digestion and low-emission spreading; digestion would reduce blockages, and full-width spreading should give more even distribution and facilitate substitution of mineral N.

The other benefits that would accrue from the developments listed above would be:

- A reduction in slurry spreading smells
- An improvement in vehicle exhaust emissions from biofuel use
- A secured outlet for recycled vegetable oil (RVO) and tallow
- A start made to the development of technologies which will undoubtedly be required in the future
- A contribution made to compliance with EU requirements in relation to greenhouse gases and acid precursor emissions, air quality and liquid biofuel substitution.

In all these areas, technologies are now well established and in practical use in other EU countries. Such incentives as have been available in Ireland to date to stimulate renewable energy production have not been sufficient to stimulate the establishment of viable projects. To allow a beginning to be made, two changes are needed immediately: a reduction or remission of road excise on biofuels and an increased price for electricity from biomass. Since the size of the biomass resource is limited and no exchequer costs are incurred until the renewable energy is produced, these measures could be introduced with very little risk to the economy.

6. SUMMARY

This paper addressed three inter-linked problems related to energy in agriculture:

- The energy used in farming and ways of reducing it
- The options for the reduction of greenhouse gas and acid-precursor emissions
- The possibilities for renewable energy production.

Engine fuel (almost 0.3 Mt) is agriculture's main direct energy input. Since there is likely to be a slight reduction in animal numbers and some diversion of land out of agriculture, as well as some improvement in energy efficiency, a reduction of 15-20% in this input over the next five years would appear to be a reasonable target. In the longer term, a continued gradual reduction is the most that can be expected.

Nitrogenous fertiliser (N) is the biggest indirect energy input. With greater precision in N use, and an increased substitution of slurry for mineral N, a reduction of 20% over five years without reducing output should be achievable.

With agriculture contributing over one-third of national greenhouse gas emissions, pressures for reduction must be expected as the effort to achieve Kyoto targets intensifies. Some abatement of ammonia emissions is also required to comply with other international commitments. To achieve both of these targets without reducing output, digestion and low-emission spreading of animal slurry to minimise methane and ammonia emissions are the most promising options.

If liquid biofuel crops (for vegetable oil or ethanol) were grown on the existing set-aside area, it could supply about 10% of the agricultural fuel demand. To meet the full agricultural fuel demand, an area of about 0.3Mha (6% of the farmed area) would be needed.

Where the whole of an energy crop is utilised in a heating or CHP plant, about 0.5Mha would be required to meet 10% of the total national primary energy demand. This could be set as a medium-term target that could be achieved

without major disruption of the existing levels of food and feed production. At the extreme, the total farmed area could produce an amount of energy roughly equivalent to our national primary energy demand.

Waste or by-product materials such as wood residues, straw, tallow and recovered vegetable oil would produce relatively small amounts of energy, but as reasonably-priced feedstocks they could help get biofuel industries started. Animal manures have a large potential, and their digestion could play a key role in the reduction of methane and ammonia emissions. Digestion of all pig and some dairy slurry should be a medium-term target.

The most promising technologies for the conversion of farm biomass to energy are:

• Vegetable oils and animal fats as engine fuels in vehicles or CHP plants: this would entail the conversion of either the fuel to biodiesel or the engine.
• Ethanol as a replacement for MTBE in petrol, either converted to ETBE or used directly: this might be produced from sugar-beet and sugar processing by-products, from cereals, or eventually from wood-waste.
• Methane production from animal slurries, used in heating or CHP plants.
• Direct combustion or gasification of wood or other energy crops in heating or CHP plants or as domestic fuel.

In all these areas, technologies are now well established and in practical use in other EU countries.

REFERENCES

Convery, F., Roberts, S., 2000. *Farming, climate and the environment in Ireland.*

Cumby, T., Nigro, E., Sandars, D.L., Canete,C., Williams, A.G., Scotford,I.M., Audsley,E., 2000. The environmental impact of farm scale anaerobic digestion of livestock wastes. Paper 00-AP-024, AgEng Conference, Warwick, July 2000.

Donnelly, L., Crosse, S., 1999. A perspective of the dairy industry 2010. Proc. Agri-food Millenium Conference. Teagasc, 19 Sandymount Ave, Dublin 4.

Downey, L., 1999. What will the agri-food industry look like in 2015?, Proc. Agri-food Millenium Conference. Teagasc, 19 Sandymount Ave, Dublin 4.

Environmental Resources Management, 1998. *Limitation and Reduction of CO_2 and other greenhouse gases in Ireland.* Government Publications Sale Office, Molesworth St., Dublin 2.

Hansson, P.A., Lindgren, M., Noren, O., 2001. A comparison between different methods of calculating average engine emissions for agricultural tractors. *J. agric. Engng. Res*, 80,1:37-43.

Irish Bio-energy Association, 2000. Strategy for Anaerobic Digestion Development in Ireland. IrBEA, c/o Tipperary Institute, Thurles, Co. Tipperary.

O'Kiely, P., McNamara, Forristal, D., K, Lenehan, J.J. 2000. Grass silage in Ireland. *Farm and Food,* Winter 2000, pp. 33-38.

McGettigan, M., Duffy, P., 2000. *Emissions to air 1990-1998.* Environment Protection Agency, Johnstown Castle, Co Wexford.

Pellizi, G., Cavalchini, A.G., Lazzari, M., (editors), 1989: *Energy savings in agricultural machinery and mechanization.* Elsevier Applied Science Publishers, Crown House, Linton Rd, Barking, Essex 1G11 8JU, England.

Pothoven, R., van Dasselaar, A., 1994. Extensief kost energie: energieverbruik in de akkerbouw. *Landbouwmechanisatie*, 45 (6) 38-40.

Rice, B., Bulfin, M., Kent, T., Frohlich, A., Lenehan, J.J., 1997. *Potential for Energy Production from Agricultural and Forest Biomass in Ireland.* Teagasc, 19 Sandymount Ave., Dublin 4.

Rinaldi,M., Stadler, E., 2002. *Trends im Abgasverhalten landwirtschaftlicher Traktoren.* Berichte 577/2002, Forschungsanstalt fur Agrarwirtschaft und Landtechnik, CH-8356 Tanikon TG, Switzerland.

United Nations, 1999. Draft Protocol to the 1979 Convention on long-range transboundary air pollution to abate acidification, eutrophication and ground level ozone. ECE/EB.AIR/1999/1. UNECE, Geneva.

Wegener, U., Koch, H.-J., and Miller, H., 2001. Effect of long-term reduced tillage on the energy balance of sugar beet and winter wheat crops, Proc. 65th Congress International

Sustainability through local self-sufficiency

by Folke Günther

Modern agricultural is a device to convert large amounts of fossil fuel into human food. It is therefore very vulnerable to energy scarcity and supply disruption. Making it more sustainable requires nutrient recycling and that people live near where their food is grown.

Sustainability is a multi-levelled quality in which some of the constituent qualities are more basic than others. If a basic quality is not fulfilled, the fulfilment of less basic qualities is not enough to bring sustainability about. To explain, take the concept seaworthines, which is also multi-levelled. The most basic need for the seaworthiness of a ship is that it doesn't sink. Next, it should withstand the weather at sea. If it can't float, weather resistance is superfluous. Next, navigation capacity is necessary, and so on. All the new qualities need the more basic ones to be fulfilled if they are to be of use.

The same goes for sustainability. Some qualities are basic, others are necessary but not basic. All the basic qualities must be fulfilled for a higher-level quality to have any effect.

Sustainability is also long-term. A hundred year sustainability is not worth the name.

Like many scientific theories, sustainability is easiest to test with the help of zero-hypotheses such as - 'if this requirement is not fulfilled, is the system still sustainable?' If this approach is used, sustainability does not generally need to be defined but any factor can be tested for its effect on the general sustainability of the system. This method is used to identify the crucial factors for local sustainability in this study. Vulnerability could be said to be the inverse of sustainability. An effort to increase the sustainability of a system is often equivalent to reducing its vulnerability. One of the more basic requirements for a sustainable society is that it cannot be dependent on storage for its survival.

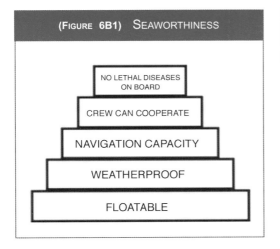

(FIGURE 6B1) SEAWORTHINESS

NO LETHAL DISEASES ON BOARD

CREW CAN COOPERATE

NAVIGATION CAPACITY

WEATHERPROOF

FLOATABLE

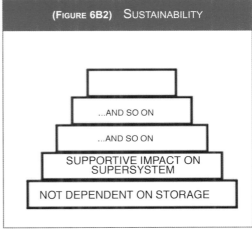

(FIGURE 6B2) SUSTAINABILITY

...AND SO ON

...AND SO ON

SUPPORTIVE IMPACT ON SUPERSYSTEM

NOT DEPENDENT ON STORAGE

BEFORE THE WELLS RUN DRY

PART 6: HOW A RENEWABLE ENERGY ECONOMY WILL AFFECT RURAL LIFE.

If it is, its sustainability cannot last longer than the contents of the store.

STORAGE DEPENDENCY

Storage dependency is frequent in our society and a real threat to its sustainability. Two such dependencies will be discussed, dependency on stored energy, and dependency on stored nutrients, especially phosphorus.

All societies are dependent on agricultural production and today's agriculture is heavily dependent on fossil fuels. In developed countries, the input of fossil fuel energy to agriculture equals or surpasses the output of energy in the food supplied for human consumption (Hoffman, 1995). This is why industrial agriculture has been described as a black box for

converting fossil fuel energy into edible food energy.

The implicit assumption underlying this conversion is that fossil fuel and the other necessary inputs will always be so cheap that they will not increase food prices beyond what the public can afford. This assumption can be questioned.

Energy prices are hard to calculate. The price for, say, gasoline at a filling station changes almost daily, as do the wages of many of those who buy it. Therefore, it is hard to say if the energy is 'cheap' or 'expensive'. One way to handle this problem is to calculate how long time a person has to work in order to get a certain amount of energy.

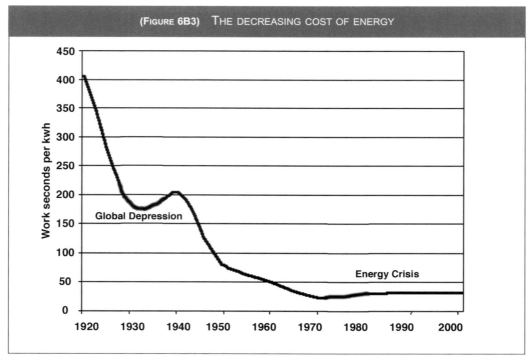

(FIGURE 6B3) THE DECREASING COST OF ENERGY

The price of energy, in terms of the hours worked to earn KWH, has fallen to a tenth of its 1920 level. This means that the access to energy has increased tenfold. Note the events ('general depression, 'energy crisis') during energy price increases.

The result of such a calculation is shown in Figure 6B3, where the price for gasoline (in SEK/kWh) in Sweden is divided by the salary (in SEK/hour) of a 'general' worker. This shows the availability of energy in the form of gasoline to the worker in hours/kWh. The working time needed to purchase one kWh of gasoline in 1995 has diminished to about 0.1 of the time needed about 1920, i.e., the availability has increased ten times.

As can be seen in figure 6B4, about half of the world's reserves of crude oil have already been used up (873 of 2027 GB in 2002 *(ASPO Newsletter 25, January 2003)*. The remaining reserves present two problems:

• With the increasing scarcity of the resource, extraction can be expected to require more energy for each unit of energy produced than those units produced already. In other words, the energy yield per unit of energy (YPE) used in the extraction will fall.

• After the peak has been reached in the rate of extraction, energy output capacity will be below the demand, a serious problem which will be discussed later.

Calculations made from the verified crude oil reserves indicate that its availability will be of a relatively short duration, less than 50 years for conventional oil, about 60 years for all oil liquids, given the current rate of resource use

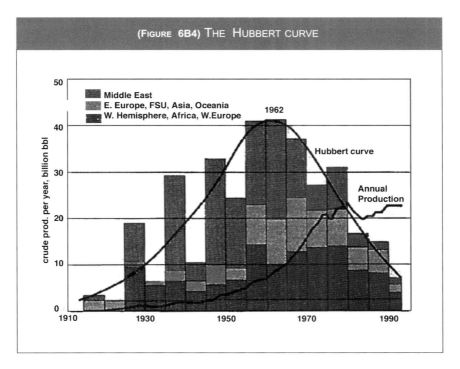

The 'Hubbert curve' displays the discoveries of crude oil during this century. They follow a bell-shaped figure with a peak around 1960. After that, no major fields were found. The total amount of extracted oil (the space under the curve 'Annual production') can never exceed the space under the Hubbert curve. If the time lag of the two curves holds, a peak production can be expected 2000 - 2005. (Adapted from Ivanhoe, 1995)

BEFORE THE WELLS RUN DRY

PART 6: HOW A RENEWABLE ENERGY ECONOMY WILL AFFECT RURAL LIFE.

(FIGURE 6B5) ESTIMATES OF WHEN OIL PRODUCTION WILL PEAK	
Year of peak	**Author and publication date**
2003	Campbell, 1998
2004	Bartlett, 2000
2007	Duncan and Youngquist, 1999
2019	Bartlett, 2000
2020	Edwards, 1997
2010-2020	International Energy Agency, 1998
2012	**Average of the above estimates**

today. As long ago as 1994, Masters published a review of global oil discoveries this century that showed a definite peak of discoveries around 1960 and a definite decline thereafter. Ivanhoe (1995) referred to the weighted average of the global oil discoveries, a typical bell-shaped curve, known as the Hubbert curve, after King Hubbert, who pioneered these calculations. The actual extraction of oil tends to follow a similar curve to that of the discoveries but with a lag of about 40 years.

These curves have recently attracted considerable attention but among geologists and engineers rather than economists. Different observers have produced different estimates of the time of the peak (Figure 6B5) Since 'you cannot use oil that has not been found' the remainder of the extraction curve can take one of three principally different shapes (Figure 6B6):

A. An extraction increase, followed by a steep drop. This curve doesn't seem realistic, as only a few states (mainly Saudi Arabia, and to some extent Iran, Iraq, Kuwait, UAE, Venezuela and Nigeria) actually have the potential to increase extraction.

B. A constant extraction rate, followed by a

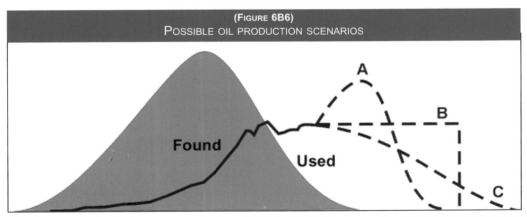

(FIGURE 6B6)
POSSIBLE OIL PRODUCTION SCENARIOS

Since the area under the 'used' curve can never be larger than that under the 'found' curve, three principally different extraction principles emerge.

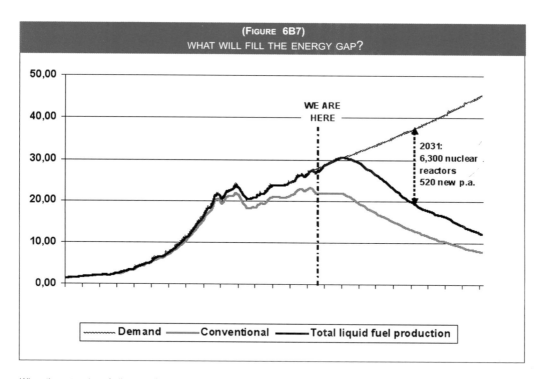

(FIGURE 6B7)
WHAT WILL FILL THE ENERGY GAP?

When the extraction of oil can no longer meet the demand around 2012, a sharp increase in price can be expected. The theoretical demand is assumed to increase 1% annually after 2004. To fill up the demand gap, about 6,300 new nuclear reactors would be needed by 2031, and the production of an additional 520 annually thereafter. Data from C. Campbell 2003. The calculations are mine.

production crash. This curve is unrealistic since YPE (energy yield per unit of energy) falls in ageing fields. However, a curve of this general type could be expected from efforts to prolong the plateau phase.

C. Dwindling production. This type seems to be the most realistic.

ENERGY AND ECONOMIC ACTIVITY

Since the world economy largely is powered by easily accessed energy, a decrease in energy availability might explain the recent global economic slowdown. The curve in Figure 6B8 has a relation to the curve in Figure 6B4 that does not seem entirely accidental.

BEFORE THE WELLS RUN DRY

PART 6: HOW A RENEWABLE ENERGY ECONOMY WILL AFFECT RURAL LIFE.

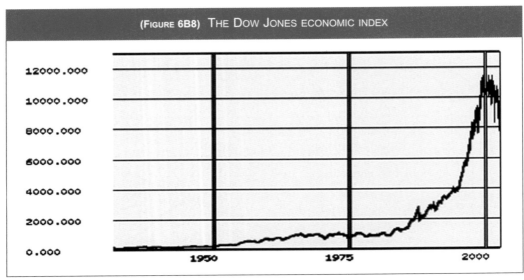

(FIGURE 6B8) THE DOW JONES ECONOMIC INDEX

Figure 6B8 The Dow Jones economic index shows a curve similar in shape to the curve of energy extraction from oil (Figure 6B4).

GAME THEORY ANALYSIS

Prediction is very difficult, especially about the future - Niels Bohr

There is at least a theoretical possibility that in some 15 or twenty years some *deus-ex-machina* solution will provide the same amount of energy, at the same price, as that which comes from the extraction of fossil fuels today, although this does not seem likely. Game theory provides a way to evaluate different risk-possibility scenarios. 6B9 is a simplified game-theory analysis of the energy depletion problem. It is restricted to a 2 x 2 guess, cheap energy / expensive energy, right / wrong. The result is convincing enough.

(FIGURE 6B9) A SIMPLIFIED GAME-THEORY ANALYSIS OF THE ENERGY PROBLEM

Energy future	Outcome	
	Right guess!	**Wrong guess!**
Guess 1: Energy will always be cheap (fossil?)	OK (?)	✝ RIP
Guess 2: Energy will be expensive (solar derived?)	OK	OK (embarrassing?)

NUTRIENTS

The elements that constitute terrestrial biological life can be divided into two groups, those that have gaseous phases (e.g. H, O, C, N and S) and those that don't (e.g. P, Na, K, Ca and so on). The fundamental difference between these two groups is that elements with gaseous phases can be distributed by air movements, but those without must be transported in liquid or solid form. The latter type of transportation is much slower, which is why such elements are prone to an uneven distribution and local deficiencies.

Nutrients are the small amounts of essential elements that constitute our bodies. Most of them occur in much higher concentrations in the earth's crust than in animal or plant bodies, so that deficiencies do not easily occur. There is one exception: phosphorus is about ten times more abundant in our bodies than in the earth's crust. This means that this element has to be concentrated from the surroundings. In water, phosphorus is available everywhere since the ions are transferred by the water itself. It is easy to find, even if the concentration is low. On land, however, the situation differs. Phosphorus has to be brought to where it is needed and any continuous leakage will be lethal. Recycling of phosphorus is thereore a typical quality of a mature ecosystem. A development period of about 400 million years of evolution has refined this capacity.

Since phosphorus is extremely important to the metabolism of biological systems (e.g. in DNA and ATP, both essential to biological functions), a lack of available phosphorus limits their capacity to use other resources, such as sun, water etc, even if they are available in profusion. Phosphorus cannot be substituted by the elements most like it, nitrogen and arsenic, which are above and below it in the periodic table; it cannot be replaced. It is not an exaggeration to claim that phosphorus is the most important nutrient.

The modern food system is not built upon the recycling of phosphorus as it loses them as the products leave the farm. A constant supply of phosphorus is therefore vital to farms that export more than they import (i.e. those specialized in plant production).

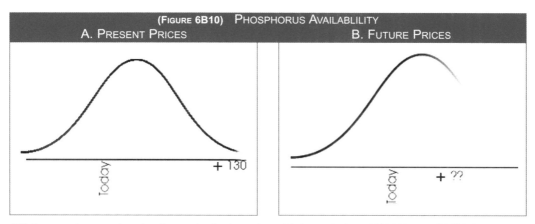

(FIGURE 6B10)   PHOSPHORUS AVAILABLILITY
A. PRESENT PRICES   B. FUTURE PRICES

With the present energy price, phosphorus extraction from mines might have a horizon of 100-150 years (A). This horizon will come closer in a situation with increased energy prices (B). This ought to call attention to the necessity of phosphorus recycling.

BEFORE THE WELLS RUN DRY

PART 6: HOW A RENEWABLE ENERGY ECONOMY WILL AFFECT RURAL LIFE.

The price of phosphorus is today about 15 SEK/kg, and the price of the energy required for its extraction is about 3 SEK. As the richest deposits are exhausted, ores that require more energy for extraction will have to be used. If energy prices rise at 5% per year in real terms and the amount of energy required for extraction rises at 3% a year because of poorer ores, the mere energy cost for extraction would exceed 400 SEK/kg within 75 years, an increase of two powers of ten.

At the present energy price, phosphorus mining might continue for around 130 years. Higher energy prices will shorten this period. (Figure 6B10). This is clearly an unsustainable situation. In other words, energy shortages will significantly restrict the current method of phosphorus use in our society.

ENERGY VULNERABILITY OF THE FOOD SYSTEM

When farms become more specialised, agriculture usually becomes less diverse and develops an increasingly vulnerable structure. Half a century ago, it was common for farms to grow a large part of the feed for their animals and to keep a wide range of them. Cows, pigs, horses, geese and chicken could be found on the same farm, together with a variety of crops and refinement procedures. Today, this situation is very rare. Farmers are forced by the increased price for their inputs and the decreased price for their produce to specialise on products that can be produced in large quantities at a low unit cost. In such a situation, the importance of the distribution system increases. Transportation lines are longer, which increases vulnerability.

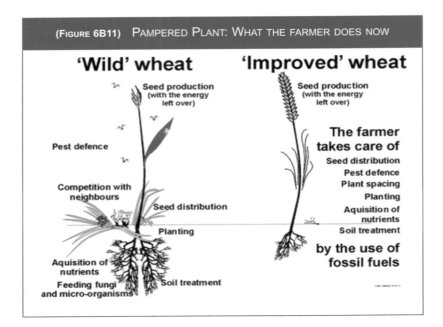

(FIGURE 6B11) PAMPERED PLANT: WHAT THE FARMER DOES NOW

In order to survive and propagate, a wild plant has to carry out a considerable amount of work with the solar energy acquired. Only a fraction of this is carried out by the domesticated plant. The rest is done by the farmer, with the use of fossil fuels. This means that the domesticated plant can put much more energy into seed production.

Moreover, the development of specialised breeds of animals and plants has generally increased the energy dependency of farms.

Consider a 'wild' wheat plant. It has to carry out a substantial amount of work in order to flourish, grow, and maintain itself. What is left over of the collected solar energy is used to produce seeds. In modern agriculture, cultivars have been developed - to be lazy!

With the help of fossil fuels, the farmer carries out a lot of the work that wild plant has to do using solar energy. This enables more of the solar energy collected by the 'improved' plants to be transformed into seeds, although the capacity of the improved plant to collect solar energy has not been increased. (Figure 6B11) The same thing goes for domesticated breeds of animals. Modern agriculture therefore needs a secure and steady supply of cheap energy and a well-functioning transportation infrastructure. However, a large-scale system dependent on specialised units and a long-distance transporta-tion system is not only more likely to fail compared to one with shorter transportation lines and more self-sufficient production units supplied with solar derived energy but the effects of failure will be more severe.

ENERGY VULNERABILITY OF A FAMILY

Consider an ordinary four-person family. If they live in a Swedish house constructed according to the Byggnorm 80 standard, their house will require around 17 000 kWh per year for heating and household machinery. Assume they want to reduce the energy requirements for their housing as much as possible. They exchange their house for a super-insulated one. By that, they can reduce the energy needed by about 8 000 kWh per year (The grey area in the left bar in Figure 6B12). Changing the car to one with the smallest fuel consumption available may result in a reduction of about 6 000 kWh, assuming they use it to the same extent (15 000 km/yr).

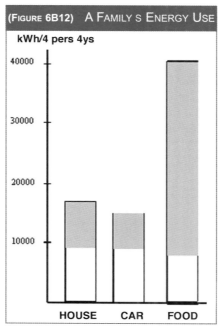

Figure 6B12 Different energy requirements of different activities for a typical family. The grey areas are the theoretical reduction potentials.

BEFORE THE WELLS RUN DRY

PART 6: HOW A RENEWABLE ENERGY ECONOMY WILL AFFECT RURAL LIFE.

The food system is more complicated. A person always needs around 1 000 kWh per year, a figure that it is not possible to reduce by negotiations or increased efficiency. The energy needed for the four persons will therefore always be about 4 000 kWh. However, the energy conversion factor in the food system is about 0.1 (Hirst, 1974; Hall, 1992; Uhlin, 1996). This means that the energy requirements to feed these four persons is about 40 000 kWh! This is mainly because of the extensive transportation, handling and packaging of most foodstuffs. Even if the human body cannot be expected to increase its efficiency, the capacity of the food system to do so is huge:

•Assume that the food comes from a general Swedish agriculture with an energy conversion factor of 1.04.
• Assume, further, that the worldwide food system is replaced by a more localized food system, which uses the same amount of energy that was required to produce the food to process and store it.

• Then, the energy needed for the food supply system could diminish to 8 000 kWh/yr from 40000 kWh/yr for the family, which implies a reduction capacity of more than 30 000 kWh/yr.

The current food system is very energy demanding, and therefore very vulnerable to energy price increases. After the big rollover, the cost of the energy required to grow food, process it and deliver to the consumer could easily become unaffordable if the current system is used.

WASTE WATER MANAGEMENT

What is generally called 'waste water' is often a mixture of two different types, grey and black. (Figure 6B13) Fairly clean rain water run-off also gets into the waste stream in many systems.

Grey water is the largest constituent of the waste water, about 65 cubic metres per person

(FIGURE 6B12) WHAT WASTE WATER CONTAINS					
				Waste water treatment	
	Urine	Faeces	Greywater	before purification	after purification
Volume (1*pers^{-1}*day^{-1})	1.12	0.15	199[1]	397[2]	396
N (g* pers^{-1}*day^{-1})	11.0	1.5	1.0	13.5	10.2
P (g*pers^{-1}*day^{-1})	1.0	0.5	0.6	2.1	0.1
Volume (1*pers^{-1}*year^{-1})	409	56	65 386	145 023	144 658
N (Kg*pers^{-1}*year^{-1})	4.0	0.6	0.4	4.9	3.7[3]
P (Kg*pers^{-1}*year^{-1})	0.4	0.2	0.2	0.8	0.1
N-conc (mg/l)	9 810	9 811	5.0	34.0	25.6[16]
P-conc (mg/l)	892	3 270	3.0	5.3	0.4
N/P-ratio[4]	*11*	*3*	*2*	*6*	*72*
Notes	Originally sterile	High content of pathogens. High dry matter content.	Low pollution	External input of water	Risk for pathogenic amounts of viruses, risk for nutrient pollution and loss

Normal amounts of P, N and volumes in wastewater in Sweden. Note that the 'purified' water is less clean than the original grey water, and of almost double volume.

per year. This is the water from bathing, showering and washing. It is only lightly polluted and easy to purify locally. If unpolluted by toxic detergents, it is excellent for watering plants.

Black water is the toilet flush. It has a low volume, about 50 litres per day. This water contains human urine and faeces, about 1.5 litres in volume. Most of this water was originally drinking water. The urine contains most of the nutrients (67% of the phosphorus and about 90% of the nitrogen). If urine is mixed with water in the ratio of 1:12, you get the same nutrient concentration as used as the standard solution in plant growth research laboratories. Pathogens (organisms that may have the capacity to cause diseases) are only found in faeces,

a comparatively small part of the total waste water volume, as they only amount to about 50 litres per person per year. Only 33% of the phosphorus and 10% of the nitrogen are found in faeces although the concentration is rather high. Mixing urine and faeces almost immediately creates a foul smell generated by the bacterial content of the faeces. We have an instinctive reaction against it. This is sound; it keeps us away from pathogens.

Current waste water management can be described as the MIFSLA-method (MIx First and Separate LAter), Figure 6B14.

The MIFSLA approach to waste water management may be described in the following way:

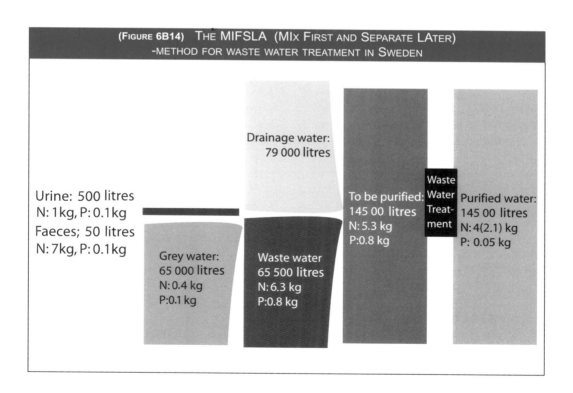

(FIGURE 6B14) THE MIFSLA (MIx First and Separate LAter)
-METHOD FOR WASTE WATER TREATMENT IN SWEDEN

Drainage water:
79 000 litres

Urine: 500 litres
N: 1kg, P: 0.1kg
Faeces; 50 litres
N: 7kg, P: 0.1kg

Grey water:
65 000 litres
N: 0.4 kg
P: 0.1 kg

Waste water
65 500 litres
N: 6.3 kg
P: 0.8 kg

To be purified:
145 00 litres
N: 5.3 kg
P: 0.8 kg

Waste Water Treatment

Purified water:
145 00 litres
N: 4(2.1) kg
P: 0.05 kg

BEFORE THE WELLS RUN DRY

PART 6: HOW A RENEWABLE ENERGY ECONOMY WILL AFFECT RURAL LIFE.

1. Clean water is mixed with urine and faeces to become a polluted and polluting mixture of plant nutrients and pathogens.
2. This mixture is in turn mixed with fairly clean grey water.
3. The resulting mixture is diluted with drainage water in an extensive web of sewage pipes. The initially high amount of wastewater (more than 170 litres per person a day) is increased to about 340 litres per day due to this water leaking or being deliberately put in.
4. Finally, the mixture is purified to a quality comparable with that of the original grey water, but the volume has now doubled.

Hence, the actual function of the waste water treatment system turns out to be the removal of urine and faeces from the grey water, a job that can be more easily done by using source-separating toilets. To be fair, the development of this management method has historical roots and is not the result of a deliberate design. It has however severe consequences:

• Comparatively clean grey water, which otherwise is easy to purify, is heavily polluted by its mixing with urine and faeces.

•The end product of this system is a contaminated, phosphorus-rich sludge and contaminated water from the waste water treatment plants. The phosphorus is, on the whole, impossible to recycle due to HEAP effects[5] (Günther, 1997), which makes the method even less sustainable because the phosphorus has to be replaced from the limited stocks in the mines. HEAP stands for Hampered Effluent Accumulation Process which happens when a constant flow into an area leads to a natural build-up and, later, to an equal but diffuse leakage.

Thus, the current waste water treatment system severely restricts the possibility of nutrient recycling.

SOLVING THE PROBLEM

It is better to be prepared for a possibility and not have one than to have a possibility and not be prepared - Witney Young

How can the energy scarcity and phosphorus availability sustainability problems we have identified be solved?

A. ENERGY

Two routes can be followed to deal with energy scarcity - one can either attempt to find new energy sources or to limit energy demand. If the second route is chosen, one has to find a method that hurts as little as possible.

a. Finding new energy sources

There are certainly alternatives to liquid fuels but since liquid fuels are such an important part of our present energy system, bridging the gap between the depletion curve and that of increasing demand shown in figure 6B7 is a tremendous task. If the gap[6] could be filled with electricity instead of liquids, it would require one new nuclear reactor to be opened every day[7]! So the problem is not only to find a new energy source, but also to develop it fast enough. If you prefer wind to nuclear just multiply the number of reactors needed to fill the gap by about 1000 to get the number of wind turbines required. Moreover, the building of both wind turbines and nuclear plants requires the input of fossil fuels, given the methods used today.

It is theoretically possible to extract large amounts of energy from renewable sources, perhaps even as much as we use today, but this type of energy never will be as cheap as the energy we use today in terms of the time people have to work per kWh. This means that both the transition to renewables and general energy depletion will have profound effects on our society.

b. Increasing energy efficiency

It is often argued that the coming energy short-age could be met by increasing the efficiency with which energy is used. This seems convincing, since the gains in particular systems are often as large as 40-50%. The problem is that the pace at which machinery is changed is rather slow and the adjustment needs to be quick in order to deal with the depletion problem. Furthermore, increasing efficiency does not necessarily lead to an overall reduction in energy use. This was observed by the economist and mathematician Jevons in the 19th century in a study of increasing efficiency in coal-powered industries. Increasing efficiency, he found, only increased the number of industries using the new method (Jevons; 1990) and ultimately increased total energy use. This is referred to as the rebound effect.

c. Decreased access to energy

This is, perhaps, the most realistic scenario so we ought to prepare for it. If it is an overreaction, well, see Figure 6B9. According to the analysis referred to in Figure 6B12, the food system seems to be characterised by high energy use and high vulnerability to decreased energy access. Furthermore, a shortfall in the food system has worse effects than shortfalls in other domestic activities, except possibly water supply. The most energy-demanding activities in the food system are (in no special order)

a. Agricultural inputs such as fertiliser
b. Agricultural traction - ploughing etc
c. Transport from farm to dinner table (farm - industry - retailer - shop - home)
d. Industrial processing (slaughterhouses, mills, industrial food processing, packaging)

Of these, c and d seem to be most easily reduced by changing societal systems while a and b could be cut by changing farm production methods. If it takes 1.04 units of energy as input to produce one unit of energy in food, b and c

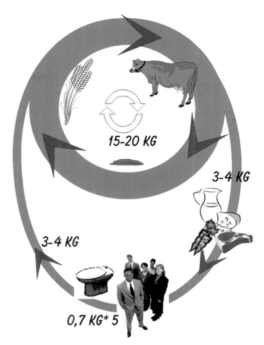

Figure 6B15 The relation of a balanced agriculture to a group of people. About five people are in nutrient balance to one hectare of balanced agriculture (figures in kg phosphorus per hectare)

seem to account for a very large part of the total energy expenditure in the food system. Both c and d could be cut by shortening the distance, both geographically and systemically, between the farmer and the consumer. Agricultural traction, b, is a very large part of the agricultural energy use. Jansen (2000) however shows that energy crops converted to tractor fuel would use the same land area as the growing of feed for horses doing the same work. The difference is that tractors need an industry to be reproduced whereas horses are self-replicating and are therefore more suitable for an agriculture less vulnerable to changes in oil prices.

B. NUTRIENT RECYCLING

Because non-airborne nutrients are very precious, and molecules don't wear down, recycling such nutrients is the best way to maintain

BEFORE THE WELLS RUN DRY

PART 6: HOW A RENEWABLE ENERGY ECONOMY WILL AFFECT RURAL LIFE.

fertility and one used since terrestrial ecosystems developed about 400 million years ago. As our present waste management system does not allow efficient recycling, it is imperative for sustainability to change mainstream agriculture, the food system and the waste management system to make it so.

To become a sustainable settlement, nutrient recycling is just as important as becoming less dependent on fossil energy use. The whole society must be involved.

a. Balanced agriculture

In pre-industrial times, almost all agriculture was based on the use of animal manure as a nutrient source for plant production to feed the animals. The number of animals kept depended on the farm's capacity to produce their food. This was a balanced agriculture. Today, though, agriculture has been split into animal husbandry and crop production. Animal feed has to be imported by farmers raising cattle and this gives rise to an excess of nutrients in farms specialising in animal husbandry and a lack of nutrients in farms where crop production is the speciality. In order to recycle nutrients, a balanced type of agriculture is necessary but this is not enough for complete nutrient recycling. The nutrients going to consumers must be recycled too. (Figure 6B15).

b. Nutrient recycling from human waste

Even a balanced agriculture loses nutrients, as it exports food for people. This amount can be estimated to 4-5 kg of phosphorus per hectare (Figure 6B15) This is rather little compared with the losses in specialised crop production, which is 15-20 kg of phosphorus per hectare. However, in the end, even this small quantity could lead to a phosphorus deficiency. Food production must therefore be balanced by a matching return of nutrients. Recycling nutrients from the population is not very complicated if the MIFSLA approach is avoided. A fur-

ther benefit of avoiding this system is also that greywater is kept as clean as possible, which makes this water simple to purify and recycle locally. To mix all the nutrients with bacteria and large amounts of fairly clean water in order to pump it long distances and, after that to try to separate it in its original parts again is stupid from a sustainability perspective. It wastes valuable nutrients and energy simultaneously.

There are many different methods to correct this folly. The easiest way is to use some type of source-separating toilet. What the different types have in common is that they avoid the pollution of grey water, and that they make recycling of nutrients possible.

Many models exist today, with (wet type) and without (dry type) water flushing of faeces, with inside or outside emptying of faecal compost, or with vacuum systems.

- The 'dry' type is the least resource demanding and easiest to install, but requires a cellar or some other space under the house.
- The 'wet' type is more expensive to install and manage but more like the current type of toilet system so 'toilet training' is not so necessary.
- In an existing building, extensive alterations can be avoided by using either a dry type without a floor passage or a vacuum-type toilet.

The choice of type depends on one's individual preference and the type of house in which it is to be installed. It is most important to avoid the unnecessary pollution of greywater. Urine and faeces should be returned to the area of food production.

Unpolluted greywater can be use for watering a greenhouse or purified using simple biological methods such as the 'Wetpark' system used in Kalmar Technical High School[8] or the 'Living

Wall' system for confined areas. The management of the toilet system does not necessarily need to be the responsibility of the inhabitants of the house. It can also be done by an agreement with specialists or with the farmer.

How can the nutrients in the food be returned from the settlement to the farm? The local production and supply of food would permit the use of low-energy methods throughout the entire food system and minimise the effect of oil-price shocks. This raises the question: What is local? Naturally, that depends on the energy resources available. In a situation with an abundance of very cheap energy, 'local' could be within hundreds of miles. With expensive energy, 'local' could mean within sight. The closer production is, naturally, the less need there is for both transportation and industrial processing.

'Localisation' should therefore be adapted to the amount of energy expected to be available with due regard for the precautionary principle.

TACKLING NUTRIENT AND ENERGY PROBLEMS SIMULTANEOUSLY

The sustainability problems around fossil energy dependence and the failure to recycle nutrients can be alleviated by the local production of food and the local recycling of nutrients supplemented by local water management including grey water recycling. Together these steps would improve the local economy and strengthen the local community but would require extensive changes to a lot of the existing infrastructure.

FOOD PRODUCTION

Even the most efficient transition to a source-separating toilet system and a well-organized

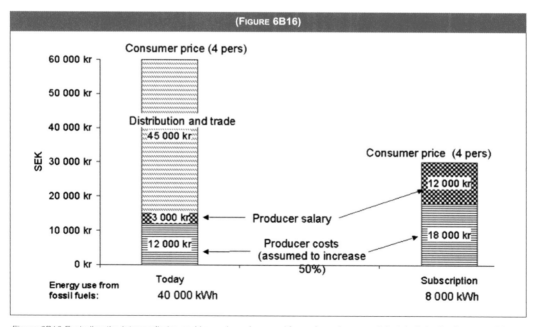

Figure 6B16 Excluding the intermediaries and becoming a 'personal farmer' may be a good deal, both for the farmer and the consumer group. Simultaneously, the energy use will be considerably reduced.

BEFORE THE WELLS RUN DRY

PART 6: HOW A RENEWABLE ENERGY ECONOMY WILL AFFECT RURAL LIFE.

return of nutrients to agricultural land would not create a nutrient cycle. Such a cycle also requires that local agricultural food production (from a balanced agriculture) fulfils a large part of the needs of the community. The psychological effects of local consumption and recycling may be quite large. Knowing where the nutrients are being returned to leads to a general sense of inclusiveness in the food system. A person involved in recycling them can point at a field and say: "My bread grows there".

In the localised system outlined here, the primary object of the farmer is to provide a local community (including himself) with food. Surpluses may be sold at the market but this is not the main goal of the agriculture which also involves the recycling of nutrients in manure and humanure and the production of feed for animals. Perhaps grey water recycling should be considered a farm activity too.

This is a much more diversified task than the management of a farm is today. However, a change to a more organic type of farming is essential for sustainability in any case and since off-farm intermediaries are largely excluded, it might be more profitable (Figure 6B16) and offer better prices to the consumer. Since the food bought in a shop today is priced at about four times higher than the farmer receives, a group of consumers can easily offer him double the normal payment and still have a good deal. Even if the farmer has to invest 50% more to change from a mono-production system to poly-production, he will still have a large increase in salary. This is a win-win relation particularly as the energy cost/dependency decreases to about a quarter of its current level

THE BALANCED SETTLEMENT: MEDIUM SCALE

The implementation of these solutions is compatible with intermediate size settlements. Settlements with their associated farms can form groups of 800 - 1,200 persons and an associated agricultural area of 160 - 240 hectares. If areas also are used for the improvement of local ecosystems, 170 - 260 hectares can be expected to support these people. This population size is large enough for the establishment of a common social infrastructure, such as primary schools and small service business. However, it could be argued that this size of settlement is not enough for non-agricultural production, such as cultural needs and service provisions, and that this may generate an increased need for transportation. For the sake of discussion, however, imagine an area where such settlement types cover the land. In such an area, ignoring lakes, mountains etc., there would be a population density close to 500 people per square kilometer, which might be enough for a diversity of direct social interactions, although not the amount we are accustomed to in high density urban areas.

RURALISATION

Nutrient circulation becomes increasingly expensive with increasing spatial distribution ranges (Günther, 1998). The energy requirements for distribution of food also tend to increase in quantum leaps when the distribution pathways require extensive packaging and preservation of the products. As pointed out earlier, solving these energy requirements by means of fossil fuels, increases the vulnerability of the society above the level required for human and environmental security. The only solution left compatible with such security would be to maintain basic energy flows from renewable sources, i.e. solar-derived, and to reduce the external energy requirements for all sectors to the lowest level possible.

The means of providing agriculture with its ultimate raw material, phosphorus, would also need to change. A system of linear flux of phosphorus through society over a prolonged time is

(FIGURE 6B17) RURALISATION OVER FIFTY YEARS

YEAR 0. URBAN POP. 33,000 RURAL POP. 3,000

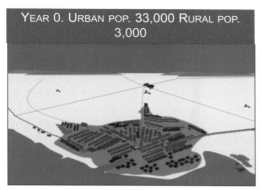

YEAR 12. URBAN POP. 24,000 RURAL POP. 12,000

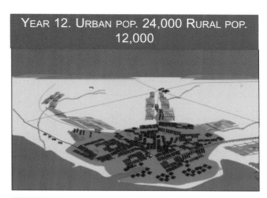

YEAR 25. URBAN POP. 12,000 RURAL POP. 24,000

YEAR 50. URBAN POP. 3,000 RURAL POP. 33,000

Figure 6B17 'ruralisation' strategy in a hypothetical, medium-sized city. Instead of replacing old houses in the urban core, balanced settlements would be created in the surrounding area.

both wasteful and insecure. Therefore, to attain nutrient circulation and at the same time reduce energy support requirements in large societies, a different societal structure should be chosen: the current trend towards increasing agricultural specialisation combined with urbanisation should be replaced by a closer integration of farms and settlements.

A name for such a strategy could be ruralisation, as opposed to urbanisation. This development strategy implies a successive replacement of houses in need of extensive restoration or rebuilding. Instead of building new houses in existing urban areas, small settlements integrated with agriculture as outlined above would be created in the hinterland of the urban areas. Many of the problems discussed above could be alleviated by such a strategy.

CONCLUSIONS

In this overview, I have argued that agriculture's *structural problems* cannot be alleviated by further changes along current lines because they reflect recent structural changes in society and must therefore be resolved by *new structural solutions.*

The problems include:

- dependency on stored energy support
- constant input of nutrients and other materials from storage
- inescapable loss of nutrients, which is an effect from
- linearity of the nutrient handling system

BEFORE THE WELLS RUN DRY

PART 6: HOW A RENEWABLE ENERGY ECONOMY WILL AFFECT RURAL LIFE.

They are aggravated by the following factors:

- ongoing specialisation of agricultural units-
- decreasing population working with agriculture
- urbanisation
- a dependency on cheap energy
- a probable increase in fossil fuel prices

I have argued that these problems could be alleviated by 'ruralisation', a closer integration of agriculture and the places where people live. This would:

- minimise dependency on industrial energy by shortening supply lines
- increase nutrient circulation by a changed nutrient infrastucture
- increase integration between agriculture and other social activities
- improve and support the natural enviroment

The economic and social benefits of this transformation are likely to be considerable, especially if fuel prices rise. The vulnerability of agriculture to energy supply disruption and nutrient loss would be greatly reduced. Indeed, it is hard to conceive of a sustainable society that is not principally powered by solar energy and which neglects to recycle those nutrients whose loss would reduce its carrying capacity.

REFERENCES:

Bartlett A. A., 2000, An analysis of US. and world oil production using Hubbert-style curves. *Mathematical Geology, v. 32,* no. 1, p. 1-17.

Campbell, C. J. 2003, *ASPO Newsletter* 25, January 2003.

Campbell, C. J., 1998, Running out of gas: *The National Interest,* Spring. p. 47-55.

Campbell, C_J, and Laherrere, J.H., 1998, The end of cheap oil. *Scientific American,* v. 278, no. 3, p. 78-83.

Duncan, R.C. and Youngquist, W, 1999, Encircling the peak of world oil production. *Oil and Gas Journal,* v. 8, no. 3, p. 219232

Edwards, J. D., 1997. Crude oil and alternative energy production forecasts of the twenty-first century. The end of the hydro-carbon era: *American Association of Petroleum Geologists Bulletin,* v, 81, p, 1292-1305
Günther, F., 1997. Hampered Effluent Accumulation Processes: Phosphorus Management and Societal Structure. *Ecological Economics,* 21, 159-174. Elsevier

Hall, C.A.S., C.J. Cleveland & R. Kaufmann, 1992. *Energy and Resource Quality.* Wiley Interscience
Hirst, E., 1974. Food-related Energy Requirements, *Science* 184:134-38

Hoffman, R. 1995 Jordbrukets energibalans - En analys av energiflöden i Svenskt jordbruk 1993 och jämförelse med åren 1956 och 1972. KSLA Tidskrift nr 6: Lantbrukets energibalans - Energiflöden i Jord- och Skogsbruk. Sammanfattning från seminariunm 19/4 1995, Stockholm.

International Energy Agency. 1998, World energy prospect to 2020, Paper Prepared for the G8 energy ministers' meeting Moscow, 31 March-April 1.

Ivanhoe, L. F., 1995; Future world oil supplies: There is a finite limit; *World Oil,* October 1995, p. 77-88.

Jansén, J., 2000. Agriculture, Energy and Sustainability; Case studies of a local farming community in Sweden. *Agraria* 253 Dissertation. Swedish University of Agricultural Sciences.

Jevons, F., 1990. Greenhouse - A Paradox. *Search 21* (5) p. 171-172
Magoon, The big rollover, http://geopubs.wr.usgs.gov/open-file/of00-320/of00-320.pdf

SNV 4425, 1995. Vad innehåller avlopp från hushåll? Swedish Environment Protection Agency.
Rapport. Naturvårdsverkets förlag.

Sundberg, K. Samhällstekniska avdelningen, Vattenskyddsenheten, SNV 1994-02-21 Fosforflödet vid A-anläggningarna 1992, baserade på miljörapporter för 1992., The phosphorus flux at the A-plants, based on the environmental reports for 1992)

Uhlin, H-E, (1996): Energiflöden i livsmedelskedjan. SNV report 4732

Youngquist W,, 1999, The post-petroleum paradigm and population. *Population and Environment,* v.20, no.4, p.297-315.

Hydrocarbons versus carbohydrates: the continuing battle in the United States

by David Morris

Recent political and technological changes have enabled plant materials to replace some of the petroleum compounds used by industry. Farmers will only benefit significantly, though, if they own the companies that turn their crops into the chemicals that industry requires.

Vegetable matter and minerals have competed with each other to become the dominant industrial input for almost 200 years. For the first 150 years, significant advances occurred in the use of both types of material. Then, for a quarter of a century after World War II, hydrocarbons took over almost completely but since the 1980s, carbohydrate-derived industrial products have been sweeping back as a result of technological and political developments.

In 1820, the United States was a carbohydrate economy and Americans used about two tons of vegetable matter for every ton of minerals. Fifty years later, 70 percent of the country's energy was still generated by burning wood. Even as late as 1891, only two of 161,000 miles of railroad tracks were made of metal.

The battle between hydrocarbons and carbohydrates began when scientists developed methods to recover and purify organic chemicals such as phenol, benzene, naphthalene from the tars and gases produced when coal was turned into coke for the steel industry. On the carbohydrate side, scientists relied on cotton lint (the short fuzz left on ginned seeds), and after the mechanical process for making paper was introduced, wood pulp.

Before the Civil War, ethyl alcohol (ethanol) from grain was one of the nation's leading chemicals, used chiefly as a solvent and an illuminant. In 1828 Michael Faraday made ethanol from coke-oven gases but making alcohol from agricultural feedstocks was much cheaper.

In 1869 two New Jersey printers, John and Wesley Hyatt modified nitrocellulose to make a highly successful commercial plastic they called celluloid, a word derived from cellulose, the largest single component of plants. A modified celluloid became the basis for the photography industry and films. To this day Hollywood still calls its movies "celluloids" although one would doubt that even Steven Spielberg knows why.

In the 1890s the first synthetic fibre, rayon, was made from wood pulp. In 1910 Leo Baekeland began commercial production of Baekelite, the world's first thermoset plastic. Charles Kettering later declared he would not have perfected electric starting, lighting and ignition systems, devices that revolutionized motoring in 1911, without this plant-derived plastic. The first film plastic, wood pulp-derived cellophane, was introduced in the 1920s.

TAXING BIOCHEMICALS TO DEATH

One reason that carbohydrates lost ground to hydrocarbons is that they were handicapped by one of their most desirable features - products derived from them often can be pleasurably ingested. In 1861, to pay for the Civil War,

Abraham Lincoln imposed a $2.08 spirits tax on alcohol and, almost overnight, the ethanol industry disappeared. Forty-five years later, The New York Times [1] editorialized, "It is only the heavy tax imposed by the United States that has prevented the use of a large number of vegetable products for the manufacturing of an exceedingly cheap and available alcohol". In 1906, under pressure from Theodore Roosevelt, one of big oil's most prominent critics, Congress finally freed industrial alcohol from the onerous tax. The ethanol industry revived and made rapid progress only to be killed off again in 1919 when the US adopted a constitutional amendment that banned the production and sale of beverage alcohol. The amendment was overturned in 1933.

Although at the end of the 19th century, Americans used about one ton of carbohydrates for every one ton of hydrocarbons, by 1920 the ratio had changed dramatically to about two tons of hydrocarbons for every one ton of carbohydrates. But the fight was not over.

World War I had brought major advances in industrial fermentation techniques for making products like acetone. By 1918, ethanol production rose to a new high of 60 million gallons a year. In 1920, Baekelite constituted 30% of all plastics made in America and an additional 25% were made of cellulose acetate.

Advances in both hydrocarbon and carbohydrate chemistry came quickly. The average price of non coal tar chemicals dropped by a factor of three from the 1921 level. Production of organic chemicals derived from petroleum rose from 21 million pounds in 1921 to 3 billion pounds in 1939.

On the carbohydrate side, the price of acetic anhydride dropped from $1.25 a pound in 1930 to 35 cents in 1939. That spurred the growth of acetate plastics. Injection molding of cellulose acetate was introduced in the early 1930s. By the start of World War II production exceeded 50 million pounds per year.

In the mid 1920s, a remarkable coalition of scientists, farm leaders and industrialists came together to promote a carbohydrate economy. It began with the publication of a long article entitled 'Farming Must Become a Chemical Industry' in the *Dearborn Independent* in 1926. The author was William Hale, the husband of the daughter of the founder of Dow Chemical and a renowned organic chemist. The number of reprints distributed rapidly exceeded 500,000, spawning what came to be known as the chemurgy movement. [2]

Dr. Hale summed up the reason for the movement from the chemists' perspective when he wrote: "We chemists felt sincerely that the whole sphere of chemical activity had become distorted. What waste and destruction in the birth of coal tar! What frightful losses in breaking of seals to valuable hydrocarbon reservoirs! Surely an all-seeing Providence has provided man with better means of advancing chemically and in simpler fashion and with no depletion of resources."[3]

SUPPORTING THE FARMER

Henry Ford summed up the reason for the movement from the perspective of industry. "If we industrialists want the American farmer to be our customer, we must find a way to become his customer. That is what I am working for."

Hale realized that theirs was an uphill struggle. "The prohibition plague set this country back fourteen years in organic technical progress", he observed. "It is absolutely impossible for us to advance in organic chemical operations without low-priced basic organic compounds such as alcohol."

BEFORE THE WELLS RUN DRY

PART 6: HOW A RENEWABLE ENERGY ECONOMY WILL AFFECT RURAL LIFE.

In 1935 the First Conference of Agriculture, Industry and Science took place. By the late 1930s some 30 regional chemurgic councils were studying crops peculiar to their areas. In 1941 Congress appropriated $4 million to establish four regional centres to research industrial applications for plants. These centres still operate today.

As early as the Model A, Ford cars were equipped with an adjustable carburettor designed for alcohol as well as gasoline. By 1940 the Ford automobile plant included one of the largest plastic molding facilities in the country. More than 21,000 tons of soybeans were used to make the plastics that went into Ford cars. In 1941 Ford unveiled a cream colored car whose body was 70 percent cellulose and 30 percent resin binder. It needed no painting or polishing. Minor bumps sprang back into shape. The cellular organic material was cooler in summer and warmer in winter than its steel equivalent. It also reduced noise.

In 1942 the government awarded $650 million in contracts to 25 major oil and chemical companies to produce 800,000 tons of oil-based synthetic rubber. When these companies failed to produce the materials needed, the government ordered the nation's whiskey distilleries to make industrial alcohol. By 1944 the U.S. was producing nearly 600 million gallons of alcohol a year. About one half was used for making synthetic rubber. The rest was used for aviation and submarine fuels and medicines. The federal rubber director, William Jeffer declared at the time that without alcohol produced from grain "the invasion of France could not have been accomplished at the time it was."

"As late as 1944", writes W.J. Reader in his history of the giant British chemical corporation, Imperial Chemical Industries (ICI), "ICI apparently gave relatively equal weight to coal, oil, and molasses as feedstocks for the production of heavy organic chemicals" [4] After World War II, however, the battle for supremacy between the carbohydrate and hydrocation appeared over. Federal support for carbohydrate chemistry disappeared. The chemurgy movement faded out. By 1949 less than 10 percent of industrial alcohol was made from grain. By 1970 two thirds of US textile fibres were made from petroleum, over 80 percent of electricity was generated from fossil fuels and not a drop of transportation fuel was derived from plants. The result? By 1980 Americans were consuming 8 tons of minerals for every ton of material derived from plants. [5]

And then the pendulum began to swing back for political and technological reasons. Politically, the introduction of environmental regulations made plant-derived products increasingly competitive. For example, when jurisdictions began banning non-degradable plastics for certain applications, starch-based plastics entered the market. Technologically, advances in the biological sciences reduced the cost of producing bioproducts. The cost of making industrial enzymes, for example, dropped by more than 75 percent between 1980 and 1995. The cost of absorbable sutures made from milk-derived lactic acid was as much as $250 per pound in 1991. By 2002, the cost of corn-derived polylactic acid dropped to less than $1 per pound.

These changes meant that natural fibres' share of the textile market had moved above 50 percent again by 1989. By 2002 over 2 billion gallons of grain-derived ethanol were being used in vehicles. Moreover, vegetable oils were replacing mineral oils in inks and hydraulic fluids.

In 1998 President Clinton declared a goal of tripling the quantity of biofuels and bioproducts used in the country by 2010. In 2002, the U.S. Congress' Biomass R&D Technical Advisory Committee which advises the Secretaries of

Energy and Agriculture and whose members were mostly appointed by President Bush, established even loftier goals[6].

In 1990, 55 years after the first chemurgic conference, another was held. Fittingly, Wheeler McMillen, President of the Farm Chemurgic Council in the 1930s and chair of the first conference, delivered the keynote. "We have experienced nearly six decades of political attempts to strengthen agriculture, with much hope hanging on foreign markets", he declared. "But we know them to be fragile, susceptible to competition or to collapse from other causes. In contrast, new industrial markets for our crops will have the virtue of permanence."

I coined the term "the carbohydrate economy" in the 1980s to describe an industrial economy where farmers would participate in the value-added step in the production chain. "A carbohydrate economy walks on two legs: a dramatic expansion in the market for industrial products and fuels made from plants; and an equally dramatic expansion in local and farmer-owned manufacturing capacity".

LOCAL OWNERSHIP

This idea - that in the carbohydrate economy, ownership matters as much as market expansion - began to guide certain public policy makers. In 2002, the Biomass Advisory Committee delivered its first report to the Secretaries of Energy and Agriculture. Among its conclusions was, "Expanding the use of biomass for non-food and feed purposes will benefit farmers and rural areas only indirectly and modestly. A

more significant development would occur if farmers themselves were able to produce the biofuels or bioproducts, either on the farm or as owners in a local production plant."

The best example of this theory put into practice occurred in Minnesota. In the early 1980s Minnesota created an incentive that mirrored that of the federal incentive—a partial exemption from the state tax on gasoline. That incentive succeeded in creating a demand for ethanol, but the demand was met entirely by ethanol imported into the state from very large plants owned by global agribusiness corporations like Archer Daniels Midland.

In the mid 1980s Minnesota converted its state ethanol incentive from a market-oriented excise tax exemption to a producer payment. Rather than reduce state gasoline taxes by a couple of cents a gallon, the state instead paid the equivalent directly to the producer, 20 cents a gallon, for ethanol produced within the state. The incentive was paid only for the first 15 million gallons produced (a typical ADM-owned ethanol facility produces over 100 million gallons a year). The incentive encouraged the formation of many small and medium-sized plants, the scale of which enabled widespread farmer ownership.

By 2002 Minnesota boasted 15 ethanol plants, 12 of which were owned by more than 9,000 Minnesota grain farmers. These were providing the fuel for almost 10 percent of all Minnesota transportation. And the state was moving into the next phase: the use of 85 percent - ethanol/gasoline fuel blends rather than 10 percent ones. So the race between carbohydrates and hydrocarbons is on. Again.

ENDNOTES

1   New York Times. May 22, 1906
2   Hale, William. The Farm Chemurgic. The Alpine Press: Boston, 1934.
3   Borth, Christy. Modern Chemists and their Work. The New Home Laboratory: New York, 1942
4   Spitz, Peter. Petrochemicals: The Rise of an Industry. John Wiley and Sons: New York, 1988
5   Morris, David; Ahmed, Irshad. The Carbohydrate Economy: Making Chemicals and Industrial   Materials from Plant
    Matter. Institute for Local Self-Reliance: Minneapolis, 1992
6   Vision for Bioenergy & Biobased Products in the United States. United States Department of
    Energy: Washington, D.C., October 2002

Maximising the returns from growing biomass

by Michael Doran

Farmers should not expect to find that simply growing energy crops will prove very profitable. They must also use such crops to meet needs besides those for heat and power which people will pay them to fill.

Rural Generation is a small private limited company formed in 1996 by John Gilliland, the current President of the Ulster Farmers Union, to commercialise an R & D project undertaken by the Department of Agriculture in Northern Ireland involving gasifying willow chip to produce heat and power. Mr. Gilliland had been looking at alternative land uses from the 1990s and had planted some willow coppice in 1994 in association with the Horticulture and Plant Breeding Station at Loughgall, Co. Armagh, on his Brook Hall Estate in Co Derry. Further plantings have taken place since and we now have 45 hectares of which 15 hectares are harvested each year.

Willows may be planted from March to June, and planting can be by hand or by automatic planter, which is normal on areas greater than one acre. The planter shown is capable of planting four rows at a time. Willows are usually planted in double rows, with cuttings 70cm apart in each row, with a space of 1.4m between double rows. A cutting 20cm long is taken from a rod approximately 3m long. The cutting is put into the ground vertically without an established root system. Cuttings are usually planted at 14,000 to the hectare.

Willows will grow in most soils, except highly organic. Ground preparation is important, and includes ploughing, power harrow and rolling. Rabbit fencing is critical for the first six months of growth, until the willows are established. The only pest that is likely to cause problems at the early stage is the leatherjacket, which will eat the cuttings unless treated.

Typically in the first year the willows will grow to a height of approximately 1.5m. They will grow as a single stem. It is normal to mix 5 or 6 different clonal types when planting. Willows are susceptible to attack by rust, which will affect the leaves. While rust will not actually kill the plant it will effectively destroy the willows' ability to transpire through the leaf and will severely stunt growth. The use of polyclonal types will completely eradicate damage from rust.

In the winter at the end of the first year of growth the willows are cut back to ground level, usually using a finger bar mower. When the plant re-grows in spring of the second year it will "multi-shoot" and 5 or 6 stems will be

Planting willows

reproduced from the original single stem plant. This coppicing is done to increase the yield. After cut back the willow will usually grow 3-4m in the first year. It will continue to grow for another two years after which time it is harvested. Further harvesting usually takes place every three years. This has been found to provide the best yield because if crops are harvested every one or two years their bulk yield is small while past year three, the percentage increase in bulk yield is marginal.

Willows on Brook Hall Estate

At Brook Hall Estate we use a modified Claas forage harvester that makes chip. This is fed directly into trailers and taken back to the farmyard. Our willow normally yields approximately 30 dry tonnes of chip per hectare per harvest. As the harvest is only done every three years this equates to 10 dry tonnes per hectare per annum. The harvester can cut up to 8 hectares per day in good conditions. Even though the harvesting is usually carried out in January or February the ground tends to be dry as a result of the willow establishment.

Traditionally willow is harvested by rod. This can be carried out by using a strimmer, or by a mechanical rod harvester. The main benefit of rod harvesting is that is avoids the necessity for drying the willow before combustion. At harvest time willow is usually about 55% moisture content. If chipped, the chips will have to be dried or the biomass will effectively create a compost heap, with a considerable loss of com-bustible material. If rod harvested, the rods can be stacked at the end of the field, and by early summer they will have dried naturally to approximately 35% moisture content without any degradation of the fuel.

Rod harvesting is labour intensive and is impractical for large areas. However, for smaller plots, and where drying facilities are not available, rod harvesting is far more cost effective.

(Figure 6D1)
ESTABLISHMENT COSTS OF SHORT ROTATION COPPICE WILLOWS ACTUAL COSTS PER HECTARE

Ground preparation	**98**
Ploughing, power harrow and roll	
Mechanical planting	**448**
Carriage, tractor and step planter hire	
Willow cuttings	**1,386**
15,000 cuttings/ha, carriage and cold store	
Rabbit fencing	**611**
Labour and material	
Cut back, after first year's growth	**41**
Reciprocating finger bar mower	
Weed and pest control	**424**
Including pre ploughing and post cut back	
Total establishment costs	**€3,008/ha**

Figure 6D1 gives an indication of the cost of planting willow coppice per hectare. The total indicative cost is approximately €3,000 per hectare. This includes for mechanical planting, cuttings, fencing and weed control which is important in the first year of growth. Planting costs in Scandinavia are approximately €2,000 per hectare because their industry has established a "critical mass" which ensures economies of scale particularly with regard to the cost of cuttings and the hire of mechanical planters. As the industry develops in this country we expect these establishment costs to fall.

BEFORE THE WELLS RUN DRY

PART 6: HOW A RENEWABLE ENERGY ECONOMY WILL AFFECT RURAL LIFE.

(FIGURE 6D2) WILLOW COSTS PER ROTATION		
1.	Harvest Cost - depending on system employed	€490 - €815
2.	Weed Control	€116
	Weedazol, 10 litres per hectare; simazine, 4 litres per hectare	
3.	Fertiliser - optional	€103
	100kg of nitrogen per hectare	
	20kg of phosphate per hectare	
	100kg of potash per hectare	
Total of Rotational Costs		€709 - 1034/ha

Figure 6D2 shows the typical cost of maintaining and harvesting the willows per rotation. The harvesting cost depends on whether it is by hand or by machine and on the volume i.e. a large area, in excess of 10 hectares, harvested by machine is likely to be around €600 per hectare.

USING WILLOW AS A BIO-FILTER

Rural Generation Limited has developed the use of willows as a bio-filter to treat dirty water or effluent. In 1998 an EU research project was set up a Culmore in Co. Derry to monitor the effects of disposing of dirty water and sludge onto willow coppice. Regulations for the disposal of wastewater and sludge are becoming stricter and environmentally acceptable options must be found for dealing with these wastes.

Four hectares of short rotation coppice were planted in May 1998 adjacent to Culmore Water Treatment Works. This is a relatively large treatment plant servicing the equivalent of 120,000 people. A ground water irrigation system was installed consisting of 28mm diameter pipes with holes at 8m centres. The flow of effluent through the pipes is controlled by pumps and motorised valves.

The site is divided into separate plots, one control plot receives no irrigation, a second plot receives irrigation with pure water, a third plot receives the sludge, a fourth plot receives irrigation with waste water at 1 times the potential evapotransperation (PE), a fifth plot at 2 x PE and a sixth plot 3 x PE The site was harvested early in 2002 and yields were measured, as well as chemical and microbiological ground water, pests, disease and weed problems.

(FIGURE 6D3) CULMORE SEWAGE TREATMENT WORKS, 1999-2001 DIRTY WATER TREATMENTS		
1.	5,000,000 l/ha of wastewater,	114kg/ha N, 24kg/ha P, 99kg/ha K.
2.	10,000,000 l/ha of wastewater	228kg/ha N, 48kg/ha P, 198kg/ha K.
3.	15,000,000 l/ha of wastewater	342kg/ha N, 72kg/ha P, 297kg/ha K.
4.	No treatment	None.
5.	10,000,000 l/ha of clean water	None.
6.	Sludge	

During harvesting the irrigation pipework was only damaged twice and this was repaired easily.

Figure 6D3 summarises the results. The volumes of NP & K were recorded as well as the total volume of effluent, which was only applied during the growing season.

Figure 6D4 indicates the yields from the various trial plots. It is interesting to note that the control plot which received no irrigation has in fact yielded greater mass than the plots which received 1 x PE waste water, 2 x PE waste water and 1 x PE clear water. We do not have an explanation for this.

it was the willows or the ground filtering that was absorbing the nutrients. By selecting a site with a high water table we were able to establish that no detectable levels of nitrate, phosphate or heavy metals were entering the ground water.

Generally there was a trend towards greater biomass yields as the volume of wastewater irrigated rose. There are practical limits as to how much effluent can be absorbed by willow and potassium (P) is normally the limiting factor. It is also likely that effluent with a Biological Oxygen Demand (BOD) in excess of 500 can be adequately treated using willow as a bio-filter.

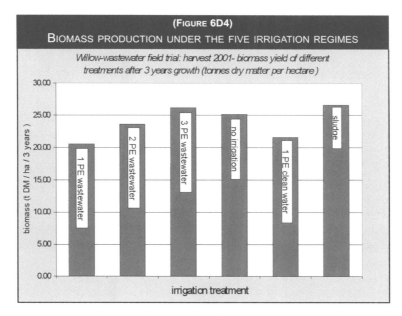

(FIGURE 6D4)
BIOMASS PRODUCTION UNDER THE FIVE IRRIGATION REGIMES

Willow-wastewater field trial: harvest 2001- biomass yield of different treatments after 3 years growth (tonnes dry matter per hectare)

One of the reasons why the site at Culmore was chosen was because the water table in the ground is only 60cm below ground level. When monitoring the capability of the willows to absorb nutrient we were particularly concerned that effluent was not flowing through the willows and entering the ground water. Therefore, had we selected a site with a water table deep below the surface we would have been unsure if

HEAT FROM BIOMASS

This section is concerned with the combustion of willow chip and wood chip in solid fuel boilers, and also with the combustion of waste agricultural products such as chicken litter and spent mushroom compost.

Rural Generation Limited has taken on the Irish

BEFORE THE WELLS RUN DRY

PART 6: HOW A RENEWABLE ENERGY ECONOMY WILL AFFECT RURAL LIFE.

agency for Farm 2000 boilers. There are several different boiler types within the range including Big Bale boilers, High Temperature boilers and automatic feed Swebo boilers. Big Bale

Big Bale, Multi fuel, Farm 2000 Boiler

boilers, as illustrated, were originally designed to accommodate full size round bales. It is now more usual to burn waste products such as timber, cardboard or paper than to burn materials that have a value such as straw.

The automatic feed Swebo boilers consist of a full storage hopper, a combustion chamber and a modified boiler. In automatic feed mode the wood chips or willow chips within the hopper are delivered to the round combustion chamber by a screw auger. The rate of combustion and the amount of heat produced can be regulated by the auger speed. Full combustion takes place

within the ceramic pot, and a flame is then fed into the boiler chamber, where the water is heated.

The automatic feed systems can also be operated in manual mode, where the fuel is fed directly into the boiler through the usual door. This allows the operator to use a range of waste fuels such as cardboard, paper, logs etc. While it is labour intensive it can be cost effective if the fuel has little or no cost. Figure 6D5 shows the comparative cost of wood chips versus oil. For example, if wood chips are being purchased at €73 per ton, and heating oil is costing 34.5 cents per litre then the heating bill for a system running on wood chips will be 54% of the comparative bill for an oil fired systems.

It is worth noting that these costs are based on wood chips with 30% moisture content. However, the willow chips produced by Rural Generation typically have moisture content of approximately 10%. Therefore, the savings will be greater because the calorific value of timber rises as the moisture content falls. Taking the €73/34.5 cents per litre oil scenario, for wood chips at 10% moisture the comparative cost would be 34% i.e. heating by wood chip would be 34% of the cost of heating by oil.

(FIGURE 6D5) WOODCHIP HEAT/ENERGY COST COMPARISON							
Woodchips (30% moisture) Delivered cost per tonne into Boiler/silo	Energy cost from Woodchip (approx. Efficiency 75%) in cents/kWH	Oil 22c /litre	Oil 25c /litre	Oil 28c /litre	Oil 31.5c /litre	Oil 34.5c /litre	Without VAT Heat cost in cents/kWh at 75% efficiency
		4.98	5.70	6.41	7.13	7.86	
49	1.75	57%	50%	44%	40%	36%	
57	2.03	66%	58%	52%	46%	42%	
65	2.33	76%	67%	59%	53%	48%	
73	2.61	86%	75%	66	60%	54%	
82	2.91	95%	83%	74%	66%	60%	

Rural Generation Limited has recently installed one of these boilers into an alcohol rehabilitation unit in Co. Donegal. They run the system in both automatic feed and manual feed mode depending on the availability of labour. Rural Generation also supplies willow chip to a community centre in Derry. Another manufacturer supplied the boiler in Creggan Community Centre, but the quality of chip provided by Rural Generation proved to be a better fuel than anything else they could obtain.

A gasifer was built under a Non Fossil Fuel Obligation (NFFO) contract at Brook Hall Estate in Derry with a capacity of 95kWe and 200kWth. It has been producing heat and power for the past six years. The gasifier has been modified continuously as part of a managed development programme and is now capable of producing 200 cubic metres of wood gas per hour. This wood gas is used to drive a diesel engine that in turn is linked to a generator. The generator produces electricity, which is export-ed to the Northern Ireland grid via the transformer. The gasifier comprises a 9cubic metre stainless steel hopper, which holds wood chip or willow chip. This feeds a down draft gasifier that is linked to an Iveco diesel engine. The system runs in batch mode and typically operates for 12/14 hours per day producing electricity and thermal energy. The thermal energy (hot water) is used to dry cereals on the 400-hectare Brook Hall Farm. The heat is also used in the winter months to dry willow chip that will subsequently be used in the gasifer.

The capital cost of the gasifier is approximately €2,000 per kW. This includes containerised units, hopper, control system, electricity generating system, safety mechanisms, heat exchangers on the engine exhaust and the engine cooling system and all installation and commissioning. The cost does not include for structural modifications to accommodate the CHP unit, compressed air supply, fuel storage silo or grid connection costs.

LOOKING AHEAD

I have already discussed the work that Rural Generation has done with regard to bio-filtration, heat and power generation from willows and heat only applications. We are however continuing to push forwards to find holistic solutions to other problems.

Northern Ireland produces approximately 200,000 tonnes of spent mushroom compost every year. This is becoming increasingly difficult to dispose of, as the traditional route of land spread becomes less viable due to legislative changes. Rural Generation has developed a system for co-combusting spent mushroom compost with dried willow chip. The heat generated can then be recycled to heat the mushroom house.

Gasifier and Generator Building with Grid Connection, Brook Hall Estate

Spent mushroom compost typically has a 80% moisture content. Virtually all other attempts to reduce this moisture content to a level at which the compost will satisfactorily burn, (usually about 40%), have required a greater energy input than is subsequently derived from the combustion. I.e. you have to expend more energy to reduce the moisture content than the compost subsequently produces on combustion. Rural Generation has found a solution to this problem.

Rural Generation has also successfully combusted chicken litter in their boiler systems. Tests are now going on to ensure that emission levels, particularly of ammonia, are reduced to an acceptable level. Rural Generation has also been involved in trials using "fine" willow chip as a bedding material in chicken houses. While this is still at an experimental stage early indications are that the salicylic acid in the willow can substantially reduce the amount of ammonia in the chicken litter. This is always a prime concern for chicken farmers who are trying to reduce "hock burn" by keeping levels of ammonia as low as possible. If our tests are successful this will open up a new market for willow chip. The chicken industry in Northern Ireland currently relies on imported wood shavings for the bulk of its litter.

The future lies in integrated environmental solutions and not in energy alone. Rural Generation believes that while the production of willow as an energy crop can generate profits for the farmer of the order of €250 per hectare, the profitability of the venture is enhanced significantly when the coppice has supplemental use. If short rotation coppice is used as a bio-filter for sewage sludge the profit margins are likely to be increased significantly. Similarly if willow chip is used as chicken litter the value of the chip is likely to be greater than the market value for chip as a fuel which is currently around €65 per ton.

We believe that farmers and commercial growers should look at all the options which willows offer before committing to a course of action. Traditionally farmers have produced a product. They deliver the product to the farm gate and by the time that product has reached the consumer it will have increased in value or cost by a factor of around 4. If farmers commit the same sin when producing willow, by stopping at the first interface in the supply chain they will prevent themselves from maximising value from their product. This is probably the most difficult aspect of willow cultivation for farmers to grasp. They are comfortable with production only scenarios. They need to increase their involvement in the supply chain to maximise returns and to add value to what is a relatively simple product.

Willows ready for harvest

The case for returning to real live horse power

by Charlie Pinney

Replacing tractors with horses would enable farms to significantly reduce their fossil energy use. Growers who have already made the switch report reduced soil compaction, increased yields and improved harvesting times.

In the past few decades, while the search for new energy sources to replace fossil-based fuels gone on, some people have continued to use a self-replicating, intelligent, user- and planet-friendly, environmentally appropriate power source that has been known about and taken advantage of for at least 8,000 years.

These people have been farming, logging and doing a wide variety of jobs using draught horses. As long as the grass grows, and their horses and other stock continue to recycle that grass to fertilise and grow the next year's crop, then oil scarcity or energy price hikes will leave them unscathed, they can become increasingly smug about their minimal-pollution farming methods and reflect that soil compaction and erosion problems on their farms are minuscule in comparison with those of their tractor-driving neighbours.

Is theirs a naive and simplistic approach to a very serious problem facing us all? Perhaps, but

Bailing hay with modern horse-drawn equipment

there are some valid reasons why animal draught could and should be re-evaluated now as a serious proposition. It is important for us to consider all the effects, environmental and economic, that both horses and the internal combustion engine have on the supporting ecosystem.

Ironically, the widespread nostalgic appeal of the draught horse often proves to be the biggest hindrance to its popular acceptance of its serious worth as a farm, forest and transport tool. Whenever you approach an individual or a government to suggest that the working horse can make a worthwhile contribution to a sustainable future for us all, you are almost invariably greeted with scorn or disbelief. You are dismissed as a dreamer, an idealist with no grasp of contemporary realities, an equine-obsessed Luddite who is actively spurning all the miraculous advantages that the scientific development of agriculture has bestowed upon us. The reason for this damning rejection is simple enough: the cart horse is invariably presented to the public at shows or in the media as a piece of living history, a relic from a museum of country life, a be-ribboned dinosaur lumbering out of the mists of our collective past.

SUSTAINABILITY

Fortunately, it is not too difficult to marshal some convincing arguments in favour of living horse power to dispel this backward-looking

BEFORE THE WELLS RUN DRY

PART 6: HOW A RENEWABLE ENERGY ECONOMY WILL AFFECT RURAL LIFE.

and limited view. Any energy source intended to reduce reliance on the world's finite resources of fossil fuels should not only be viable in the long term but offer immediate benefits as well. Here the cart horse towers with noble head and powerful shoulders above all other power sources on offer. Being a naturally-occurring living organism, albeit selectively bred (without resort to genetic modification) during domestication for special purposes, the draught horse manufactures its own replacements even while at work, a process that tractors cannot attempt. Better still, a horse can be bred and fed locally, using locally-produced sources of renewable energy - grasses and cereals.

The horse has a long working life during which 1/3 of the energy it consumes as food is reusable as manure whereas 2/3 of the fuel energy used by a tractor is lost as heat and exhaust fumes (Ref 1). The cart horse usually starts productive work at around three years old and continues until its mid 20s, after which its carcass is recyclable as meat and leather. Few of today's highly complex and sophisticated tractors will survive as long without major and expensive repairs. And to recycle the metals in a scrap tractor is itself an energy-costly process in comparison, though it may have a less adverse impact on social sensibilities in some countries.

It is sometimes argued that if horses were to be used again in large numbers on farms and elsewhere, then an unacceptably high proportion of land currently used for the production of crops directly consumable by the human population would have to be given over to the growing of food for the horse. While it is true that a working horse needs high-energy cereals as part of its diet - an amount varying widely according to its workload and breed characteristics - it is interesting to note that there are roughly similar numbers of horses in the UK today as there

were in the 1930s, yet large areas of arable ground are non-productive set-aside.

Of the approximately one million horses in the UK (the figure cannot be more precise as horse owners are often even more reluctant to complete census forms than farmers) it is estimated that 98% are leisure horses and 2% "workers", an almost exact reversal of the relative proportions that existed 80 years ago (Ref 2). One study (Ref 1) suggests that when horses were prime movers on the land, 18% of locally-produced crops were devoted to meeting their gross energy requirements. To what extent that proportion would be acceptable in the future, when perhaps the horse is again a key component of any form of agricultural activity, is open to debate. Put another way, if and when conventional fuels become unavailable or too expensive or even too tightly rationed for agriculture to continue to rely on tractor traction alone, then the price to be paid in terms of cultivatable ground resources allocated to maintaining a horse-powered alternative may, in reality, be not so unacceptable. There may be little choice.

Taking the Republic of Ireland as an example, one can calculate the approximate area that might be needed for feeding horses if agriculture were to employ large numbers of them once more. This figure will be pretty speculative because it does not take into account the improved productivity of horses using modern and different types of machinery, a factor that will affect the old, accepted horse-per-hectare ratio. Nor does it allow for the horses that would be needed outside agriculture for local transport or forestry work which would also need to be fed from the land. The estimate also fails to distinguish between mainly arable and mainly livestock farms although the theoretical horse-per-hectare ratio for each farm type is very different. A livestock farming region is likely to have fewer horses than an arable one.

For what it is worth, the calculation for mixed farms goes like this. When farm horse numbers were at their highest, the generally-accepted horse-per-hectare ratio was around one pair per 10ha., with that number increasing by one horse per each 10ha increment in farm size. If the average farm unit is 40ha it therefore needs five horses.

Each horse needs around 0.89 ha for maintenance (Ref 1) but this figure is not set in stone as so much depends on soil fertility, fertilisers used, crops grown, horse size etc.

Thus, taking the Republic's good quality grassland and arable area as 3.9 million ha, we have 97,500 farms of 40a, on which 487,500 cart horses are trundling around, ploughing, harvesting, carting things and so on. These horses will need 433,875ha for their fodder requirements, or 11.12% of the total hectares.

An interesting side to this is to recalculate using a recommended stocking rate for modern organic farms where the optimum livestock unit/ha is 500kg/ha. (Ref 6). The organic route may become obligatory if artificial fertilisers become unavailable. If we assume the farm horse will weigh 750kgs - a figure experience suggests is the best balance of weight/power output - then each horse will need 1.5ha for fodder and grazing. In an artificial-fertiliser-free Republic, 731,250ha (18.75%) of its best ground would be have to be committed to our equine assistants. However, this rather gloomy figure does not take account of the real world, in which a large proportion of the grazing requirements of the horse population could be met from marginal or lower quality ground, thus releasing some of the better soils for other cropping purposes. In other words, horses can make good, productive use of land which may not be suitable for arable use. Horses happily graze hillsides that tractors can't climb.

Suggestions have been made that tractor fuels could be economically sourced from biomass production such as oilseed rape, but this scenario would also remove land from human-consumable food production. Biomass fuels may prove to be an option of limited value for two reasons. Firstly, every process in the transformation of energy into some other, more useable form consumes energy itself. In the case of the growing, harvesting, refining and then using of biomass-sourced fuels in a tractor, the number and complexities of the transformation processes are significantly higher and more wasteful of overall energy reserves than a horse munching grass. Secondly, when you add in the energy costs of mining, refining and processing iron ore to make the tractor in the first place, you begin to wonder why on earth - literally - we bother with tractors at all, if we are genuinely concerned with responsible use of the total resources available to us within the global biosphere in which we all live.

So if it is accepted that a sensible aim for the future is to make the most efficient use in the least polluting way of the sun's energy, in whatever form, to power our agricultural prime movers, then the horse, even if simply viewed as a mechanism for turning one form of energy into another more accessible one, has a lot to offer. It can directly transform the photosynthetic reserves available in grasses and cereals into useful work with the least number of energy-wasteful processes. It is easily and relatively quickly multiplied to supply the units necessary according to demand. We already are expert in the production, feeding and utilisation of the horse. Although there is considerable scope for refining and developing some details of these aspects of horse work, such research will be vastly less expensive and time-consuming than the development, let alone the practical implementation of, other, non-fossil fuel dependant alternatives.

BEFORE THE WELLS RUN DRY

PART 6: HOW A RENEWABLE ENERGY ECONOMY WILL AFFECT RURAL LIFE.

PRODUCTIVITY

A horse, compared to the smallest of tractors, is a low-powered device able to deliver a high proportion of its body weight as power for a very short period but only around 15% of that weight as a sustainable tractive effort. The classic example of the initial power of the horse was demonstrated at the Shire Horse Show in London in 1924. Two 16 cwt shires, Umber and Vesuvius owned by Liverpool Corporation, were hitched to a dray weighing 18 tons, which they moved easily. Not content with that, they were later harnessed to a dynamometer in tandem. Umber started to pull before his companion got going, and registered a pull of 50 tons before breaking the dynamometer's needle. (Ref 3)

Horses get tired, though, while tractors don't. Horses need regular feed breaks and rest periods but a tractor can be driven continuously with the briefest of refuelling stops. Horses have one, relatively inflexible speed - the walk - most commonly employed in heavy draught work, whereas the tractor has a wide speed range. Tractors, when idle, happily depreciate in a shed unsupervised, but horses need feed and care on a daily basis whether they are working or not. Horses need specialist training and handling to maximise their draught potential while almost anyone can drive a tractor.

But the horse is intelligent and able to learn routines where it is capable of remote control by the use of the voice. This is extremely useful, especially in stop-start work at which the horse excels. Tractors don't start, turn or stop no matter how loudly you yell at them. The horse is infinitely more manoeuvrable than any tractor so, for example, headlands and turning areas can be very small, leading to a greater number of crop plants per acre. It is well-suited for row crop work. Many farm and horticultural activities are best performed at a low forward speed -

harrowing, rolling, hoeing, planting and the like - so the tractor's higher speed is not always a pre-requisite of an efficient work rate. The horse is ideal for forestry thinning where it can manoeuvre between standing timber in a way impossible using mechanical harvesting methods. Its impact on the forest environment is minimal. The horse is inherently stable, with a low soil compaction effect and has permanent "four wheel drive" enabling it to work on steep, wet or otherwise difficult terrain inaccessible to conventional systems. It can also to perform some operations at times where soil conditions would not permit the use of heavy machinery.

Two studies (Ref 4) undertaken in the 1980s suggest that for short-haul delivery work in urban areas, a pair of horses and a wagon, and a small motor lorry cost much the same to operate. It is interesting to note that the average traffic speed in London is now lower than when all that city's transport was horse based. Also, it is recognised that continuous stop-start traffic movements, such as are now common-place in any urban environment, cause the maximum pollution of the environment and wear and tear on the vehicles involved. The horse, with its high starting torque, low speed and limited radius of operation is ideally suited for city work. Indeed the by-products of its combustion processes are often eagerly sought after by the urban population in contrast to those of the motor vehicle.

Critics of the use of horses in agriculture, forestry or industry usually base their arguments on the low work rates of the horse compared to a mechanised system. Horses are usually seen to be most efficient in relatively small-scale operations. It would be absurd for example, to attempt to run a large arable farm of an agri-business type using horses in today's economic climate. The skilled labour needed, the requisite number of trained horses and the associated machinery necessary could not easily be obtained at present. And today's agriculture is inexorably moving, for reasons of economic and political pressure, towards ever larger units on which it would be extremely difficult to employ horses.

However, such large-scale intensive agriculture relies heavily on fossil-based energy sources for its mechanisation, fuels, fertilisers, sprays and so on. If we look at a scenario where such energy sources are diminishing in availability and quantity, it is likely that the nature of agricultural policy and practice will have to change radically. If the movement of produce over long distances becomes too expensive, if low labour input but high energy consuming mechanical and chemical-reliant practices become impractical, then farming may have to revert to higher labour input, smaller holdings selling produce locally. For example some crops may have to be weeded by hand or hoed by horse instead of drenched with herbicides - the sprays being too expensive or unobtainable.

Any reduction in the present high level of mechanisation on farms would lead to more people having to work the land to maintain its output. Such a change of scale and management system would of course have widespread social implications but need not imply per se a return to a primitive, impoverished and exhausting lifestyle for the population thus affected. Indeed it could be argued that a return to a less frenetic lifestyle incorporating the steady plod of a cart horse might be welcomed.

A recent study shows that both horse and tractor systems "use nearly the same amount of energy to generate any given amount of food but the quality of the energy source and its impact on the environment differ a lot" (Ref 5). Importantly, a horse-based system could rely on 60% of its total energy needs (including fodder, labour, equipment) from local renewable sources; a tractor-based system only 9 %. - its

locally bred driver and mechanic! (Ref 1) The implications of these figures are clear if non-renewable sources of energy are in increasingly short supply.

There is a large body of evidence - mostly anecdotal at the moment although an important university research project is currently assembling data (Ref 5) - which suggests that even today, when the draught horse is viewed with sceptical nostalgia by some, that those farms relying on living horse power do function as economically viable units. They would not remain in business long if they didn't. It is not a case of special pleading. The reduced soil compaction, increased yields and improved harvesting times on one large vegetable farm in Germany are all directly attributable to a recent change-over from tractors to horses. (Ref 5). In the U.K. and the rest of Europe there are farms (mine and many others), market gardens, forest management enterprises (particularly in England, France, Germany, Norway, Sweden, Belgium and Luxembourg) and urban delivery networks (such as those of the breweries) using horses in various ways. Horse work is therefore successful even in today's hectic, highly mechanised world. And if such work is possible and profitable now, how much more so will it become when the fossil fuel dependant element of life as we know it is threatened or eventually disappears altogether ?

PRACTICAL CONSIDERATIONS

What examples exist today from which one can get some idea of what horse-based agriculture might look like in the future? The small but steadily increasing number of operations in Western Europe which use horses to a greater or lesser extent as a power source have one important feature, apart from the horse, in common - they receive much popular support. Whatever the theoretical, economic objections to horse work, the reality is that vegetables grown on a

BEFORE THE WELLS RUN DRY

PART 6: HOW A RENEWABLE ENERGY ECONOMY WILL AFFECT RURAL LIFE.

horse-drawn farm are in great demand. People love to see horses extracting timber without destroying the forest fauna and flora. Urban delivery horses are given carrots and caresses throughout the working day. The evident benefits of animal traction for the care and maintenance of conservation sites are greeted with enthusiasm by local ratepayers. There is no reason to suppose that if such activities were to become more widespread, the approval of the voting public would diminish - something which might give heart to politicians teetering nervously on the edge of giving official encouragement to horse-based alternatives.

The gradual increase in horse use in Western Europe has led to and in turn been stimulated by a range of new specialised horse machinery being developed and produced for sale. Some of these machines are purpose-built, single function implements such as rowcrop equipment or timber handing machinery and others, such as the hitchcart, provide a means of linking the horse or horses to existing tractor tooling. While it is true that multinational tractor manufacturers are probably not quaking in their shoes at the prospect of their products being displaced by huge numbers of glossy horses pulling shiny new machinery for the present, it is worth noting that serious, and successful, efforts are being made to bring the draught horse up to date even in high-tech European society.

In addition, the Amish and similar communities in the USA and Canada farm large tracts of land very effectively using horses as the prime mover. However, there are certain dangers in taking the example of the Amish communities as a role model for a modern world in which the horse is the main power source. There are many differences, social, climatic, soil type, cropping possibilities, field size and so on between this agrarian, mid-western, highly organised religious society and the current norms applying in

Europe, which make the blanket imposition of an Amish blueprint for a horse-drawn future inappropriate. The differences are complex and fascinating but to detail them here would be outside the scope of this paper.

Nevertheless, there are lessons to be learned. Though relying on animal traction, the Amish farms are at least as productive as their conventional neighbours. The use of horses as prime movers does not result in a lower level of output. Indeed, although in part this is attributable to their unique social structure, the Amish are a prosperous and expanding community in contrast to many "normal" American farms. In general, the Amish farms are not specifically geared to organic food production using old implements and methods. On the contrary, they have developed ways of adapting the very latest of modern cultivation and harvesting implements to be pulled by horses and they have to compete with conventional farms for their share of the market place.

In many cases, this adaptation, like some of the new European developments, involves the use of small petrol or diesel engines to operate an implement while a team of horses actually pulls it along. This is instead of using "ground drive transmission", the rotation of the wheels to power the mechanism as traditional horse machinery used to do. This seemingly contradictory or even illogical combination of living and mechanical horsepower actually works very well. The size of the power unit involved is considerably smaller - and cheaper to buy and run and less polluting - than the engine unit that would need to be used in a heavy, complex tractor which has to haul itself along as well as the implement it is attached to. But if in the future even these small auxiliary engines cannot be used because the fuel to run them has run out, then a return to ground drive technology would be necessary. In any case such technology would be an appropriate and logical integral feature of future exploitation of the environ-mental and fossil-fuel free benefits of the draught horse.

But it has its limitations, like any physical sys-tem. Ground drive renders some of the modern farm equipment whose development has pro-foundly affected modern farm practices virtual-ly unworkable. Some implements seen as key tools on modern farms need to continue to be powered when stationary, and require a very high initial torque imput to start them up and cope with fluctuating loadings. Neither of these requirements can be met easily by ground drive alone. For example, if the power to the working parts of a round baler stops when the horse pulling it stops, it's not possible to wrap the formed bale with its netting. Also, ground drive transmission is liable to speed fluctuations as a result of the horses tiring and slowing or encountering difficult terrain. This drop in input speed can result in speed-sensitive devices not working at all.

So, if we are to use draught horses in an agri-cultural context where fossil fuels are of limit-ed availability, and we cannot therefore afford to supplement living horse power with an aux-iliary engine, then this will inevitably change, or at least powerfully influence, those current agricultural practices which depend on some of the latest advances made in implement technol-ogy. It may well be that new crop management techniques, and the machines to work them, will have to be developed - or even reinvented - to exploit the strengths and limit the weakness-es inherent in "pure" animal draught work. But compared to managing the vast social and eco-nomic upheavals implicit in future reduced or non-existent availability of fossil fuels which at the moment offer inexpensive and effortless transport, food production and a host of differ-ent aspects of our daily lives, a re-think of farm-ing practices along horse lines will be compar-atively straightforward. It should be remem-bered that present production methods have been developed under conditions of economic expansion, population growth, expensive labour and plentiful energy. A change in any one of these factors will affect these production meth-ods. We should address this issue now and develop the appropriate machinery while we still have the industrial capacity to do so easily and cheaply.

Another practice frequently employed on Amish farms is the use of big teams of horses to pull large implements. In Europe historically, the normal working unit was one man and a pair of horses. This became established when labour was cheap and plentiful but today if one sug-gests to a farmer that he should, let alone could, pay a normal farm wage to a ploughman whose efforts yield one acre of ground ploughed per day with his team, the answer will usually be negative, if at all printable. However the Amish and others have developed ways of hitching together teams much larger than we in Europe are used to, under the control of one driver. Here the output per man is immensely greater, if that should remain an important considera-tion in a future society where more of the labour force may be obliged to be employed directly in food production. For example a 12 horse team, generally accepted as the biggest that can easi-ly be hitched and driven single handed, will plough in excess of one acre per horse in a working day and operate other machinery at a similar rate. A limitation of such hitches in Europe at present is often simply the availabili-ty of sufficient trained horses and, in certain areas, the physical sizes and shapes of the fields.

However, this extreme example makes a vital point in favour of the horse compared to the tractor. The tractor is a single, indivisible device, capable of performing only one task, however complex, at a time. A big team of hors-es can together perform startling amounts of

BEFORE THE WELLS RUN DRY

PART 6: HOW A RENEWABLE ENERGY ECONOMY WILL AFFECT RURAL LIFE.

work one day and on the next, be subdivided into much smaller units to carry out a large number of different tasks at the same time, provided of course there are sufficient drivers available. The inherent flexibility offered by the big hitch system could be of immense value to future developments in horse farming. It is not too difficult to imagine local groups of small farms, each equipped with their own horse numbers adequate for the routine work on the individual holdings, combining those horses together to work as big teams to cover large tracts of land at key moments in the farming calendar such as harvest time or when big acreages have to be ploughed and sown. Farmers working together? Perhaps an unlikely scenario today, but it might be a necessity in the future.

A HORSE-DRAWN SOCIETY

At present it is probably idle speculation to attempt to describe in detail what life would be like if we once more were to use large numbers of that pleasant, companionable, self-sustaining, eco-friendly, agile and appropriate power source, the horse. However, certain implications are clear and some suggestions worth making.

Firstly, the infrastructure required. On a national level, we should now be researching, designing and manufacturing the implements and other equipment necessary for the most efficient use of the horse in the future. Such designs should obviously be made with both the characteristics of horse draught in mind and also, importantly, the possibility of sustained manufacture when existing production methods are affected by the inevitable changes in industrial energy and other resources which will take place in the foreseeable future. Possible climatic change and predicted energy resource change (limited supplies of fuels, fertilisers and sprays etc) will inevitably alter agriculture as we now

know it anyway, and so we should be looking at ways in which we can best diminish the adverse effects and maximise the positive ones by developing agricultural practices that fulfil population requirements in conjunction with methods of farming that are possible with horses.

An upsurge in demand for horse traction should be addressed nationally too, as well as on a local level. The selection and breeding of appropriate types and numbers of horses, from heavy draught horses to lighter, faster ones for delivery and transport purposes should receive government support and funding, although the practicalities of the business should be left to expert horsemen and well away from bureaucratic interference.

Locally, there will be an increase in labour demands to care for and work the horses, labour which will need training as well as recruitment. The migration of labour away from the land as society has changed from an agrarian one to an industrial one may be reversed in the future. If there is a signicant change in the relative costs - let alone the ready availability - between oil and labour, then this will have an impact on agricultural strategies (Ref 1). Harness makers and farriers will have to increase in number too and appropriate training programmes put in place to make these skills far more widely available than they are at present.

One dramatic effect of decreased fossil fuel availability will be the effect on personal mobility and the cheap movement of goods and products, a feature of life so much taken for granted today. Here there may well be a lesson to be learnt from the past. The upsurge in draught horse numbers in the UK from the mid 19th century to the early years of the 20th was stimulated largely by the development of the railways. The railways needed a locally-based transport system to transfer goods and people to and from the national network, and relied heavily on draught horses to carry locally-made products to the stations for onward transmission and to deliver other products from the stations to local consumers. A similar strategy could work once more. The draught horse could collect and distribute people and goods locally to and from a national network of long distance, high speed transport systems be they rail, road, sea or air, thus offering economies of scale and resource use which may become a pre-requisite of a society whose current high levels of dependence on non-renewable energy sources will be severely curtailed in the future.

SUMMARY

We should be debating whether a renaissance of the draught horse, prompted by a crisis in the supply of cheap fossil fuels and by a desire to limit pollution, is a realistic, sustainable option, and moreover one which should be evaluated now when there remains time available to put in place the necessary infrastructure to optimise such a change.

At some point, we are going to have to decide how we are going to use the last barrel of oil. Are we going to turn it into fertiliser so we can grow more food or use it for some other process where it cannot easily be substituted? Or waste it as fuel to power a tractor when there is a perfectly good replacement for the tractor looking patiently at us over the farm gate?

No one should have any illusions about working with draught horses. It is physically demanding, and has to be highly skilled if it is to be effective. It is also labour intensive. A proposition that the agricultural industry,

already in crisis prompted by other factors, should give up its cost-saving machines, sprays and fertilisers will be greeted with groans of despair and snorts of cynical disbelief. It may seem unwise to suggest that a larger portion of the population may have to become involved in food production at a time when manual labour of any kind is increasingly viewed as unacceptable by some segments of society. In fact to invite our highly mechanised western world to seriously contemplate using a wilful, feeble, mortal device in need of constant care and attention, one who is subject to as many fits, sulks and diseases as its handler and moreover one which can kick, bite or merely tread heavily on you, when press-button tractor technology is freely available, at least for the moment, might appear to be a mere flight of fancy.

But these facts are clear and beyond dispute: living horse power is cheap and readily available. We can breed horses, without limit, without endangering the planet. We know a lot about them and how to use them. They can pull things for us, carry us, help support our society, feed it and enable it to function. They can do so far better than they did so in the past if we take advantage of some of the technical advances made in agriculture and machinery design. They can be fed from our fields. They don't destroy the environment but enhance it. They create employment, not replace it. They are a source of companionship in the workplace, a source of pride and pleasure when seen to be working to perfection in harmony with man and his surroundings.

So why on earth don't we use them, then?

References

1. Agriculture, Energy and Sustainability. Jan Jansen. Doctoral thesis. Swedish University of Agricultural Sciences. Uppsala 2000.
2. British Horse Society.
3. Diana Zeuner, editor, *Heavy Horse World.* Personal communication.
4. *Heavy Horse Haulage in the 1980s:* report of the investigation into the comparative costs of horse and motor transport for local deliveries. Pub: Shire Horse Society .Webster, I.C. 1981 & update 1985.
5. Peter Herold. University of Witzenhausen. Personal communication
6. *Handbuch fur den biologischen Landbau.* G.E.Siebeneicher. Augsburg 1993.

Useful references and links

History with a future ed. Keith Chivers. Pub: Shire Horse Society and Royal Agricultural Society of England. 1988.

Heavy Horse World, editor Diana Zeuner. U.K. draught horse specialist magazine. Website: www.heavyhorseworld.co.uk

Rural Heritage, editor Gail Damerow. U.S.A. magazine specialising in animal draught farming and logging. Website: www.ruralheritage.com

Starke Pferde, editor Erhard Schroll. German draught horse magazine. Website: www.starke-pferde.de

Carthorse Machinery, Europe's longest-established manufacturer of modern draught horse equipment, supplies and training courses. Website: www.carthorsemachinery.com

Univecus, a German manufacturer of new designs of row-crop horse machinery. Website: www.univecus. com

Hypro AB, a Swedish manufacturer of modern horse and tractor logging equipment. Website: www.hypro.se

A single horse used for mowing hay with a mower mounted on a Pintow platform.

Moving towards zero-impact building materials

Tom Woolley

Many of the 'green' buildings being built at present aren't green at all. To stop using more resources than we can sustain, we really have to adopt different construction methods but even these should only be used if existing buildings cannot be adapted satisfactorily.

Let's consider the real implications of the global issues that underlie the interest in renewable energy. First, what actually is sustainable or green? The word sustainability can mean almost anything to anybody and is in danger of going the way of the word community. There is too much "greenwash" about because no one is very clear what the definition of sustainability actually is. There is also a fair amount of propaganda about how we all need to do our little bit, but that's not enough. We have to go a lot further than doing a little bit.

Sustainability is in danger of becoming a marketing device rather than a genuine commitment. Just because you can come up with a product or a solution that helps to save some energy and is financially viable, it doesn't necessarily mean that it is going to save the planet. The development of renewable energy is being driven by business interests that want to make money out of generating more energy when we are already using far too much in developed countries. The real priority is to reduce the amount of energy we consume. However most of the conventional methods of achieving energy efficiency use fossil fuel based insulation products and are often also dangerous. They can be fire hazards, give off toxic fumes, refuse to biodegrade when land filled and tend to pollute the atmosphere during manufacture. As a result, many conventional energy efficient buildings can also suffer from sick building syndrome.

We rely far too much on glues, sealants, membranes and so on which are synthetic, toxic, pollute the environment and often make disassembly very difficult. Many materials that are used in construction today are non-renewable; they leave holes in the ground and cannot easily be recycled. If we continue to consume resources at the present rate, particularly in the construction industry, we will need three or four planets to sustain the current rate of growth. Even if they run on renewable energy, conventional buildings represent an excessive amount of resource consumption.

FOOTPRINT ANALYSIS

Recent studies based on ecological footprint analysis techniques and mass balance studies indicate just how profligate we are in terms of resource use. After grossly misusing non-renewable resources to feed the construction industry, we then go on to waste a tremendous amount of the material that goes onto building sites. Construction waste is one of the biggest contributors to landfill, itself an environmental problem.

We have a huge number of empty, disused or underused buildings that could meet many of our needs and yet we are under tremendous pressure to build new buildings. A lot of work is done to design new green buildings but these represent only a very small percentage of the stock. Although the real problem is what to do

BEFORE THE WELLS RUN DRY

Part 6: How a renewable energy economy will affect rural life.

with existing buildings and how to make them less damaging to the environment, surprisingly little work is being done on this. Re-using existing buildings and therefore saving the embodied energy bound up within those buildings and reducing the amount the demolition waste is incredibly important.

There is a real conflict between people in the green design movement who concentrate on energy efficiency and those who feel that health and toxicity is just as important. I feel that the environmental impact of material production both in manufacturing and when installed in buildings is a key issue. We need to think very seriously about what happens to materials when they come to the end of the line, so that they can be dismantled or reused instead of causing pollution through landfill. Many insulation materials are not biodegradable.

POOR PROJECTS

One of our difficulties is that there are now a growing number of demonstration projects that are very much seen as exemplars of the way forward but are in danger of being 'off-message'. In other words they are not necessarily giving the public the right signals about the future. In a way it might seem a bit unfair to attack particular projects when they have worthy intentions. Nevertheless, we have been doing research at Queen's University which has involved looking at a range of innovative projects which are promoted and claimed to be sustainable, green, environmentally friendly, ecological or whatever. When you try to work out what's gone into those projects - and how far they actually come up to the claims they are making - you start to become a bit sceptical about how much they are really helping to tackle environmental problems.

There are a number of very expensive demonstration buildings throughout the UK that have

used Millennium funding to provide a demonstration of renewable energy. However, our analysis of these projects has shown that they are not good examples of best practice in many other aspects of green design. Most fail to make good use of passive solar energy and although millions of pounds was spent on the use of renewable energy, they still only meet 75% - 80% of their energy needs from these sources. A lot of concrete and heavy materials were used in their construction on the basis that thermal mass was required. Rarely was the timber in them from properly certified forests

We have got to get these things right if we are going to teach people what needs to be done in the future. We need to adopt a holistic approach in which we look at the upstream and the downstream impacts of everything that we do. There is no magic to this. You could come along and pay us a lot of money at the University to calculate lots of things like embodied energy, and to do lifecycle analyses and ecological profiling but the basic principles are very simple. If people were to follow them in a very practical and down to earth way you wouldn't necessarily need to do a lot of calculations. It's a question of thinking through the impacts of the decisions that you are making and having a genuine commitment to being as green as possible. Unfortunately, at the end of the day most architects and clients want to get the building up more than anything else, so that how it is done often becomes secondary.

But I would argue we need to go even further than buildings that are a good attempt at being green, we need to look at how close we can get to zero impact. If we are consuming more resources than we can sustain over the next decades then we have to look at different ways of doing things. It's not necessarily going to be that easy to achieve zero impact buildings. But at least if we set that as a benchmark, as a target, something we are trying to work towards,

Solar energy building in Ontario, Canada, built with hemp walls. Photo - C. Dancey

Hemp-walled houses in Haverhill, designed by Modece Architects. Photo - Tom Woolley

BEFORE THE WELLS RUN DRY

PART 6: HOW A RENEWABLE ENERGY ECONOMY WILL AFFECT RURAL LIFE.

then we can have some kind of basis on which to judge how far we are able to achieve that aim.

All buildings inevitably are going to use some resources. Do we have to use as much as we normally do and are there other alternatives? Many of the assessment systems currently available to us to evaluate projects are essentially based on existing practice. They are trying to push things a little bit further along, but are not based on a fundamental critique of the way we do things now.

So what sort of things do we need to move towards zero impact building? We can use renewable materials. Renewable means renewable! In other words those materials that can be replaced within a realistic timescale. A lot of people assume that timber is renewable and there are big advertising campaigns like "Wood for Good" which says that timber is sustainable, but what does that mean? If you cut a tree down, it's going to take 60/70 years for another tree to grow. You can't get away from that, you can't just get trees to suddenly pop up.

If we carry on chopping down forests at the rate that we do, we are going to have serious problems because we are going to have to wait 60/70 years to replace them, even if they are supposedly being managed in an environmentally friendly way. At least with the Forest Stewardship Council (FSC) we have got some kind of benchmark of good practice but those sorts of methods are not available for other materials.

Materials have got to be responsibly sourced. That means not getting them from the other side of the world! I recently talked to some people at a trade exhibition at the RDS in Dublin who were selling granite products and doing extremely well. There is a big upsurge in interest in granite, particularly from the public sec-

tor replacing kerbstones in nice urban upgrading schemes. But the granite is coming from China!

Using recycled materials is important but it mustn't lead to the demolition of existing buildings in order to generate high quality architectural salvage when those buildings perhaps themselves ought to be retained and used.

CLAY AND MUD

If we try and create a carbon neutral building, reducing energy as much as possible, there are a range of possible materials which can be used which I would characterise as low impact materials, but not necessarily zero impact materials. For instance, earth. We can use clay and mud forms of construction. This can replace a lot of the materials that we currently use from quarried and highly processed production processes like cement. But earth is not a renewable material, once you have dug it up out of the ground it isn't going to reinvent itself although in small-scale developments you can maybe use the earth that's underneath the building that you need to dig up anyway. So earth is only a low impact material, it is not a zero impact material. On the other hand it has a tremendous potential as a building material and should be considered at all possible times when you are looking for an alternative.

Then there are an awful lot of materials that are made from waste materials such as fly ash. Glass is a material that, if recycled, can be used for building and road construction. There is a lot of work going on around the world using rice husk ash to replace cement and produce very good quality materials. Then there is quite a lot of very interesting work going on using bio-composites and eco-composites.

At Queen's, we've been researching materials that are genuinely renewable such as the use of

Houses in Shettleston, Glasgow, heated by solor and geo-thermal energy. Architect, John Gilbert. Photo - Tom Woolley

House in County Down, converted from ruined stone building. Rachel Bevan Architects. Photo - Tom Woolley

BEFORE THE WELLS RUN DRY

PART 6: HOW A RENEWABLE ENERGY ECONOMY WILL AFFECT RURAL LIFE.

hemp as a building material. We have done quite a lot of work on straw bale building. It's still regarded as a bit of a joke in the UK and Ireland but straw bale building has now become mainstream in the US.

Farmers have had tremendous problems with what to do with the wool from all their sheep but it could be used as an insulation material and there are a number of companies developing that now. Bamboo is perhaps the most renewable material that you could possibly get. It can grow so quickly that you can actually watch it growing! So if you cut down bamboo it can regenerate itself within 2 to 3 years. There are some remarkably interesting exciting buildings and building products using bamboo. Bamboo can be grown in temperate climates as well. It doesn't just have to be seen as a tropical material.

We have been seeking funding for "The Grow Build Project" where the idea is to see whether it is possible to grow your building. This is not meant to be seen as some kind of peripheral project, but it's to be something that could be part of mainstream construction.

HEMP AND LIME

There is no reason why the kind of experiments we have been doing couldn't be duplicated on a much larger basis, and we have been very excited about the possibilities. We are using composite mixes of hemp and lime, and also hemp and earth. Apart from being a very good, highly insulating and breathable walling material it can also provide an alternative crop for the rural economy and it is adding a great deal of value to something that otherwise is currently just being sold as horse bedding.

In the UK there has been a surge of companies trying to put ecological and environmental building materials onto the market and we have been doing a study funded by the UK Engineering Research Council into the opportunities and obstacles they face. They range from Natural Building Technologies, the Green Building Store that supplies a wide range of products to a company called Eco Solutions that makes a non-toxic form of paint stripper.

A lot of people assume that ecological building solutions will cost more but if buildings are designed and specified correctly from the start there is absolutely no reason why there should be any extra cost. Some materials do, on the face of it appear to cost more, but those costs are going to come down as soon as there is a much bigger take up. If local authorities, for instance, were to really seriously implement green purchasing policies, particularly in the construction sector, that would create a much, much bigger market for the kinds of environmental products which are now becoming available. If they were taken up on a large scale then you would find the cost would come down significantly.

In theory, many renewable products would cost much less than the expensive fossil fuel based synthetic and quarry products.

I am trying to challenge you to think about building in an environmentally responsible, low impact way. We have to make radical change in the way we build our buildings and what we use to make them if we are really going to start to reduce resource use and materials.

REFERENCES

Building Research Establishment Environmental Assessment Method (BREEAM). http:// products.bre.co.uk/breeam/default.html

Caleyron N and Woolley T (2002) Overcoming the Barriers to the Greater Development and Use of Environmentally Friendly Construction Materials CIB Sustainable Building Conference Oslo, September.

Centre for Green Building Research. www.qub.ac.uk/arc/research/GreenBuilding/. Centre's Contact: Tel/Fax. 0044 2890 335466. Email. t.woolley@qub.ac.uk

Construction Resources. http://www.ecoconstruct.com/

DETR. (2000) *Building a better Quality of Life.* DETR, London. http://www.sustainable-development.gov.uk/ann_rep/

Egan, J. (1998). *Rethinking Construction.* DETR, London. http://www.m4i.org.uk/publications/rethink/

EU. Construction Product Directive. http://europa.eu.int/comm/enterprise/construction/

Fairclough, Sir J. (2002). *Rethinking Construction Innovation and Research.* DTI, London. http://www.dti.gov.uk/con-struction/main.htm

Forest Stewardship Council. http://www.fsc-uk.demon.co.uk/ FSC

Greenpeace. http://www.greenpeace.org/. Greenpeace Ancient Forest Campaign. http://www. greenpeace.org/pressreleases/forests/2002feb25.html

Kennedy J F , Smith M G and Wanek C. (Eds) (2002) *The Art of Natural Building*, New Society Publishers, Canada

Malin, N. (2002). Life-cycle Assessment for Buildings: Seeking the Holy Grail. *Environmental Building News.* March, p.10

National Green Specification (NGS). http://www.greenspec.org.uk/. Brian Murphy, contact: BrianSpecMan@aol.com. Fax: 01733 238148

Woolley, T., S. Kimmins, P. Harrison, R. Harrison, (1997) *Green Building Handbook,* Vol. 1. Spon, London.

Woolley T, Kimmins S, (2002) *Green Building Handbook* Vol 2 Spon Press, London.

Ireland's Renewable Energy Resources and its Energy Demand

Kevin Healion

Two elements are crucial to the development of renewable energy sources in Ireland – the quality of the resource and the quality of the people involved in developing it. This article and those that follow it in this section review both resource and the obstacles the people face.

Renewables could meet a quarter of Ireland's energy needs by 2010 but developing liquid fuels for the transport sector will be a major challenge.

Some energy sources are obviously better at meeting particular energy needs than others. This makes it necessary to examine the ways in which Ireland uses energy and the trends in those uses before the contribution that renewable energy could potentially make to filling the needs represented by those uses can be assessed.

ENERGY TRENDS

Figure 7A1 below shows the Total Primary Energy Requirement (TPER) of the Republic of Ireland, broken down by fuel type, over the period 1990 to 2000 (ESRI, 2001). Estimates for the period 2001 to 2010 are also included. The data is presented in units of kTOE (thousand tonnes of oil equivalent), where 1 kTOE is equal to 0.0419 PetaJoules (PJ). Analysis of Figure 7A1 shows the following key trends:

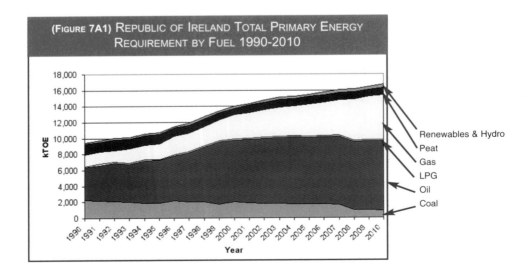

(FIGURE 7A1) REPUBLIC OF IRELAND TOTAL PRIMARY ENERGY REQUIREMENT BY FUEL 1990-2010

• a rapidly increasing energy demand over the period 1990 to 2000
• a projected continued increase in energy demand over the period 2001 to 2010
• a high dependence on two fuels: oil and natural gas

Where does the energy go?

Figure 7A2 below shows the sectors in which the energy supply is used (for the year 2002). Energy is used in the heat, electricity generation and transport sectors. Figure 7A2 shows both the amount of energy actually used by consumers in the form of electricity, and the amount of energy lost in the transformation sector. This transformation sector is primarily the generation of electricity - only about one third of the energy input to electricity generation is delivered to consumers in the form of electricity. Energy is lost as waste heat in power generation and from electricity transmission and distribution lines. It should also be pointed out that there are losses in the heat and transport sectors too - due to the inefficiencies involved in converting heating fuel to thermal energy or transport fuels to vehicular motion.

THE CONTRIBUTION OF RENEWABLE ENERGY

Renewables contributed about 1.8% of TPER in 2000 (250 kTOE out of a TPER of 13,591 kTOE; equivalent to 10.5 PetaJoules out of 569 PJ). Figure 7A3 shows a breakdown of the different renewable energy resources to the total renewables contribution of 1.8%. The single largest contribution is provided by wood (or 'biomass') – this is wood used to provide heat in the domestic sector and in the wood processing industry. Hydro electricity, electricity generation from landfill gas and wind power were the three other major renewable energy sources contributing to energy supply in 2002. It should be noted that the sources of geothermal, liquid biofuels and solar thermal also provide some supply but were not recorded in the sources used to produce Figure 7A3.

LOOKING TO 2010

The projected energy demand in 2010 is 18,700 kTOE (see Figure 7A1). The Renewable Energy Information Office of Sustainable Energy Ireland (2002) estimate that "renewable energy sources could practically supply a quarter of Ireland's energy requirements in 2010" (over

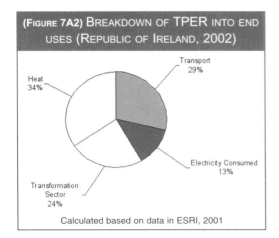

(FIGURE 7A2) BREAKDOWN OF TPER INTO END USES (REPUBLIC OF IRELAND, 2002)

Transport 29%
Heat 34%
Electricity Consumed 13%
Transformation Sector 24%

Calculated based on data in ESRI, 2001

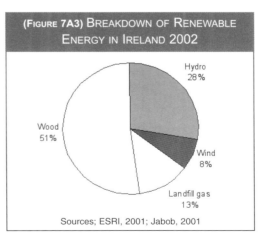

(FIGURE 7A3) BREAKDOWN OF RENEWABLE ENERGY IN IRELAND 2002

Hydro 28%
Wood 51%
Wind 8%
Landfill gas 13%

Sources; ESRI, 2001; Jabob, 2001

4,000 kTOE of renewables). Biomass, wave and wind in particular are considered to have significant potential for further development. It can be concluded therefore that a mix of renewable energy sources could make a major contribution to the energy supply of the Republic of Ireland in the near future. A particular challenge will be to develop transport fuels based on renewable resources – the transport sector is almost entirely dependent on oil. It is important that government policy and development efforts promote the required mix of renewable energy sources across the electricity, heat and transport sectors.

SUSTAINABLE ENERGY ASSOCIATIONS

The conference which led to this book was notable not only for the range of national and international speakers on the programme, but also for the fact that it was supported by all the associations dealing with sustainable energy in the Republic of Ireland. These were the Association of Irish Energy Agencies; the Geothermal Association of Ireland; the Irish Bioenergy Association; the Irish Hydro Power Association; the Irish Solar Energy Association; the Irish Wind Energy Association; and Meitheal Na Gaoithe. Collectively, these organisations comprise a key resource in the development of renewable energy in Ireland, as the papers which follow show.

REFERENCES

Thanks to Mr. Joc Sanders for production of Figure 1 while working on contract for Tipperary Institute.

ESRI, (2001). *Energy Demand Projection Model.* Economic and Social Research Institute. Dublin.

Jacob, J. (2001). Answer to Dáil Question No. 30, 20th June 2001. Minister of State in the Department of Public Enterprise. Dublin.

Sustainable Energy Ireland, (2002). Renewable Energy Research, Development & Demonstration Programme - Programme Strategy, Dublin. Available from http://www.sei.ie

Bioenergy for Planet, People and Profit

An overview of bioenergy in Ireland - potential and barriers

Seamus Hoyne,
IrBEA Secretary 2002

Ireland is one of Europe's laggards in developing its bioenergy resources,
despite their versatility. One reason for this is that no single government
department has accepted responsibility.

1.0   BIOMASS AND BIOENERGY TECHNOLOGIES

1.1   SOURCES OF BIOMASS

Plants convert sunlight into plant matter (biomass), which is stored energy. This energy can be released for our use with the right technology. Biomass can be sourced from a wide range of materials as outlined in the table below.

There are a range of technologies which can then be utilised to produce energy from these biomass sources. This energy (bioenergy) can be in the form of heat, electricity or transport fuels. This is a vitally important factor given the fact that the Total Primary Energy Requirement (TPER) for Ireland can be equally divided between electricity, heat and transport fuel usage. Bioenergy is the only renewable energy which can meet all parts of the 'energy pie.'

(FIGURE 7B1) SOURCES OF BIO ENERGY		
Farm	**Forestry**	**Other**
Slurry	Firewood	Food Processing Wastes
Agri Residues	Forest Residues	Sewage Sludge
Energy Crops	Short Rotation Coppice	Landfill - gas
Firewood	Wood Industry Residues	Wood Waste
	Tree Surgery Residues	Food and Green Waste

1.2 BIOMASS TO ENERGY TECHNOLOGIES

A number of technologies can be utilised to capture the energy in biomass sources. Only a brief comment on each technology is provided here as it is not within the scope of this paper to describe each technology in detail. More information on these can be supplied by the Irish Bioenergy Association if required.

• Anaerobic Digestion (AD)

This is a process where organic material is placed in a sealed vessel or tank in the absence of air (anaerobic) and bacteria work on the material. It is broken down and the resulting reaction releases methane gas, which is then captured and can be utilised in a boiler or combined heat and power (CHP) plant. AD plants can range in scale from individual farm-based units to large centralised units taking material from a range of sources. AD is growing dramatically in Germany and other EU countries.

• Combustion

This is a well known technology generally but modern systems and equipment which are fuelled by wood and other biomass sources are new to Ireland. Systems are available to suit all sectors from domestic to industrial and these are well proven in other European countries.

• Gasification

This is still a developing technology. It differs from combustion in that, when dealing with wood in particular, a gas is produced from the fuel by controlling the air intake, and the temperature and pressure within the gasification chamber. This gas can then be utilised in an engine or a turbine, linked to a generator, to produce heat and electricity. Gasification has particular opportunities when seeking to develop small scale CHP projects (<1MW).

• Pyrolysis

The next step on from gasification is pyrolysis where instead of a gas an oil can be produced from the biomass material. This technology is still very much as the development stage and there is little work ongoing in Ireland at present.

• Processes to produce liquid biofuels

Energy crops and waste materials (such as vegetable oils and tallow) which can be used to produce transport fuels will come more and more into focus in the immediate future. This will be driven by the increasing cost of traditional transport fuels (petrol and diesel) and the need to comply with an EU Directive on Biofuels. The production of these fuels is well proven in other EU countries and it is generally accepted that market development is dependent not on technical breakthroughs but on financial supports such a reduced excise duty on biofuels.

2.0 IRISH BIOENERGY ASSOCIATION

Given the diverse nature of the biomass sector and the need for a range of actors and interested bodies to co-ordinate efforts a group of people came together in 1998 to form the Irish Bioenergy Association (IrBEA). The Association's mission statement is:

The Irish Bioenergy Association (IrBEA) is an organisation which seeks to maximise the use of bioenergy and the awareness of its benefits on the island of Ireland. This will be achieved by influencing Government policy and public opinion, project facilitation and the provision of support to existing and potential bio-energy users and producers.

Its key visions are that:

1. Integrated and favourable Government poli cies for bio-energy will be developed and implemented
2. There will be wide-spread support for the development of the bio-energy sector
3. There will be a wide-spread wish from the market and buyers to purchase bio-energy products
4. Conditions will exist in which bio-energy can be economically sustainable
5. Conditions will exist in which bio-energy can be financially sustainable
6. Developed market structures for bio-energy products will be in place
7. Economically sustainable supply structures for bio-energy feedstocks will be in place
8. That bio-energy will be developed in a sus tainable manner
9. IrBEA will play a central role in the develop ment of the bio-energy sector
10. IrBEA will be a strong, representative, transparent, effective, efficient, organisation
11. A range of proven production and conver

sion technologies will be commercially available

Its key activities are in the following areas:

• Awareness creation
• Influencing policy
• Promoting project implementation
• Networking and information sharing
• Promoting the interests of its members
• Liasing with similar interest groups

IrBEA is also affiliated to AEBIOM, the European Biomass Association.

3.0 STATUS AND POTENTIAL OF BIOMASS USE

At a European level biomass has achieved a considerable share of the energy market. Figure 7B2 (Kellett, 2002) illustrates the annual use of biomass across Europe. It is evident from this picture that Ireland is lagging significantly behind in its exploitation of the resources out-lined in Section 1.

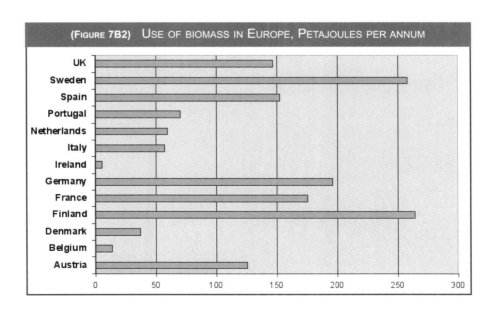

(FIGURE 7B2) USE OF BIOMASS IN EUROPE, PETAJOULES PER ANNUM

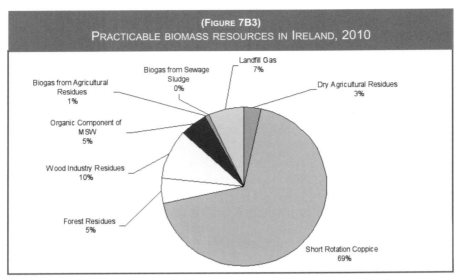

Data in the Sustainable Energy Ireland Renewable Energy RD&D Programme Strategy shows that the scope for development of biomass in Ireland is significant, and spread across many sectors. This chart illustrates a percentage breakdown of the various biomass resources.

4.0 SO WHAT'S HOLDING THINGS UP?

If the potential is there and bioenergy can meet a number of different market needs (electricity, heat and transport) then there must be barriers which are restricting development. These barriers have been summarised in a number of key categories:

• Benefits in multiple sectors

As noted, biomass can be obtained from a number of sources and also can meet the requirements of different sectors e.g. waste management, climate change, enterprise development, alternative agricultural enterprises. As a result it is often difficult to find, particularly at government level, a department which can take control of bioenergy development. This 'control' is important as without it both policies and financial support cannot be maximised.

• Requires integrated push

There are multiple policies at international, European and national level which have an impact on the development of bioenergy. These include the Kyoto Protocol, EU directives on electricity from renewable energy and biofuels, waste management and water quality Directives and the Irish National Climate Change Strategy and Green Paper on Sustainable Energy. Unless these policies are integrated, barriers to development can be 'unwittingly' put in place. However, through integration and synergy it may be possible to maximise the development of the resource. This requires communication and dialogue, in particular at a national level.

• New to Ireland

While the majority of technologies have been well proven in other EU countries they are still new to Ireland. There are few demonstration plants and a lack of markets and supply systems for fuels. Indeed, access to finance at reasonable rates is a particular issue given the perceived level of risk. In addition, there is a continued need for information and awareness creation in the whole bioenergy area.

• **Scale factors**

Bioenergy projects can vary significantly in scale and the drive for larger (>3MW) renewable energy projects which has occurred generally under the Alternative Energy Requirement (AER) programme in Ireland does not always suit bioenergy projects. In addition, the effective utilisation of the heat produced from the bioenergy plant can significantly increase the financial viability but having a use for the heat is not always possible. Small scale plants could be developed across Ireland if the issues of grid connection costs and technology are addressed.

• **Lack of support for Heat and Transport Fuels**

To date the support mechanism of the AER process has concentrated solely on electricity production. There is a need to support and develop projects which are heat only or CHP based. In addition, the support and development of the biofuels industry is vital, in light of the biofuels directive from the EU.

5.0   What's Needed Now?

To overcome these barriers there are a number of policy and technical issues which can be addressed in the short to medium term, including:

• **Simple access to the grid and billing systems for small projects**

Small scale projects often cannot carry the cost of grid connection. Net-metering or similar mechanisms need to be developed to facilitate smaller scale projects (<1MW).

• **Acceptance and recognition that bioenergy can generate >90% of time**

While IrBEA accepts that the wind energy industry has developed significantly in the past five years, a significant problem exists with regard to the availability (percentage of time electricity is actually exported to the grid) of wind energy to the grid (typical values of between 30-40%). Most bioenergy projects which generate electricity have availabilities in the region of 90%. This is of vital importance when addressing such issues as power quality and meeting peak demand.

• **Reassessment of suitability of AER**

The AER process has failed to develop bioenergy apart from landfill gas sites. There is an urgent need to revise this approach and develop a new mechanism which can support the multiple benefits of bioenergy and therefore support project development in other sectors.

• **Promotion of bioenergy for heating**

Currently 1% of Ireland's TPER comes from wood fuel (used domestically and in the wood processing industry). This can be increased and systems exist for the domestic and commercial sector but these are capital intensive compared to traditional fossil fuel based heating systems. Support is required, perhaps modelled on the UK grant and installer accreditation system.

• **Removal of Excise Duty on biofuels**

This can be done with immediate effect. The mechanism which was in place under a previous Finance Bill was not properly advertised and supported. The industry is now better placed to utilise such a support mechanism.

• **Demonstration projects**

The SEI Renewable Energy RD&D Programme should address this issue partly but more supports will be needed in the future.

• **Monitored results, technical information and support**

Data and information from demonstration projects must be made available to the industry to allow it to improve and modify applications to Irish conditions. This must be coupled with the provision of quality technical information and support structures.

• **Integrated policies**

The need for these has been highlighted above and can only be addressed through the relevant government departments.

• **Develop fuel supply systems**

While demonstration plants and projects can be established it is vital that the fuel supply systems are also supported. Systems for the supply of fuels to wood or anaerobic digestion (AD)

plants need to be developed and proven economically.

6.0 CONCLUSION

The development of the practical bioenergy resource in Ireland is a challenge which will take considerable effort to achieve. Developing the industry can meet a range of policy targets and solve a number of problems. There are opportunities for some 'quick wins' but support mechanisms are needed if these are to be achieved.

Given that the technology has been proven in many other EU countries, many of the current barriers are non-technical and relate to financial and infrastructural issues. A co-ordinated strategy, which engages the relevant government departments and other relevant bodies, can assist in moving the industry forward.

Information and education of policy makers, financiers and potential project owners and developers is vital and an immediate need. For the industry to develop the existing and potential developers will need to lobby and this can be most effectively done through the Irish Bioenergy Association.

CONTACT DETAILS:

Irish Bioenergy Association
C/o Tipperary Institute
Nenagh Rd, Thurles, Co. Tipperary
Tel: 0504 28105   Fax: 0504 28111
Email: khealion@tippinst.ie (Kevin Healion is Secretary of IrBEA for 2003)
Web: www.irbea.org

REFERENCES:

IrBEA (2002), Irish Bioenergy Association Strategic Plan.
Sustainable Energy Ireland (2002), *Renewable Energy RD&D – Programme Strategy,* Dublin. Available from http://www.sei.ie
Kellett, P (2002), Introduction to Renewable Energy - Presentation to Certificate in Renewable Energy students, Tipperary Institute.

IRISH HYDRO POWER ASSOCIATION

Small hydro:
the potential to grow but no incentive

David Miller
IHPA and President, European Small Hydropower Association

*Ireland could almost double the amount of electricity it is getting from
small-scale hydro projects. Unfortunately, the real price being paid for
hydro power has been falling for over twenty years and would need to rise
to make investment attractive.*

The term "small hydro" in this paper refers to hydro power projects of less than 10 MW electrical output. Before 1984 there were 20 MW of small hydro capacity owned by the ESB in Ireland, and less than 2 MW in private ownership.

In 1984 a comprehensive survey of hydro power potential in the Republic of Ireland was published. The survey identified a resource of 48 MW of low head small hydro and 40 MW of high head small hydro in remote areas, giving a total small hydro resource of 88 MW. Since 1984, 5 MW of low head potential and 6.6 MW of the high head potential have been developed. The total installed capacity of small hydro power projects in the Republic of Ireland at present is therefore 33.6 MW (22 MW installed pre 1984 and 11.6 MW installed post 1984).

The capacity of small hydro power remaining to be developed is estimated in the table below.
Of course there are also environmental and/or financial constraints surrounding the development of even the 30 MW of potential capacity. There are concerns about the potential environmental impacts on fish life, for example, although there can be a difference between the perceived environmental impacts of a potential small hydro power project and the impacts in reality when proper design and impact mitigation measures are implemented. The EU Water Framework Directive (Directive 2000/60/EC) is now a relevant part of the policy context of small hydro. It states that *"Further integration of protection and sustainable management of water into other Community policy areas such as energy, transport, agriculture, fisheries, regional policy and tourism is necessary."*

	MW
Total potential for small hydro	88
Existing capacity installed	33.6
Undeveloped potential remaining	54.4
Eliminated due to financial or environmental constraints	20
Potential capacity for development	30

Though it would appear that as long as there is no significant impoundment by small hydro, the Directive is much more concerned with the pollution caused by industry, domestic sewage and agriculture.

There are also financial constraints to the development of the small hydro capacity in terms of the price available for the electricity produced. The principal options used by hydro power generators in the Republic of Ireland to sell their electricity to date are:

- Self-supply with sale of surplus to ESB based on avoided fuel cost
- Sale to ESB under a Power Purchase Agreement (PPA)

Prices paid to renewable suppliers who do not have a power purchase agreement are based on ESB's avoided fuel cost. This option is only suitable to provide additional income for projects where the main objective is self-supply.

The principal mechanism at present for supporting the development of small hydro projects is the Alternative Energy Requirement (AER) scheme run by the Department of

Communications, Marine and Natural Resources, the government department with responsibility for energy. The AER provides successful bidders with a long-term Power Purchase Agreement (PPA) under which electricity is sold to the ESB. The Department is responsible for setting the cap prices and the amount of capacity offered under each round of the competition. The first round of the AER was held in 1994. Before then contracts were negotiated by project developers directly with the ESB although the price paid was common to all small hydro supplied and was set by the government.

The lower line in the graph below (Figure 7C1) shows the purchase price for small hydro production from 1981 to 2002. The price payable if the 1981 price had been fully index-linked is shown by the upper line. The price in 1981 was based on avoided fuel cost plus a bonus for regular winter supply. In 1991, an agreement was reached between the Irish Hydro Power Association and the Department of Energy which based the price on ESB avoided fuel cost, operating cost, avoided transmission losses and a small premium for being green.

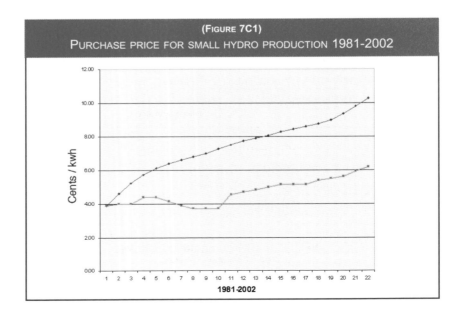

(FIGURE 7C1)
PURCHASE PRICE FOR SMALL HYDRO PRODUCTION 1981-2002

In the rapid and successful development of wind power in certain EU countries, political *price* has been a clear winner over political *quota*. Central to this has been the recognition that the generator must be allowed to make a profit to compare with alternative investments. The concept of a "Profitability Index" is being used increasingly as a basis for tariff structures. The development and the sustaining of small hydro in Ireland could benefit greatly from this approach.

To calculate a Profitability Index, data on the following parameters is required:
• A discount rate
• A period of years
• An investment cost
• A net annual revenue or cash flow
The Profitability Index is then calculated as follows:
Present Value = Cash Flow discounted over 15 years at 6.5% (or other rate)
Net Present Value = Present Value - Investment cost

Profitability Index = $\dfrac{\text{Net Present Value}}{\text{Investment Cost}}$

Figure 7C2 below shows the price required at 50% overall hydro plant efficiency to achieve a

profitability index of 0.3 (upper series of data points). This 0.3 index is considered to provide a reasonable return to the project developer. The smaller the installed capacity of the hydro power project, the higher the electricity sale price that is required to maintain an index of 0.3. Figure 7C2 also shows the maximum price that is presently available under the AER (lower series of data points). It is clear that the present maximum price available under the AER is not sufficient for small hydro projects to make a reasonable profit on the investment required. It is concluded therefore that improved government policy is required to assist in the development of the remaining small hydro potential in the Republic of Ireland.

The Irish Hydro Power Association is the representative body for the operators of small hydro power projects in Ireland. It is affiliated to the European Small Hydropower Association (ESHA). The ESHA website (http://www.esha.be/) provides much useful information on renewable electricity generation from small hydro power projects.

The IHPA may be contacted on telephone 0902 57660.

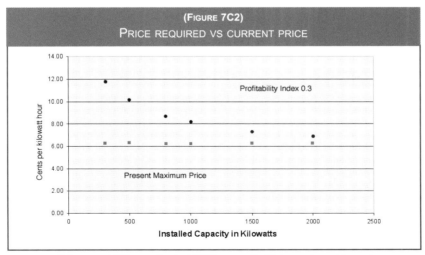

Price per kWh required at 50% overall efficiency to achieve a profitability of 0.3, versus current AER price available.

THE GEOTHERMAL ASSOCIATION OF IRELAND

Ireland's geothermal resources are ideal for space heating

Brian P. Connor

Only low-grade heat can be expected from geothermal sources in Ireland. Research is required to find sites to supply industrial and horticultural heating needs.

Geothermal energy is the earth's natural heat. Heat is transferred to the earth's surface by conduction through rock and via convection in moving fluids. Heat flow is highest in regions of active tectonism and volcanics and lowest in stable shield areas. Geothermal energy can be used for (a) electricity production or (b) direct heating applications. Geothermal energy available on demand, unlike wind energy which is only available when there is sufficient wind speed.

Geothermal energy systems can be classified into four categories:

1. hot dry rock system
2. high enthalpy systems
3. low enthalpy systems
4. shallow geothermal energy

The geographical extent of potential hot dry rock systems is limited. The system involves a temperature of over 200°C at a depth greater than 3km (5-7km). Water is injected into the hot rock through deep boreholes and the hot water or steam returns up another borehole to be used for electrical generation. This system does not have potential in Ireland but experiments have been conducted in Cornwall in the UK.

High enthalpy systems are associated with active tectonic and volcanic areas. These are water or vapour dominated systems. The temperature of the source is over 200°C. These systems are generally used for electricity generation. They are not suitable for Ireland due to the geological conditions in the country.

Low enthalpy systems are applicable for stable geological areas e.g. North West Europe. Suitably warm rocks occur at depths of up to 2km with temperatures up to 100°C. This system is used for direct heating in, for example, the Paris basin and in Southampton, England. Applications include industrial and horticultural heating. This system has potential in Ireland but research is needed to locate suitable sources of this geothermal heat.

Shallow geothermal energy uses geothermal energy with a source temperature of about 10°C. The temperature is increased using heat pumps. There are four main production configurations currently in use in Ireland - horizontal loops, vertical loop, groundwater and building foundations. Current applications include space heating in commercial buildings, private houses and swimming pools. The most common configurations use horizontal loops or the direct use of aquifer water. There are 500-600 installations in Ireland at present.

The status, needs and potential for future development of the geothermal resource in Ireland can be summarised as follows:

Low temperature geothermal using heat pumps
Status at present
- technology developed
- demonstration installations are available for inspection
- limited number of installers

Required to develop use of technology on a large scale
- promotion of technology
- training of installers
- regulation and certification of installers

Potential of resource
- most sites can support installations using locally available geothermal energy

Low enthalpy systems
Status at present
- no development in Ireland

- lack of data on potential aquifers that could be developed to produce geothermal energy

Required to develop use of technology on a large scale
- study to evaluate resource
- demonstration of technology to develop and use the resource

Potential of resource
- unknown at present until preliminary evaluation studies are carried out

The Geothermal Association of Ireland was founded in 1997. It has over 30 members, with representation from academic institutes, energy management agencies, consultants and contractors. The association is the Irish representative on the European Geothermal Energy Council. The objectives of the Geothermal Association of Ireland are as follows

- Promote the use of geothermal energy in Ireland
- Carry out research on geothermal energy in Ireland.

The activities of the association include:
- lectures on current development worldwide on geothermal energy
- provision of training courses for installers of geothermal energy systems
- organising site visits to geothermal installations.

The secretary of the Geothermal Association of Ireland can be contacted through Cork County Energy Agency,
Spa House,
Mallow,
Co. Cork.
Ph: +353.22.43610
Fax: +353.22.43678
e-mail: mallowre@eircom.net

Power from the Sun is accessible to all

Douglas Gordon - Chairman, ISEA

*Every property owner has the opportunity to use the energy from the sun
for heating and generating electricity. Loans at the same rate of interest as
house mortgages would enecourage them to do so.*

In June 2002 the Renewable Energy Information Office, Bandon, Co. Cork and Sustainable Energy Ireland organised a conference in Tralee entitled *'See the Light, no bills from the Sun'*. This was a brilliant conference with some of the top European experts on the subject of solar energy. The outcome of the conference was a meeting of delegates to decide on how best to represent the entire industry, meaning not just suppliers and installers, but also professionals and the consumers. After an hour of heated discussion it was agreed to have a follow-up meeting in Thurles to agree the setting up of an association to represent as a many aspects of the industry as possible.

By August 2002 a not for profit limited company was established with nine directors and this is now the Irish Solar Energy Association Ltd., ISEA for short. Its remit is threefold

• To promote solar energy
• To raise awareness throughout the whole population.
• To improve quality in all aspects of solar technology

You may ask what do we mean by 'solar'? The level of ignorance on this subject in all sectors is astonishing considering that solar energy is so crucial to our everyday living. We just take solar energy for granted and ignore the huge benefits to be derived from developing this virtually free resource. Solar is about:

• Solar panels for domestic/commercial hot water
• Photovoltaic panels for electricity generation
• Heat pumps for space heating and cooling
• Passive solar gain construction

Most people have some understanding of conservatories on houses and they would be familiar with solar domestic hot water roof panels, but they certainly have no experience in Ireland with town and village district heating systems derived from solar farms, which can be seen in Denmark. Interestingly Denmark is roughly on the same latitude as Ireland, so why have we in Ireland taken so long to embrace this abundant source of energy?

Has anybody thought of using photovoltaic

panels as a substitute for standard roof tiles, while having the benefit of generating their own source of electricity?

Heat pumps are a greatly misunderstood technology that is only just catching on in Ireland. This is a way of harvesting the rich source of solar energy at shallow depths under the garden grass or from a borehole or other water sources 365 days of the year and at night or day time. All of this translates into a huge move away from hydrocarbon-based fuels and the possibility of meeting our Kyoto commitments with ease.

However, the current level of ignorance at all levels of Irish society means that we have an uphill battle that presents a really exciting challenge for those involved in the industry.

WHAT DOES THE ISEA PLAN TO DO?

There is so much to do, so the discipline is where to start and what to leave out at the beginning. On the best advice from our European colleagues who went through this pain threshold many years before us and learnt a lot of hard lessons, we have a short list as follows:

- To run a PR campaign to raise the awareness among the general population
- To develop training courses and to have a code of practice for installers
- To affiliate with other renewable energy organisations
- To lobby the government to bring in incen tives for solar systems.

I would be the first to say in the current difficult economic climate that the government is not going to provide any financial incentives or VAT reductions. Instead can I suggest that the financial institutions be encouraged to provide both capital and low cost loans similar to the current mortgage rates of 3.9%. Grants and VAT reductions smack of dependency culture, which is not what this €700 million industry needs. We need the best financial resources available in this country and the best management, and that means private enterprise.

The unique aspect of the ISEA is that it is essentially a bottom up organisation unlike the wind energy industry which is the preserve of business interests as it is very capital intensive. How can the man in the street get involved in wind power except by being a consumer or an environmental objector? With solar energy every man, woman, child, company, farm and institution has a role to play in helping to make Ireland not only self-sufficient in energy, and that is a reality which our politicians have not realised yet, but we should also be seriously considering how we can establish Ireland as a world leader in solar applied technology with huge export potential in design, consultancy, manufacturing and installations. With Ireland's worldwide connections this should be just as big an export potential as our computer industry. Is anybody prepared to take note of this simple fact? Is anybody interested in creating wealth and jobs? The ISEA has already had an approach from sources close to the Indian Government to get involved in technology transfer to India with a market value of €5 billion.

The ISEA is a national representative body concerned with the following:
- To help the public to contact competent installers
- To provide training and accreditation for member installers
- To increase confidence in both the government and in the public regarding the serious advantages of solar energy

The address of the ISEA is 17, Kildare Street, Dublin 2. Alternatively, you may contact the Association using my e-mail - douglasgordon@ eircom.net

IRISH WIND ENERGY ASSOCIATION

Wind energy in Ireland, the present situation

Inge Buckley
IWEA committee member and former chairman

Wind farms have been established in Ireland far more slowly than either the government wished or the resource warranted. The Alternative Energy Requirement approach has not worked well and is likely to be reformed or abandoned shortly.

While Ireland and Scotland have the best wind resources in Europe, Ireland has by far the lowest prices in the EU for the electricity that wind can generate. As a result, only 120MW of wind energy has been installed since Ireland's first commercial windfarm was built at Bellacorrick in Co. Mayo in 1992. In 2001 only 7MW was installed and in 2002 only 14MW. Just one further one windfarm is under construction.

The Irish wind market has been led by the government's Alternative Energy Requirements (AER) programme. AER1, AER3 and AER5 dealt with wind energy.

AER1 offered Power Purchase Agreements (PPA) from the ESB for a 15 year period. Contracts for 70MW were offered and 46MW of capacity was built, a success rate of 66%. AER3 in 1997 offered contracts for 137MW, but was a huge failure as only 28% of this capacity, 38MW, was built.

Under AER5 in 2001, those tendering had to have full and final planning permission for their proposed farms for the first time. Contracts were offered for a massive 355MW of capacity in late February 2002. By November 2002,

however, none of these projects had been offered a Power Purchase Agreement as the industry was still waiting for the energy minister to sign an order allowing the ESB to buy the electricity under a Public Service Obligation (PSO). In other words no project had been able to draw down project finance from a bank.

AER6 was launched in November 2002 seeking 470MW of renewable electricity from wind, 25MW from biomass and 5MW from hydro. Bids had to be in by April 2003. Few people expected that it would be any more successful than AER5 and the minister even announced on the day of its launch that his department, the Department of Communication, Marine and Natural Resources, would be consulting the industry and others about how the sector could reach the EU target of 13.2% of Ireland's electricity coming from renewable sources by 2010. This would require approximately 1800MW to be installed.

The government's 1999 Green Paper on Sustainable Energy set a target of an additional 500MW installed capacity of renewable energy by 2005 on top of the 177MW installed or about to be installed at the time. This additional

500MW is vital for the government's National Climate Change Strategy.

CONSTRAINTS ON THE DEVELOPMENT OF WIND ENERGY:

1. Availability of Power Puchase Agreements (PPAs): The competitive and restrictive way in which PPAs are offered under the AER programme has meant that at least one site has seen its planning permission expire because construction couild not go ahead without a PPA.

2. Poor Prices: At roughly 4.8 eurocent per kWh, the price offered under the AER programme is by far the cheapest in Europe, and is lower than the price at 5.2 eurocent per kWh currently paid to ESB Power Generation for its electricity from its portfolio of power stations. This figure excludes the price paid for electricity generated which is purchased under a separate Public Service Obligation (PSO).

3. Inadequate Indexation; Although AER1 and AER3 contracts were subject to full Consumer Price Indexation (CPI), the AER5 price is subject to only 25% indexation, a source of discontent within the IWEA. In contrast ESB Power Generation not only gets its higher price of 5.2 eurocents but also gets full indexation and is allowed to pass on any increases in its fuel costs.

4. Planning Problems. Overall, the IWEA feels that obtaining planning consents from county planners is not a major obstacle to the development of wind energy, even though individual members of the IWEA contend that certain local authorities are anti wind. Our major problem is with An Bord Pleanala, whose decisions often are seen as a lottery. However, with the 355MW of contracts offered under AER5 it has by and large overcome the planning issues. Since the industry started it has 700 MW inshore wind projects with full planning permission.

5. Grid connections; Connection to the ESB grid is increasingly becoming a major issue as wind projects compete for access to the network. The capability of the Distribution and Transmission network to connect wind energy onto the system is limited in most places, particularly in the more outlying regions of Ireland, where the wind resource is often the best.

6. Financial issues: With the prices paid for wind generated electricity so low, there is enough cash flow to service the bank loan element of the typical financial model with 20% equity and an 80 % bank loan, but no money to allow for any return on the equity component. The result is that the wind industry is forced to avail of whatever tax incentives are available and what clever tax experts can engineer.

WHAT HAPPENS NEXT?

Although the Programme for Government stated that tax incentives would be made available to the renewable energy industry; this may not happen in the present financial climate and the whole industry could grind to a halt unless either full indexation is restored to the AER5 and AER6 prices or these are improved marginally.

The de-regulated market will continue to grow and companies selling green electricity may offer Power Purchase Agreements to independent developers. If new players enter the market and existing players grow bigger, these private PPAs may become attractive enough to compete with the government-supported ones.

The government committed itself to the development of offshore wind in the Programme for Government and contracts for 50MW were reserved for this sector in AER6 offering considerably higher prices - 8.4 eurocents or possibly more – than for onshore wind developments. A lot of activity has and is taking place

THE IWEA ITSELF

The IWEA was established as an association in 1993. It now has two arms. One is a company with charitable status whose objects are to promote wind energy and to undertake research. The other is a limited company to deal with the IWEA's commercial aspects and revenue-generating activities.

The IWEA offers different types of membership running from Ordinary to Associate and Corporate. It has an elected Council, which elects a chairman. Under the Council there are a number of committees, which each has a chairman, who must be a member of the Council. The current committees are: Administration, Planning, Grid, Market Regulation and Policy, Public Relations, Off-Shore and Finance.

The IWEA has a fulltime staffed office in Arigna, Co. Leitrim, serving 200 ordinary members, 11 corporate ones, 20 associates, 5 directors and 22 Council members. Key activities include organising two annual conferences, issuing newsletters, maintaining a website, preparing consultation papers and submissions and involvement in external groups. These include close contact with government departments, the Commission for Energy Regulation, international and EU links. The IWEA has two representatives on the Council of the EWEA (European Wind Energy Association). It is represented on the IBEC Energy Policy Committee and was part of the government's Strategy Group for Wind Energy and the Grid Investment Group. The IWEA has close links to the Renewable Energy Information Office and the local energy agencies.

IWEA, Arigna, Carrick-on-Shannon,
Co. Roscommon, Ireland
Tel: +353-(0)71 9646072,
Fax: +353 (0)71 9646080,
email: office@iwea.com

offshore but the implementation of many of the projects will depend on the construction of a interconnector to Great Britain.

Green Credits/ Green Certificates/ Emission Trading are in their infancy throughout Europe and some trial trading is already taking place. However, they are not yet a bankable commodity against which we can borrow to finance our farms.

WHY DOES WIND ENERGY NEED GOVERNMENT SUPPORT?

As will be seen from the above, government support is really in the form of longterm contracts and the security that banks and investors like. Wind energy has a very high upfront cost of approximately 1 - 1.1 million euros per installed MW. Once built, the fuel cost is nil and the turbines will continue producing emission-free electricity for at least 20 years. It should be noted that wind energy is not alone in requiring secure off-take contracts; The Commission for Energy Regulation (CER) has recently published a consultation paper which may very well result in the ESB PES (Public Electricity Supply) being asked to offer guaranteed off-take contracts to new gas-fired power stations.

Finally, it is about time the "official" government bodies recognised the potential and the opportunities that the wind industry offers in terms of rural development, income generation and employment generation. It creates consultancy jobs, construction jobs, and manufacturing jobs as well as extra income for the legal and financial sectors. At present there is full planning permission for in excess of 1,000 MW of wind power, representing an investment of in excess of 1.1 billion euros, most of it from indigenous Irish companies. The potential of the sector is huge.

Companies' wind power investment plans dashed

There was widespread disappointment among firms hoping to develop wind farms in Ireland when the results of the sixth – and probably the final – round of bidding for contracts under the Alternative Energy Requirement (AER) scheme were announced in early July 2003. The Minister for Communications, Marine and Natural Resources, Dermot Ahern gave major contracts to supply wind electricity to just three firms. Out of a total of 330MW of contracts to supply the state-owned Electricity Supply Board, the ESB, with electricity generated from the wind, 63MW went to a wholly-owned subsidiary of the ESB, Hibernian Wind Power, and 158MW to Saorgus Energy, a Kerry-based company.

"In total, the ESB and Saorgus have secured 82% of the contracts awarded. This cements the ESB's monopoly position in the Irish market as the ESB currently has 88% of the electricity generating capacity in the country" Tim Cowhig, the chairman of the Irish Wind Energy Association (IWEA) said in a press release headed 'Government kills the Irish Wind Industry: Potential investment of €2bn by private sector is now seriously jeopardised.'

Of the nine contracts given for supplies from large (over 5MW) onshore windfarms, only one, the smallest, went to a company other than Saorgus and Hibernian Wind. Both the offshore contracts went to the Kish Consortium in which the ESB has a one-third stake and Saorgus Energy two-thirds.

Many companies could not understand why they had been unsuccessful. "The Minister has refused to release the prices associated with the winning bids," Mr. Cowhig said. "The IWEA is considering taking legal proceedings or appealing to the Competition Authority in terms of national legislation or European competition law. In addition, we may seek a judicial review or an appeal to Europe to seek an injunction preventing the Minister from awarding the contracts to the ESB."

Speaking in August 2003, Mike Barry, a director of Saorgus, denied rumours that the ESB had a financial stake in his company. "They don't and they never will," he said. His company had been successful because its bids had been lower. This had been possible because its projects were in parts of the country with high windspeeds. "Our project with the highest price was on a site with lower speeds and only just scraped through."

Mr. Cowhig said he wondered how many contracts would actually be fulfilled as the price being paid for the power was too low to give a proper financial return. "We know the Hibernian Wind Power projects will go ahead" he said, "but if the others do, a lot of us will have to eat humble pie."

Mr. Barry was confident that Cowhig would have to do so. "We've already ordered the turbines for the site where we are getting the lowest price. Work will start there in another few weeks and we are negotiating contracts for another site where work will start in six months," he said. "AER VI is a success because projects are happening." This was a reference to the failure of AER V. None of the firms offered contracts under that bidding round had installed any turbines by spring, 2003.

Mr Ahern obviously realised that the allocation of contracts would be badly received. His press statement read: "The Minister recognises that there will be a number of disappointed bidders due to the overwhelming interest in the competition and the quality of the bids received. He is aware of the hard work and expense which bidders put in to the seeking of planning permission for their projects and the submission of bids. He has therefore announced his intention to immediately seek state aids clearance for an additional 140 megawatts capacity to be offered in large-scale wind, small-scale wind and biomass categories."

Three months earlier, at an IWEA conference in Cork to celebrate the tenth anniversary of Ireland's first wind farm at Bellacorrick, Co. Mayo, Mr. Ahern had stated that the European Commission's directive on the promotion of new and renewable sources in the internal electricity market had set a target for Ireland which he regarded as the minimum the country must achieve. "Clearly, to achieve those targets huge private sector investment will be necessary. And clearly, if investment conditions are not right then we won't meet those targets" he said. "In developing the Terms and Conditions of AER VI, it was therefore an imperative for me to put in place an open and transparent mechanism that would be attractive to investors. I believe that the package I have put on offer for AER VI achieves that goal."

Nevertheless, he thought that "the current AER mechanism might not be the optimum support measure to bring us to the 2010 target. Other systems in place elsewhere seem to have delivered much more. The German system, the French system and the pure market approach of the Renewable Obligation Certificate system in the United Kingdom are examples. The challenge is to find a system that gives certainty to investors while at he same time taking account of cost reductions in the various technologies."

AER VI also offered contracts for power from biomass (34MW, mostly wood-fired CHP) and hydro (1.3MW). The higher prices paid by the ESB for electricity purchased under the AER system are covered by the Public Service Obligation which is added to all electricity bills. It is estimated that €74.8 million will be raised by the PSO in 2004. Of this, €58.4 million will be paid to the ESB to cover the additional costs it incurs by buying power from the peat-fired Edenderry Power and from a peat-fired power station being constructed by the ESB at Lanesboro in Co.Longford. The balance - €16 million - will be used to cover the extra cost of the AER power programmes.

Part Eight
The Way Ahead

The Editor's conclusions:
So little time and so much to do

It is crucially important to make massive investments towards bringing about the switch to renewables now, before oil and gas production peaks, so that enough fossil energy is available. Waiting a few years could condemn millions to misery.

Where did humanity go wrong? When did we take a path which, because 'one path leads to another' in Robert Frost's phrase, inexorably led us to becoming totally dependent on a grotesquely unsustainable energy system? To put this another way, why is our way of life under threat from the way we generate our livelihoods?

The story of humanity's relationship with energy records a progression rather than progress, although if we stick with the latter term, the qualifier 'rake's' comes to mind. Its key feature over many centuries is that people have moved from simple ways of organising themselves and supplying their needs to much more complex ones. For example, the shift 10,000 years ago from hunter-gathering to depending on settled agriculture was obviously a step from a simple to a more complex way of life. It was also a step that, in turn, allowed even more complex ways of living to develop. It led to towns and cities, to specialists and priesthoods, to the development of the notion of private property, and, as a result of that notion, to the rule of the many by the few. With settlement came crafts such as pottery, and then literature, science, most music and art, each an example of greater complexity.

Complexity can be measured. One way is to count the number of roles that people play. Hunter-gatherer societies are said[1] to contain no more than a few dozen distinct social personalities, while modern European censuses recognise 10,000 to 20,000 unique occupational roles, and industrial societies may contain more than a million different kinds of social personalities overall. Another way of measuring is to count the number of different artifacts in daily use. Compare, for example, the number of lines sold in a typical shop in an Indian village – salt, sugar, rice, beedis, matches and very little more – with that in a modern European or North American supermarket which could well have 15,000 different products on display. Sainsbury's flagship store on the Cromwell Road in London sells 40 different types of apple, six varieties of caviar, 50 different teas, and 400 forms of bread. "Someone came in on Christmas Eve and asked for banana leaves," a keen young manager told a journalist[2] recently "and you know something? We had them."

The transition from one level of complexity is always marked by an increase in energy use. In earlier days, this usually meant that people had to work harder. Farmers had to spend more time growing food than hunter-gatherers had had to spend on collecting it. Bushmen apparently[3] only had to collect food every third or fourth day.

There's no evidence that the transition from hunter-gathering to settled agriculture was the fatal mistake we are looking for in the sense of it marking the start of a system that would have eventually proved unsustainable. After all, it did survive for thousands of years anyway, despite many local unsustainabilities along the way, such as the steady decline of irrigated farming yields in Mesopotamia because of the increasing salt content in the soil. (The lower crop yields caused by the salt meant that the human energy required to run the complex system could not be maintained. There was too little food to operate the Sumarian bureaucracy and, more importantly, its army, which led to the state's conquest and collapse[4].)

It can be argued that the wrong turn was taken in England in the 16th Century as the population began to recover from the Black Death. The increased numbers – a rise from 1.6 million to 5 million in less than 200 years - naturally put greater pressure on resources and caused communities to have problems living within the limits imposed by their local environments. In 1631, Edmund Howes described how this had forced them to start to burn coal:

Within man's memory it was held impossible to have any want of wood in England. But …such hath been the great expence of timber of navigation, with infinite increase of building houses, with great expence of wood for household furniture, casks and other vessels not to be numbered, and of carts, wagons and coaches, besides the extreme waste of wood in making iron, burning of bricks and tiles, that at this present, through the great consuming of wood as aforesaid, and the neglect of planting of woods, there is so great scarcity of wood throughout the whole kingdom that not only the City of London, all haven towns and in very many parts within the land, the inhabitants in general are constrained to make their fires of sea-coal or pit coal, even in the chambers of honourable personages and through necessity which is the mother of all arts, they have in late years devised the making of iron, the making of all sorts of glass and the burning of bricks with sea-coal and pit-coal.[5]

That was it. The thin end of the wedge. The slippery slope. For the first time, humanity was starting to depend on a non-renewable, and hence unsustainable, energy source for its comfort and livelihood. It was understandable that it did. Which of us would have worried about the long-term consequences of burning black stones collected from beaches in Northumberland, or which had been dug out of shallow holes in the ground?

As the demand for coal increased, the easiest, shallowest mines were soon exhausted, and deeper and deeper pits had to be dug. This posed enormous problems since, if a shaft is sunk below the water table, it floods and a pump has to be installed to keep things reasonably dry. The early pumps consisted of rags or buckets on continuous chains which were turned by horses or, if a stream was handy, a water wheel. However, the deeper a shaft went, the longer the chain had to be and the more friction the horse or the wheel had to overcome. As this placed a real limit on how deep a mine could go, mine-owners were keen to find other ways of powering their pumps. Around the time Edmund Howes was writing, coal-fired steam power began to be used for the first time for pumping water out of mines. In a somewhat incestuous way, coal energy was being used for mining coal.

The first steam engines just moved a piston back and forth, which was all that was required to work a cylinder-type pump. It was only during the following century that the piston was attached to a crank to turn a revolving shaft, an innovation in response to a demand for rotary power from cotton mills unable to find additional sites for their waterwheels. This was the type of engine, of course, that powered the industrial revolution and led with an alarming inevitability to the problems we have today. It was steam power, in fact, which made the widespread use of machines both necessary and possible.

The essence of industrialisation is that it produces lower-cost goods by using capital equipment and external energy to replace the skilled, and thus relatively expensive, labour used in hand crafts. Since less labour is used per unit of output, unemployment develops unless sales expand. The mechanisation of sock and lace production in the English midlands led to such widespread job losses that riots broke out in 1811 and 1812. Troops were sent to the area to stop the Luddites, as the bands of destitute working men were called, from breaking into the new factories and destroying the machines. Indeed, had the Napoleonic War not ended in 1815 allowing the factories to increase their sales in Europe and elsewhere, the disturbances might have become serious enough to kill off the industrial revolution. Without wider markets, firms using powered machinery would have either consumed themselves in a competitive frenzy, or seen their technologies banned as a result of popular unrest.

Eventually, British imports put most continental craft producers out of business and left the remainder with no alternative but to adopt more fossil energy-intensive methods too. In some cases, the surviving producers received state grants to help them re-equip, such as those given to the ironworks and engineering companies owned by the Cockerills in Belgium after that country became independent from France in 1830. More generally, however, governments, or leading public figures, helped them acquire the new technology by organising - and sponsoring - demonstrations of the latest British equipment. Tariff barriers were maintained to allow the new continental industries to build themselves up until they could not only compete with their British rivals but had acquired export markets in which to sell themselves. It was the need for exclusive external markets to solve the problem of mass unemployment at home that led the European powers to scramble to assemble competing empires and eventually to confront each other in the First World War.

A TECHNOLOGY PYRAMID

The early participants in a sales pyramid get rich because they receive commission on the goods they sell to people whom they have persuaded to become dealers too; dealers who, in turn, can earn a commission from others they induce to join the pyramid as dealers later on, who themselves recruit and stock further dealers. And so it goes on, setting up a situation in which everyone in the pyramid can only fulfill their income aspirations if the pyramid does the impossible and expands indefinitely, eventually involving infinitely more people than there are in the world.

The fossil-fuel-based production system became dominant by expanding on exactly the same lines. Just as British factories had needed to take over the markets previously served by craft-scale manufacturers in Europe to survive, industrial Europe had to oust artisanal producers elsewhere in the world, and the British sold them the machinery to do so. As each successive group of countries was forced to adopt mechanised production methods themselves in the hope of escaping poverty, so those who had mechanised earlier sold them the equipment. And so the industrial pyramid grew and grew until it reached the point some years ago when there were no more markets supplied by craft producers to take over. This left firms in the pyramid with no one to displace but each other, and since then, international competition has become much more intense.

Firms have adopted two strategies to survive: one is to automate, eliminating the need for human labour almost entirely. The other is to move production to countries where labour is cheap. The combined result of the two is that the share of industrial revenues being paid in wages and salaries has fallen rapidly and larger and larger numbers of people are being left without the financial means to buy many manufactured products. In more than 100 countries, average per capita incomes are lower today than they were 15 years ago, and more than a quarter of humanity - 1.6 billion people - is worse off now than it was then. In Britain, the proportion of national income being paid in wages and salaries fell from 72% in 1974 to only 63% in 1995, an unprecedented fall in so short a time.

In short, the machine-based production system is proving itself to be unsustainable on two counts. One is that, because manufacturing companies are racing against each other to achieve ever-lower costs, the system is progressively denying its worker-customers the incomes they need to buy its products. It is thus curtailing its own markets and imploding. With surplus production capacity in almost every sector, the world is now poised on the brink of an economic collapse more serious than that in the 1930s. It is not that there is no demand for the additional products the factories could produce. The potential market is huge. It is just that because of the low wages and high levels of unemployment, those who would like to consume more do not have the income to express their demand.

The second source of unsustainability is the topic of this book. It is that the fossil energy which made mechanisation and globalisation possible will soon begin to get scarce. As John McMullan shows in his paper, there is still plenty of the fuel that powered the Industrial Revolution in the ground. However, the amount of energy required to sink a mine, extract the coal and then turn it into useful heat, light or power has climbed and climbed. It has been calculated that American strip-mined coal only produces 2.5 times the amount of energy required to mine it when it is burned in a power station if scrubbers are fitted to remove sulphur dioxide from the smoke so as not to cause acid rain.

The same is true for oil – the amount of energy required to find and extract it is taking an increasing share of the energy it delivers. This is the reason that Colin Campbell expects the world's oil production from conventional sources to peak within the next five or six years. Output, he thinks, will then fall away so that by 2050 it will be just over half its 2010 level, as Figure 8A1 shows. Even if the serious environmental problems with unconventional oil sources like the Athabaska tar sands can be overcome and the energy in/energy out ratio can be greatly improved, it would only ease supplies for a few more years. With gas, world output is expected to peak around 2040 and then go into a steep decline, as Figure 8A2 illustrates.

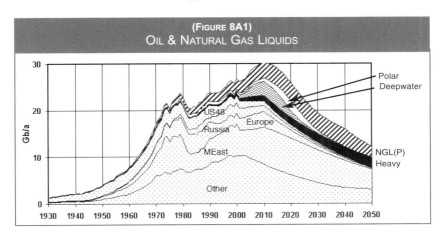

(FIGURE 8A1)
OIL & NATURAL GAS LIQUIDS

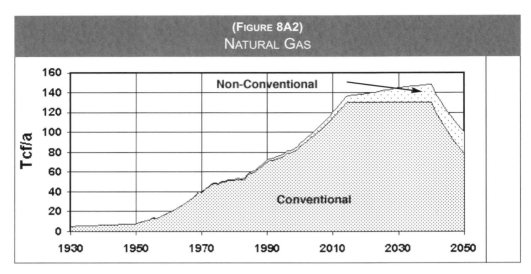

(FIGURE 8A2)
NATURAL GAS

If we put the two graphs together to show the total amount of energy that oil and gas can be expected to deliver over the next century we get Figure 8A3. This shows that the rising amount of energy available from gas will be unable to declining in 1979 although in some countries, notably the US and China (and Ireland) the amount per person was still increasing until very recently. This means that many countries are already adjusting to having less energy

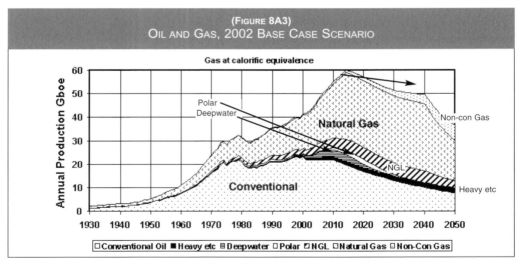

(FIGURE 8A3)
OIL AND GAS, 2002 BASE CASE SCENARIO

compensate for the declining amount from oil after 2015 or thereabouts. After that, in roughly twelve years' time, the overall decline will begin.

In fact, the amount of oil being consumed by the average person around the world began available and the slower rates of economic growth and higher levels of unemployment they have experienced compared with the 1950s and 1960s, when per capita energy use was growing fast, are symptoms of this. But their adjustments are tiny compared with those that every country will have to make to avoid complete breakdowns in the future. All the fossil-energy-intensive systems of production and distribution that have been built up over the past two centuries are going to have to be radically changed, and, as we discussed in the Introduction, there is only a limited amount of usable fossil energy left that can be diverted to bring this about. The key question is, then, how should the fossil energy that can be made available be used? In what types of energy supply projects should it be invested? There are four alternatives. Tar sands, coal, nuclear and renewables. Let's look these in turn.

We'll take tar sands and coal together. In my view, expanding the output of these fuels would be a mistake for two reasons.

1. Both contribute seriously to global warming and the Intergovernmental Panel on Climate Change has warned that carbon dioxide emissions and consequently fossil fuel use needs to be cut by around 80% to prevent a possibly catastrophic climate change. It would therefore be

madness to develop energy sources which would increase these emissions, to go further up a dangerous cul de sac which we know we need to leave as quickly as we can. The fact that John McMullan could report that world coal use has gone up 47% in the past 25 years is very worrying indeed. It means that humanity is heading rapidly in the wrong direction. This is not to say that the type of super-efficient, ultra-high temperature and pressure coal-burning power stations that he discusses should not be built, but, if they are, it should be as part of a programme to reduce coal consumption rather than to increase it. Of course, sequestration might enable the output of both these fuels to be increased while simultaneously cutting carbon dioxide emissions. However, this would require both the use of more energy as capital to build the equipment, and also the expenditure of energy as an input to compress the gas before pumping it down an oil well or into the sea. The net energy gain from the combustion of both fuels would be seriously reduced, making other sources more attractive.

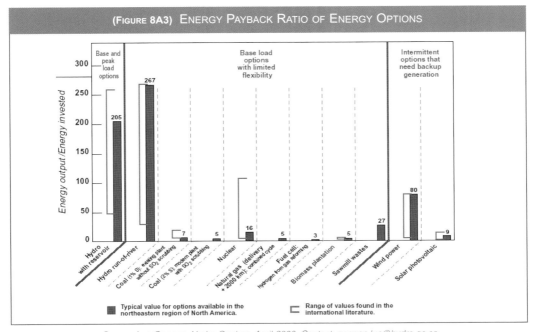

(FIGURE 8A3) ENERGY PAYBACK RATIO OF ENERGY OPTIONS

Source: Luc Gagnon, Hydro Quebec, April 2000. Contact: gagnon.luc@hydro.qc.ca

2. Even if the serious environmental downside to the development of both fuels could be overcome, we ought to reject their expansion anyway because, quite simply, they already give a very poor return for the energy we would have to invest in producing them and sequestration could only make matters worse. The situation without sequestration is shown clearly in Figure 8A4, which comes from the Quebec Hydro website already mentioned by Dave Elliott. It shows that an investment of energy in coal will only give 11-25 times the amount of energy out, whereas an investment in hydro will give 205 times the amount of energy and an investment in wind or nuclear will give you 15 times. Basically the same information is given in the table below and, of course, in the much more extensive one compiled by Ian Hore-Lacy in his paper.

(FIGURE 8A5) LIFE CYCLE ENERGY RATIOS FOR VARIOUS TECHNOLOGIES	
	Input as % of lifetime output
PV polycrystalline silicon	124
PV amorphous silicon	67
Coal	30
Lignite	17
Gas (Combined Cycle)	17
Nuclear (PWR)	7
Wind	7
Hydro	4

from Voss 2002

So if we heed the figures in the three tables and reject investing energy in developing coalmines and building the plants required to extract oil from tar sands because of their poor rate of return and the effect their exploration would have on the gobal climate, that leaves us with two possibilities – nuclear and renewables. Nuclear power has the big advantage over the leading renewable, wind, because the electricity it produces is always available, not just when the wind blows. To make wind comparable, some way of storing the electrical energy a turbine captures has to be provided. This, as Werner Zittel said, is where the hydrogen economy comes in, but providing the additional equipment for that does require the investment of more energy as capital. So, in energy investment terms, nuclear power apparently gives more bang for your buck.

And it might do just that, too. I think nuclear has to be rejected on five grounds:

1. The risk factor. The nuclear industry is unable to get commercial insurance cover and governments have had to step in, taking on the burden instead. This is a massive subsidy.

2. The type of society that would be created. Nuclear reactors make wonderful targets for terrorists. Just having them could lead to a police state. There is also the problem of providing the materials for the proliferation of nuclear weapons.

3. The need for the long-term care of the waste. We don't know that our descendants will have the capacity to provide it continuously for the next 10,000 years.

4. Uranium is in very limited supply, as Hore-Lacy pointed out, and the use of fast breeder reactors does not get around the problem very convincingly. They entail considerably higher energy investments but could, theoretically increase the energy available by a factor of 60. But as the UK Atomic Energy Authority wrote in 1989, 'In practice, it is now not clear how [the use of fast breeders] would be achieved on an expanded global scale without encountering basic plutonium shortages, not to mention serious problems with waste disposal, power plant decommissioning and nuclear weapons proliferation."

5. The number of nuclear stations that would be

required is too large to be feasible as Folke Gunther pointed out. 1,700 nuclear stations would be required just to make up the decline in oil and gas output between 2015 and 2040 and if we wished to provide the capacity for world economic growth to continue at 2% beyond 2015, that would take another 5,000 stations. So, over the 25 year period, between 6,500 and 7,000 stations would have to come on stream – that's five every week. There would be real problems in finding suitable sites outside earthquake zones where the cooling water would not

sions) in OECD countries and the annual increase in their incomes. Roughly 50% of all energy used around the world is invested in trying to generate economic growth and then more energy has to be spent as income on a continual basis to work the new systems. The rate at which a country's economy can grow, if it does not use extra energy, is equal to the rate at which it can increase energy productivity and that might not be very fast because energy is needed to make and install the equipment required to take advantage of whatever energy-

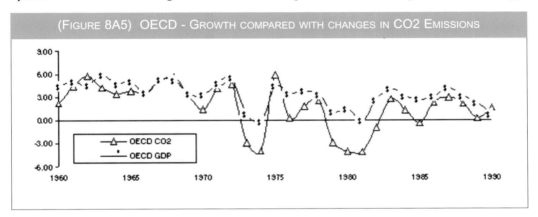

(FIGURE 8A5) OECD - GROWTH COMPARED WITH CHANGES IN CO2 EMISSIONS

harm the marine environment. And given that most stations take ten years to build, work would have to start now.

ARE RENEWABLES ADEQUATE?

Rejecting the nuclear option just leaves us with wind and the other renewables. Let's consider the size of the task we are setting them. We not only want them to make up for the declining amount of energy that oil and gas will start to deliver in around twelve years' time but also to provide the increasing amounts of energy required to raise incomes – in other words, for economic growth if not in the wealthy countries then in the poorer parts of the world.

Figure 8A5 shows the very close relationship between the annual increase in energy consumption (expressed as industrial CO_2 emis-

saving technologies come along. In other words, just as an energy scarcity will limit the pace at which we can develop additional supplies of renewable energy, it will also limit the pace at which we can introduce technologies to conserve it and the pace of economic growth.

Renewables currently supply only 0.6% of the world's traded energy so their rate of expansion is going to have to be very rapid to prevent an overall decline in the world's energy supply and a consequent fall in the level of economic activity. That's a major task in itself but will it be possible to expand them even more rapidly still to enable the extra amount of energy required for, say, a 2% rate of economic growth to be produced as well? If not, no other energy source can do so either because coal and tar sands take more energy to develop than renewables

In view of the magnitude of the task, it should not be surprising that the papers by David Crane and Laurence Staudt, Olaf Hohmeyer and David Fleming all conclude that renewables will not be able to supply enough energy for economic growth to be able to continue at anything like the current rate. This means that the OECD countries will no longer be able to say to the rest of the world 'Open up your economy to international investment, work hard and you too can be like Ireland, doubling your income (and hence your rate of resource consumption) in less than ten years.' The energy to permit that just isn't going to be there. Moreover, if the wealthy countries continue to use fossil energy from the limited supply to try to grow themselves, they will be denying the use of that energy to other, poorer, people, thus keeping them in poverty. Growth therefore needs to be abandoned as a developed-country aim. This would allow half of the energy saved to be invested in renewable energy generation projects or in increased energy efficiency and the balance freed up for use in other parts of the world.

Growth might not be achievable anyway if, as I suggested earlier, the world is on the brink of a depression of similar depth to that in the 1930s. If a depression develops, investment will stop and energy use will fall but, as it will not fall to zero, we'll still be eating into potential energy capital and spending it as income. With low oil prices in a buyers' market, excess generating capacity and very little money about, a situation could easily arise in which no-one will either want, or find it commercially feasible, to invest in renewable power.

CURING A DEPRESSED ECONOMY

The only way to get a seriously depressed economy moving again is to restart investment but firms are not going to plough funds into building more plants producing conventional goods until their existing capacity is taken up – in other words, until demand reaches the level it was before the depression began. That situation might take many years to develop because there's a chicken-and-egg situation here – without investment there won't be demand, and without demand there won't be investment.

New products are therefore needed to create the new demand. Towards the end of the 1930s, the demand for arms restored full employment and got investment moving again. This time, the new demand could – should – be connected with achieving energy sustainability. There will both be the manufacturing capacity and the need – at least from the sustainability perspective if not from the supply side – to make investments in renewable energy supply systems. And we will never have such abundant supplies of fossil energy to be able to do so on the same scale again.

If we let the chance to make massive renewable energy investments slip, when the world eventually moves out of the depression, oil and gas output will be declining and, as demand strengthens, both fuels will become come increasingly expensive. Two scenarios are possible then. One is that the wealthy parts of the world use their wealth to commandeer bio-energy resources from the economically weaker parts, just as they already do on a large scale. Indeed, as I will mention later, the EU is already planning to do so and talking about the benefits that the new trade opportunities will bring to developing countries. If this goes ahead, besides the plantations and ranches that already grow food, beverages, raw materials, flowers and animal feedstuffs for export to the EU and other parts of the wealthy world, more land will be taken up producing vegetable oil for fuel and industrial inputs to replace petrochemical ones. Those displaced from their land by this change will move to the cities to join the millions already living in hardship there because the higher energy prices that scarcity will bring will have pushed up the cost of their food.

The second scenario is that, as the world economy recovers from the depression, the five big OPEC producers – Saudi Arabia, Kuwait, Iraq, Iran, and the United Arab Emirates – take advantage of their growing share of the world's oil production and put up prices sharply. This could give them such a huge increase in their earnings that they will be unable to spend it all on additional imports. If so, as in 1973, they would have no option but to lend their surplus back to the countries from which it came by depositing it in western banks. The problem with this is that the money might stay in those banks rather than being lent out again because, unless countries and corporations can see some prospect of being able to repay additional loans, they will not take them on. Interest rates might be cut to encourage them to do so but, as Japan has shown in the past five years, even zero rates might not be low enough to make extra borrowing attractive. Without the extra borrowing, however, the global money supply would contract, returning the world to the depression from which it had just emerged, while simultaneously cutting oil demand and bringing its price down.

In other words, under a business-as-usual scenario, there is a real chance that the level of global economic activity will contract in step with the decline in oil supplies. Constant contraction and depression could be the norm. Even the oil producers would not do well out of this because for a lot of the time, their output would be being sold in depression conditions. There might be no way that the free market could break out of this cycle once it started because the peak oil price – the level that tipped the world into depression - might not be high enough or maintained for long enough to encourage investment in renewable energy sources. Then, once the depression had begun,

oil would be cheap again and the market would provide no incentive to countries to reduce dependence on the fuel, at least on a significant scale. The world could descend into chaos and misery, unable to help itself.

If such a scenario is a possibility then the energy markets need to be modified in some way so that they can deliver a better result. How? Well, what does a group of dishonest antique dealers do before an auction? They decide who is to bid for each item and the maximum he or she is to pay and then, afterwards, they hold a private auction among themselves to determine who actually gets what. The point of this ploy is to ensure that the extra money which would have gone to the vendor if the dealers had bid against each other in the original auction stays within the group and does not leak away unnecessarily to a member of the public. Something similar could be done for oil. A buyers' ring could be set up to prevent excess money going to fossil fuel producers in times of scarcity and plunging the world into an economic depression.

CONTRACTION AND CONVERGENCE

A digression is necessary to explain how this might work. If a country is to enjoy the maximum sustainable level of economy activity, it needs to decide which scarce resource places the tightest constraint on its economy's development and expansion. It should then adjust its systems and technologies so that they automatically observe the limits imposed by that constraint. In terms of our discussion so far it might seem that oil and gas were the scarcest factors of production at present but I don't think that's true. Labour and capital are not the critical factors either. There is unemployment in most countries and, in comparison with a century ago, the physical capital stock is huge and under-utilised. On the other hand, the natural environment is grossly overused especially as a sink for human-made pollutants with the result that a runaway global warming is a real possibility. In other words, the Earth's capacity to remove greenhouse gases from the atmosphere is the scarcest resource and the economic system should be adapted accordingly.

Contraction and Convergence (C&C) is a way of doing so. It is a plan for reducing greenhouse gas emissions developed by the Global Commons Institute[8] in London that involves the international community agreeing how much the level of the main greenhouse gas, carbon dioxide (CO_2), in the atmosphere can be allowed to rise. There is considerable uncertainty over this. The EU considers a doubling from pre-industrial levels to around 550 parts per million (ppm) might be safe while Bert Bolin, a former chairman of the IPCC, has suggested that 450 ppm should be considered the absolute upper limit. Even the present level of roughly 360ppm may prove too high because of the time lag between a rise in concentration and the climate changes it brings about. Indeed, in view of this lag, it is worrying that so many harmful effects of warming such as melting icecaps, dryer summers, rougher seas and more frequent storms have already appeared.

Whatever CO_2 concentration target is chosen automatically sets the annual rate at which the world must reduce its present greenhouse emissions until they come into line with the Earth's capacity to absorb the gas. This is the contraction course implied in the Contraction and Convergence name.

Once the series of annual global emissions limits have been set, the right to burn whatever amount of fuel this represents in any year would be shared out among the nations of the world on the basis of their population at an agreed date – 1990, perhaps. In the early stages of the contraction process, some nations would find themselves consuming less than their allocation, while others would be consuming more, so under-consumers would have the right to sell their surplus to more energy-intensive lands. This would generate a healthy income for some of the poorest countries in the world and give them every incentive to continue following a low-energy development path. Eventually, most countries would probably converge on similar levels of fossil energy use per head.

But what currency are the over-consuming nations going to use to buy extra CO_2 emission permits? If those countries with reserve currencies such as the dollar, the pound sterling and the euro were allowed to use them, they would effectively get the right to use a lot of their extra energy for free because much of the money they paid would be used to provide liquidity for the world economy rather than purchasing goods from the countries which issued them. To avoid this, Aubrey Meyer of GCI and Feasta[9] devised a plan[10] under which a new international organisation, the Issuing Authority, would assign Special Emission Rights (SERs, the right to emit a specified amount of greenhouse gases and hence to burn fossil fuel) to national governments every month according to their entitlement under the Contraction and Convergence formula.

SERs would essentially be ration coupons, to be handed over to fossil-fuel production companies in addition to cash by their customers - electricity producers, oil refineries, coal distributors and so on. An international inspectorate would monitor producers to ensure that their sales did not exceed the number of SERs they received. This would be surprisingly easy as nearly 80 per cent of the fossil carbon that ends up as manmade carbon dioxide in the earth's atmosphere comes from only 122 producers of carbon-based fuels[11]. The used SER coupons would then be destroyed.

Such a system is not an impossibility. Considerable work has already been done towards the development of an international trading system in carbon dioxide emission rights both at a theoretical level and in practice.

AN ENERGY-BACKED CURRENCY

Besides the SERs, the Issuing Authority would supply governments with a new form of money, emissions-backed currency units (ebcus), on the same per capita basis. It would announce that it would always be prepared to sell additional SERs at a specific ebcu price. This would fix the value of the ebcu in relation to a certain amount of greenhouse emissions and make holding the unit very attractive as other monies have no fixed value and SERs are going to become scarcer year by year.

The ebcu issue would be a once-off, to get the system started. If a power company actually used ebcus to buy additional SERs from the Issuing Authority in order to be able to burn more fossil energy, the number of ebcus in circulation internationally would not be increased to make up for the loss. The ebcus paid over would simply be cancelled and the world would have to manage with less of them in circulation. This would cut the amount of international trading it was possible to carry on and, as a result, world fossil energy consumption would fall. On the other hand, there would be no limit to the amount of trading that could go on within a single country using its national currency provided it kept its fossil energy use down.

Governments could auction their monthly allocation of SERs from the Issuing Authority to major energy users and distributors in their own country and then pass all or part of the national currency they received to their citizens as a basic income. (Something along these lines would be necessary as the price of energy would go up sharply and the poor would be badly hit) They could also sell SERs abroad for ebcus. The prices set by these two types of sale

would establish the exchange rate of their national currency in terms of ebcus, and thus in terms of other national currencies.

The use of national currencies for international trade would be phased out. Only ebcu would be used among participating countries and any countries which stayed out of the system would have tariff barriers raised against them. Many indebted countries would find that their initial allocation of ebcu enabled them to clear their foreign loans. In subsequent years, they would be able to import equipment for capital projects with their income from the sale of SERs, thus helping the depressed world economy to revive.

Setting up this type of dealers' ring would ensure that, rather than a lot of money being paid to the producer-countries for scarce oil and gas as a result of competitive bidding between prospective purchasers, it would go instead to poor countries after an auction for their surplus SERs. This money would not have to be lent back into the world economy as would happen if the energy producers received it. It would be quickly spent back by people who urgently need many things which the over-fosil-energy-intensive economies can make.

So, rather than debt growing, demand would, constrained only by the availability of energy. Suppose it was decided to cut emissions by 5% a year, a rate which would achieve the 80% cut the IPCC urges in thirty years, the sort of goal we need to adopt. Cutting fossil energy supplies at this rate would mean that the ability of the world economy to supply goods and services would shrink by 5% a year minus the rate at which energy economies became possible and renewable energy supplies were introduced. Initially, energy savings would take the sting out of most of the cuts – there's a lot of fat around - and as these became progressively difficult to find, the rate of renewable energy installations should have increased enough to prevent significant falls in global output.

The global economy this system would create would be much less liable to a boom and bust cycle than the present one for two reasons. One is that, as the shape of every national economy would be changing rapidly, there would be a lot of investment opportunities around. The other is that the supply of the world's money, the ebcu, would not fluctuate up and down as happens now, magnifying changes in the business climate. Their amount would be stable or, if the demand for fossil fuels rose so much that the emissions target was threatened, in slow decline.

Under C&C, investors in renewable energy projects could be sure of keen demand. The poorer parts of the world would get the resources they need to follow low-energy development paths. And the spreading out of purchasing power would open new markets for manufacturing companies. Everyone, even the fossil fuel producers, would benefit from the arrangement and, as far as I am aware, no other course has been proposed which tackles the problem in a way which is both equitable and guarantees that emissions targets are met. What is certain is that the unguided workings of the global market are unlikely to ensure that fossil energy use is cut back quickly enough to avoid a climate crisis in a way that brings about a rapid switch to renewable energy supplies.

MODIFYING MARKET MECHANISMS

As C&C is a world solution, it will take several years to put into effect. Until it is, Europe must not rely on the market to decide whether or not it should invest in renewables and, if so, which ones, on what scale and where. We – the people of Europe – have to decide what we want to do and then design the legislative framework within which the market can then be allowed produce the desired results.

The only sustainable target for the EU would involve it achieving energy sustainability within its own borders and not meeting its energy needs through imports, whether of fuels or products which took a lot of energy to make. As Hohmeyer's paper shows, this goal can be achieved by 2050 and enough energy delivered to enable all the people of the 15 current member states of the EU to live at the present Northern European level.

Ireland's role in such a Europe should be to become a net exporter of wind, wave and tidal energy to its partners because it has a much better resource base than most. The EU is slowly forcing the country to move in that direction. A particularly hefty push came in October 2001 when the directive requiring 20% of all the Community's electricity to be produced from renewable sources by 2010 was passed by the Council of Ministers. Another shove came in April 2003 when the Council of Ministers approved the Biofuels Directive, which envisages 20% of all transport fuel coming from non-oil sources by 2020.

The electricity directive has already forced the Irish government to raise its sights. Its 1998 Green Paper on Sustainable Energy suggested that only 5.6% of electricity would come from renewables by 2010. However, in the table below which accompanied the directive, the European Commission says that Ireland's target is now 13.2%. This 240% increase must have been offered by (or at least extracted from) the government.

Even so, it is still aiming far below the EU average of 22% and Austria's target is an amazing 80% of its electricity from renewables by the end of the decade. The low goal is due in part to the fact that rapid economic growth rates have caused electricity demand to rise by around 6.5% a year for several years and it is assumed that this will carry on. If that turns out to be correct, the amount of electricity generated from renewables would have to increase by the same percentage just to maintain its present market share. The sector would have to run to stand still.

While the renewable electricity directive can be welcomed wholeheartedly, the Biofuels Directive is a serious mistake for three reasons. The first is that it will do little to achieve its own objectives because it will neither lead to a significant reduction in greenhouse gas emis-

tricity from the wind. Thus the transport system will remain almost entirely dependent on oil which, as the Commission points out, will be supplied in 2020 almost entirely from the perennially unstable Middle East. This level of dependence is too high for the Commission's liking and it wants to reduce it by a further 10% by having more vehicles powered by natural gas. In 2020, however, gas will be largely sourced from equally unstable places like Algeria and the countries around the Caspian Sea.

(Figure 8A6) Member States targets for the proportion of electricity to come from renewables by 2010		
	Percentage	**TWh**
Austria	78.1	55.3
Belgium	6.0	6.3
Denmark	29.0	12.9
Finland	35.0	33.7
France	21.0	112.9
Germany	12.5	76.4
Greece	20.1	14.5
Ireland	13.2	4.5
Italy	25.0	89.6
Luxembourg	5.7	0.5
Netherlands	12.0	15.9
Portugal	45.6	28.3
Spain	29.4	76.6
Sweden	60.0	97.5
United Kingdom	10.0	50.0
European Union	22.1%	674.9

sions nor will it do much to reduce the EU's dependence on imported oil. The second is that it is likely to increase world hunger. And the third is that it will require resources that would be better employed developing other ways of powering vehicles.

In the documentation accompanying the directive, the Commission projects that biofuels will provide 8% of the fuel for the EU's road vehicles by 2020 and that a further 5% will come from hydrogen, perhaps produced using elec-

Biofuels suitable for transport include methane from the digestion of organic wastes, ethanol from the fermentation of sugar beet and oil from crops like rape. Unfortunately when crude oil is $25 a barrel they cost about 0.3 euro per litre more to make than oil-based fuel so the Commission suggests that governments compensate by lowering the tax road users have to pay. At present, users pay the same tax whatever the fuel type. The tax reduction would essentially be a subsidy liable to produce the same waste of fossil energy that we noted in the

Introduction had happened in Minnesota.

Another serious objection to the directive is that the rich who want fuel for their cars will start competing for arable land with the poor who need food for their stomachs. Food prices will go up, so that people already struggling will be able to buy even less. The document supporting the directive even talks about the possibility of using cereals for fuel. The directive itself does not stipulate that biofuels must come from EU sources to qualify for the proposed tax breaks. Quite the contrary – the supporting material talks about the new trade opportunities that will be created for 'developing' countries. Almost inevitably, this means that biofuel production for the EU will increase hunger in the rest of the world.

Because it is uncertain whether fossil energy would actually be saved by growing crops to turn into biofuels, the only clear advantage of switching part of the transport sector from imported oil to domestic biofuel is that it would create fifty times as many jobs, mostly in rural areas, as would be required to process the same amount of energy in an oil refinery. Policies to mimimise the need for transport could do far more to improve energy security and cut greenhouse emissions.

The Commission states that biofuels can never provide more than a fraction of the energy required for the transport system. In other words, they are merely a stop-gap until the switch to hydrogen-powered vehicles can be made. And, if that is the case, wouldn't the tax reliefs proposed to encourage biofuels be better spent on encouraging the production of hydrogen using renewable energy? "Go straight for goal" as Jack Charlton says in his television advertisement for a used car dealer.

Official Ireland's reluctance to develop renew-able energy is incomprehensible. The country has the second best wind regime in Europe (after Scotland) from a power generation perspective. An Irish university is a world leader in the development of wave power. Its coastline offers enormous potential for tidal power, generated not by environmentally-damaging barrages but by turbines anchored to the seabed. Wood chips from short rotation forestry, regular forestry waste, and biogas from animal dung and vegetable waste, all offer excellent potential for producing heat and electricity combined. Even solar energy could play an important role.

A report assessing the amount of electricity Scotland could generate from renewables was published in 2002 by the Scottish Executive. It looks at how much would be available, where it would be generated and how much it would cost given current technologies. Agricultural and forestry wastes, energy crops and gas from municipal rubbish are all explored but dismissed as minor sources. Land-based wind turbines have the ability to deliver much more power at a lower price. They could produce 125% of the country's current electricity consumption for less than 2p (Sterling) a kilowatt hour.

Offshore wind kicks in next and could produce three times Scotland's current electricity output for around 4p a unit. Wave power could become as important as onshore wind at prices above 4.5p, the same price as required for electricity from tidal streams and from energy crops. All told, Scotland could produce 5.6 times as much electricity from renewables as it is using at present, and twice the amount used in the entire UK, if the price to producers was about 4.5p/kwh. The Scottish report can be downloaded from www.scotland.gov.uk/who/elld/energy /srs2001vol1.pdf A similar one is badly needed for Ireland.

THE CASE FOR INVESTING NOW

There are five reasons for calling for massive, immediate investments in renewable energy systems. There is the environmental one - we need to limit climate change. There are two practical ones – first, that oil and gas are running short and we won't have the fossil energy so readily available to invest in the transition ever again, and secondly, that renewables – wind and biomass – give out more energy for each unit of energy invested than either nuclear power or coal. There is the economic reason – we need new products, or new ways of producing old ones, like electricity, if we are to get the economy out of the looming depression. And finally, there is the moral one – we need to free up resources for use by poorer countries and succeeding generations.

A return to a renewables-only powered economy would put the world back on the sustainable path it so mistakenly abandoned when the British began to burn coal four hundred years ago. If a determined start is made on restructuring the energy economy now, while oil and gas are still relatively abundant, renewables have the potential to take us to a sophisticated, sustainable world with a high degree of equality and complexity. If we delay the change, however, even by just a few years, it will remove most of our choices and make life for the majority of people in future terribly simple. And nasty, brutish and short. Taking the right path now is therefore vitally important.

ENDNOTES

1. J.A. Tainter, *The Collapse of Complex Societies,* Cambridge: Cambridge University Press, 1988. See also R. H. McGuire, 'Breaking down cultural complexity: inequality and heterogeneity' in *Advances in Archaeological Method and Theory,* Volume 6, ed. Michael B. Schiffer, pp. 91-142. New York: Academic Press, 1983.

2. Andrew O'Hagan, *The Guardian,* 26 March, 2001.

3. Richard G. Wilkinson, *Poverty and Progress,* London: Methuen, 1973, p42.

4. See Clive Ponting, *A Green History of the World,* London: Sinclair-Stevenson, 1991, for a detailed account.

5. Quoted by Wilkinson, p115.

6. John Gever, Robert Kaufmann, David Skole and Charles Vorosmarty, *Beyond Oil,* Ballinger, Cambridge (Mass.) 1987.

7. MuseLetter 135, May 2003, downloaded from
http://globalpublicmedia.com/ARTICLES/richardheinberg.museletter.petroleumplateau.2003-05.php

8. See http://www.gci.org.uk/

9. See http://www.feasta.org/

10. What next for slowing climate change? *Feasta Review,* No. 1, Dublin, 2001, pp 158-173

11. *Kingpins of Carbon: How Fossil Fuel Producers Contribute to Global Warming,* Natural Resources Defense Council and others, New York, July 1999.

13. Voss A. 2002, 'LCA & External Costs in comparative assessment of electricity chains' *Proceedings,* Nuclear Energy Agency, Paris.

Rules and Guidelines for Energy Challenge

Jackie Carpenter

This game was played one evening at the Thurles conference by several dozen of the participants. It proved very popular. Players remarked afterwards that it had made them think about the choices involved in planning a country's energy future

This version of the Energy Challenge aims to get the players to look in a light-hearted way at possible energy balances for a hypothetical future when the Republic of Ireland is powered by 100% renewable energy. Whilst it is not meant to be technical or detailed (for example it does not ask them to go into issues of power or to carry out an economic assessment), it demonstrates a process which may need to be carried out "for real" sooner than we think.

It is a team game and part of the exercise is for the players to co-operate and agree on each issue. If they need help with any aspect of the exercise there will be a facilitator on hand to answer their questions. The challenge to each team is to place on the wall a poster it is proud of that depicts how its 100% renewable energy solution would work.

How to Play

Your team's aim is to produce a renewable energy scenario for the Republic of Ireland, based on an assumption that ALL energy must come from renewable resources. You must produce a poster that details your scenario and these will later be put on display. You may wish to go through your sheet personally in advance of the programmed exercise, calculating some numbers and filling them in pencil, ready to discuss with your team.

Steps in the Exercise

1. Plan the use of your time and which member of the team is going to carry out which task. You may wish to identify an "artist" to make an early start on the presentation. You could also appoint a "recorder" to jot down your ideas and assumptions and a "calculating officer" to do the sums. However everyone is encouraged to participate in the formulation of the final scenario.

2. Go through the exercise sheet filling in the boxes as you go. You can do this individually and then discuss your results and fill in a team sheet, or you can go straight for the team sheet. At the end of this you will have decided how much energy the Republic of Ireland will use and how it will be generated. This isn't just about developing enough renewable energy to meet the energy demands of today. Energy efficiency and energy conservation can be utilised to reduce the actual amount of energy that is required. Come up with some ideas and figures, but don't be too serious!

3. Market your scenario. Be dramatic! Be positive! Make your posters outstanding, inspired and eye-catching!

• The scenario must be based on 100% renewable energy.

• We would like you to work in terawatt-hours (TWh). One unit of electricity, as shown on your electricity bill, is one kilowatt-hour. A terawatt-hour is a thousand million kilowatt-hours i.e. a thousand million units.

• Use pencil to fill in the boxes so you can go back and change your figures as the ideas develop.

• The data in grey boxes is for your help and information. It is only meant to act as a guide to the technologies available today. **If you feel that there can or should be great advancements in these energy sources, or completely new technologies, feel free to add creative ideas.** Try to justify this in your final presentation.

• Consider why have you chosen your particular figures. What will be the costs and benefits to Ireland? What problems might you encounter and what related issues might you need to tackle? How can your ideas lead to more jobs and a vibrant local economy? Think about the role of renewable energy as a positive force for regeneration and change. Try to make the idea of 100% renewable energy as realistic as possible. Record three or four key bullet points for your team.

• Make a display that will sell your ideas to the other delegates. This will include the filled-in team sheet and one flipchart sheet. You may lay this out as you wish. Have fun!

LAND USE STATISTICS

Look at the current land use and population statistics for the Republic of Ireland and then decide what the values will become in your future scenario.

Land Use 100 ha = one square kilometre	Now Hectares (ha)	Future Scenario
Urban and wasteland		1,877,245
Agricultural	3,840,230	
Grass		
Crops	601,525	
Total		4,441,755
Forest and woodland		570,000
Total		**6,889,000**

People and Houses	Now	Future Scenario
Population	3,600,000	
Households	1,100,000	

For simplicity, details about public buildings and public transport are not included but you can make some general assumptions here, e.g. "more", "many more", or "fewer" large buildings.

Public Buildings	
Public Transport	

ENERGY USE (Figures from CSO)

Energy is currently delivered to the consumer as (figures in TWh/yr):

Coal	Peat	Briguettes	Oil and Petrol	Gas	Renewables inc. hydro	Electricity	Total
6.1	2.1	1.4	78.1	18.5	1.6	20.1	127.9
4.8	1.6%	1.1%	61%	14.4%	1.3%	15.7%	

The current energy split between the following sectors is (figures in TWh/yr):

Industry	Transport	Residential	Commercial	Agricultural	Total
30.8	45.4	30.0	17.8	3.9	127.9
24.1%	35.5%	23.4%	13.9%	3%	

Now plan the demand in your future scenario. Think about satisfying *energy;* don't worry about power.

Reducing demand:

Improvements in domestic, industrial and commercial efficiency can easily result in a 20% reduction in energy consumption. Could we do more?

Transport energy usage is another area where substantial energy reductions can be made. It's up to you to decide how much can be done.

Our team's future energy split between the following sectors will be (figures in TWh/yr):

Industry	Transport	Residential	Commercial	Agricultural	Total Demand
%	%	%	%	%	

IN YOUR FUTURE SCENARIO 100% OF DEMAND MUST BE MET BY RENEWABLE SOURCES

Which renewable energy technologies will your scenario employ? If you feel that the Republic of Ireland can produce more energy than it needs, you could export the surplus. Go through quickly to get a feeling for the possibilities, then your team needs to agree a figure for each white box

Wind

Turbine	Blade diameter (m)	Rated Output	Output (TWh/yr)
Very Small	0.5	60W	0.00000025
Small	5.5	6kW	0.000014
Large	40	600kW	0.0015
Very Large	66	1.75MW	0.004

Some sample calculations to help you on your way:
One small turbine for half of the 1,100,000 dwellings would provide 7.7 TWh/yr.
One large turbine per square kilometre would result in 68,890 turbines providing 103 TWh/yr.
5000 very large turbines spread across the country would produce 20 TWh/yr

WIND	**POWER SCENARIO**	
Turbine	**Number in Scenario**	**Output (TWh/yr)**
Very small		
Small		
Large		
Very Large		
		Total

PV

The average yearly insolation is 1000 kWh/m²/yr. PV can collect 10% and the average available domestic roof area is 12–20 m² per dwelling. You may also decide to install PV along the edges of all roads or covering brownfield sites in urban areas.

One ha covered with PV would supply 0.001 TWh/yr – and the country has 6,889,000 ha.

PV systems could also be installed on all current commercial and public buildings.

Some sample calculations to help you on your way:

PV installations of 15m² on ALL dwellings would provide 1.65 TWh/yr.

PV SCENARIO	**Total Output (GWh/yr)**

Biomass

SRC has an energy yield of 0.000070 TWh/ha/yr. Forestry thinnings provide 0.000012 TWh/ha/yr. There are currently 4,441,755 ha of land used for agricultural purposes in the Republic of Ireland. Think about what percentage could be used for SRC.

Some sample calculations to help you on your way:

500,000 ha of Short Rotation Coppice (SRC) would provide 35 TWh/yr

500,000 ha of Forestry thinnings would provide 6 TWh/yr

BIOMASS SCENARIO	**Total Output (GWh/yr)**

Hydro, Tidal & Wave

The estimated hydropower potential for the whole of the UK is 1.8 TWh/yr. Compared with this you can estimate the possible amount for Ireland.

The estimated tidal power potential for the whole of the UK (including the Severn estuary) is 29 TWh/yr. Compared with this you can estimate the possible amount for Ireland.

500 kW shoreline wave generators, in areas where the wave power is between 15-25 kW/m, could provide 0.0015 GWh/yr. Near shore wave generators operating in 15m of water, have a capacity of 2 MW. This could provide say 0.005 TWh/yr.
Some sample calculations to help you on your way:
2000 shoreline wave power generators of 500kW capacity could provide 3 TWh/yr
5000 near shore wave power generators of 2MW capacity could provide 25 TWh/yr

HYDRO, TIDAL & WAVE POWER SCENARIO	Total Output (GWh/yr)

Waste

Each tonne of waste could produce 550 kWh. The UK produces around one tonne of household waste per household per year – it assumed that the figure for the Republic of Ireland is approximately the same. Remember that this figure can change in your future scenario. All the domestic waste in the Republic of Ireland could produce 0.6 TWh/yr.

WASTE POWER SCENARIO	Total Output (GWh/yr)

Solar hot water, other sources, novel sources

One 4 m² domestic solar hot water installation can provide 1,500 kWh/yr.
Solar hot water installations of 4 m² on HALF of all dwellings would provide 0.8 TWh/yr.

OTHER	Total Output (GWh/yr)

Now put your totals for each kind of energy into the table below. If your figures do not add up you will have to go back and reassess the demand, production or imports/exports accordingly.

Energy Source	Energy Produced (TWh/yr)
Wind	
PV	
Biomass	
Hydro	
Tidal	
Wave	
Waste	
Other	
Import	
Total	
Total Demand	
Surplus for Export	

The Energy Challenge was devised by Energy 21 (www.energy21.org.uk).
Energy 21 can provide facilitators and background data.

Hail . . . . .

Pádraig Culbert, Chief Executive, Tipperary Institute, welcomed those attending the Ireland's Transition to Renewable Energy conference with these words:

Distinguished guests, ladies and gentlemen. My function this morning is to welcome you to Tipperary Institute and to officially open this conference.

In doing so I would like to pay tribute to our partners in organising this conference, the Renewable Energy Information Office of Sustainable Energy Ireland and FEASTA, the Foundation for the Economics of Sustainability. In particular I would like to thank Richard Douthwaite, the main organiser. I gratefully acknowledge the support given to the conference by ESB Independent Energy, Airtricity, GE Wind, COMHAR (the National Sustainable Development Partnership) and the Green Group in the European Parliament. Without the support of our sponsors this conference would not have been possible.

One might wonder why Tipperary Institute is involved in organising this major event on renewable energy, so I shall explain. The Institute has been given a mission by the Irish Government to promote the sustainable socio-economic development of the region. In all our development work in Tipperary Institute the concept of sustainability is paramount. One of the key areas of economic activity that raises issues of sustainability is energy production and usage. It is clear that our present reliance on non-renewable fossil fuels is unsustainable on a number of levels.

The Tipperary Institute has therefore been active in the sustainable energy sector since its inception. The Institute has particular focuses on community-involvement in renewable energy development and on bioenergy – a number of projects on these topics have been successfully completed. Under the leadership of Ciarán Lynch, three staff from the Rural Development Department, Clifford Guest, Kevin Healion and Seamus Hoyne, are actively working on the topic of sustainable energy and have been involved in the organisation of this conference. The Institute is also a partner with North Tipperary County Council and South Tipperary County Council in the Tipperary Energy Agency, a local energy agency whose establishment was supported under the EU SAVE programme. The agency promotes energy conservation and renewable energy.

I would like to acknowledge the input of the Institute staff who have assisted in the organisation and preparations for the conference, and who will be involved over the duration of the event.

The conference brings a number of different perspectives to the debate on the future of energy supply for Ireland - petro-geology, the oil industry, the nuclear perspective and, of course, the renewable energy perspective. I am certain that we can look forward to a challenging and informative conference. I am delighted that we in Tipperary Institute have you as our guests for the three days of the event, and I hope that you find the conference valuable and enjoyable. I thank you in advance for your active participation and contribution to the success of the event.

. . . & Farewell

The conference closed by passing the motion below unanimously. It had been proposed by Richard Behel.

We call upon the Irish Government to take the lead in the EU as a matter of urgency in calling for a form of Marshall Plan to fund the research and implementation of a renewable energy future for Europe and the entire world.

The environmental sickness of the Earth and the looming shortage of polluting, conventional fossil fuels makes it clear that our dependence on them cannot be allowed to continue any longer. Yet private enterprise alone cannot provide the solution within the timeframe required.

The EU should therefore set up a task force of scientists, engineers and environmentalists with a multi-billion euro budget to bring about the rapid transition to renewable energy for the benefit of all mankind.